# The Sovereign States, 1775–1783

JACKSON TURNER MAIN

*The Sovereign States, 1775-1783*

NEW VIEWPOINTS

A Division of Franklin Watts, Inc.
New York
1973

*Text design by Elliot Epstein*
*Cover design by Nicholas Krenitsky*
*Maps by George Buctel*

LIBRARY OF CONGRESS CATALOGING IN PUBLICATION DATA

Main, Jackson Turner.
  The sovereign States, 1775–1783.

  Bibliography: p.
  1. United States–History–Revolution.
I. Title.
E208.M33   1973   973.3   75-190137
ISBN 0-531-06355-0
ISBN 0-531-06481-6  (pbk)

# *Preface*

The publishers and I intended this book as a brief, readable summary of existing knowledge about the American people and their state governments during the Revolutionary War years. The writer of such a survey, absolved of the necessity for precise language which the research monograph requires, can sacrifice exactitude in the interest of style and can hazard interesting generalizations far in advance of the evidence. In return for this freedom, he abandons any claim to be taken seriously by scholars.

It turned out that our knowledge did not permit such a book. Indeed, only a considerable number of detailed studies would justify the breezy confidence that the writer of a textbook assumes. Therefore several chapters and parts of every chapter depend largely upon original research, and ought properly to be couched in the cautious terminology of the scholarly genre. The bold language should not mislead my historian colleagues into thinking that I intend finality. The specialist will find most nearly original the material on the interim governments in Chapter 4 and some of the information in Chapters 7, 10, and 11. My interpretation of the ideological division and its practical implications, developed in Chapters 4 and 5, differs somewhat from the current view. A bibliographical essay indicates the major sources for the book as a whole and for each chapter.

The book owes much of its readability to my wife's conscientious editing. Kathy Carney and Jacqueline Liebl intelligently and patiently typed successive drafts. Every reader will realize that a book of this sort depends for its mere existence upon the whole community of historians.

J. T. M.

*Setauket, New York*
*July 1972*

# Contents

Preface, v

1. American Society in 1776, 1

2. Making a Living in the Country, 37

3. Making a Living in the Towns, 67

4. The Political Background, 99

5. Conflicts over the Constitutions, 143

6. The New Governments, 186

7. Economic Changes During the War, 222

8. Loyalism in the Thirteen States, 269

9. Social Changes in the Revolutionary Era, 318

10. Northern Politics During the War, 349

11. Southern Politics During the War, 396

12. Retrospect and Prospect, 439

A Note on Sources, 455

Index, 482

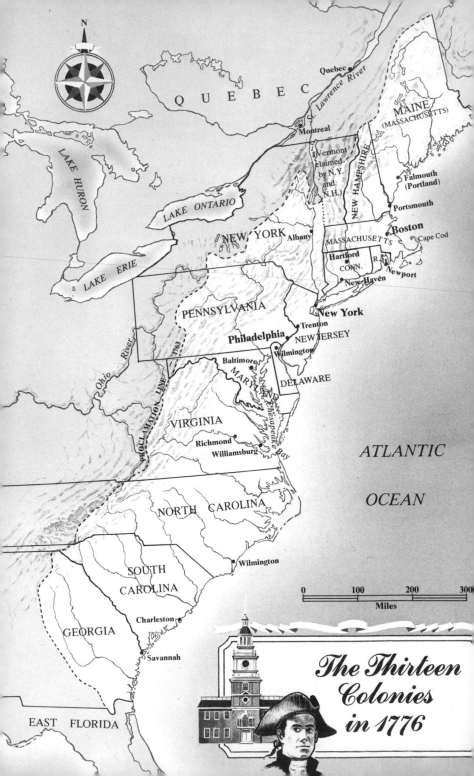

The Thirteen Colonies in 1776

## Chapter One

## American Society in 1776

THE two and a half million people who risked their lives, fortunes, and sacred honors in 1776 scarcely knew one another. They were scattered over an area twelve hundred miles long and two hundred miles wide, averaging ten persons to the square mile. Nine of these ten lived in the country. The largest towns (Boston and Philadelphia) contained only thirty thousand apiece, scarcely enough to make a decent showing in a modern ball park. If you lined up the Boston men four abreast at a comfortable interval you could walk past them all in ten or twelve minutes. Most towns contained only a few hundred houses, and everyone knew everybody else.

One's circle of acquaintances did not extend much beyond the locality. Almost every person from his early teens worked hard six days a week to support himself, and even on the seventh farmers and artisans and laborers and slaves must care for the animals, houses, personal needs, and their patch of garden. Many of course went to church. Certainly they could not simply drop everything and go off sightseeing. Since nobody had a vacation and nobody "retired," leisure time scarcely existed. Only rarely did men leave their farms or shops. People lived all their lives in the same sort of neighborhood. The young man might move from his father's house to a less crowded area, and perhaps repeat the trip, for Americans were mobile then too, but he planted himself again in the same environment. The head of the family visited the market town to buy and sell, and rode to the county seat on court day, but he seldom, perhaps never, saw a city or traveled more than a few score miles.

One did not travel for fun. Slaves, servants, laborers, and in the North even some of the poorer yeomen lacked a horse. After all, it cost several months' work and then must be fed and cared for. Even with a horse, few men liked to travel more than a day's journey. The only cheap and easy means of transportation was downstream by boat, but who goes down must go back up, and often the rivers impeded rather than assisted transportation. Travel by coach or ship cost too much for all but a few of the people. And nobody moved during the winter or in rainy spells. Probably most of the boys of '76, like the modern GIs, saw more of the world in a few months' service than they would see the rest of their lives.

The world the soldiers knew, despite the isolation, the poor transportation, and the undeveloped character of its economy, was a land of opportunity. It contained six or seven geographic regions, each including parts of several states, all with great natural resources and each made up of distinct subsections. These regions were, from northeast to southwest: northern New England, the Long Island Sound–

[2]

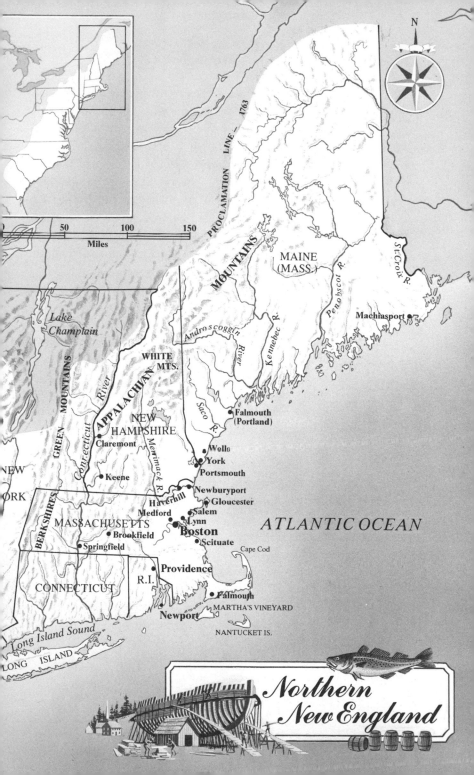

N

50 100 150

Miles

Lake
Champlain

PROCLAMATION LINE — 1763

MAINE
(MASS.)

St. Croix R.

Penobscot R.

Machiasport

MOUNTAINS

Androscoggin River

Kennebec R.

WHITE
MTS.

APPALACHIAN

GREEN MOUNTAINS

Connecticut River

NEW
HAMPSHIRE

Claremont

Keene

Merrimack R.

Saco R.

Falmouth
(Portland)

Wells

York

Portsmouth

Newburyport

Haverhill

Gloucester

Medford

Salem

Lynn

Boston

Scituate

ATLANTIC OCEAN

Cape Cod

NEW
YORK

BERKSHIRES

MASSACHUSETTS

Brookfield

Springfield

Providence

R.I.

CONNECTICUT

Falmouth

Newport

MARTHA'S VINEYARD

NANTUCKET IS.

Long Island Sound

LONG ISLAND

*Northern
New England*

Hudson River area, the Delaware River basin, the lands adjoining Chesapeake Bay, a somewhat amorphous region between the James and the Pee Dee rivers, and the southern-most settlements given unity by Charleston. To these might be added trans-Appalachia and perhaps a northern frontier.

The most northerly and easterly region reached from Cape Cod to Machiasport on the Canadian border, west to the New York line, and south to northern Connecticut and Rhode Island. The economic hub of this extensive empire, Boston, lay two hundred miles nearer England than did New York, a considerable distance under sail. The town acted as distributing center for the dozens of lesser trading towns and fishing villages in the sheltered harbors along the coast. Geography encouraged trade in northern New England. The area contained so little fertile and accessible soil that symptoms of overpopulation had long since appeared in eastern Massachusetts and New Hampshire. Rural New England, indeed, would supply no less than half the soldiers for the Continental Army. Most farms included fewer than a hundred acres, valued at about £300. These produced enough to supply the people's needs but only a small surplus for export: Boston even imported food. The traveler who struck out into the hilly interior found larger farms but with less land under cultivation, and worth only half as much as in the east. Lumber, the principal resource of northern New England's land, needed cheap transportation which existed only near the coast or along some of the rivers in New Hampshire and Maine. The people of Massachusetts and New Hampshire continued to push westward and north-ward in search of profit, but not until they spilled over into New York after the Revolution did they find agricultural wealth.

The men north of Cape Cod therefore turned to the sea.

New York and Southern New England

The ocean produced silver and gold in three ways. First, the fish and whales enabled New Englanders to extract wealth from the West Indies and southern Europe. Second, the forests produced lumber, which the people exported as a raw material primarily to the West Indies. Lumber also furnished barrels for fish and other products, and ships to earn even greater profits. Finally, the trading centers carried on a valuable re-export business, the most familiar version of which involved importing sugar and molasses and exporting rum, but which also included the re-export of British manufactured goods and a lively coastal trade in miscellaneous products. These maritime activities supported directly such manufactures as shipbuilding and cooperage, and indirectly a great variety of arts and crafts essential to the towns. Northern New England therefore formed an economic unit, potentially almost self-sufficient, diversified, producing enough food for her own needs, manufacturing many essentials and some surplus, and earning money by commerce. The people also shared social and cultural characteristics. Almost everyone had come from England during the great migration of the seventeenth century. Thereafter few people arrived, so that the people remained English, and the original Congregationalism continued as the dominant religion. On the other hand, a division of interest separated the prosperous commercial towns along the coast from the agricultural, financially dependent villages of the interior.

Southern New England, together with New York and eastern New Jersey, composed a second major geographical region. Dominating the area was the system of navigable waterways leading into Long Island Sound and New York Bay. The Housatonic, the Connecticut, the Thames (with New London at its outlet), and Narragansett Bay open up the north coast of Long Island Sound, while the Hudson, the

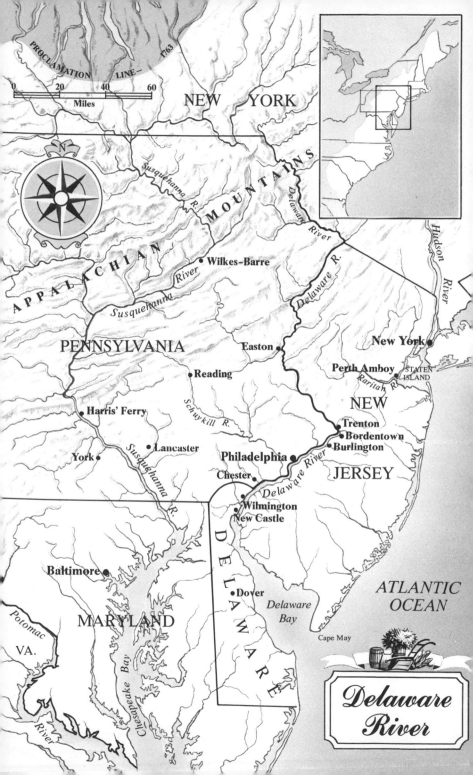

Passaic, and the Raritan rivers combine to form New York Bay, around which lay New York City, Staten Island, Brooklyn, and several counties of New Jersey. The Hudson and the Connecticut led far northward into an agricultural hinterland. The region greatly exceeded the northeastern area in economic potential and already contained more people.

Almost the entire area lay near the coast or along navigable streams. The people found the soil more productive than farther north and the growing season longer, so they enjoyed larger and more profitable farms. By 1776 they were exporting iron, rum, and some lumber, but above all foodstuffs, especially to the West Indies. Manufacturing exceeded that of Massachusetts. Commerce centered in New York City and Newport, the other port towns pursuing a small overseas trade and a large local one. The economic growth of New York had been restricted, until 1763, by wars with the French and the Indians as well as by a short-sighted land policy which repelled immigrants; but the colony then expanded rapidly, almost doubling in population during the next twelve years. This section had always been culturally more diversified than northern New England, with a substantial Dutch minority, while Quakers, Baptists, and Anglicans challenged the Congregationalists in Connecticut and Presbyterians elsewhere.

Southwest of the Long Island–New York Sound region lay the Delaware River area, including the colony of Delaware, West Jersey, and eastern Pennsylvania. Its population equaled that of the two sections to the north and its wealth probably surpassed either. The fertility of the land, its proximity to markets, the absence of any major impediments to transportation, and (by contrast with the Hudson Valley and more southern regions) the relative absence of huge

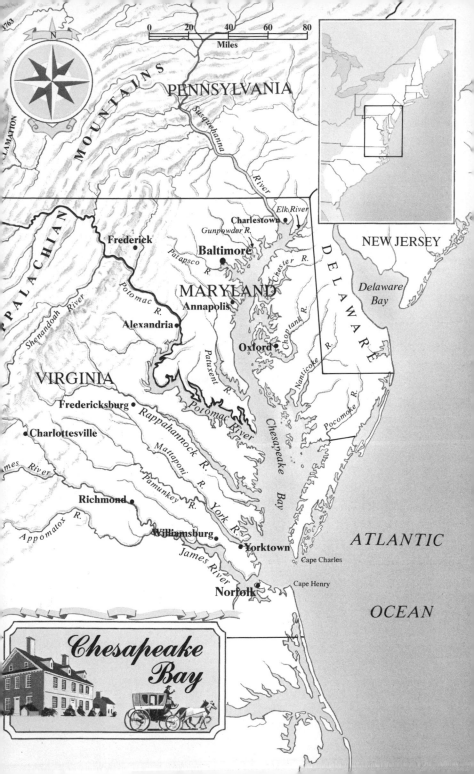

estates combined to produce numerous substantial farms of two hundred acres or so. These exported wheat, corn, flour, and beef, which, with lumber products, rum, iron, and miscellaneous articles, enabled Philadelphia to buy as much from England as all the New England ports combined. Many artisans found economic opportunities, and the huge immigration testified and contributed to the growth of the Delaware region, leading also to the famous expansion into western Pennsylvania. Philadelphia had become the largest and probably the richest city in the British colonies by 1776, though Charleston may have exceeded it in per capita wealth. The Delaware basin contained by far the most diversified population socially and culturally, with half the people being non-English and a corresponding admixture of religious groups.

West and south of the Delaware lay the larger and even more populous area of the Chesapeake Bay. Into that bay flowed the Susquehanna, the Potomac, the Rappahannock, and the James, together with such significant lesser streams as the Elk, Chester, Choptank, and Nanticoke on the eastern side, the Gunpowder, Patapsco, and Patuxent on Maryland's western shore, and in Virginia the tributaries forming the York. Half a dozen of these rivers might have supported major centers of population, but before 1776 the two largest towns, Baltimore and Norfolk, had reached only six thousand each. As we know, the people heeded the lure of rich soil and hastened upstream, spreading out over the farm country and leaving behind a few scattered little villages. The abundance of good land, a long growing season, and easy transportation permitted large-scale commercial farming, for only near the end of the Colonial period did the settlers penetrate into the less favorable terrain of the Appalachian mountains. Tobacco, of course, became the earliest

staple. In addition, Maryland and Virginia outranked all the other colonies combined in the export of oats, peas, wheat, and corn (though not flour), and they led in beef and pork. This surplus enabled the Chesapeake settlers to import more goods than did any other colonists. The failure to develop shipping and to realize their potential in manufacturing may have reduced profits in the long run, but the agricultural wealth permitted a generally high standard of living. As in New England, the basic population was almost entirely English, and the increase depended upon the birth rate rather than upon immigration. The addition of Negro slaves contributed a new element, which by 1776 amounted to more than two-fifths of the people.

A fifth, very extensive area consisted of the region between the James and the Pee Dee, including the settlements along Albemarle and Pamlico sounds, Cape Fear, and the interior of North Carolina. Many of Virginia's southern counties belonged to this section, for the Roanoke and Nottoway rivers pass through the "Southside" on their way to Albemarle Sound. The Pamlico and the Neuse, entering Pamlico Sound, and the Cape Fear River furnish harbors and access to the interior. But unlike Long Island Sound, which offered a highway to the sea, the harbors of North Carolina were blocked by an almost continuous island, the openings through which were narrow, shallow, and shifting. The absence of major port towns and of rivers navigable by oceangoing vessels hampered the region's economic development. Only a few small trading towns such as New Bern, Edenton, Beaufort, Bath, and Wilmington had developed, each containing no more than a few hundred families.

In other respects, however, this vast area, reaching for 250 miles along the coast and an equal distance to the mountains, contained great potential wealth. Long before 1776 a

Miles
0    25    50    75    100

VIRGINIA

APPALACHIAN MOUNTAINS

N

*Yadkin R.*

NORTH CAROLINA

*Catawba R.*

*Yadkin R.*

*Cape Fear River*

Cheraw •

*Little Pee Dee R.*

*Pee Dee River*

*Saluda River*

*Broad R.*

• Camden

*Wateree R.*

*Broad R.*

SOUTH CAROLINA

*Oconee R.*

Augusta •

*Ogeechee River*

*Edisto River*

*Black*

*Santee R.*

• Georgetown

*Ocmulgee River*

GEORGIA

*Savannah River*

• Charleston

*nnouchee R.*

Eden •

• Beaufort

ATLANTIC
OCEAN

Savannah •

PROCLAMATION LINE — 1763

*Altahama River*

Brunswick •

South
Carolina
and
Georgia

EAST FLORIDA

Virginian complained that his Southern neighbors had become lazy and shiftless because the land supported them without hard labor—a quality never imputed to New England's soil. Most of North Carolina produced wheat and corn, with large herds of cattle and pigs. In addition the northeastern farmers, who migrated from Virginia, specialized in tobacco while some of those along the Cape Fear coast grew rice. The most important exports were lumber and naval stores (tar, pitch, and turpentine). North Carolinians lived far enough south so that their livestock required little care during the winter. They let the cows and pigs run wild, drove them to market when weather permitted and streams ran low, raised enough food for their own tables, and exploited the forests when they felt like it. They sent tobacco, tar, and pitch to England and lumber to the West Indies. The profits brought in little hard cash but did pay for essential imports. This region contained a population of fewer than six persons to the square mile, less than half that of the Chesapeake Bay area; almost the entire state was a frontier. The people owned only a fourth as many slaves as did the Virginians, and the relatively few large "plantations" were limited to the northeastern and Cape Fear counties. The typical North Carolina farmer held three hundred acres, but since he depended entirely upon his family for labor he improved only a small part of this. On the whole, North Carolina remained economically underdeveloped.

The last major region of the thirteen states in 1776, excluding trans-Appalachia, stretched along the coast from the Pee Dee River valley in northern South Carolina to the Altamaha River in Georgia, and thence northwest about 160 miles. Fewer than 200,000 people lived there in 1776 (a population smaller than North Carolina's), and of these more than half were slaves. Almost all the blacks and half the whites clustered within a few miles of the coast, where the deltas of the Pee Dee, Santee, Cooper, Edisto, Savannah, and some lesser streams formed an almost continuous belt of fertile, alluvial soil. The superb port of Charleston dominated the entire area, serving as an export center not only for its own extensive hinterland but for the farms reached by way of Georgetown, Beaufort, and Savannah.

Rice brought gold, silver, and slaves to the coastal parishes. Half of this went to England, while the West Indies and southern Europe bought the rest. Other plantations produced indigo. The rice and indigo planters raised most of their own food and a small surplus of forest products but, like other Southerners, manufactured little. This section differed from the Chesapeake and North Carolina regions in that it furnished a significant part of its own shipping. Alone among all of the colonial areas, the Charleston region enjoyed a favorable balance of trade with England. This happy situation enabled the planters to accumulate the new nation's heaviest concentration of slaves and the greatest per capita wealth.

The back-country contributed to this prosperity. Although its major growth had just begun, the farmers of the interior were already exploiting its great natural resources. These included lumber and provisions, exported primarily to the West Indies, and naval stores sent to England. Both South Carolina and Georgia contained some large cattle ranches. The major rivers and their tributaries such as the Broad, Catawba, and Wateree led easily into the interior, which now received an overflow of population from the north as well as from the coast. The Anglican English, who predominated throughout the Southern Tidewater, mingled in the west with a heterogeneous mixture, less diverse than in the Middle states but far more varied than New Englanders in religion and national origin.

These six regions, taken collectively, contained every essential for a diversified and rich economy. The rainfall was ample, the climate never extreme, with sufficient variation to permit the growth of all crops except the tropical. Although most of the wealth was agricultural, manufacturing supplied many of the peoples' needs plus an increasing surplus for export, notably from shipbuilding, iron manufacturing, and milling. Locally built vessels dominated every branch of commerce except the direct trade with England. The economic growth made possible payments on several million pounds' worth of credits advanced from England and generated perhaps ten times as much capital internally. The rapid increase of population contributed to this expansion, as did the gradual occupation of the western lands.

The men who now boldly strove to create from this wealth a victorious army and a nation found among the gold one layer of dross: the fragmented nature of the economy. The capital, though large, was scattered among thousands of business and farming enterprises. The half-dozen regions developed almost independently of one another and indeed tended to consist of semi-autonomous subsections. Thus the Chesapeake Bay area, geographically an entity, contained the eastern shore, which lacked any central focus; the northern Chesapeake, which Baltimore was beginning to dominate; the separate area of the Potomac Valley, which in turn lacked communication with the counties along the Rappahannock and the James; and finally Virginia's southern Piedmont. Northern New England intersected with the Long Island Sound region at a few points only, primarily by the road from Boston to Providence and along the Connecticut River valley. Boston did conduct a coastwise trade, but most of it was limited to the country north of Cape Cod: for example, all of New England imported only .0004 per cent of the tobacco raised in America. The commerce of other ports was equally restricted, and one can quickly exhaust the list of contact points between regions. The fact is that each of these areas exchanged goods, as well as ideas and people, with the British Isles and the West Indies more than with each other. The people of the thirteen states sought to create a nation, but they were united neither economically nor socially.

The most mobile and the most isolated Americans lived on the frontier. There were two quite different kinds of frontier communities, which might be called the squirearchy and the democracy. The former resembled the Scottish Highland clan or the border march. One man or a few families obtained from the government a large tract of land, moved out with servants and tenants, and established a baronial estate. The government gladly encouraged the project because it helped to settle and to defend the country. Indeed, the settlement's leader often held high office. Other men unconnected with the original plan moved into the area because they appreciated its military protection, economic advantages such as a mill and transportation facilities, and companionship. The people often admired the leader for his ability, wealth, influence, and prestige, and he in turn usually tried to care for the general interest which in fact coincided with his own. This frontier contained great economic, social, cultural, and political distinctions. At the top stood the squire, owning much of the wealth, with a big house, cultural pretensions, and power. At the bottom were servants or slaves and hired help, often a majority of the people. Above them stood tenants and artisans dependent upon the great landowner; and finally the community might contain some independent farmers and others such as a minister or a shopkeeper, frequently allied with the squire.

Frontier societies of this sort appeared in every colony. In one South Carolina district (part of "East of the Wateree") John Chesnut, with 126 slaves and nearly ten thousand acres, and Joseph Kershaw, owning more than twice as much land and seventy slaves, held about a fourth of the wealth. Kershaw, an immigrant from Yorkshire, had moved west in 1758 with capital earned in Charleston by himself and a brother, establishing an extensive trade, various manufactories, and the town of Camden. Chesnut, a Virginian, got his start in Kershaw's store and eventually branched out as an independent merchant. Both men held important offices during the Revolution, in which Kershaw suffered heavy losses. Along the Mohawk River valley in New York, Sir William Johnston imported six hundred Highland Scots. Indian agent and entrepreneur, the owner of an immense tract, Johnston and his fellow speculators dominated western New York. The Johnstons remained loyal and lost their property, but Philip Schuyler, who developed a huge estate north of Albany, joined the Revolution and increased his fortune. In both cases the tenants and yeomen followed the same political course as their leader.

Virginia's frontier contained variants of the same social order. In the northern end of the Shenandoah Valley the descendants of Thomas, Lord Fairfax, and the great planters who bought land from him—including the Washingtons— held much of the property of Berkeley County. Lord Grenville acquired a huge section of North Carolina, enabling some of his employees to become economically powerful. One agent, Thomas Person, acquired more than eighty thousand acres and another, Robert Jones, left a rich estate to his son Willie. Person and Jones took opposite sides during the Regulator troubles, the former supporting the back-country farmers and the latter the government, but by 1776 both had emerged as powerful leaders of the western democracy.

The frequency with which the ordinary folk followed these frontier squires seems to contradict the hypotheses that the west bred democracy and that the men of '76 preferred liberty to authority. One should therefore cite, as evidence to the contrary, instances in which the people challenged rule by the elite. Dramatic cases exist, such as the Regulation in both Carolinas before the war, a tenant revolt on Livingston Manor during it, and Shays' Rebellion after it. The fact is, however, that these cases are exceptional, and that they usually arose not out of a simple class conflict but in response to more complex circumstances. The great majority of these leaders retained the loyalty of the humbler folk.

The reason for this social harmony lies in a mixture of economic, social, cultural, and political factors. No one can doubt the economic influence of the frontier squires. They had most of the money, so if one needed to borrow, one went to them. Often they owned the saw or grist mill, tannery, or smithy. Even more important, they controlled the trade, so that the people bought and received credit at their stores and relied upon them to find markets for the community's surplus. Many Americans acknowledged as a matter of course the right of their superiors to rule (just as the Scots Highlanders followed their chiefs), and the rest admired and deferred to the successful. Wealth in America has rarely handicapped the candidate for office. In addition, the man of property was or became culturally superior. Once the pioneer reached his new home he found himself isolated, without a school or books or newspaper or perhaps even a church. He depended for information and guidance upon the local elite. They alone could hire a tutor, subscribe to a newspaper, buy some books, learn how to write and speak effectively, and travel to the source of knowledge. Their broad experience enabled them to transcend the locality, to become cosmopolitans. They alone had the connections and the prestige and ability to win concessions from the government. The frontier leaders inevitably and naturally supplied the justices of the peace, the sheriffs, and the high-ranking militia officers, and the people habitually sent them to the legislature. It was not strange but natural for the frontiersmen in such a society to follow a Kershaw, a Johnston, a Person, a Schuyler, or a Washington.

This kind of frontier community developed only under particular conditions. The essential requirements included fertile land, a system of land grants that encouraged large estates, and transportation good enough to attract the entrepreneurs. Some speculators acquired huge tracts (for example, in Maine and southwestern Virginia) but lost or sold them to farmers without ever moving into the wilderness themselves. If we were to locate on a map the residences of the bona fide frontier squires we would find them bunched along a few major rivers: the Santee and its extensions, the James, the Potomac, the Hudson-Mohawk, and the Connecticut. Elsewhere the frontier produced a very different social order.

The usual frontier settlement in 1776 consisted of small property owners and free laborers. Characteristically, the frontier consisted not of miscellaneous individuals scattering through the forest but of groups moving slowly and keeping, as it were, within shouting distance of each other. They formed a community for worship, mutual aid, protection, or because of geographical circumstance. The religious motive, which we tend to associate with New England, affected groups of Christians all the way to Georgia, for many people insisted upon settling near others of the same faith even when they could not form a church. Most pioneers also bought their farms near neighbors because they could not survive alone. Some men could build houses, fell trees, clear land, feed themselves, and condemn their wives and children to perpetual loneliness, but most needed the physical and psychological help of neighbors. Group cooperation outranked individualism as a qualification for survival on the frontier. If one had grain to grind, a rifle to repair, salt to buy, a barn to raise, an infant to bear, or a hog to sell, one needed some form of social organization. And almost every frontier community in 1776 confronted danger from Indians or local banditti, and huddled together for safety. Geography also contributed to the community type of settlement. The settlers naturally concentrated along the streams and in the valleys where they found water, fertile soil, and a link with the civilization they had left behind. Thus few settlers lived entirely alone. They seldom sought to escape from mankind, but tried to conquer the wilderness while remaining part of society. The Ordinance of 1785, which required the pioneer to buy a 640-acre tract instead of encouraging settlement in groups, may have been rational, but it certainly was not reasonable.

The typical Southern frontier of this period differed from the Northern in that Southern land claims were quite large and many settlers took slaves along with them. The two sections were alike, however, because most of the people were or quickly became farmers, and property was widely held, not concentrated in a few hands. Lunenberg County, in the southern Piedmont of Virginia, illustrates the westward movement of the tobacco frontier. In 1764 more than five hundred white men had moved into the district. Nearly half had not yet secured title to land, but most of these were working on their family's farm. During the next twenty years about four out of five became landholders. From the start, half a dozen men had obtained more than two thousand acres apiece, and land was so plentiful and so cheap that the median farm exceeded three hundred acres. The wealthiest 10 per cent of the landowners held 38 per cent of the real property, a figure that contrasts favorably to the 67 per cent for the South Carolina frontier district. Washington County, farther west, contained much the same sort of society in 1782. A few men obtained large speculative estates, but the richest 10 per cent held no more than 36 per cent of the wealth. Only a few farmers owned slaves.

The Northern farms ran much smaller primarily because of population pressure on the limited amount of good soil. Well-to-do pioneers were rare, slaves and servants equally uncommon. The Berkshire County settlements in Massachusetts generally contained just two classes: the small farmers and the farm laborers, the latter including only a third of the men. A town might contain a few substantial residents, perhaps a local shopkeeper, justice, large farmer, minister, or country lawyer, but all these together would own only a fourth or a third of the property and certainly did not form an upper class. At the other end of the social scale, the laborers seldom remained dependent but, as in Virginia, quickly acquired farms. A fair guess is that in 1776 not more than one out of twenty whites in these frontier settlements failed to improve his position. Most frontiers, then, were characterized by equality and mobility.

As an area lost its frontier qualities, its economy developed along one of three lines. Sometimes it remained relatively isolated as a semi-subsistence farming region. It might instead become a highly developed commercial farming community; more rarely, the frontier settlement might grow into a town. The first type of economy characterized large sections of the country in 1776, especially in the Northern states. Such a region had failed to progress economically much past the pioneer stage—it was a frontier in arrested development. Several factors might contribute to this situation. If the people lacked capital or labor they could not engage in profitable commercial farming. Their small farms, depending upon the labor of the owner and his sons, produced little surplus. Horses or oxen might help with the plowing, but the sowing, harvesting, and processing required human labor. By 1776 someone with capital could obtain slaves or servants or hired hands, but few farmers had enough money and seldom could borrow it. In addition to the shortage of labor, poor soil inhibited profitable farming, and in some areas the high cost of transportation ate up the profit. Therefore over large parts of the country the farmers and their sons did their own work, selling what they could at market and providing most of what they needed.

Although the subsistence farm society resembled that of the frontier in many ways, it differed in one crucial respect: it was static rather than dynamic, offering only a limited chance for the poor man to improve his position. Once the people had taken up the good land, sons and newcomers found their ambitions frustrated. Even established residents could not acquire wealth but might become at best substantial, respected citizens. The result was a very high rate of movement out of the area, involving both a surplus of native sons and disappointed immigrants. Probably most of these moved west where they could still obtain cheap land.

The people who remained depended upon the soil. At any one time in a New England rural village about two men out of five did not have farms but furnished hired help for the property owners. Many of these workers were grown sons who presently would inherit land. Nearly half the men were farmers producing a decent but not luxurious living. Finally, one man in every ten was neither a farmer nor a farm laborer, but an artisan (such as a miller, blacksmith, or tanner), a shopkeeper, a minister, a doctor, or a lawyer. The 10 per cent holding the most property owned at most two-fifths of the total wealth. That is a low figure: a hundred years later the richest tenth of the people in the United States held 60—some say 70—per cent of the property. The rural New Englanders perhaps rejoiced in belonging to a society with so few class distinctions, but the surplus sons, or the man who sought fame and fortune, went forth into the world.

These subsistence (more accurately, semi-subsistence) farm societies were much the same everywhere. All shared an equalitarian social structure and a wide distribution of property. All were quite isolated, comparatively poor, and culturally backward. The ambitious young man moved out to the frontier, the town, or during the war the army. The people who remained could not afford much schooling and saw little utility in higher education. They read few books, rarely traveled, suspected outsiders, idealized farm life, preferred to govern themselves, and focused their attention on the locality rather than on the world.

The rest of the rural folk depended in much greater degree upon the sale of surplus crops. These commercial farmers tended to specialize in some staple, employing a large labor force and investing considerable capital. The key to such an economic system was access to market. Commercial farming therefore developed around sizable towns, most of which lay in the North, or along navigable rivers leading to an important export center. The climax of commercial farming was reached in the familiar Southern "plantation."

Certain South Carolina parishes furnish a sort of caricature of the species. St. James, Santee, in 1787 contained forty-nine white taxpayers and 1,979 slaves. From the masters' point of view their society might fairly be called democratic, since almost three-fourths of the white men owned land and several of those who did not held slaves. The richest 10 per cent of the whites owned about half the wealth. From our modern standpoint, however, considering slaves as people, the parish contained roughly four hundred men of whom 90 per cent belonged to a propertyless labor force. This was a society in which 10 per cent of the people owned all of the property, including most of the other people. Charles City County, typical of Virginia's highly developed Tidewater, illustrates a similar though less extreme kind of social structure. Of the white population, half of the approximately four hundred men lacked land, although many belonged to a landowning family or held other property. Probably one-fifth were laborers unrelated to the farmers. About one-tenth were "planters" holding five hundred acres or twenty slaves, and the rest owned medium-sized farms. Ten per cent owned half of the total wealth. But now we must consider the 2,400 slaves, of whom presumably one-fifth, or 480, were adult men. Including these, Charles City's landless laborers, white and black, totaled more than five-eighths of the people. Thus the richest 10 per cent of the male population, all whites, held three-fourths of the property.

These are extreme examples, but they serve to emphasize the essential characteristics of a commercial farm society. First, the labor force (even in areas of free labor) considerably exceeded that in noncommercial agricultural areas, generally including half the population. These workers enjoyed little opportunity for advancement partly because so many were servants or slaves and partly because they needed capital to acquire property. For this reason the social order was more stable than on the frontier. Large property owners, rarely found on the frontier or in subsistence farming communities, were the most conspicuous social class. After the first generation most of them inherited their position. These men owned much of the best land, and many engaged in economic activities other than farming, such as milling, trading, speculating in land, and money-lending. A community of this sort, if not near a town, would support its own artisans, professionals, and shopkeepers. It would also contain, finally, many small but prosperous farmers, each producing a marketable surplus. These men usually entrusted political power to the great landowners—to the successful leaders of the neighborhood.

The social milieu of a commercial farm community differed in several important respects from that of the subsistence and frontier societies. Blessed with an income above the subsistence level and (thanks to the labor force) with some spare time, the more prosperous landowners acquired formal education, "culture," and knowledge of the world. Their often extensive business experience combined with travel and high political office diluted their rural parochialism and transformed the leaders, at least, into cosmopolitan men. Culturally and politically the society of a commercial farming area stood between the subsistence farm environment and the towns.

Urban society resembled that of the commercial farming areas in several important ways. The traveler who admired the fine homes of the countryside around Philadelphia, and who noted also the presence of numerous servants and hired hands, would remark the same phenomena in the city, where rich and poor still lived side by side. The urban upper class in 1776 consisted of merchants and other entrepreneurs such as distillers and shipbuilders, the most successful professional men, and the owners of valuable real estate. These held at least three-fifths of the wealth. Below them a middle-income group of small property owners included the "artisans and mechanics"—the skilled workers, often with their own shops, together with the lesser tradesmen, most of the professionals, and even some farmers. Finally, half the men were laborers such as sailors, wage workers, servants, and slaves, generally without property.

Such a concentration of wealth and extremes in social rank suggest the plantation type of society, but there were two obvious differences. The city contained a far greater variety of people engaging in specialized jobs unknown to the farmers: scriveners, chaisemakers, venduemasters, mariners, ropemakers, carters, sugar bakers, shipwrights, barbers, wigmakers. Because these jobs existed, and because most of the towns had been growing, opportunities for advancement exceeded those of rural areas except in parts of the frontier. The towns, from Boston down to Springfield, from Charleston to Beaufort, contained only a fraction of the total population, but their dynamic growth, their vital economic functions, cultural contributions, and political role made them crucial to the civilization of the thirteen states.

Though all these four types of societies resembled one another in their basic characteristics, yet the traveler would perceive much diversity as he toured the new country. Boston, like New England generally, consisted almost entirely of English Congregationalists. One might notice in the streets an occasional Negro, pass an Anglican church, and hear a Scottish or Irish brogue, but most minorities faded into the basic population. Even these fragments disappeared to the north and west of Boston save for a few Scottish-Irish settlements and some religious nonconformists. Religious controversies, while important to the debaters, all took place within a shared theological framework and to the outsider seemed minor. The obvious contrasts were economic and social.

Nowadays if one bows to Sam Adams's gravestone and walks on past Boston Common, everyone appears to be on the same economic level. Barring the obviously very poor, one can rarely distinguish affluence or occupation: that man has the clerical garb of a minister, and that black coat may cover a lawyer, but one passes without clue the tailor, businessman, clerk, carpenter, and millionaire, all shopping; even in Durgin Park where the people wear their working clothes to lunch, one must look closely for social differences. In contrast, colonial Boston, like every other eighteenth-century town, conspicuously identified its gentlemen. They and their wives and children wore elegant imported silks and satins carefully fitted to order by tailors and dressmakers, who together with wigmakers, staymakers, milliners, hatters, and silk drapers kept the elite fashionable. These properly dressed Bostonians bought carriages for their families (they would cost a year's wages for the ordinary worker), and fine furniture, glassware, and silver for their lovely Georgian homes. These men were worth at least £2,000 (local money) each, the equivalent of a hundred thousand dollars today, and earned the £500 or more which it took to live in some style. A queer kind of revolutionary! Indeed, the class supplied numerous Loyalists, and few among the rebels expected or desired any change in the established order, other than to remove a major obstacle to their own continued supremacy.

The Boston elite derived little of its wealth from land. A few earned fortunes through the law, a few by profitable enterprises such as a shipyard, a distillery, or a ropewalk; but almost all of them were merchants, like the loyalist Governor Thomas Hutchinson and his family (just departed on a British warship), James Bowdoin, and John Hancock. Practically all had been born in Massachusetts, and about half were descended from middle-class parents, whereas the loyalist elements generally inherited their money. These circumstances, combined with their superior education, Atlantic-wide contacts, and ability, probably account for their continued leadership during the Revolutionary years.

Some of those who dressed in the same style hoped to achieve by attire a status which their wealth did not justify, assisting the process by assuming the title of "gentleman" and aping the English dandies, or "macaroni." As a rule, however, Bostonians of the second rank dressed soberly, in durable working clothes devoid of frills, practical and frank —the garb of John Hurd or Paul Revere in Copley's famous portraits. Such men formed a class of substantial citizens, hard-working, ambitious, and were as capable of leadership as their more affluent neighbors. They included most of the lawyers, doctors, officials, and ministers, prosperous artisans with their shops (like William Dawes, Revere's co-rider, or Benjamin Edes, the printer), the reputable innkeepers, and men in trade who had not yet made their fortunes. City-born, of respectable colonial stock, they differed little from the patriot elite and generally joined with them during and after the war.

Just below them in property and prestige came the skilled

workers and the lesser businessmen, the small property owners of the period. These men earned enough for decency,
usually bought their own houses, and formed the rank and
file of the famous town meetings. The carters, painters,
housewrights, coopers, shoemakers, shipwrights, tailors, bakers, and sailmakers formed a respectable "middling sort,"
clearly differentiated from their betters by their marginal
standard of living. In Boston these men owned or rented
their own small shops, but seldom employed any help, and
they often worked for others.

At the bottom of the town's social order were the almost
propertyless workers. Some of these lived as servants, slaves,
and apprentices in the house of a master; others, including
mariners and semi-skilled laborers, slept in rented rooms
when in towns, and earned a sum just sufficient to exist but
rarely to save. Three out of ten Bostonians paid no taxes in
1771, and another tenth owned less than £50 worth of
property. Poor though they were, Boston's "inferior sort"
cannot be compared with present-day slum dwellers. They
were not segregated into slums, but lived at home with or
among the rest of the people; poor relief protected them
from starvation; the helpless among them boarded with families, their upkeep coming from town taxes; and, except for
slaves (5 per cent of the people), they might end as successful men. Only the infrequent periods of general unemployment created the serious hardships that might lead to vio-
lence. The years of the Revolutionary War were prosperous
after the British left.

Leaving Boston, a traveler would pass through the eastern
agricultural towns which fed the metropolis. Each of these
communities, such as Roxbury, Milton, Newton, and Dedham, contained two or three hundred families clustered
around the village center or in the countryside. Social dis-

tinctions were well marked but, compared with Boston's, rudimentary. A few families would own large estates, with farms containing several hundred acres and a fine house. Often the local doctor, lawyer, miller, minister, or store-keeper belonged to this local elite, but most of them de-scended from several generations of hard-working farmers who had thriftily accumulated property. In the village cen-ter lived a few artisans, and each community also contained laborers, sometimes sons who would one day take over their fathers' farms, often migrants who drifted in and out again. The number of such people had been steadily increasing as the result of population pressure on the land, and by 1776 they made up probably one-third of the people. Their pros-pects were not very good—rather worse than in Boston, for these towns were not expanding in size and furnished few new jobs and no additional land. This lack of mobility, and the entrenchment of a small proportion of the people hold-ing more than half the wealth, suggests a somewhat aristo-cratic, static social order, the leaders of which might reject any radical economic or social change.

Much more typical of New England were the hill towns a few miles further inland. These held almost as many farm laborers who, like their eastern counterparts, tended to move around, but large property owners were very rare. Thus the social structure was much more equalitarian, property more evenly distributed, the average wealth only half that of the lowland town. Farms remained about the same size, but the soil being poorer and the markets more distant, the owners had seldom prospered. The people here might well benefit from almost any change of circumstance.

As one traveled westward toward New York, across Wor-cester County, the Connecticut River, and the Berkshire Hills, one saw everywhere the same social order as in these agricultural villages: few large farms, many small, some very poor ones. The only fortunes made came not from the land but from trade or the law. Here were almost no slaves, seldom servants, but a considerable number of farm laborers, generally young. These did not make much money and their chances for self-improvement were rather poor, but at least they had enough to eat and were discontented rather than desperate. They would furnish plenty of rebel soldiers.

As one crossed the Berkshires and the Taconic hills—a frontier region then—and dropped down to the Hudson River valley, one saw for almost the first time since leaving Boston a truly fine home. The Livingstons, Van Rensselaers, Phillipses, Beekmans, and Robinsons dominated the eastern bank of the river as far down as Westchester County, where equally powerful manor lords owned great estates. On and between these huge tracts lived numerous independent farmers and tenants, often more prosperous than the New England yeomanry but sharply differentiated from the landlords. The proportion of poor people, including slaves, exceeded that in rural New England. Across the river in Ulster and even more in Orange County, however, large estates were rare and the social structure resembled that of the richer New England towns. New York farms ran much larger in size than did those of the eastern colonies, produced far more food, and probably supported a higher standard of living.

New York City also revealed the regional differences between the Middle and New England states. The streets nearest the water were filled with a similar busy medley of gentlemen and workingmen, but one heard more unfamiliar accents and saw different churches, for New York received a larger immigrant population. The rest of Manhattan remained Dutch in language, architecture, and customs, with fewer propertyless workers and more substantial burghers. Another element almost unknown in Boston were the great landowners and their relatives living in or visiting the city. This highly varied population lacked the town meeting and probably that sense of community which so distinguished the Yankee capital.

The societies of New Jersey and Pennsylvania also differed from those of New England. Although many little villages dotted the countryside, these were much smaller than the eastern towns, for most farmers lived not in village centers but out in the country. The average farm was twice the size of New England's, the houses more often of brick or stone, the wealth somewhat greater, and differences between rich and poor more marked. Moreover, the Middle colonies presented greater variety among localities. Different areas were dominated by Germans or Dutch, by Quakers or Presbyterians; the exciting, vital city of Philadelphia contrasted with the great estates and these with the lonely farms, as the big mansions of the merchants and landlords did with the increasing number of poor cabins. But if the New England visitor was struck by the opulence of this society, the traveler from abroad saw there instead a relative equality. A New Jerseyite could write quite honestly that all the people were "upon a levil" and that "gentlemen and servants" ate together. Much depended upon the point of view: the society did feature gentlemen and servants. Burlington County tax lists show well over half the men holding no land, while those who did have real estate averaged nearly two hundred acres of improved land. The most prosperous owned upwards of five hundred acres and as much as 60 per cent of the total wealth.

The major change as one rode southward through young America appeared after one crossed the Delaware into

Maryland and traveled along the shores of the Chesapeake to the Potomac, the James, and the Roanoke. Towns became scarcer and smaller: after Baltimore, which itself was only a fifth the size of Philadelphia, one would pass through no town of more than a few hundred families until reaching Charleston, several weeks' ride away. Farms grew still larger —generally more than two hundred acres, and one out of five landholders owned more than five hundred. These plantations were the most conspicuous, for they lay along the lines of communication and grew big houses as well as ample crops of tobacco or wheat. Conspicuous too were the slaves, almost half of whom lived on the large estates, so that the sharp divisions in Southern society, the wealth and poverty, struck the traveler most forcibly. In other parts of the South, to be sure, he would see more farmers working their land without slaves, as in the North, but even here he would not think himself in New England. The occasional big plantations, the distances, the lack of towns, churches, and schools, the higher average wealth combined with the greater number of poor people, clearly identified this as a distinctive society.

When the traveler finally reached Charleston, the contrasts to Boston appeared total. Blacks outnumbered whites in this city of fourteen thousand. Half of the artisans—all those who amounted to anything—held slaves: one barber owned five, a baker six, a mason eight, a silversmith nineteen, and even a shoemaker who left little property besides a flute, had his black. While the city was thus disfigured by a class of poor laborers twice as numerous as Boston's poor, it also displayed mansions more richly furnished than those of any other colonial city, for in Charleston the greatest poverty coincided with the greatest wealth. Here, during the summer, the rice planters joined the merchants and lawyers and other men of property to create the highest of all colonial high societies.

What was the future of this American society, "so various, so beautiful, and so new"? It contained the seeds of an equalitarian social structure, as some men longed for, as well as of an aristocracy, as others desired. The potential for a society of equals, an "agrarian society" as men called it, appeared most of all on the frontier and in subsistence farm societies, but one saw it too in the regions characterized by small commercial farms and in the lesser trading centers. As we have seen, these contained few wealthy families, and the number of poor people seldom exceeded the community's ability to care for them decently. Most of the thirteen states, moreover, could furnish vacant lands for the excess population, and people deprived of opportunity in crowded areas could migrate quite easily into newly established settlements. The larger trading centers also afforded a chance to rise which probably exceeded the usual situation (whatever that may be). The evidence points to a generally high vertical mobility at least into the ranks of independent yeomen and artisans. It appears that the distribution of wealth, taking the country as a whole, was democratic in that the small property holders owned a greater share than had been true in England and than was to be true a century later. Finally, the general standard of living favored an economic democracy in that relatively few men lived either in affluence or below the subsistence level. These facts anticipated the possibility of that idyllic utopia in which every man lived in comfort and could look every other man in the eye.

But there were other facts. In many commercial farming areas and in the larger towns, wealthy men contrasted with a class of propertyless laborers which included half of the people. As the country developed economically, the areas characterized by inequality steadily increased. All signs pointed to a growing gap between rich and poor. The opportunity to rise probably had been diminishing as the country matured. No such opportunity whatever existed for the slaves, comprising nearly one-fifth of the people. The distribution of wealth had become less equal as frontier and subsistence farms grew into commercial farms and towns, indicating that the present comparative equality would be succeeded by a society in which a tenth of the people held 60 or 70 per cent of the wealth. Such a trend would finally re-create the worst European conditions: a static social order in which a few lived in luxury and the many in want.

Thus independence meant to some men abundance for all, to other men riches only for the successful. The resolution of this conflict over social goals depended partly upon the structure of power and partly upon economic realities in the new nation.

# Chapter Two

## Making a Living in the Country

MOST American men in 1776 owned a farm. Two out of five made their living entirely by farming, and others—traders, craftsmen, innkeepers, ministers, doctors, even many ordinary laborers—owned and worked some land as a supplement to their other activities. Several hundred thousand men who had no land were farm laborers, and raised food on small plots owned by someone else, as the slaves sometimes did. Since many townspeople came from farm families, and since a few minutes' walk from every town took one into the country, every American knew about farming and farm life.

Three basic kinds of people made their living by agriculture: small farmers, including almost two-fifths of the entire population, farm laborers, numbering perhaps a third, and large landowners. Besides them, rural America contained professional men, skilled workers of various kinds, traders, and miscellaneous others. Each of these affected in important respects the economic, social, cultural, and political history of the Revolutionary years.

Although the category of small farmer encompasses quite a variety of persons, some generalizations are valid about most of them. The farm family owned a couple of hundred acres (more in the South, fewer in the North), but half of that remained unimproved, serving as wood lots or given over to livestock. How much the farmer could cultivate depended upon his labor force, since everything must be done by hand or with cattle and horses. Roughly speaking, one man alone could handle four or five acres of plow land, depending upon the crop and the soil. The families of Malden, Massachusetts, tilled on the average only three and one-half acres each. Farmers relied for help on their sons or hired extra hands, and they aided one another at harvest or whenever cooperation was more efficient than individual work. Thus a family might till a few acres intensively and thirty or forty superficially, plowing in the spring with oxen or horses, weeding a small part, cultivating not at all, and harvesting with outside help. The farmer would also use about the same quantity of pasture and meadow land and plant an orchard of several acres. The minimum necessary to support a family in New England was about fifty acres, and probably this just sufficed for the rest of the country: thus the common fifty-acre qualification for voting separated the self-sufficient from the dependent farmer.

Even when the small farmer specialized in a particular product, he diversified his activities, varying with the climate and soil. Grain served as the common staple. Wheat brought the best price, but several diseases had almost eliminated it in certain areas, notably New England, and it had other disadvantages. The farmer must harvest it promptly, yet he could reap no more than an acre a day. Then he had to carry it to a mill, for few families ground their own small grains. Naturally he had to pay the miller. People living in the deep South found that wheat spoiled easily. By 1776 most of the wheat was produced in the Chesapeake, Delaware, and New York regions, where farmers sold thousands of bushels at four or five shillings per bushel. An acre might produce ten bushels, so a one-family farm might earn £20 or so annually—a tidy sum, but of course the family itself consumed part of this.

Corn had displaced wheat as the staff of life in every colony except Pennsylvania and had become an important export crop in the South. It had several advantages. Farm animals could fatten on the stalk, leaves, and husks whereas wheat provided little fodder. The cultivation demanded less labor and the harvest could be delayed or protracted, permitting more efficient use of the labor force. Corn kept well, could be cooked in many tasty ways, required simple processing, and in general cost less than wheat to raise. Most farmers could grind up their own corn into coarse flour whereas other grain crops needed professional treatment. The market price of corn was only half or two-thirds that of wheat, so the latter remained the more profitable cash crop while corn fed the family. Farmers also raised rye, oats, and barley, while along the southernmost coast rice replaced other grain. They planted peas and beans, exporting twenty thousand bushels to the West Indies in 1772 (mostly from Virginia), and they supplied their tables with cabbages, potatoes, and other vegetables, flavored from an herb garden in the older communities. Orchards were almost universal, and one finds tenants required by lease to plant and maintain fruit trees. In parts of New England the value of an acre was measured by the barrels of cider it could produce. In the absence of refrigeration fruits did not last well except during the Northern winters, so people turned the apples, pears, peaches, and plums into potables (usually alcoholic) or preserves.

The rural American ate meat every day. Every farmer kept a dozen or more animals. The Northern winters forced the settler to play nursemaid to his livestock for many months, a task so burdensome and expensive that he kept only a few: the rugged oxen, a horse used for both farm work and transportation, two or three cows primarily for milk, butter, and cheese, and a few sheep and pigs. He never turned these animals loose but pastured them in summer and brought water and hay into their barn during winter. The highest-priced part of a farm was its good mowing and marshland. The more temperate Southern climate allowed animals to run freely, foraging in the woods. The planters seldom worried about furnishing hay or tending sick animals. As a result, Southern cows and horses and pigs were poorer than those in the North, but Southerners owned more of them. Most Virginians had several horses: even the landless rode one, and the larger planters kept five or more. Cattle outnumbered men eight to one, the average farmer raising nine or ten and the substantial planter at least twenty. All Southern folk took for granted that enough hogs for their meals were running around in the woods. Chickens, commonly called dunghill fowl, and sometimes ducks or geese cluttered up the home lot. If the farmer wanted variety for his table, he might hunt or fish.

Joshua Hubbart of Franklin, Massachusetts, owned a typical New England farm of eighty acres. On it he had raised, when he died in 1782, a pair of oxen, a mare and her two colts (one just born), five cows of which two were yearlings, six sheep, and about twenty bushels of Indian corn.

The corn, the three yearlings, and perhaps some of the sheep, together with some pine and oak lumber, probably comprised his surplus for the year, worth £10 or so. Of course he may have previously sold some other products such as cider (he owned an empty cider barrel). Samuel Carne, a prosperous South Carolina farmer, left a good deal more property when he died, including two Negro men, three "wenches," a young girl, and three children, worth five-sixths of his personal estate. These enabled him to produce seventy bushels of rice for market and 150 bushels of corn, probably consumed on his plantation. He also had twenty-four head of cattle (collectively worth much less than the New Englander's seven), six horses, four colts, and six hogs. He therefore produced for sale, in rice and live-stock, about £10 or £12, to which perhaps should be added the slave children, valued roughly at £35, and who would one day be worth £50 each. Both of these men lived simply, the Massachusetts man owning considerably more household goods, clothes (the climate), and books.

How much money did farmers make? These two inventories suggest a sufficient cash income for an adequate standard of living. The South Carolinian periodically invested a tidy surplus in slaves while Hubbart just maintained his family comfortably. About half the farmers owned less property than Hubbart. We find them most often in the subsistence farm communities, but some of them lived everywhere. Apparently they earned a cash income which during normal years enabled them to break even—about £10 or £12. That money, together with some extra hours of work, paid for the essential manufactured goods—firearms, great coat, brass kettle, iron pot, axe, wedges, hoes, saw, cornmill; for necessary foods, salt and rum above all; for the occasional services of a doctor, blacksmith, shoemaker, weaver, or other artisan;

for the local tax which supported a minister, the village poor, and perhaps a schoolmaster; and finally for the county and provincial taxes. There would be little left over, and any additional expense or loss of income meant trouble. A decline in the price of his cash crop, an unusually heavy tax, a drought, sickness, or other calamity, would plunge him into debt, probably to the shopkeeper or some other man of means, or to the tax collector. Court suits and the sheriff's sale followed. On the other hand, he could weather inflation very nicely, since he could stop buying almost entirely for some months while selling his surplus at a higher price. Such a man could provide for his first-born, but the other children would have to shift for themselves when they reached maturity.

The implications of the small farmer's economic situation extended to every aspect of his life. Since he enjoyed almost no surplus income he could not acquire a formal education, purchase books other than the bible and an occasional religious tract, subscribe to a newspaper, or broaden his mind by travel. Therefore his outlook remained narrow and he relied for his ideas primarily on his minister, his representative to the legislature, or another local leader such as a doctor, country lawyer, or justice of the peace. With an education limited to the practical, his utilitarian prejudices condemned art for art's sake, nor could he afford paintings, architects, or tickets to a concert; the theater he considered immoral. He enjoyed folk hymns, pictures which simply recorded how things looked—he'd have delighted in a camera—and a house fit for living. Religion he usually took seriously, emotionally, and enthusiastically. His economic ideas served to justify his needs: pare government costs to the bone, shift taxes to someone else, make cheap, long-term credit available, grant relief to debtors, and expect the legislature to otherwise leave him alone. This laissez-faire attitude implied a government that would protect the farmer and carry out his desires but otherwise remain passive. Since men like himself made up a majority of the voters, the farmer advocated rule by the majority, as we shall presently see. Yet he did not insist that government officials consist exclusively of farmers. He still retained, not always but often, a concept of society which acknowledged the superior ability of a few men who would govern in the best interest of all. He therefore tended to select the local leaders, even if they were not farmers, so long as they did in fact implement his objectives. Thus the farmer's beliefs reflected both his environment and his inheritance.

The more substantial farmers, who could market a larger crop, fared better and thought somewhat differently. Toward the top of the yeomanry, just below the class of large landowner, stood Theophilus Faver of Essex County, Virginia, with his eleven slaves—four men, three boys, a woman, and three girls. His large family (the house contained four beds) probably consumed most of the surplus from his fourteen cattle, twenty sheep, ten dunghill fowls, and eighteen geese, though, one trusts, not all of his seventy-five gallons of brandy. His cash crop consisted of £58.15.3 worth of tobacco. To this should probably be added some of the fifty hogs, seven horses, and more than ninety-two barrels of corn, giving him an income of around £100. This enabled him to furnish his house with over £80 worth of necessities and a very few luxuries: his books were worth only sixteen shillings and his clothes £3.2. Men such as Faver enjoyed a cushion which the ordinary farmer lacked, and which separated the two types in other ways as well.

At the top of rural society stood the large landowners, lord of hundreds, even thousands of acres and master of men, servile or free. In New England anyone with five hundred acres or more might qualify if his estate were intensively developed. Some men owned extensive tracts: James Gordon, who died in Boston, held nearly four thousand acres stretching from Braintree near Boston to Hampshire County. Gordon leased nine farms to tenants and left an estate valued at £5,000. A Cohasset man owned a 746½ acre farm worth nearly as much, and in Rutland, James Caldwell's thousand-acre estate was appraised at £3,393. Caldwell also owned five slaves and fifty head of cattle. Many such men lived in the Middle states and even more in the South.

Representative of the Southern planters was Thomas Mitchel of Prince George's Parish in South Carolina. Mitchel left, when he died in 1768, a personal estate valued at £32,020.10 Carolina money, or £4,574.7 sterling. Probably his land came to as much more. Mitchel owned eighty-four slaves, including a cooper, a carpenter, two indigo workers, and four babies. He had a schooner, two riding chairs, a mill house, an overseer's house, and his own home containing two mahogany and three other beds, a desk and bookcase, fifty-five gallons of rum and some wine, a silver watch, and an eight-day clock. Outside were eight pair of oxen and seventy-two other cattle, seventeen horses, fifty sheep, and twelve hogs. Two bushels of indigo seed reveal his plans for the future. As to the past, the inventory lists no indigo (already sold?), but he had produced rice worth £228 sterling and corn valued at £57.

The estates of most other large landowners would include fewer slaves and more money loaned at interest, but Mitchel's inventory points up some important characteristics of these men. They operated large-scale business enterprises with considerable investments of capital. The Virginia "planter" with a thousand-acre estate generally held about £2,000 worth of property, including some thirty slaves. Of their land only a small part would be planted to tobacco or wheat, probably not more than four acres per hand, and since most of those thirty slaves would be women and children, the planter might actually be relying on twenty or twenty-four acres to produce his cash crop of £160 or £200 currency (£100 to £150 sterling). To this might be added the sale of surplus lumber products, the profit from storing and handling his poorer neighbors' crops, charges at his saw or grist mill, land rented to tenants, fees received from local offices, and interest from money loaned. We are dealing, then, not simply with farmers but with businessmen.

Business ledgers have columns for debits as well as for credits. The slaves cost something to maintain—perhaps £4 a year each—and the landowner must pay for certain goods and services even as did the smaller farmer. Above all loomed two uncertain items: the expenses of his own household, generally higher than necessary or prudent, and interest charges on his debts. The well-to-do American could not resist erecting a more elaborate house than he needed, buying a four-wheeled phaeton instead of a two-wheeled chair, ordering some expensive clothes, wines, silver, and china, or investing in a few more slaves than he really needed, for use as house servants. Since he almost never had cash for all this, he bought, like his descendants, on credit, in anticipation of a bumper crop and good prices. When that good fortune came to pass he bought more; when it did not he suffered like his poorer neighbors. But there was this significant difference: a suit for debt might oblige the ordinary farmer to sell his very farm, whereas the large landowner could pledge a part of his property and continue to live much as before.

This fundamentally different situation contributed to a set of attitudes which clearly distinguished the two types of farmers. Because the great landholder enjoyed an income beyond subsistence, he could send his son to school or hire a tutor, buy books, subscribe to a newspaper, and travel. He usually lived near a town or along the main lines of transportation. He entertained visitors or went to the local trading center on court days, to attend the legislature, for business, or just for fun. These experiences widened his horizons. To be sure, some men of broad acres remained isolated in mind and body, but most became, by comparison with the rest of the country folk, cosmopolitan and urbane. The same advantages made the large landowner more appreciative of the arts: he built his house according to a book on architecture, ordered some stylish furniture from England, hung up a portrait of his wife, heard a performance of chamber music (Washington himself played the flute), and attended a play. In many ways he felt himself more like the well-to-do townsman than like the ordinary yeoman. He preferred a religion not too confining to his moral or economic life, decorous, rational, and supportive of social order. He recognized his special fitness as a social and political leader of the community, accepting office as his due and exercising power without direction from the electorate. Often holding some post of profit, and believing strongly in social order, he perceived the need for an effective government, even a strong one if he held the reins. His economic attitudes differed markedly from those of smaller farmers, for he was as often a creditor as a debtor, as much a businessman as an agriculturalist, spanning both the agrarian life and the wider world of the trader.

Second in number only to the farmers in the rural parts of the thirteen states were the laborers. One out of three

Northerners and almost half the Southerners held no land and little property of any kind, but worked for others who did. They included a variety of persons: free wage workers, indentured servants, and slaves.

The free laborers themselves consisted of several groups. More than two out of five were junior members of land-owning families who might eventually inherit part of the estate. In Lunenburg County, Virginia, in 1764, nearly half the landless whites were related to farm owners. Some of these left the county, but the great majority remained and became landowners themselves. This was a newly settled area with characteristically high mobility. In old Chester County, Pennsylvania, on the other hand, the batting average of success for the landless stood at a little over .500. We may suppose that until the young men took over the ancestral farms, their material—if not their other—needs were met by the family.

The rest of the free laborers hired themselves out. If one lived by himself the going wage of two shillings a day enabled the frugal to save a little money if he worked every day. But unfortunately the laborer could not hope for steady work, since the farmers needed extra help only now and then. Therefore he benefited most from boarding with his employer, receiving his room, "diet," and a wage of £15 annually. In this way he could save a few pounds a year and perhaps in time acquire land. On the frontier, almost anyone in good health could acquire land. In the east, where land cost more, rather fewer than half of the rural wage-workers succeeded, the failures being the least skilled, who accordingly made up a small class of permanently poor hired hands.

We know little about these free laborers, except those rare ones who later rose to prominence. Few contributed to society intellectually or artistically, for they lacked education. They created little wealth because they produced scarcely more than their own keep. Politically they seldom could vote, and we cannot with assurance separate their ideas from the farmers'. Military historians have not complimented them as soldiers, and the student of court records sees them too often. Yet they did help to meet the demand for labor, and many eventually became independent yeomen.

Indentured servants—men or women under contract to work for a period of years—had originally furnished much of the extra labor, but by 1776 they were partly displaced by slaves and free wage-earners. The Richmond County, Virginia, inventories of eighty-five estates during the early 1760's show 452 slaves but only nine white indentured servants, four of them female. The whites were appraised at about £12 each, the slaves at £36. Nevertheless, merchants continued to import them, and as late as 1775 a shipload of 130 arrived at Leeds, Virginia, representing twelve trades as well as farmers and laborers. New England had never attracted many, but in Pennsylvania, New York, and New Jersey they remained numerous, composing 8 or 10 per cent of the population. Most of them had emigrated from Germany and Ireland.

During the first decades of the century these servants seem to have remained as they were in the 1600's—a sorry lot. Many had been exiled as convicts; the rest came from the class of society least skilled, quite likely least intelligent, and apparently least adaptable: relatively few made good. After 1760, however, the colonies attracted people of a superior type. The danger from Indian attacks diminished, the trip over was faster and easier, and the odds in favor of a good life rose decisively. Although we still find some horror stories about the ocean crossing and bitter introductions to the new world, the colonies had become less a refuge for the desperate and more an opportunity for the ambitious. Servants advertised as runaways in the Virginia newspapers during 1775 included four skilled workers to every convict. We do not know how many rose into the propertied class, but probably at least half succeeded. During the period of their indenture they contributed substantially to the economy, for they cost the farmer little to support and added the productivity of a skilled and sometimes willing hand. Probably the master netted at least £10 per person per year unless the servant became ill, refused to work, or ran away. These servants, like the free laborers, were politically and socially unimportant during the Revolutionary years.

During the period of their indentures the white servants fared better than the black, despite their lower initial cost. The advantage probably resulted from a mixture of race prejudice and status, since the servant had been born free and would again become free. The frequent newspaper advertisements for runaways, generally couched in terms uncomplimentary to the servant, indicates a natural dissatisfaction with the servile status, and scattered court records contain cases of excessive punishment by the master. The servant's experience, however, may be considered as a species of schooling in which the pupil resisted his workload, but which was really advantageous to him in the long run since he acquired the skills necessary to future success. If the master sometimes lost his temper, let the parent consider that the relationship between the father and his grown but still-dependent son has always generated tension on both sides.

The simile of father and son cannot be applied to the blacks, free or slave. Whatever the origin of race prejudice, its reality in 1776 was almost universal among the white majority and served to depress the status of all colored folk.

Nineteen out of twenty blacks were slaves, and among the exceptions many were servants. Thus Willoughby Newton of Richmond County, Virginia, left to his children thirty-nine slaves, three white servants, and four free mulatto men, also indentured and evaluated at about the same as the whites. Some free Negroes held small farms or other property, but a higher proportion were laborers than among whites probably because they were less able to obtain the credit necessary to become independent.

The blacks' economic contribution remains uncertain despite attempts to measure the profitability of the slave system. During the years before 1776 they unquestionably helped to relieve a shortage of labor and thus to hasten the development of commercial farming in the South and perhaps in a few Northern counties. According to one estimate, a slave rented for £12 per year, and the return on rice or tobacco field hands must have been nearly that. The estates accumulated by the slaveowners testify to the profit, even taking their debts into account. Needless to say, the masters did not share the wealth with their labor force. Thus the free and slave laborers of 1776 had helped to create an agricultural prosperity much enjoyed by the prosperous farmers, who were not likely to permit a revolutionary assault on so comfortable a status quo.

Farmers and their laborers, as we have seen, did not provide all the necessities for rural America. Every country society needed skilled artisans, a few professional men, and a trader. The number of these varied from place to place with the degree of self-sufficiency, but in most communities one out of ten families and sometimes more contributed a nonagricultural skill. Groton, Connecticut, contained, according to the 1783 tax list, more than five hundred men, including a lawyer, a doctor, eight shopkeepers, fifteen innkeepers, nine blacksmiths, seven shoemakers, a clothier, two tanners, a goldsmith, fifteen carpenters and joiners, five tailors, and thirteen millers (ministers were not taxed), who made up about one-seventh of the population. On the other hand, in Winchester, a more nearly subsistence farming community, all but about one person in eleven were farmers or farm laborers. Even these figures exaggerate the nonfarm element, for many of these men had land: in Winchester the blacksmith, both millers, a shoemaker, and an innkeeper were farmers as well.

Reciting some of the most common English names announces the important rural artisans: above all Smith and Miller, then less certainly present Carpenter, Weaver, Shoemaker, and—depending on the area—Tanner or Cooper. The miller ranked among the leading members of rural society, often as one of the wealthiest. Farmers growing wheat, oats, rye, or barley needed a gristmill desperately, and the community sometimes gave away valuable millsites with land attached. Often several men united in raising the capital, and shares in the mill passed from father to son as valuable inheritances. In other cases a large farmer, favorably located, would construct the dam and mill, perhaps hiring a millwright. Since the miller received part of the grain as pay, he had no problem collecting money; employment was steady, and the enterprise was profitable. The largest operations (called merchants' mills) might grind thousands of bushels and net a profit of hundreds of pounds. Owners of sawmills also prospered. Millers therefore often became large landowners and political leaders for the community. Thus in Winchester Captain Benjamin Benedict, owner of a sawmill, paid the sixth highest tax, and the third highest taxpayer was Samuel Hurlburt, miller and innkeeper.

Blacksmiths performed a service just as essential, one

which required less capital but more skill. They did not, typically, produce original articles for sale, though the owners of ironworks sometimes referred to themselves as smiths and may have begun as such. The village or country blacksmith ran a small shop, not a foundry, and repaired local articles, occasionally making simple products such as nails or hoes. For example, Joseph Cook of Harwinton, Connecticut, shoed oxen and horses (a full job cost three shillings two pence), sharpened shears, axes, and hoes, mended plows, scythes, forks, and chains, and in addition sold wood, pork, and cider. On an average the smith owned £300 worth of property, about the same as his neighbors. He almost always farmed some land, relying on his customers to supply labor for him if he himself lacked time.

Tanners, like millers, needed a substantial amount of money to start their business. Later they might accumulate more property than any other country artisan. There seems to have been a division among them comparable to the difference between the smith and the iron manufacturer, the ordinary miller and the owner of a merchant mill: about half had small tanyards worth, with the land, a couple of hundred pounds, while others ran a big business with hired hands. Thus a tanner in Keene, New Hampshire, acquired a nice estate of £617 while another in Henniker left property worth only £100. The prosperous tanner, like the miller, occasionally showed up in the legislature, whereas other rural artisans almost never did so.

Shoemakers, called cordwainers in New England, existed in most farm societies because the people seldom knew how to make shoes. Since every pair must be fitted to the individual, the country-dweller was forced to seek a specialist, which meant that one shoemaker was needed for every hundred people, or thereabouts. Rural cordwainers seldom acquired more than a modest estate and often owned no land at all. It seems likely that they realized only a small profit from customers demanding the cheapest and most practical foot-covering. A good many abandoned their craft as a primary source of income and turned to farming, practicing their old trade during the winter. It was not uncommon for the American farmer to retain some vestiges of a former calling, and we find their inventories listing tools of many trades.

The word "carpenter," for some reason, does not occur in New England, where the terms "joiner" or "housewright" identified those specialists. Although the colonial American learned many crafts, only the pioneer approached complete independence, at considerable cost to his time and comfort. When the men of 1776 replaced their frontier cabins with decent homes, they hired an expert for the tricky parts and another for comfortable or attractive furniture. Carpenters made about the same incomes as other artisans of the middle ranks: five or six shillings a day, or at least twice what an agricultural laborer earned. Needless to say, such men built a home for themselves, and their pay enabled them to acquire property about on a level with small farmers.

The weaver and the cooper, like the carpenter, performed services that farm communities could not do without, though their numbers varied depending upon the local cash crop. They too were generally men of moderate means with only a few pounds' worth of tools. A long time would elapse before the weaver would become a textile manufacturer, and in this period they still served only their neighborhood. The cooper, however, prospered if the people needed a lot of his barrels to carry away their products, as they often did.

Thus one man in Leicester, Massachusetts, acquired 258 acres and left a tidy estate of £905, quite likely because of the excellent Worcester County cider.

Rural communities might include other skilled workers depending upon local needs: a millwright where numerous mills were built, a fuller where the people raised flax for cloth, a potash manufacturer in lumbering centers, or an occasional tailor, generally poor. In New Jersey, Pennsylvania, Maryland, and Virginia, blacksmiths often grew into iron founders, and other artisans also worked in the furnaces and forges. All of these men earned an income ranging from bare subsistence on up to a comfortable livelihood, but almost none became really large property holders. The exceptions engaged either in milling or those branches of manufacturing that required considerable capital, involved hired hands, and produced for export. One man, for example, owned a saw mill, grist mill, and ironworks in East Kingston, New Hampshire, together worth more than £2,000. A miller in Cumberland County, New Jersey, left an estate of £1,699, not including his house, land, and four mills. These men had clearly risen out of the artisan class and probably should be considered entrepreneurs, capitalistic employers on a par with the large landowners.

Artisans in Southern commercial farming regions belong to a separate subspecies, since they lived in a society which did not foster numerous independent skilled craftsmen. The scattered character of Southern settlements may partly account for this, as some observers have believed, yet the people needed smiths, coopers, millers, shoemakers, and the rest whether scattered or not. The primary factor seems to lie rather in the economic system of commercial farming based upon slavery. By exporting a large surplus, many

Southerners were able to import some articles which otherwise they would have manufactured locally, such as cloth. Even more important, perhaps, the commercial farmers trained their slaves to perform the functions of white artisans. One finds them not only in the fields and acting as house servants but trained to be bricklayers, coopers, various kinds of carpenters, weavers, blacksmiths, and experts in nearly every other craft. White artisans served in a supervisory capacity, as millers often did, or as teachers of the trade, but seldom worked independently. When they did appear in the records of the rural South, they seem either to have been very poor, with only a few pounds of property, probably dependent upon wages, or else they owned a respectable estate including slaves, who doubtless did much of the manual work. Thus a blacksmith in Chesterfield County, Virginia, owned personal property worth £221, including two slaves, while a carpenter in St. Thomas and Denis Parish, South Carolina, had six slaves as part of a personal estate evaluated at £275 (and which sold for £292). Another carpenter in St. Matthew's Parish owned seven blacks. In contrast, the entire property left by a blacksmith of Berkeley County, South Carolina, sold for less than £13. In various parts of Virginia two blacksmiths, a tailor, a millwright, and a carpenter combined had acquired only £127. No middle class of artisans emerged in the slave states.

Rural artisans thus included a broad spectrum of peoples about whom it is hard to generalize. They ranged from substantial property holders to the poor, from community leaders to the disfranchised. Almost all worked very hard, like their farmer-neighbors, from sunrise to sunset six days a week. Most of them—say four out of five—succeeded in acquiring land and a decent livelihood, so that they spoke as equals to the small farmers. One out of five ranked with the larger property holders of the community, and a very few achieved high social status and political leadership.

The principal men of rural society seldom belonged to the artisan class, and even large farmers did not produce as many leaders as one might expect from their numbers. The country people turned instead to their best-educated neighbors: the professional men. Of these the most important were lawyers or justices, ministers, and, on a lower rung of the ladder, doctors.

If we define the lawyer as one with formal legal training, then very few lived in rural areas except in the plantation South. There were several reasons for this. First, in 1776 few such men existed anywhere. No state contained a law school, so the prospective lawyer either must live for several years in England at a cost prohibitive for all but the rich, or serve an apprenticeship under an established colonial lawyer, for a fee of course; meanwhile he earned no money. This situation meant that lawyers belonged, with few exceptions, to the colonial elite, which fact suggests several additional reasons for their geographical imbalance. Most men brought up in comfort prefer to remain comfortable. In the colonies they stayed near the cultural centers among people of their own tastes. The rural life or the society of a village community did not attract them, and moreover the courts they attended usually sat only in the larger towns. Finally, one did not make much money providing for the legal needs of farmers and artisans, but grew rich through collecting fees from the wealthy.

The country lawyer, therefore, stood out above his neighbors as a man of education, ability, and often family. He was also conspicuous for his property, since if he did not begin with money he quickly acquired cash through fees, and then could further increase his wealth by investing his fluid capital in land, debts, or other income-producing enterprises. Samuel Livermore, after graduating from Yale, first practiced in Portsmouth, but in 1775 moved to Holderness on New Hampshire's frontier. He became the dominant figure in that area, owning a mill and upwards of ten thousand acres in ten townships, climaxing his career as chief justice of the state and a United States Senator. John Ashley of Sheffield, Berkshire County, Massachusetts, also graduated from Yale and inherited a huge landed property. In Sheffield he practiced law, ran a store, owned a grist mill, saw mill, and ironworks, and loaned money. Similarly another Yale man, Ezra L'Hommedieu, son of a Suffolk County, New York, trader, settled down in his home town of Southold, married into the local elite, acquired £1,000 worth of land by 1776, and became the region's most prominent public figure. The names of Thomas Jefferson and James Madison make unnecessary examples from Virginia's Piedmont. By 1776 many country men were passing bar examinations in Williamsburg and returning home to prosecute suits for debt.

The educated lawyer probably made more money than anyone else in the thirteen states except for the luckiest of merchants or those great landowners who avoided debts. In Virginia he might earn more than £1,000 annually, and while he often had to sue for his fees, economic prosperity followed eventually. He became an extensive landowner and frequently married into the best local family. Lawyers furnished political leadership for rural areas where most people could spend neither time nor money in public service and where education and wide acquaintanceship conspicuously recommended one for office. George Clinton of New York, Patrick Henry of Virginia, Thomas Burke of North Caro-

lina, John Sullivan of New Hampshire, and Thomas Johnson
of Maryland are a few Revolutionary governors who practiced law in small rural communities.

A broader definition of a lawyer, simply as one who
practices the law, will admit a larger number and greater
variety of Americans. Until long after 1700 educated lawyers were uncommon, and legal affairs in most colonies remained in the hands of amateurs such as James Otis's father.
Jonathan Grout of Petersham, Massachusetts, neither went
to college nor served an apprenticeship, but he practiced law
quite successfully in Worcester County. So did William
Jernegan of Edgartown on Martha's Vineyard and William
Starkweather of Lanesboro in the Berkshires, William
Wedgery in New Gloucester, Maine, Dirck Wynkoop of
Ulster County, and Peter B. Tierce of Washington County,
New York, all of whom became locally important. As a rule
these men acquired less property and held fewer major
offices than their more learned brethren. Groton, Connecticut's attorney paid a tax which was exceeded by nearly 20
per cent of the residents, and Adam Hubly in Lancaster
County, Pennsylvania, owned property about equal to his
prosperous Pennsylvania farm neighbors (though he would
enlarge it after the war). On the whole, however, the country lawyer earned more money than almost anyone else and
contributed superior leadership to his society.

Justices of the peace occupied a position halfway between
a lawyer and a judge, settling local cases by referring to a
mixture of legal precedent and the rights and wrongs of the
affair (equity). Their income from fees and the local impact of their decisions would alone have made them conspicuous citizens, but in addition the office both in England
and America had been associated traditionally with the influential country gentry. To some extent the colonial en-

vironment lessened this prestige, and some justices actually held only moderate property. In Bedford County, Pennsylvania, only two of the justices who held office in 1776 were wealthy (Bernard Dougherty and Robert Cluggage); and half of their colleagues owned only average estates. On the whole, however, up until 1776, at least, justices were selected from among the wealthier inhabitants, especially those reputed to know some law, or to be generally well educated. The office itself was profitable, so justices usually were or became part of the economic and social upper class.

Socially and culturally ministers ranked with lawyers, but their lower incomes suggest a declining status. The country clergy usually received much less than did those in the towns, indeed sometimes their "living" was scarcely enough to live on. Such were the "clerk" of Petersham, Massachusetts, who left an estate of £94, of which all but £87 consisted of debts owed to him; the minister of Newcastle, New Hampshire, with £140 total property, and that of Hampton owning £112 in all; or, at the other end of the country, ministers of Prince William and St. Helena's parish leaving personal estates of £206 and £59 respectively. Perhaps these are individuals whom the people did not admire, but many rural communities simply did not have the money for good salaries. Ministers who lacked family or other connections generally occupied these less financially rewarding posts. The Anglican clergy, up until 1776, benefited from an English subsidy, but many still needed local support which was not always forthcoming.

One nevertheless gets the impression that the people contributed liberally to the church, considering their finances. More typical than the examples cited above were the estates left by the ministers of Hampstead and Pembroke, both small New Hampshire towns, of £805 and £1,330. In New

Jersey the ministers owned property well above the average, and the two poor South Carolinians are offset by another whose inventory of £3,707, aside from his land, included seventy slaves. The £200 settlement commonly granted by New England towns, together with the profit from a farm, use of a house, other gifts such as firewood, and a salary of £40 to £100, combined to relieve most ministers from financial worries and enabled them to live in comfort. The ministry therefore attracted, as was intended, some of the better minds of the Colonial period, men who deeply influenced the feelings and convictions of their congregations.

Doctor's incomes reflected, even more than the earnings of other professional men, the state of knowledge and the attitude toward intellectuals and science among the people of 1776. One rather small group of doctors had received the best education that the times afforded, enabling them to treat their patients under scientific auspices by bleeding or purging or gagging with nauseous medicines. These few almost never settled in the country except in the plantation South, where they would combine planting, farming, and sometimes other remunerative activities. One South Carolina doctor had managed to acquire fifty-two slaves and left a personal estate valued at nearly £2,000. Charles Drayton was one of the same colony's wealthiest men, as were Drs. George Haig and Thomas Tudor Tucker. All had studied at Edinburgh and practiced among the rich rice planters. David Stuart of Fairfax County, Virginia, a neighbor and friend of Washington, graduated from William and Mary and became far wealthier than his minister father, while William Fleming of the Valley, William Hubbard of Charlotte on the Southside, and Walter Jones of Northumberland, all Virginia Senators, had taken degrees from Edinburgh. In Maryland the prominent William Ennalls Hooper practiced medicine on the eastern shore as did Daniel of St. Thomas Jenifer on the western. As a rule, however, such trained men located in centers of population where they could extract a concentration of fat fees.

Rural areas commonly attracted physicians with less formal training or even with none, often equipped with a motley assortment of medicines, a few books, and an impressive manner. They ranged from the well-intentioned and competent to the quack. Some of these earned decent incomes. One Surry County, Virginia, doctor left thirteen slaves as part of a £681 personal estate. Two physicians in Dedham, Massachusetts, never a wealthy community, left estates worth £1,968 and £1,255. A third was worth only £327 but included medicines valued at £150—indicating a seriousness of purpose at least. The income of about half of these country doctors everywhere placed them among the well-to-do men of their societies even though they failed to achieve real wealth. This substantial and respected group, with money enough to allow them some leisure time, produced many political leaders of the country areas: New Hampshire's Councilors Ebenezer Hale and Nathaniel Peabody; in Massachusetts the Federalist leader Colonel John Brooks of Medford and Senator John Hastings of Hatfield; in the South men such as General Adam Stephen of Berkeley County, Virginia, and the army surgeon James Martin of the New Acquisition. Finally, near the bottom of the scale of wealth comes an all-too-numerous group: a physician from New Jersey with an estate of £27, one from New Hampshire with £4.6.6 consisting entirely of books, and one from Massachusetts with £4.2.9. Doctors' account books show many pounds' worth of uncollected fees, and the very low incomes of so many must often reflect the unvarnished poverty of their community.

At the very bottom of rural society, excepting only the laborers, came the schoolmasters. Few men of property taught school unless they earned a living as a minister or a farmer. Those who had no other job remained poor. Thus in Gloucester County, New Jersey, a teacher left an estate of £10, one in Cumberland County owned only £9, and a Burlington County teacher's estate was £15—and he was married. In the North, rural folk preferred to hire a local wife who would accept a pittance, or a young lad just out of school himself. Southern planters occasionally hired a tutor for their children, but the job lacked prestige. Anyone with knowledge enough to teach went to the larger towns or, better still, put that knowledge to more profitable use as a doctor or minister or lawyer or trader—anything but as a teacher, leaving behind only incompetents. As a result the country schoolmaster almost never occupied a post of consequence but died unsung and, with rare exceptions, unpropertied. One suspects that Hercules Mooney, a peripatetic New Hamsphire teacher, won election to the legislature from two different towns because he had been a military captain during the war, not as a result of his occupation.

Considered merely in their economic capacities the professional men, including local officials such as sheriffs, tax collectors, and clerks as well as justices, contributed virtually nothing to the rural community but were parasitical upon it, and indeed newspapers published attacks on them for that reason. Yet the lawyers, doctors, ministers, and teachers did return to the people most of the money received from them, because they purchased local products and services and provided capital out of their profits, and their services helped to sustain the people. The lawyers aroused resentment because they spent much of their time collecting money owed by the country folk to nonresident creditors, and because they extracted fees which they then spent in travel or the purchase of luxury articles. Yet the people appreciated their ability and chose them as representatives in the legislature.

Extracting money from the country people too, but performing even more essential economic functions were the traders and shopkeepers. The former conducted an extensive wholesale business which might reach from the port city far into the interior. They made their headquarters in some inland town with excellent transportation facilities, rarely settling in a farming community. Often they enjoyed important political and family connections within the provincial world, as did Isaac Coles of Halifax County, Virginia's Southside, whose father John had been a wealthy planter and who, after attending William and Mary College, married into the prominent Lightfoot family. On the other hand, Matthew Marable, of neighboring Mecklenburg, a fellow Burgess in 1773, immigrated from Scotland. Combining the characteristics of both, Robert Rutherford came from a good Scottish family, went to the University of Edinburgh, and acquired fortune in the Shenandoah Valley, from which he too traveled to attend the 1773 Burgesses. In the Mohawk Valley of New York, Jacobus Mynderse succeeded to his father's business as a trader and joined the legislature in 1769, at the same time that Timothy and Josiah Dwight, of an equally prominent family, were representing Hampshire County in Boston, and Jedidiah Foster, a Harvard man though a blacksmith's son, attended from Brookfield in Worcester County.

Traders were engaged in a hazardous enterprise with sudden wealth or bankruptcy equally probable. A South Carolinian left property worth £28,000 currency when he died, but most of this consisted of bad—as they called it, "desperate"—or hopeless debts. If one man in little Rindge, New Hampshire, accumulated £2,034, another in Epsom left only £129, and Somerworth's trader died insolvent. The usefulness of such men lay in their ability to sell the surplus produced by the locality. They collected tobacco from Virginia's Southside, wheat from the Shenandoah Valley, furs and flour along the Mohawk, lumber from New Hampshire, a miscellany from central Massachusetts, and transported these to the principal ports, often over many miles. Returning with a variety of manufactured goods and foods both necessary and luxurious, they sold at their storehouses to the retail shopkeepers or direct to consumers. They obtained credit for their own purchases and then passed on the credit to the country people, furnishing in this way much of the capital for expansion. Successful traders almost always bought and sold land and often engaged in manufacturing as well, especially as millowners. They were, in short, the principal entrepreneurs of their area.

The more numerous storekeepers lacked opportunities for great wealth, but were just as useful as the traders. They supplied the many articles that farmers or artisans needed: pins, rum, nails, cloth, iron pots, pewter plates, harnesses, tea, ribbons, salt, bibles, bullets, sugar, thread. The shopkeeper recorded every transaction in his big ledger, and on the opposite page appeared the record of payment, rarely of coin, sometimes of a service performed (help with the harvesting, a horse shoed, some timber cut), or of an article received. The value of the storekeeper's stock might be quite small, perhaps only £30 or £40. He expected a profit of at least 40 or even 50 per cent above costs of transportation, and renewed his stock twice a year. He might also sell to his wholesale supplier the articles which his customers paid in to him, such as peas, shingles, livestock, tobacco, corn, or flaxseed. Thus Connecticut's Governor Jonathan Trumbull, when he was a shopkeeper in Lebanon, drove the area's surplus cattle to Boston. Some ambitious men risked considerably more capital and invested yearly profits in land, mills, or money-lending, finally acquiring quite substantial estates like the Halifax County storekeeper whose personal property sold for £2,147 just before the Revolution.

The economic contributions, at least of the more enterprising shopkeepers, seem to have been recognized as such by the people they served. Although they sued for long-overdue debts, they seldom charged interest on their ordinary accounts and provided many free services. Aroused farmers directed their animosity rather against the nonresident wholesalers who extracted money without obvious return. The connections formed by local shopkeepers with the outside world and the prestige associated with economic success often led to their assuming political leadership in the Revolutionary years.

A quite different sort of trade also produced some leaders. Innkeepers sold rooms, meals, care of horses, liquors, and, in the absence of another local retailer, other supplies. While the records disclose some poor ones, and travelers often complained bitterly, many innkeepers flourished and by opening their rooms to politicking became influential. A New Jersey tavernkeeper left £894 in personal property together with three houses and nearly two hundred acres; an innholder in Kingston, New Hampshire, died worth £1,000, while in South Carolina the sale of an innkeeper's estate netted over £350 sterling, not including many debts receivable and some land. The Massachusetts legislature in 1765 contained three tavernkeepers; others would join them during the Revolutionary years.

The rural community of Revolutionary America had little

need of the outside world. It produced nearly all its essentials and necessary skills. Farmers grew food, cut lumber for dwellings, furniture, and fuel, and supplied wool, linen, and leather for clothes. Millers, smiths, and other artisans contributed their skills, laborers their time. Professionals met spiritual, medical, and other noneconomic needs. What the people could not supply themselves, they bought by selling their surplus. A New England farm town containing a couple of hundred farm families might have available for such market activity more than a thousand pounds in value not in specie but in yearly profits. Most of this "surplus" went to pay for the services of the local minister, lawyer, doctor, teacher, and various craftsmen. Some bought from the traders the sugar, salt, tea, coffee, rum, and other articles necessary or desirable. The semi-subsistence farming community might earn, after necessary consumption and depreciation, a small margin for further investments or a slightly higher standard of living. To a war for independence it could contribute little money, some supplies for the army, and many men. A commercial farming area, like those in the rich lands of the Middle states and in some of the plantation centers farther south, produced several times as much. This annual margin between income and necessary expenses, when added to that of the towns, enabled the country to support a long and costly war.

## Chapter Three

## Making a Living in the Towns

EVERY town in the thirteen states had its own personality: Boston with its crooked streets, capitol hill, spires, and Common; New York on an island, English around the shores and Dutch in the middle; Philadelphia along the river, broad streets and plain folk; and Charleston, West Indian and British, black and white. Each lesser town was unique, too, from the part–fishing villages, part–port cities like Falmouth and York in Maine to the inland distributing centers such as Lancaster and another York in Pennsylvania and the Southern tobacco marts of Alexandria and New Bern. Even the small ones performed for their people and their country neighbors the vital functions of any city: each was a seat of government, a focus for social life, a custodian of culture, and, above all, a center for essential economic activities.

Large or small, the towns of 1776 contained several basic

kinds of people earning a living and through their labor creating a dynamic economy. Slaves, servants, and wage-workers toiled at hard, menial, unpleasant, poorly paid tasks. Above them came the skilled laborers, from the journeymen up to the master craftsmen and the owners of larger manu-factories. Professional men concentrated in the towns and so did traders, including the modest owners of small specialty shops and the great merchants. By 1776 the cities had also produced a class of gentlemen who lived at leisure by their investments in debts or in land and houses.

What we would today call the labor force made up nearly half the population of the port towns, and perhaps a some-what smaller proportion of the inland centers. The most numerous segment of the urban working class in the South was the slave, who performed household chores for white families of average property below the Mason-Dixon line and for the more prosperous farther north. By 1776, as we have already seen, many slaves had become highly skilled, so that white craftsmen often used black labor not simply for cleaning shops but to help with the most important jobs. One suspects that the Charleston shipwright with twelve slaves, the wheelwright with four, and the barber with six led rather leisurely lives. Southern townspeople probably could have done without black help. Slaves were essential only to the plantation economy, founded as it was on scarce cheap labor; in the towns they were just luxury items. Even in Charleston Negro men formed considerably under half the adult male population, whereas in the nearby parishes they outnumbered their masters five or six to one. Most of the functions they performed, especially in the North but everywhere, were really noneconomic, satisfying the white's desire for status, relieving the mistress from household drudgery, and enabling the master race to enjoy some leisure. One suspects that from a financial point of view the urban slaves did not increase the white's earning capacity. Most of them were, so to speak, consumer durable goods rather than part of the labor force.

Less visible but much noisier, the sailors formed a colorful part of the seacoast people. Most of them were young men. Few became ancient mariners—if the sea failed to end them, war or disease did. Most stable and with the best survival record among the sailors were the fishermen. Some of these built their own small boats and sailed daily to banks offshore. They avoided the worst storms simply by staying home. Raising their own food and providing for other necessities, they earned enough to live decently. The only way to riches, if one persisted in fishing, lay in owning a big vessel and voyaging far out to the productive Gulf Stream, especially to the famous northeastern banks. The venture might be profitable, but it was hazardous and expensive, too risky and too costly for the ordinary fisherman. Men with capital built the ships and absorbed the occasional losses, hiring others as ordinary sailors, mates, or masters. The wages just sufficed to support a family, assuming that one survived, but the major profits went to the owners. Of course, some men did start as common fishermen and like the lucky mariner work up to the higher rewards of a master, buy shares in a fortunate voyage, and end as a shipowner, but one was much more likely to fail somewhere along the way: the apt adjective modifying fisherman was "poor."

Colonials seldom joined the navy, and indeed few men deliberately did so, for the poor food, low pay, harsh discipline, and high mortality rate attracted only the desperate. Rather, officers seized lads who promptly deserted when they could and signed on to a merchant ship. The difference seems slight to the modern observer, yet civilian shipowners found crews without kidnaping them. Common seamen earned £2 or £3 per month on the trading vessels, enough for a young man to save and settle down. Few did so, partly because they did not work constantly, and partly because they squandered their wages at once. Even in good times, port cities harbored a sizable floating population of rough, penniless jack-tars, and in bad times the sailors became dangerous, the raw material for mobs. Those mariners who saved some money left the sea and settled down, perhaps after rising to the rank of mate or captain. At that point they began to invest in part of a cargo or buy a share in a vessel. Once economically independent, they could multiply their capital as traders instead of hoarding a few pennies as sailors. The profits went to the landlubber, not to the men before the mast.

Those wage-earners who remained on shore lived longer and had a better chance of acquiring substantial property. The familiar sequence of apprentice–journeyman–master craftsman continued during the Revolutionary era. The indentured servant just ashore from Europe and the local teenaged boy began by joining a group of the permanently unskilled at the lowest economic level. Servants and apprentices lived in the master's house or a small outbuilding, and in exchange for room, board, clothing, and other expenses did what they were told. Ideally the relationship included, on one side, a parental obligation to cherish, educate, Christianize, and protect, and, on the other side, filial love and obedience. Long before 1776 the ethical content of such agreements had largely evaporated. The master neglected his obligations and sought instead to recover his investment with interest, while the servant, lacking any reason for gratitude, malingered or fled. The law protected the worker against manifest ill treatment, he did receive on-the-job training, and he did get enough to eat. The appeal and opportunity of independence, however, often exceeded the advantages of security: servants generally preferred liberty to order. The master also came to prefer a free labor force over a servile one, because by hiring workers only when he needed them he eliminated fixed costs as well as twinges of conscience. During much of the Colonial period no reservoir of labor existed to meet sudden demands, so the employer was forced to sacrifice his ability to hire and fire in order to secure his labor supply. By 1776 the size of the labor force was increasing, unemployment became endemic, and the worker's position was deteriorating. Fortunately for him the war years created a demand for labor and wages skyrocketed temporarily.

We do not know how many of these servants, apprentices, and common laborers became independent craftsmen. Individual instances of rags to riches, and many more of rags to respectability, do not prove a trend. The key to economic success undoubtedly lay in acquiring a skill. Until the worker completed his term or apprenticeship, he earned no income which could establish his independence. The basic wage of the free laborer scarcely enabled him to buy necessities. The ordinary urban wage-earner seldom owned land or a house but had to rent a room, and probably had to eat out and to purchase his other necessities instead of providing for himself as the farmers did. That was why even the free men so often lived with their employers. One could not readily buy a farm, and the towns therefore contained a steadily growing number of almost propertyless workers. They combined with the sailors in the Revolutionary "mobs" and continued to be a disturbing force in the new nation.

The skilled workers, called "craftsmen," "artisans," or

"mechanics," had a much better chance for economic advancement. They included three major groups: wage-workers, small independent shopowners, and those operating large-scale establishments.

By 1776 the important towns contained many master craftsmen who hired skilled "journeymen," and some sizable manufactories with large amounts of capital and many employees. As a rule of thumb, the occupations requiring the least skill and the lowest investment in tools and labor returned the least profit. The basic daily wage of employees varied from not much above that of rural workers, which meant bare subsistence, up to two or three times the minimum, which enabled one to accumulate property. The man who owned a shop and worked alone might just break even. As he hired workers he profited not simply from his own labor but from that of his employees, producing a greater volume and perhaps a more complex product. As a final step he might supplement the output of his own shop by importing and selling similar articles, and end by becoming a merchant. The sequence, therefore, went as follows: poor tailor, master tailor with apprentices and journeymen making to order cloths of the best quality, and finally a clothier, importing and selling to other tailors high-grade cloth. Similarly, the general carpenter, worth three shillings per day, becomes a housewright, earning four or five shillings, then builds a house, hires men, builds more, and dies leaving an estate of £1,000.

As the artisan increased his skill and income, his social status also improved. Neighbors reserved their highest esteem, however, for the craftsman whose art was neither smelly (like the tanner's or butcher's), menial (barbers and carters), nor laborious (coopers and shipwrights). Most respected and usually most profitable were the gentlemanly crafts requiring the greatest skill and education, such as those of the gold- and silversmith, the printer, and the joiner; ranking with these were owners of enterprises requiring capital and managerial skills, such as shipyards, ropewalks, or distilleries.

Some of these activities enabled the community to survive but did not create wealth for the state. Bakers and butchers, for example, performed functions which country folk did not need but which townspeople found necessary. Other craftsmen catered to the demand for luxury, neither extracting money from nor adding wealth to the town: such were barbers and staymakers. But many craftsmen did produce articles for export which brought in substantial profits. Some made possible the sale of the nation's agricultural surplus (sailmakers), others created value independently, anticipating the industrial expansion to come, like tanners and various ironworkers. An additional clue to the relative importance of these craftsmen and manufacturers is provided by their growing political role. Within a few years, for example, Philadelphia would be sending to the legislative assembly a brickmaker (William Coats), a sugar refiner (F. A. Muhlenberg), and a shipmaker (Emanuel Eyre); New York a gunsmith (Isaac Stoutenburgh) and a mason (John Stagg); Charleston a carpenter (Daniel Cannon), a blacksmith (William Johnson), and a mason (Anthony Toomer); and Boston a mason (Thomas Daives) and a ropemaker (Benjamin Austin).

No cooper appears on this list, yet during 1771–1772 the colonies must have exported nearly a million barrels, worth several hundred thousand pounds. A cooper needed more than a day to produce a barrel, even with help; the work was arduous, and large-scale cooperages had not appeared despite obvious opportunities. Instead, numerous individual coopers produced several barrels per week.

Housewrights and joiners created products equal in value to the barrels, but their work does not appear among the export statistics. Instead we read that New York City contained 1,500 houses around 1730, 2,000 in 1761, and 2,500 or 3,000 by 1776, while Boston added more than 500 between 1765' and 1786. Masons and bricklayers also benefited as recurrent, disastrous fires drove the people to using stone or brick walls, and by 1776 some masons had acquired large properties. Increasingly, the prosperous homeowner filled his rooms with the beautiful chairs, beds, cabinets, and desks of the local turners, carvers, upholsterers, and chairmakers.

Even more common than housewrights, in the towns, were tailors and shoemakers, who also satisfied only a local demand. Whereas in the country most people made their own clothing, townsmen tended to rely on specialists. In Philadelphia one out of seven artisans was a tailor, usually poor. Like housewrights and masons, tailors and shoemakers seldom confronted British competition because they made shoes and most other articles of clothing to order, and sold them more cheaply. But they in turn could not produce for export or even tap an extensive domestic market: the cordwainer fitted his customer's feet with "lasts" while his neighbor cut the cloth to the man. Hatters and stockingmakers could and did manufacture in advance of sale, but neither contributed significantly to foreign trade.

Less numerous but equally important were the various smiths. Blacksmiths lived not only in the villages but in the towns, where they tended to specialize. The farrier concentrated on the care of horses, cutlers made knives and the like, while gunsmiths became especially important after 1775.

Whitesmiths worked in tin, braziers with brass. During the Colonial period these artisans struggled against cheaper and often superior imported products, and faced high labor costs as well. Yet Benjamin Clarke, a Boston brazier, by 1770 could spend £1.17 a year for "dressing and Shaveing" performed by a wigmaker. The advent of war suddenly elevated these metalworkers into citizens of real consequence, so that within a decade Clarke more than doubled the expenditure lavished on his head.

Quite a different category of smith worked with silver and gold. From a purely economic point of view they contributed less than those skilled in iron. Rarely producing for export, they brought no money into their country, and their raw material came not from local mines but through foreign imports. They acted, in one capacity, as savings banks, where men could deposit coins and receive, in lieu of interest, "plate" more valuable than the original because more artistically designed. Thereafter, however, the investment brought in no return. The goldsmiths and silversmiths also loaned money during these years before banks came into existence. The successful craftsmen often began to import finished silverware from England, thus transforming themselves into merchants. Moreau Sarazin, a Charleston goldsmith, silversmith, and engraver, prospered and expanded his activities by purchasing five hundred acres and fourteen slaves. His son Jonathan continued to work as an artisan, employing a "Number of Hands," and he also imported and sold plate, jewels, and watches, marrying into two mercantile families. He bought out a competitor for £810, purchased a 1,296-acre rice plantation and a £3,000 house, became a state senator after the war, and ended as a merchant. Sarazin's career has parallels, and illustrates an important fact about "manufacturing" in this period: artisans seldom became wealthy and important men until they engaged in trade or money-lending.

Each of the enterprises described so far required essentially only one master craftsman, who might or might not hire some assistants, and who needed relatively small amounts of capital, depending for profit on his skill rather than on his investment of money. By 1776, however, large-scale manufacturing had developed, employing many skilled workers and requiring a substantial fixed-capital investment. These entrepreneurs contributed to the new nation's economic growth by relieving the people to some extent from dependence on foreign imports, and by producing valuable materials for overseas sale. The men who founded these businesses often began as artisans, drawing on their own savings, but some of the larger establishments attracted outside capital and their owners acted as managers rather than highly skilled workers.

Among these manufacturing enterprises, shipbuilding loomed largest in the lives of the people in the Northern towns. Southerners constructed some small river and coastal boats but relied upon other people, primarily the British, for shipping. In contrast, Northerners furnished most of the transportation for themselves and others as well. To do so they built each year several hundred vessels worth £200,000, earning £500,000 annually. The oceangoing ships, snows, brigantines, and schooners averaged between two hundred and three hundred tons each, requiring an investment of hundreds of pounds and the employment of numerous specialists. The shipyard, therefore, drew upon and benefited a whole community: shipwrights, of course, "walkers" working in the ropewalks, sailmakers, riggers, caulkers, blockmakers, joiners, smiths, painters, chandlers, and instrumentmakers, together with the even more numerous supporting

[76]

cast of bakers, butchers, carters, shoemakers, and so on down to the laborers. The shipwrights themselves earned just-average wages, but the owners of the yard prospered, probably because they often engaged in overseas trade. Ropemakers also ranked high on the economic ladder: the walk itself took up a good deal of space and required several walkers.

Almost as important as shipbuilding in sterling value was the distilling industry. It affected Negroes, Indians, fishermen on the Great Banks, sailors, soldiers, and practically everybody else. This was almost exclusively a Northern enterprise. Southerners contributed to it only as consumers, importing from the West Indies a million gallons in 1772. Northerners bought, and presumably drank, even more; but they also purchased 4.5 million gallons of molasses which, when distilled, enabled them to export as much rum as they received. From the point of view of the country as a whole, the universal taste for rum was very expensive, as publicists were beginning to make clear, but New England's economy benefited enormously. Distillers ranked near the top of urban society in terms of prosperity, and their product played a vital role in commerce.

Several other enterprises also required considerable capital. Sugar bakers often imported their raw material and sold the finished product, thus profiting both as traders and manufacturers. Isaac Roosevelt, ancestor of the famous family, began as a sugar refiner and presently became one of New York's wealthiest merchants. The demand for paper, satisfied primarily by importation, as Charles Townsend well knew, led men such as Benjamin Franklin to encourage paper mills, while other entrepreneurs manufactured carriages, glass, and—especially after 1775—gunpowder.

Located in the country, but financed by townsmen, the

ironworks added both wealth and strength to the infant nation. Although slitting mills and forges were often small, smelting furnaces could cost thousands of pounds and effectively excluded the man with only a skill to invest. A good many ironmasters failed, not because of British restrictions, which the colonists ignored, but because costs of labor and transportation ate into profits. Yet the Leonard family dominated parts of Bristol County, Massachusetts, John Potts of Pennsylvania left an estate of more than £20,000, while Charles Ridgely's Baltimore forge employed seventy-three slaves and was valued by the tax assessor at £12,000. Ridgely, whose other property raised his total worth to nearly £30,000, inherited much of this estate from his merchant father. Like John Hancock, he became an ardent revolutionist, and despite his wealth acted thereafter as a principal spokesman for the agrarian party. These iron manufacturers operated businesses which anticipated in size the factories of a later era. Isaac Zane employed 150 hands, and entire villages sprang up around a furnace. Managers and highly skilled founders, earning £100 a year, supervised a company of hired workmen, slaves, and indentured servants who, among other tasks, cut wood, dug ore, and hauled the finished product to market. When the thirteen states united they became one of the world's leading producers of iron. These furnaces and forges furnished a surplus for export and were fully able to supply the country's wartime requirements.

Last, the most important of the craftsmen, the printers, occupied a unique place in urban society. They did not, like the manufacturers, add directly to the country's income. Yet their economic contribution extended into every aspect of moneymaking. They published advertisements for merchants, shopkeepers, and artisans, notices of ships' arrivals and departures, price data, information concerning markets, and how-to-do-it articles including the latest agricultural techniques. Their almanacs contained much useful information, such as the times of high and low tides. They made and sold all kinds of business papers and forms as well as account books, paper money, laws, and broadsides. Governments could not act efficiently without them, and their almost complete disappearance in the Carolinas and Georgia during the middle years of the war made an organized military effort almost impossible. For their part the printers benefited from the governments, one in each state deriving a nice profit from official publications, and such a subsidy guaranteed the success of a newspaper. Without state aid, newspapers became marginal enterprises, depending upon advertisements rather than subscriptions, sometimes successful but often failing. The major cities supported several, towns of the second rank one. Printers also kept trying to sell magazines, but these never became profitable. They published books, of course, and the sale of business forms and the like provided a steady income. They rarely acquired real wealth, but they usually prospered. In 1771 Boston's printers all ranked above most artisans on the economic scale, and one stood among the large property owners as did Benjamin Franklin in Philadelphia.

The Revolutionary craftsmen, artisans, mechanics, and manufacturers comprehended a wide range of individuals. Some owned almost no property; indeed, even among the skilled workers one out of four had no real estate. Shoemakers and coopers in particular tended to live in poverty. Yet others belonged to the economic elite. Boston's 1771 assessment list identifies a dozen aritsans among the wealthiest taxpayers, including a ropemaker, a housewright, a brazier, a feltmaker and hatter, and seven distillers. Philadelphia's richest residents in 1765 included a distiller, a tanner, a clock-maker, two carpenters, two brewers, an ironmaster, two button manufacturers (sons of Caspar Wistar), and Franklin. Below these, yet still well-to-do, ranked another printer (David Hall) and a variety of craftsmen and manufacturers, including three or more tailors, goldsmiths, skinners, hatters, distillers, tanners, and brewers.

Curiously, these economic leaders seldom intersected with the urban commercial and professional upper class. The successful artisans came from artisan families, occasionally from farm backgrounds, but rarely were they sons of traders. Similarly, well over half the well-to-do merchants and professional men had merchants or professionals as fathers, another sizable group started as large landowners, and only one in six began as an artisan. In all probability we are dealing here with a social prejudice on the part of gentlemen toward men who worked with their hands, an inherited class bias which New World mobility might weaken but which continued powerful and had important political consequences. Thus these craftsmen, however they differed among themselves in economic rank and perhaps in status, formed a distinctive element in urban society.

The economic contribution of the artisans and mechanics appears less in the export figures than in domestic consumption. Exports of rum, barrels, ships, and iron certainly helped, but above all the people manufactured a vast quantity of products which they must otherwise have purchased, and indeed had imported in the past. The thirteen states had not yet achieved self-sufficiency, but in 1776 they gambled successfully on sustaining themselves independently from the mother country. With few manufactured products reaching them through the British blockade, they supplied their own and the army's necessities. Craftsmen, regarded as socially inferior to other sorts of people, suddenly became the recipients of admiration and state aid.

At the same time they entered politics. Rural artisans may have conceived of themselves as merely part of their community, lacking any sense of separate identity; but urban craftsmen emerged as a unique force. They resembled the small farmers in that both were small property owners, with standards of living often marginal and never luxurious. Both received little education, paid little attention to cultural matters, and traditionally deferred to the local better sort. Both often contracted debts and might suffer seriously from low prices. Neither had entered politics except at the lowest levels, leaving weightier matters to their superiors, but both now prepared to seek political power. The farmers and artisans therefore might join together as members of a social and economic middle class and as aspirants for a democratization of government.

On the other hand, circumstances equally important separated urban craftsmen from farmers and united them with other townspeople. They bought most of their food, so tried to keep farm prices low, while the country folk wanted cheap manufactured goods. They depended upon commerce, either directly by producing for export or by selling to men in trade. An intricate network of debt as well as habits of deference and mutual trust bound them to the urban merchants and professional men who furnished intellectual and political leadership. In 1776 they were beginning to assert their independence from the urban elite, yet a basic community of interest would preserve a now uneasy alliance.

Craftsmen worked with their hands; professional men with their heads. Craftsmen formed part of the ordinary folk—as we might call them, the working class; professionals were gentlemen. These distinctions suggest separate social origins, economic rank, and political attitudes.

At the bottom of the professional pecking order, in the towns as in the country, stood the schoolteachers in shabby gentility. College teachers formed the exceptions, but in 1776 they numbered a mere handful. The president of Harvard earned £250, as much as the rest of his faculty combined. Yale paid its president £150 plus a house; the professor of divinity also received a house and £113.5.8, but the senior and junior tutors earned only £65.1.4 and £57.1.4, and all four of them had to petition occasionally for their money. These salaries, for the profession's most respectable positions, barely sufficed to support a family in middle-class decency, and certainly did not encourage luxurious living, though they might drive one to drink. College teachers today receive three or four times as much in equivalent prices. In order to make ends meet, the faculty moonlighted, tutoring students on the side. Schoolmasters at the secondary level earned about the same as skilled workers. Typical of the best-paid positions was the classics teacher in an Annapolis school who received £55 sterling annually plus £3 per scholar and a house. Closer to the average was the "usher" there who was paid half as much. Every sizable town contained one or more grammar schools which, through their Latin courses, prepared boys for college and by an English curriculum taught others how to make money in trade. Elementary schools transmitted the bare essentials and inculcated proper theological principles and a fixed moral code. Newspapers continually advertised these institutions, often established by immigrants who gave lessons in French, dancing, and other decorative subjects at odd hours. Apparently most of these men were young. Economic opportunities for educated young men were good in America, so they quickly

moved on to more rewarding and prestigious jobs in medicine, the ministry, the law, or trade.

Doctors, on the other hand, earned quite good incomes.
As we have seen, those in the country lacked formal training and could not charge high fees; rural people had little
money to pay. The college-educated physician in the towns,
on the other hand, recovered the considerable cost of his
training from a well-to-do clientele, and physicians' incomes of £500 sterling annually were not uncommon.
Despite their increasing prosperity and professional com-
petence, doctors had not yet achieved positions of leadership. Medical knowledge did not enable them to treat successfully many diseases, so their high fees seemed excessive.
Probably most people felt that they extracted more from
the community than they returned.

Ministers rarely appeared in the legislatures and, except
for a few conspicuous Tories and equally determined
Whigs, they kept out of the political arena. They exerted a
considerable influence privately or in sermons, where radical
ideas could be insinuated in theological language. Most of
the well-known clergymen lived in the towns, employed by
the congregations of prosperous churches. Even these earned
rather less than doctors but, on the average, they owned
fully as much property, partly because they often came
from propertied families and partly because their parish-
ioners gave them a "settlement" to invest, a manse to live in,
usually with a garden, and other support such as firewood.
Although urban ministers did not double as physicians like
many of the rural clergy, they often tutored students pre-
paring for college and served their community also by delivering sermons upon public occasions. Undoubtedly their
prestige had declined: by 1776 intellectual leadership in all
but theological questions had passed to others, especially

lawyers. The secular spirit of the age had something to do with this, as did the bitter disputes associated with the Great Awakening which, by pitting clergymen against one another, called into question all clerical authority. The ministers' contribution lay in expressing and sanctifying the shared thoughts of most Americans. From a strictly economic standpoint many people regarded them as liabilities rather than assets, and their relative economic rank suffered accordingly.

Whether urban lawyers appeared beneficial or parasitical depended upon how much property the observer owned. We do know of a very few attorneys who preferred to represent the poor, and some became political leaders of the popular party. These men, such as Abraham Clark of New Jersey, Abraham Yates of New York, George Bryan of Philadelphia, and David McMechen of Baltimore, generally lacked college training and came from middle-class backgrounds. The majority, however, prosecuted suits for the well-to-do, primarily to recover debts. Characteristically they belonged to the country's prominent families and attended college, sometimes in England. Thus associated from birth with the well-to-do businessmen and large landowners, they spoke for them politically and protected their interests in court.

Indeed, the fees which attorneys charged placed them safely above the poor man's reach, while subjecting them to sporadic attacks. Loyalist lawyers who later presented claims in England for their losses estimated their annual incomes at £500 for men with established practices, and some are on record as earning several times as much. Every pound over £500 made them financially independent. Moreover, whereas country lawyers lost an important part of their fees by allowing credit, the townspeople generally paid promptly in cash. The practice of law appealed to the sons of gentlemen for the fame that it brought, but the accompanying fortune helped. Trade might return a higher profit but involved greater risks. For this reason the Southern planters often practiced law in order to obtain cash, as did Thomas Jefferson and Edmund Pendleton. Forced to think under pressure, to speak fluently, and to reason closely, lawyers naturally served as spokesmen for their more silent allies— as James Wilson spoke for the Morrises and Binghams, as James Duane, John Jay, and Alexander Hamilton represented the landlord and merchants of New York, and as Edmund Pendleton, George Mason, and Jefferson pled for the Fairfaxes, Carters, Fitzhughs, Washingtons, and Nelsons of the Old Dominion. Above all other professional men, lawyers furnished active leadership in the young republic.

As the lawyers thrust themselves into politics, they formed the nucleus of a class of professional officeholders. The public official as a full-time occupation scarcely existed in 1776. England's civil service contained many, but in America the public had come to regard them as hostile and probably corrupt agents of Britain, as "placemen" seeking their own fortunes rather than the public good. The attacks on British officialdom undermined their prestige, and the abolition of plural officeholding rendered government posts relatively unprofitable. After Independence, however, the states found it essential to encourage skilled judges, sheriffs, collectors, commissaries, and other employees and to pay them adequate salaries. Urban businessmen and professionals applauded and profited from this process, but most people, especially small property owners, regarded officials as they did other professional men—as nonproductive if not counterproductive, who ought, as one critic remarked, to be "as few as possible; for they do not increase the power of the state; but live on the property acquired by others."

The same mixture of admiration and mistrust applied to men in trade, who like the professionals ranged from the poor to the very rich. Every town contained small retail shops, sometimes run by widows for a bare livelihood, sometimes by artisans in conjunction with their trades, others by men who hoped one day to become great merchants. By 1776 the beginnings of specialization separated several species of storekeeper. The apothecary, or druggist, often started as a physician and found selling medicines more lucrative than prescribing them. Some men sold drygoods, others (like Henry Knox) books: victualers sold food, and tavernkeepers or innkeepers dispensed drink, meals, feed for horses, and rooms. Although we lack studies of business failures, the sources of the period are full of marginal and insolvent enterprises. One Boston shopkeeper left £288 in personal property, but his debts exceeded his assets. A neighbor owned only £68, another £405 in personal estate but no land or house. A more nearly average enterprise belonged to the man with £814 all told, of which £574 was in personal property, including £405 in cash. Death probably deprived this shopkeeper of the chance to reinvest his capital and earn perhaps £100. About the same time a Boston bookseller had a stock worth £1,000 and died leaving a personal estate valued at £1,609.

Shopkeepers occasionally earned more than this bookseller did, but they seldom became wealthy because they dealt primarily at retail. They did import goods, but almost by definition they never exported. They sold in small quantities to local consumers, a few pounds—more likely shillings—at a time. Whereas wholesale merchants might dispose of their entire stock immediately and reinvest the proceeds for quick turnover of capital, shopkeepers were obliged to recover their investment bit by bit, slowly and unsurely. During good times, when money was plentiful, cash came in promptly and incomes soared. Otherwise they had to allow credit if they wished to sell at all and then, like the country storekeepers, they faced reluctant debtors. They could have charged interest, of course, but apparently never did so on ordinary transactions, or "book debts." Storekeepers, like the craftsmen, seldom controlled their own capital and were economically vulnerable to commercial recession. Although they sold to the artisans, they interlocked primarily with the merchants, whom they emulated and supported. Innkeepers, on the other hand, did not depend upon merchants for credit, had no prospect of becoming importers or exporters, and acted politically with the craftsmen.

Storekeepers and innkeepers, with their clerks and servants, all emulated the men at the very apex of urban society: the merchants. Not that all of them were great men: probably one in ten, if not one in five, died insolvent. But whereas the average shopkeeper left to his heirs £270 in personal property, the merchant left £700 and as much again in real estate. Boston contained, in 1771, around forty men with £5,000, ten of whom had fortunes of £10,000. Almost all of these were merchants. Philadelphia probably produced even more men of wealth, merchants contributing at least two-thirds. These traders characteristically derived some of their fortunes from merchant-fathers or, in some cases, parents who were professional men or landowners, about one in five being self-made men (the proportions would double during the war).

Merchants in those days meant wholesalers. In the Revolutionary period they almost invariably engaged in overseas trade, and that required capital and credit. If one began without family advantages, the usual procedure was to start as a clerk, a ship's officer, or a shopkeeper, investing in part of a cargo or a share in a vessel. The profits, if any, then permitted a larger share—a sort of double-or-nothing game. Insurance and spreading the risk over several ventures hedged the bet, and during good years one successful voyage might compensate for several bad ones. The hazards are dramatized by the career of Jonathan Trumbull, Connecticut's wartime governor. Trumbull began as a successful Lebanon shopkeeper and moved up to the big time by exporting to the West Indies and importing from England on credit. Theoretically he should have earned enough selling his imports at wholesale to pay for them, and success in the West Indies trade would make his fortune. Unfortunately he could not collect for the goods which he sold on time, and his ships to the West Indies disappointed him, so he lost his credit in England. British merchants first dunned him and then threatened to sue, and only his timely selection as governor saved his economic hide. On the other hand, George Boyd of Portsmouth began to send out ships from his shipyard, never experienced a misfortune, and presently earned more than £1,000 sterling annually. Once successful, the merchants hastened to diversify. They were in the money-lending business anyway, since they sold extensively on credit, so they expanded by advancing sums to other traders for their ventures, by loaning money to the government, or by serving as bankers to the community generally. They invested in land, sometimes speculating in newly settled areas, sometimes buying valuable farm or town properties. And they participated in manufacturing, usually the branches closely related to trade such as shipbuilding.

William Elliott, the prominent Charleston merchant, left £24,000 in personal property alone, including more than four hundred slaves, a new schooner, and about £4,600 in debts owed to him. He also owned more than 4,400 valuable acres divided into several plantations, plus property in the city, his total worth surely approaching £40,000.

The commerce that created such fortunes extended over the entire Altantic world, subject to numerous restrictions. One of the most important branches, regardless of restrictions, was the import trade from England. Just before the war the colonies were buying one or two million pounds' worth annually, consisting primarily of manufactured goods. The people could have survived without spending all that money, but only through a lower standard of living and some discomfort. This trade, which of course ceased between 1775 and 1783, had cost the colonies heavily and benefited only a few merchants. English ships transported most of the cargo, and English merchants skimmed off much of the profit. The American sometimes handled the goods on 5 per cent commission, selling for the best price he could get, usually at wholesale for quick turnover, and netting a small but safe return which might yield a nice income if he transacted enough business. Alternatively he bought in England at his own risk. He might be able to "lay out" some cash, through an inheritance or some other windfall (English or Scottish immigrants occasionally did this), or through the earnings of a preliminary voyage. The usual method, however, was to buy on credit, taking advantage of an established reputation or a letter of introduction certifying his reliability and financial solvency. The transaction might take place by mail, but generally at least one trip to England was necessary to establish the essential relationships. The importer paid costs of transportation and then hoped for a good market, meaning a markup of 25 per cent or so at wholesale, and a brisk sale so that he could reinvest the money. Merchants' letters are filled with complaints that trade was "dull," meaning that they could not dispose of goods quickly and their capital lay idle.

Importers naturally preferred cash sales, so badly needed for "remittances" to England which maintained their credit, and for a new venture. But the general lack of specie forced them to extend credit, especially when business was "dull." Their account books and inventories include long lists of "sperate" debts which they hoped to collect and "desperate" ones which they gave up for lost. They recovered some of the loss due to bad debts by charging interest, but that scarcely compensated for the interest owed to the English supplier and for legal expenses. Quite often they openly raised prices to customers buying on credit, their ability to do so depending upon their competition. As Jonathan Trumbull discovered, importing British goods did not automatically create wealth.

The other major trade route leading to the thirteen states ran from the West Indies along a whole series of paths. One network transported slaves—2,970 in 1771—to Southern ports, almost all to Virginia, Charleston, and Savannah. In addition, Northern ports received some five million gallons of molasses as well as small quantities of salt, cocoa, and cotton. Both sections bought huge amounts of rum. These products came primarily from non-British islands despite the restrictions. The traders extended their activities into Spanish-held Central and South America too, though we know little about these illegal voyages. Merchants of the newly independent states controlled virtually this entire trade. They also brought wine from the "Wine Islands" and from Europe, where they also obtained other luxury articles after British restrictions ceased; but the direct trade from Europe remained minor, as did that from Africa.

The import trade, though lucrative for individuals, suffered from two major handicaps. First, it drained money from a country already seriously short of specie. Second, it introduced luxury and even sin: articles such as fine clothes, carriages, wine, silverware, tea, and rum were a waste of money and at worst a clear evil, in either case condemned by the accepted code of ethics. The ready acceptance of nonimportation agreements and of subsequent embargos and sumptuary taxes reflected a widely held commitment, at least verbally, to the plain, simple, and moral life. The importing merchant thus became the symbol of sin, and it is no wonder that so many had departed by 1776. Those who remained stressed that part of their business that everyone recognized as beneficial—the purchase of salt, gunpowder, and other essential military supplies. At the same time they polished their image through the export trade.

The sale of American-made products obviously served the whole country and partially redeemed the merchants' moral position. The most lucrative branch of the business had been a British and Scottish monopoly during the colonial years, and consisted simply of sending tobacco to England. After 1776 the choice of markets widened but the fundamental situation remained unaltered: the English enjoyed a competitive advantage and tobacco prices were low. Not until much later did American merchants dominate the trade. England had also accepted, in exchange for that huge volume of exports, certain other commodities, above all lumber products, and ships, naval stores, iron, rice, and indigo. These, together with the "invisible earnings" of the colonial merchants, helped to redress the balance of trade and brought profits to American entrepreneurs. Still, all of the Northern colonies accumulated a balance of trade with Britain far more unfavorable than that of the Chesapeake, to say nothing of the Carolinas and Georgia, which showed a profit.

Exports to the rest of the world had become particularly important to the traders who sought money for remittances to England and to that crucial sector of the economy which was independent of British markets. Merchants shipped directly to Europe and the Wine Islands a variety of products including grain, fish, lumber, rice, and, after Independence, tobacco, and they also carried sugar and other West Indian products across the Atlantic. The trade was hazardous, partly because nobody knew anything about market conditions, but potentially very profitable. Above all, the West Indies absorbed food of all kinds and huge amounts of lumber. American merchants financed the non-English trade themselves, employed their own vessels, and kept the profits. Their ability to discover markets for American farmers and manufacturers created wealth for the whole people. Also beneficial and rewarding was a lively coastal trade connecting and strengthening the several states, and a re-export business which involved, for example, importing European manufactures and then forwarding them to markets in the West Indies.

The conduct of this Atlantic-wide commerce required considerable skill and luck. By examining many voyages in the aggregate we can generalize patterns and trade routes and balances of payment, but the individual merchant actually engaged in a miscellaneous, unstructured, and uncertain series of ventures. Sending a vessel south to the West Indies with a cargo of lumber and provisions, the owner suggested to the captain a destination based upon past experience and

obsolete information. But the captain must judge the market
—often "very dull" because another ship arrived first—and
if necessary seek out another port. The captain earned a
commission for selling the cargo, but he often "valued himself" on a local firm, splitting the commission. He then could
reload quickly and rely on the new ally to sell for the best
price. The commission merchant, again for a percentage,
filled the ship with sugar or rum. Subsequently he would
account for the sale, subtract his commissions and the cost
of the rum, and claim a balance with the owner which he
might then draw on as he might on a bank by a "bill of
exchange." The captain then proceeded according to tentative plans, perhaps to Europe, offering the new cargo at
some port where he had heard the price was high. For the
final leg he would purchase whatever he could obtain
cheaply and which might sell in America, and he would
probably bring home also, by way of profit, the much-
needed specie or a bill of exchange representing a credit with
the foreign firm. The bill might help to finance another
voyage, or the owner could sell it to another merchant;
eventually it would be presented for payment to the European commercial house just as our owner would be required,
eventually, to meet the demand of the West Indian agent.
If he failed to do so, the "protested" bill would destroy that
confidence in him so essential to success. The voyage thus
created a little legacy of credits and debits, represented by
entries in ledgers and by bills of exchange indicating money
due. Every year hundreds of such voyages generated these
bills, which served as an international currency and furnished working capital for foreign trade.

All the many different economic activities of the shipowner were potentially profitable. His ship might earn
money if he sold cargo space or if he sold the vessel itself.

He exported various kinds of goods to several merchants and carried products from one port to another. He acted as commission agent for other merchants and loaded their ships for them on request. He imported and sold a wide spectrum of goods ranging from the essential such as salt to the luxurious such as Madeira wine. He might buy or sell bills of exchange, advance credit to his customers, perhaps loan money to other entrepreneurs. The profits from trade and his money at interest then served as capital for further business activities or for investments in land, houses, or manufacturing enterprises. If therefore many Americans regarded the merchants as profiteers, the merchants considered themselves with some justice as benefactors, creators of wealth.

Certainly the townspeople admired them and looked to them for political leadership. Merchants shared power with lawyers, especially in the upper houses of the legislatures. Among the first governors of the thirteen states, Button Gwinnett of Georgia, Jonathan Trumbull of Connecticut, John Hancock of Massachusetts, Mesech Weare of New Hampshire, Thomas Wharton of Pennsylvania, and Nicholas Cooke of Rhode Island all derived their wealth from trade. The "commercial interest," with merchants at the core, drew support from professional men, many artisans, and the numerous farmers who depended upon an overseas market. It radiated out from the towns far up the great waterways, following the trade routes, and forming one of the major political influences in young America.

The states' extensive trade, and the people's getting and spending, generated a substantial flow of income. Most of it was paid in and out not in money but through paper debts. Before 1776 the colonies' total money supply probably did not exceed £5 million, of which specie formed only a part.

Hard money kept arriving from Europe and the West Indies through trade, and from Britain in the pockets of immigrants and through the army's purchases, but it flowed out quickly to pay for English imports. Country folk saw little of it while the townspeople snatched a small portion as it flowed past. An important part of the colonies' credit originated in Britain, whose merchants extended several million pounds' sterling worth. The Americans loaned even more (we really do not know how much) to one another through "book debts" recorded by shopkeepers, craftsmen, lawyers, doctors, innkeepers, and merchants, and in sizable sums loaned by men with money to those without it. The chain of indebtedness ran from the farmers and other country people through the rural shopkeepers to the city wholesalers, moving up from poor to rich and across country from farm to town. The burden was not excessive and it was not evil, for it contributed to economic growth and furnished purchasing power where that was badly needed; but several circumstances in 1776 were making the situation precarious. First, the unequal distribution of the debts meant that certain large groups of people owed substantial sums to a comparatively small number. Second, the public debt began to increase enormously. Third, exports nosedived, reducing the country's income. Finally, the supply and value of all currencies began to fluctuate, endangering the credit structure. The resultant financial crisis occupies much of our attention in later chapters.

These new circumstances merely aggravated an old problem—the shortage of money. Americans met the difficulty in their traditional way: by conducting business without cash, entering transactions in account books and settling balances periodically without charging interest. Bills of exchange served as international currency, and the IOU's of reliable

merchants circulated within the colonies. Colonial governments had from time to time authorized or condoned several
kinds of paper money which, though of course lacking any
real or intrinsic value, represented property of various sorts
and served as local media of exchange. Several of these
expedients now became crucially important.

Tobacco notes circulated only in the Chesapeake area.
These originated when inspectors, appointed by law, certi-
fied that a given hogshead contained tobacco of a stated
amount and quality. The certificate, entitling the bearer to
that hogshead, passed from hand to hand equal in value to
specie. A second type of certificate arose when someone
who owed money to the government signed a note to that
effect, as an importer might promise to pay on demand a
duty imposed on his shipment. Third, the more general land
bank notes grew primarily out of the farmers' need for
money. The government established a bank which printed
paper money and loaned it, at a relatively low rate of interest, to men who owned enough real estate for proper
security, generally double the value of the loan. The borrower would pay interest, thus furnishing revenue for the
government, and would discharge the principal over time,
the notes being gradually withdrawn or, if desired, reissued.
Meanwhile the borrower could pay his private debts or purchase necessities, the notes thereby becoming part of the
money supply. Whether the increase in money led to price
inflation, and whether the notes depreciated or maintained
their value, depended upon both their quantity and their
security. The experiences of the colonies differed. In Massachusetts, New Hampshire, and Rhode Island, land bank
notes declined in value, and the British government finally
forbade them. In South Carolina they also depreciated until
seven pounds of paper equaled one of sterling, after which

they held steady and proved useful. Maryland, Pennsylvania, New Jersey, Delaware, and New York issued controlled amounts which maintained their value, furnished revenue for the government, and probably stimulated economic growth.

A final type of familiar paper appeared when the governments desperately needed funds, usually during a war, and found the treasury bare. In this case the legislature authorized the treasurer to issue notes payable later, when taxes permitted redemption. Ideally a tax law was passed at the same time providing for the collection of enough revenue to pay these IOU's, or "tax anticipation notes" as they were sometimes called. The treasurer then used the new currency to pay the soldiers and the commissaries and quartermasters who fed, clothed, transported, housed, and armed the troops. Recipients used the notes as money. If the law permitted they might pay taxes with them. If the legislature had defined them as "legal tender," creditors were forced to accept them at a rate equal to their face value in gold and silver, and if not men could still use them to buy goods or pay debts at a market-determined discount. Generally issued for a certain number of years, and presumably paid off in gold and silver collected through taxes, the notes might be reissued and potentially become a permanent part of the money supply. Their value—whether people accepted them as they would coin—depended above all on whether the government stood ready and able to redeem them in specie at the promised time.

The use of these various methods of creating money aroused controversy before and after 1776, as we shall see. Briefly, one set of men preferred gold and silver, regarding paper currency as basically evil. If the supply of hard money proved totally inadequate, they were prepared to accept carefully limited amounts of paper. They would agree to its being legal tender only if it unquestionably would circulate at par with specie. These hard-money advocates included creditors, most businessmen, larger property owners, people on fixed incomes, and anyone else who feared inflation. Other Americans applauded an increase in the money supply even if inflation occurred. Among them were debtors, those who wished to borrow, or those who would benefit from price increases. As we look back on it, the debate pitted defenders of a gold standard against proponents of a managed currency.

The serious debate over monetary policy, just beginning in 1776, merged into a larger controversy over economic, social, and political decisions. The various economic interests of the people, their ways of life and their ideas, had long produced public contests. Now the new problems of independence would create new political alignments and new governments.

# Chapter Four

# The Political Background

THE structure of power in most of the thirteen colonies, before 1776, had strongly favored the merchants, professional men, and great landowners who made up the colonial elite. Opposed to these men stood not the rest of the people but the British government. The two forces continued almost equal in strength until 1776 because some colonials sided with the Crown, but when after Independence one protagonist disappeared entirely, the power structure shook to its foundations. At the same time, the old ideological contest which had pitted the Tories against the Whigs became irrelevant with Independence. Both the structure of power and political theory changed, sometimes radically, to fit the new circumstances. People new to politics, with fresh ideas, brought significant political changes.

Historians have tended to minimize the authority of the governors and of the executive department generally, stressing instead the increasing influence of colonial assemblies. Yet we cannot understand constitutional developments and the people's ideas about their governments unless we recognize the great power of the governors as agents of King and Parliament. However ineffectual the governor might be personally, back of him stood the whole force of the British government which, if fully exerted, would overwhelm any colonial legislature or all of the legislatures combined—even in 1776 many felt it still superior to the united weight of the American people. Behind a Dunmore or a Martin, to name a pair of governors who lost control, stood the King with all his boards and councils, the Lords, the Commons, the general opinion of most Englishmen who counted, the navy, and the army. If in practice these had not previously exerted their overwhelming weight, and if by that neglect the local legislatures had in practice gained much power, there still loomed ominously the greatest military and financial force in the world.

Indeed, in some colonies the executive branch remained supreme until the final stages of the resistance movement. John Wentworth in New Hampshire and James Wright in Georgia both dominated local affairs. The former, by preventing many towns that opposed his policies from choosing members of the legislature, retained a preponderant influence in all branches of government, while the latter enjoyed the support of a majority of the people until the very end. The authority of the proprietors in Pennsylvania, Delaware, and Maryland enabled the governors there to contend on an almost equal basis with the legislature. Governor William Bull of South Carolina had been strong enough to create a deadlock in a long dispute with the Assembly; William Franklin in New Jersey and William Tryon on New York both remained potent. Only in Virginia and Massachusetts, the two oldest and most mature colonies, had the legislature clearly become superior to the executive by the 1770's (we except here Connecticut and Rhode Island, where the people elected their governors; after every generalization concerning colonial politics one must mutter "except Connecticut and especially Rhode Island").

This executive influence acted through the "royal prerogative"—the full power of the King. The colonials felt it when laws encountered a veto, and through dissolutions of legislatures; adverse decisions of English courts and boards and councils; activities of customs officials, collectors of quit rents (for land, due in much of the South), naval vessels, and admiralty judges; or through laws of Parliament limiting currency, restraining trade, quartering troops, and asserting its own supremacy—none of which the colonials succeeded in nullifying. The governor himself in many cases expanded his local power, for example, by his right to grant land, spend the colonial revenue, collect various sums of money, determine the time, place, and duration of legislative sessions, and influence the choice of local officials. Over the years each colony had come to contain a large number of men dependent upon the Crown for profitable and prestigious positions. In theory, and to some degree in practice, men such as judges, sheriffs, and justices of the peace usually held their office from the King "at pleasure," which meant that the King might remove them. Together with other officials they formed a potentially powerful influence in support of the government. The King's advisers tried to make certain that the men who occupied these posts belonged to the best families, who were most likely to remain loyal and to exert the maximum weight on the side of law and order. In every community some of the better sort held government offices and often drew from these much of their income. Thus when the King instructed the governor to obtain a law, and the governor communicated the royal command, the legislature listened not to an individual figurehead but to the spokesman for a power elite extending from Whitehall to the county seats, and including many of the most important colonials. This powerful executive branch had complete command over the army and almost exclusive control over the spending of money. It concluded relations between the colony and the outside world, drew to itself the major judicial and administrative officials, and ran the government without interference during most of every year. Finally, it vetoed, once and for all, any act of the legislature.

A second branch of the government, now soon to be reformed, was the council. This body served both as adviser to the governor, a sort of incipient cabinet, and as one branch of the legislature (plus occasional judicial functions). Because of this dual role the council theoretically exceeded the lower house in power, though actually the reverse was true. Most of the councilors came from the topmost layer of colonial society. The British government did select a few English-born men for their loyalty, but even these officials, whom the native colonials disparagingly called "placemen," held considerable property and had joined the local upper crust. Thus Egerton Leigh, South Carolina's admiralty judge, had married the niece of the eminent merchant Henry Laurens. The great majority of councilors, however, were natives. Granted that they held high office, like the Hutchinsons, Wentworths, Bulls, and their supporters, yet they certainly cannot be classed as mere placemen, for they were the First Families of the colonies—the cream of the cream. The names of Habersham, Middleton, Fitzhugh, Dulany, Lloyd, Byrd, Carter, Lee, Randolph, Coxe, DeLancey, Van

Cortlandt, Van Rensselaer, Bowdoin, Fitch, Huntington, and Hazard—just to list a few—reverberate through colonial history. Almost all wealthy, well-educated, cultured men, they lived in the towns or on their plantations along the great rivers. Merchants, lawyers, and professional men rather than farmers or artisans, they represented the conservative, aristocratic element, defending property and the status quo. At the same time they contributed to good government by careful revisions of the laws, by a collective wisdom and breadth of vision. Through the council the colonial upper class, in its purest distillation, exercised power.

Yet the councilors did not differ radically from the members of the lower house save in their greater loyalty to the prerogative. The colonial assemblies, variously called Commons, Burgesses, Delegates, or even House of Representatives, also drew primarily from the better sort. Several influences account for the fact. Suffrage restrictions probably mattered little. As a rule the voter had to own outright a parcel of about forty acres. Practically every farmer did so, and many who were not farmers as well. Alternatively one might vote if he held other property to about the same value. These restrictions excluded slaves, servants, most wage-workers, and other poor people, especially the drifters, perhaps all told 40 per cent of the men. Few of them probably would have voted anyhow. The only considerable group of potential voters thus deprived were the townspeople of small property, and many of these voted despite the requirement (as in Boston). The lack of a secret ballot many have enabled men of property to browbeat lesser mortals at the polls, though in fact we have little evidence of it. Transportation difficulties prevented people in more remote areas from exerting their full weight, which probably favored the more mobile well-to-do folk and the town-dwellers who lived near the polling places. More important, the newly settled areas often chose fewer representatives than did the older areas. This discrimination deprived many farmer-dominated localities of their proper influence, while maximizing the political power of the towns and commercial farming areas where the upper class was strongest. The interior parts of New Hampshire, South Carolina, and Pennsylvania especially suffered. Still, the major reason for upper-class control of the legislatures was what people then called "Influence," or to use the less sinister modern term, deference.

The habit of deference to some extent was imbedded in Old World tradition and arrived in America as part of the immigrants' intellectual baggage. A society in which a few men possessed most of the wealth and power together with practically all of the higher education and broad experience naturally entrusted leadership to those few. Whether the voters did so entirely out of respect for their superiors, or whether the common people feared reprisal if they acted independently is hard to say, but the effect was to grant political office to the local elite. The circumstances of the New World only gradually modified this automatic respect for authority. If greater mobility and economic opportunities enabled humble men to achieve status, if divisions among the elite diminished their authority, if the absence of force at the center of government encouraged independence at the peripheries, and if communal consensus gave ground to separatism in religion and individualism in everything else, yet the circumstances of most men forbade their active participation in political affairs and obliged them still to entrust power to a few. Perhaps the leaders did not assume their role as automatically as did England's squirearchy, for they seldom inherited their positions, but the effect down to

1776 had been much the same: whatever the colonists could produce by way of an elite, won election to the assemblies.

The colonial representatives (Connecticut and Rhode Island again the exceptions) therefore consisted of large property owners. Merchants and lawyers made up a proportion far beyond their number in the population—about one in three representatives. Most of the others were large landowners. Many were educated, sometimes at college. They benefited from political experience and good family backgrounds. Scarcely one in five came from the "middling sort" of farmers and craftsmen. The representatives may, of course, have faithfully reflected the desires of their constituents, but they did not reflect their other characteristics.

Despite their somewhat aristocratic composition, the lower houses of the legislature had whittled away at the prerogative throughout the Colonial period. Although we have stressed the considerable power retained by the executive branch and by the councils, the assemblies had achieved equality in all but two colonies. They reached this position, as is well known, by controlling the power over taxes in such a way that the governors, in order to get money, had allowed their authority to deteriorate. The assemblies had influenced appointments, obtained laws which the governor ought to have vetoed, supervised certain expenditures, supported agents in London, and most recently organized resistence to Acts of Parliament. They had, however, failed in other objectives. They had not succeeded in obtaining regular elections free from interference. They had not relieved the judiciary and other officials from dependence on the Crown. They had failed to establish, in general, their complete control over legislative matters, nor had they reduced the executive to subservience. Thus the colonial power structure contained two elements: a powerful executive branch, deriving its authority from Britain and drawing to it some of the most prominent colonials, and a strong legislative body, chosen by property holders and consisting of almost equally prominent men.

Important though they were, the legislators and governors performed fewer services for the people than did the local governments. These maintained the roads, collected money for the churches and schools, enforced laws, cared for the poor, settled disputes, and passed a great many ordinances. The principal officials at the county level were justices of the peace, sheriffs, and county lieutenants. The executive branch chose most of these men but responded to local desires. The justices individually settled minor civil questions, generally those in which less than £5 was at stake. Collectively they heard most other cases, sitting as the Court of Common Pleas (civil) and General Sessions of the Peace (criminal). The sheriff enforced the laws, and the county lieutenant commanded the militia, holding the rank of lieutenant colonel when in service. The assessors rated men's estates for tax purposes, and collectors or receivers, aided if necessary by the sheriffs, demanded payment. These last had to be honest men of recognized reliability and property, and indeed most of these officials belonged to the prominent county families. Under the town system, the voters in town meetings chose men to perform certain of these functions, the selectmen in particular exercising extensive authority. Left to their own devices the people chose much the same kind of person as did the governors. In fact, therefore, the better sort controlled all levels of government and spoke or pretended to speak for everyone.

Yet they spoke with a divided voice. They articulated two major bodies of thought, both derived from England, neither expressing actual conditions, yet each incorporating a set of practical objectives. We shall call these the Tory and Whig ideologies.

Tory ideas became obsolete within England after the Glorious Revolution of 1689 established Parliament's supremacy. But outside of Britain the government attempted to apply their implications. Few colonials adhered to more than a fraction of Tory thought, which derived its strength by being the official position of the Crown, an integral part of the prerogative, commanding the allegiance of anyone truly loyal to the government. Tory ideology thus became in eighteenth-century America, as it had been in seventeenth-century Britain, a major political force. Confronting it, the colonials elaborated their own theoretical defense. Even when in 1776 Toryism died with the old regime, the Whigs continued to react against some of its characteristics. It serves then as a background for and an introduction to subsequent ideological disputes.

In its purest form (which never existed), Tory ideology concentrated all power in a Patriot King. A father to all his people, the King would act in the best interest of his entire realm. Benevolent and wise by definition (if not in his person then through his counselors), he brought justice, order, and efficiency, while in return the people rendered their affectionate obedience. To help him in attaining wisdom and administering effectively, the King sought advice from among the best of his subjects. The ministers who sat on the royal Council, the Board of Trade, the courts, and who occupied other executive positions, supported the prerogative and corrected inadvertent errors of judgment. After 1689 the Tories made room for Parliament. In England the King's authority now had to be diminished. In America, however, Parliament's laws became operative only as they passed through the ministers, who translated them into practical regulations, and through the colonial officials, who applied them. Thus for the Empire, the Commons, Lords, King, and ministry all acted as a unit. Their collective will became the royal prerogative, and the prerogative became the law.

The prerogative—the King's will—knew almost no limits. True, a body of traditions, rights, charters, and the like, the "constitution," bound everyone including the King, and in other respects the King had deliberately confined his sovereignty by grants, such as colonial charters. Yet even these concessions he might withdraw. The key phrase was "at pleasure": everything existed because the King willed it and ceased if he so pleased. The colonial legislatures developed not because of any right inherent in the colonists but because the King permitted, and they endured only at pleasure. That was why they met only when the governor permitted elections (the Wentworths in New Hampshire, as we have seen, issued election writs only to certain towns), when he called them, where he wished, and for as long as he chose. The King might veto any bill passed by the legislatures. By the same reasoning, all officials theoretically held office at pleasure and were entirely responsible not to the people or the legislature but to the King.

Colonial government, in the Tory view, worked like this: the King, with advice, reached a decision and transmitted his desires. The officials carried out these instructions and everyone helped to implement them. Thus he might order the governor to obtain a permanent grant of money to pay local salaries. The governor communicated the royal will in a message to the legislature, which obeyed. If the legislators felt the instructions unwise or unfair, they might express their views respectfully and petition for redress. The King's benevolence might grant concessions, and he doubtless would reconsider the wisdom of the original decision, but if upon the advice of his ministers he reaffirmed the order, then that was final. The process, called "government by instruction," bound everyone to the King's will. The royal government had not fully implemented the principle but was attempting to move toward that goal just before 1776.

Against these doctrines and against the weight of royal authority that energized them, the leading colonials opposed a set of practical objectives and elaborated theories which refuted the Tory view and justified their own goals. They needed to ensure as an inviolable right the existence of their local legislatures and to protect them against executive interference. They wanted to lodge with the assemblies as much power as possible, reducing in like proportion the extent of the prerogative. They hoped to free officials from dependence on the King and render them either subject to the legislatures or entirely independent of anyone. In brief, they sought to transfer power from England to America and within America from the governor and council to the assemblies. At the same time we must recall that these leaders were not ordinary farmers or artisans but merchants, lawyers, and great landowners, men of education and property. They therefore sought to retain power in their own hands in order that they could implement their own practical objectives. Fortunately the arguments they sought came readily to hand, for the Whigs had fought the same battle in England. The colonials therefore needed only to adopt such elements of traditional Whig thought as suited their particular situation.

English experience demonstrated to the Whig colonials that the King, far from acting benevolently and patriotic, became despotic. Indeed, history proved that any man or set of men, once they obtained power, governed for their own benefit: the single ruler became a despot, a group became an autocracy, and both established tyranny. Power corrupted, and every state tended toward despotism among its rulers and slavery for its people. Anyone searching for signs of this process in England could easily discern growing corruption in politics and tyrannical behavior toward the subjects in America, as Wilkes and other Englishmen delighted in pointing out. Even if the King himself remained innocent, around him gathered ambitious and designing men. In the colonies too, such men appeared everywhere among royal officials and aspirants for office. Two instruments supported the gradual enslavement of the people: permanent taxes and a standing army. The former enabled the King to govern unchecked, without responsibility to the people, and moreover furnished funds for corruption. The latter enabled the corrupt ministry to rule by force. The government might also use an established church to inculcate obedience.

To counteract this concentration of authority and the accompanying conspiracy against liberty, the Whigs would not without power but divide it. Most of them recognized the need for a fairly strong government. As large property owners they wished to protect property rights, including the collection of debts; as beneficiaries of the current social arrangements they approved of law and order; and as wielders of power themselves they sought to expand, not to contract, political authority. They favored taxes which would pay for defense, for courts, for order and efficiency. Some even defended an established church. Lawyers fully understood the desirability of legal codes and an elaborate court system. Merchants appreciated the protection and encouragement of trade. Large landowners recognized the importance of acts to further both commerce and agriculture, to secure their possessions and discipline their laborers. Such men would never destroy government but only reform and control it. They shared the Tory fear of chaos, admiration for efficiency, and recognition of the need for authority; even until the very end they shared loyalty to the King. As we shall see, most of them also distrusted the people.

How to reconcile their conviction that power corrupts, their growing suspicion of the ministry, with their appreciation for the value of government? The answer lay in the concept of a balance of power which supposedly characterized the British system in its uncorrupted form. One need not abolish the King, only check him or, if a republic replaced the monarchy, retain an efficient executive surrounded by necessary safeguards. The monarchical principle, characterized by efficiency, dispatch, and authority, should be incorporated into the ideal system, shorn of its placemen, courtiers, and despotic tendencies.

Until after 1776 the Whigs overreacted against the King and concentrated on reducing the executive branch not merely to parity with other segments of government but to subordination. In theory it ought to have remained equal, carrying promptly into execution the laws of the country and supervising the activity of public officials. For their model, Whig thinkers could refer to the Roman republic and similar states (being scholars and jurists, they liked precedents, the more remote the better); but they needed not to wander so far: close at hand the government of Connecticut furnished a convenient model. In that state Governor Jonathan Trumbull, who apparently intended to rival kings in tenure, was serving the colony well, providing good government without abuse of power. Indeed, the checks on him prevented any step toward despotism, for the people re-elected him every year and could retire him if they wished, as they had retired Thomas Fitch during the Stamp Act crisis. The war was to reveal certain defects in Trumbull's situation, but for the moment he and the governor of Rhode Island represented about as much of the monarchical principle as the Whigs could accept.

A second element in this balanced government, the aristocratic principle, posed difficult problems which the Whigs never resolved to their satisfaction. It brought into the system the country's best men, the wise and good, probably older men, preferably of substantial properties who need not seek their fortune. If they served for life they would never stoop to popularity nor respond to party pressure but would act independently, disinterestedly, for the good of the whole. In England this principle was embodied in the House of Lords, but of course the colonies lacked a nobility and few proposed its establishment. They did, however, contain councils which might be transformed into repositories of wisdom by separating them entirely from the executive and filling them with good Whigs. How the councilors could be made independent and yet subject to checks, how the most eligible men could be identified and selected, the Whigs were uncertain. For the moment they were trying to purge the councils of placemen and to free them of executive domination.

An executive for efficiency, a senate for wisdom, and a commons for popularity: these three institutions formed the essential parts to a balanced government and incorporated all of the balancing principles. In their prolonged contest with the King, the Whigs had insisted upon the ultimate sovereignty of the people. They denied that authority came from above, and located it instead among the citizenry. The people first formed a government and entrusted certain powers to the rulers, but the grant always remained provisional, never absolute: if the governors abused the trust reposed in them, power reverted to the people. A parallel and illuminating situation could be found in the contract theory popular among Calvinists. The doctrine of popular sovereignty supplied the necessary check upon the King and Lords, and justified revolution as a last resort. From this one could easily develop a defense of parliamentary supremacy as in fact Englishmen had done. Colonial Whigs, however, clung to a mixed government. They might agree that in the last analysis conflicts among the three branches must be resolved in favor of the representative assembly. Yet just as they feared tyranny in the monarchy or the aristocracy, they felt that the people too would abuse power. A democratic despotism was indeed the worst of governments, lacking in stability or wisdom, and tending toward a chaos from which the people would turn in relief to a Caesar. Despite their acknowledgment of an ultimate popular sovereignty, therefore, the Whigs conceived that the commons would normally contribute only its equal share to the government.

The precise attributes of the commons occasioned some disagreement. The Whigs' confidence in the people, such as it was, did not extend below the small property holders, and they preferred that a safe majority of the legislature represent the long-established areas, the regions most socially and culturally advanced. Places, rather than men individually, formed the unit of representation. They sincerely hoped that within each town or parish or county the voters would select men of property and reputation. Any effort to persuade the people otherwise they recognized as dangerous to good government. Demagogues who courted popularity sought power and office for selfish ends, and brought evil rather than good. The Whigs suspected men who actively campaigned, and even when they themselves engaged in electioneering, as they were doing in several colonies, they condemned it in their opponents. Instead the voters should choose the ablest and best leaders, the local elite, who presumably would unite for the common good. The Whigs condemned the "party spirit" which created divisions within the legislature, because they believed in a cooperative political order. If the people disliked the decisions of their legislators they might petition or remonstrate, and could displace incumbents by elections, but as long as the representatives held office they should act independently out of their superior knowledge and their willingness to subordinate particular interests to the welfare of the whole. Only as a last resort, to defend liberty against tyranny, could the voters assert their ultimate sovereignty.

Whig theory, then, recognized a democratic branch equal but not superior to the other parts of government. Should it err, or cater excessively to public opinion, the council or senate would impose its superior wisdom (acting, too, for the best interest of all), and finally the executive continued the tradition of the Patriot King, protecting the people from legislative oppression.

Public officials troubled Whig theorists. Clearly, independence from political pressures would free them from corrupt influences and enable them to act effectively, yet how could power be granted unchecked? And what branch of the government should select these important men? During the Colonial period the Whigs struggled to separate judges, tax collectors, and the like from the monarchy, to increase legislative influence over appointments, and to subordinate officials to the legislature by annual salary grants. Most Whigs agreed that popular elections meant poor choices, both because the voters lacked information and because they might select politicians rather than qualified men. Executive appointments might lead to the same corruption, subservience, and abuses of power that they were protesting. Two alternatives appeared: selection by some special, unprejudiced body created for the purpose, or choice by the legislature, in either case granting to the officials long terms and perhaps fixed salaries for independence, stability, and to attract the best candidates, while providing for removal in case of extreme misbehavior.

Whig ideology thus guarded against three evils: despotism in an individual, autocracy or plutocracy in a faction, democracy in popular rule. It justified at every step the drive of the colonial elite for power. Their attacks on the prerogative appeared now simply as efforts to restore an ideal balance. Their attempts to gain control over money, the army, and appointments became a defense of liberty against despotism. They claimed to be criticizing not the King but the perversion of the monarchical element by corrupt ministers, a development always to be expected and zealously watched. So also disputes between the assembly and the council took the form of entirely proper efforts to separate the upper house from an erroneous connection with the executive, to render it independent and purify it so that it could furnish a true aristocratic balance. At the same time the Whigs repelled despotism from above, they protected themselves against tyranny from below, for the people usually would be seen but not heard. Except for the ultimate right of revolution, in which men would resume for a moment their original sovereignty, the ordinary citizen could vote but would not himself hold more than a local office, and indeed would be represented in but one branch of government. The Whigs—the educated, the experienced, the propertied men, the merchants and lawyers and ministers and large farmers, the natural leaders of the country, the traditional objects of deference—would govern for the people.

What about the people? Did they accept their exclusion from active participation, agree with Whig ideology, and follow their betters? Most historians think so. Challenges to authority occur throughout the Colonial period, but they remain separate, without pattern, and not sufficiently numerous to affect the basic picture. Nor did these instances of opposition grow into a major challenge with the passage of time. After 1764, however, the situation changes. The Whigs no longer present a united front: some will become loyalists, a few emerge as popular leaders. Habits of deference, respect for authority, erode more rapidly. Finally, in 1774–1776, one huge segment of government collapses, taking with it Tory ideas and many of the former restraints on the people. Disobedience becomes virtuous and liberty replaces order. Sovereignty reverts momentarily to the people. Now at last some men insist that sovereignty should stay there.

Democratic thought first becomes important in 1776, and from that point replaces Tory ideology as the opponent of Whiggism. It seems to have derived from radical Protestantism, which stressed the equality of all men and democracy in church governance, and from left-wing Whiggism with its emphasis upon liberty and popular sovereignty. Something may be attributed also to Enlightenment ideas about natural rights and to the leveling elements in the New World environment, affording almost equal opportunities to free whites and creating a comparatively equalitarian atmosphere. Indeed, some Whig commentators had referred disparagingly to Rhode Island, where all these influences converged, as a "mere democracy," and had noted similar dangerous tendencies elsewhere. Thus the origins of democratic ideology reached far back into the colonial past, but had remained inarticulated.

Many of the advocates of political democracy shared the Whig conviction about man's sinful nature and the corrupting effect of power. They concluded from this not that power should be divided among an executive, an elite, and the people, but that the people should retain all authority, for while despots and aristocrats might oppress the people, the people would not oppress themselves. Other democrats believed that men were good, not bad—all the more reason for a popular government. The people themselves governed best.

The ideal political system (the Whigs would have said the worst) was a simple, pure democracy in which the freemen assembled and agreed upon matters of common interest. These local meetings should adjudicate legal disputes, make and enforce laws to keep order and regulate civil affairs, and select men to execute the resolutions. They should raise a militia for protection, impose taxes as needed, and control their own schools, churches, and economic activities. There the people would choose agents to consult with the representatives of other communities upon matters of mutual concern, problems soluble only by cooperative effort.

In selecting representatives the democrats did not intend to divide power. Power remained with the constituency, and the delegates, far from acting independently, as the Whigs advocated, merely carried out the people's wishes. One might say that both Tories and democrats believed in government by instruction, in one case by the King, in the other by the voters. One might further say that both accepted the concept of "at pleasure," but to the democrats, of course, the representative held his position at the pleasure of the people, not of some higher authority. The man thus elected would meet in an assembly and there transact all essential business. If for some reason two branches of the legislature proved superior to one—and a case could be made for this, as we shall see—the two ought not to differ in their characteristics nor in their responsibility. No aristocratic element was necessary; indeed, none should be tolerated.

The delegates should execute their own decisions, for a separate executive, like a King, might abuse power. The democrats wanted no governor to command them, but only a president to act as chairman and carry out the wishes of the legislature. He would be nothing in himself but the mere creature of the representatives, chosen by them as their instrument. Probably a council, similarly selected, should assist, advise, and keep an eye on him—one could not be too watchful!

The government must include certain officials to conduct affairs too extensive for the localities. These men should still be immediately responsive to the public will. Either the people themselves or their representatives should elect them for short terms and grant salaries annually rather than permanently, so as to assure their dependence, and forbid them to serve in the legislature while holding office, so as to preclude undue influence. Thus every person in every part of the government must obey the will of the people.

These three ideologies, the Tory, Whig, and democratic, stood opposed at every point, like this:

|  | TORIES | WHIGS | DEMOCRATS |
|---|---|---|---|
| *Location of sovereignty* | the King | ultimately, the people | the people |
| *Location of power* | the King | divided | the people |
| *Nature of the executive* | omnipotent | strong, monarchical | weak, if any |
| *Nature of the council* | advises King | aristocratic | represents the people |
| *Nature of the assembly* | passes laws desired by King | strong, democratic | all-powerful |

| *The judiciary, etc.* | exists at pleasure | independent | dependent on people |
| *Role of the people* | obedience | choose best men for Assembly | govern themselves |

During the Colonial period the Tories and the Whigs contended for supremacy in America. The democratic element, merging with the left-wing Whigs, counterbalanced the Tories but did not constitute a separate force. The first great effect of the Revolution was the elimination of the Tories from the political spectrum. This violent wrench leftward caused a radical ideological realignment and a new contest for supremacy, now between the Whigs and the democrats. The first stage of this restructuring of politics took place during 1774–1776, with the creation of Revolutionary interim governments.

At the same time and for some of the same reasons, the nature of political controversies altered just as extensively. During the Colonial period these contests took three frequent and three intermittent forms. The first, a struggle for supremacy between the colonial legislatures and the executive, involved the ideological division just discussed. Leaders of colonial rights invoked Whig ideology to justify their aspirations toward autonomy, while the governors and other supporters of the Crown appealed to Tory principles to persuade the colonists of their subordination. The same controversy appeared in the proprietary colonies. The subject hardly requires illustration, for examples abound in every colony and the revolutionary movement itself was in part the ultimate battle.

A second species of political contest opposed various factions, most often the "ins" and the "outs." We may conveniently define the faction as a group of men combining to seek power. Characteristically, factions did not differ ideologically or on any principle, nor in economic interests, social aspirations, religious affiliation, or in any other way; each simply wanted to hold office. Each, of course, thought of itself as peculiarly fit to govern and imputed to the others evil and selfish motives such as greed, lack of religious commitment, or demagogic attempts to corrupt the people, but that was all mere rhetoric. Political parties today often consist primarily of factions led by men who agree on practically everything except who should hold office.

Every colony contains illustrations. Rhode Island's politics were almost exclusively factional. The leaders of one group —the Wards—lived in Newport while their rivals—the Hopkinses—controlled Providence, but both drew support everywhere and either differed in policy. The DeLanceys and the Livingstons, who fought for control of New York, did differ in religion, but above all both wanted to rule the colony and appealed to ideology as this suited them. In Virginia's elections various large planters opposed one another, all adhering to Whig thought and all agreeing on such fundamentals as slavery, economic policy, the need for social order, and religion (Patrick Henry represented a new, nonfactional element). Factions of course competed for popular support, but it did not really matter to the people who won. On the other hand, the contest between the governor and the assembly did matter, and factions therefore often used that real issue for their own ends. As a consequence, these two major forms of political alignment often merged. In Maryland, for example, defenders of proprietary prerogatives attracted prominent colonials, rewarded them with office, and formed an in-group called the "court party." Opposed to them were other families such as the Lloyds of the eastern shore, defending local rights in the name of Whig ideology under the title "country party." Both groups consisted of great planters, with some merchants and lawyers, who differed little in economic interest or social objectives, and all were Anglicans.

The third major species of political controversy before 1776 grew out of regional differences within each colony. These took various forms. In one subspecies, people in the most recently settled areas strove for different objectives than those of the easterners, such as an aggressive Indian policy and the speedy establishment of local political and judicial units. In another variety, areas primarily agricultural contended with more commercial regions, and those characterized by small farmers conflicted with plantation-type societies. In most cases, however, sectionalism originated with fairly complex patterns of settlement and development. East and West Jersey shared some common traits, but the Quaker influence and large farms of the latter distinguished it from the dominantly Presbyterian, small-farm, partly New England character of the former. So also Connecticut's politics can best be understood as sectional, mingling religion with economic objectives and political attitudes. Kent and Sussex counties, Delaware, were purely agricultural, Anglican, and conservative, whereas commercial New Castle County contained many manufacturing enterprises, was religiously diversified, and welcomed change.

Religion, which had once caused major and continual differences, now affected politics only occasionally. It ceased to be important as a political issue in the South because the dissenting sects could not cope with Anglican dominance until after the break with England. But it did help to differentiate the back-country from regions nearer the coast.

Farther north, religion influenced the Jerseys, affected sectionalism in Connecticut and Delaware, and continued as a divisive force in Massachusetts, though there the contest probably occurred within individual towns and did not seriously affect provincial politics. An anti-Catholic reaction to the Quebec Act and hostility to the proposed Anglican bishop did more to unite than to divide the colonists.

Politics in both New York and Pennsylvania continued to be strongly affected by religion. New York contained an important Anglican element, represented politically by the DeLanceys and allied with the Crown; a Presbyterian influence, for which the Livingstons spoke and which espoused Whig ideology; and the Calvinist Dutch, who were courted by both. Similarly, in Pennsylvania the Proprietary party, attracting Anglicans and Lutherans, opposed the Quaker party with its allies among German sects, and the Presbyterians pursued separate objectives. In both colonies religion fused with other formative influences to create an intricate "party" alignment.

Class conflicts were comparatively unimportant in colonial politics. The necessary antecedents existed, notably in the case of slavery, more locally in antagonisms between landlords and tenants and between urban workers and employers. But when high mobility failed to mute these, force did. Slaves, tenants, and workers could not mount successful revolts and could not exert pressure through the polls. Almost no politician spoke for them. A case can be made that protest movements on the part of small farmers, such as the Regulation in North Carolina, involved a class conflict between large and small property owners. If that is what class conflict means to the reader, then the point can be conceded, with the proviso that other factors such as sectionalism must be considered in those disputes. But few such events took place before 1776.

Finally, politics reflected differences among interest groups, by which we mean primarily economic interests. Potentially these might have included that entire list of occupational groups which attracted our attention for two chapters, such as semi-subsistence farmers, small commercial farmers, large landowners, workers, rural and urban artisans of various types, traders, lawyers and other professionals, each with subspecies, each with appropriate objectives. As with class conflicts, however, restricted access to political power eliminated many groups from serious contention. In the most nearly democratic New England colonies, contemporaries did refer to politics as a struggle between the creditors and debtors, or the agrarian and mercantile interests. We can sometimes discover differences between the merchants, representing trading towns, and the great landholders speaking for rural constituencies. Interest groups occasionally became important when attention centered on economic issues such as monetary policy, and we see their influence in sectionalism. Minor until 1766, they would now become major, and as they did so factions would give way to parties as the primary form of political alignment. The first steps toward this metamorphosis came during the transition years of 1774–1776.

To Virginia went the honor of originating an extralegal government when in May 1774 the House of Delegates, upon its dissolution by Governor Dunmore, walked a few blocks to the Raleigh tavern where they drew up a limited nonimportation agreement and proposed a Continental Congress. A few days later, after the meeting had ended, a messenger arrived with a request from the town of Boston for a total embargo on trade with England. The Speaker then reassembled such delegates as he could reach, who agreed to meet again on August 1. But this "Provincial Convention," interesting to the student of the movement for Independence, holds less significance for us because it involved little restructuring of institutional arrangements and no internal shift of power. The people would not be holding new elections; the same Burgesses simply met as before, but now in the absence of governor and Council they held complete power.

The laurel for originality therefore belongs, of all colonies, to Maryland. There the legislature was not in session when news arrived that Parliament had closed the port of Boston to trade, and the governor naturally did not summon one. The citizenry of Baltimore, however, held a mass meeting which called for a congress of deputies. We do not know certainly whether special elections followed. The deputies who met in Annapolis on June 22, 1774, referred to themselves as consisting of committees appointed by the counties, and since half again as many attended (ninety-two) as sat in the House, we infer that elections did take place and that the voters chose some new men. This meeting promised Maryland's support for a general embargo on trade with England and threatened to boycott any merchant who raised prices.

The next major step toward a new political order came in Pennsylvania, for similar reasons but with even broader implications. When Paul Revere on the inevitable horse arrived from Boston on May 19 he found Philadelphians already excited by the Boston Port Bill. After a huge mass meeting the city's committee of correspondence requested the counties to send representatives to a general convention on July 15. Until this time the small assembly of thirty-nine men included only thirteen delegates living outside the three old counties around the capital city. Now the counties chose, we do not know how, as many men as suited them, totaling seventy-five, and since each of the eleven counties had a single vote, power abruptly shifted westward. This convention accomplished less than similar gatherings elsewhere because the Assembly, which Governor Penn summoned to meet simultaneously, retained control.

A month later New Hampshire dramatically increased popular influence in politics. The governor had dissolved an Assembly which proved intractable even though two-thirds of the towns had not been allowed to send representatives. As with Virginia, Maryland, and Pennsylvania, news of the Boston Port Bill started a nonimportation movement which, for success, required general assent. The call for a colony-wide meeting, issued this time by a Committee of Correspondence which the legislature had established, went out to all the towns, not just those previously represented. The Assembly contained only thirty-four members, but eighty-five attended the "Provincial Congress" which met in Exeter instead of the provincial capital. It chose delegates to the Continental Congress and supplied them with £200 contributed by several towns. We do not have the roster of members, but obviously this was a body composed of some new materials, chose by a far more democratic constituency.

On that same date a parallel development culminated in New Jersey. Again the Port Bill led to local meetings, of which one in Essex County called for a general conference. The counties were already adequately represented in the Assembly, and the elections therefore followed a traditional pattern. But seventy-two men instead of the usual thirty gathered. Here too, participation in politics substantially increased.

News of the Port Bill reached the Carolinas later than in more northern colonies, but they reacted quickly with similar effect. A committee in Charleston called a convention for July 6, too early for the back-country to elect representatives. The city delegates may have hoped to delay rather than to expedite a nonimportation agreement, and indeed Charleston sent 45 of the 104. The convention, however, broadened popular participation through the decision to allow universal white manhood suffrage in selecting delegates to another congress. The interior still did not have time to join, but in the Charleston area a large number of men must have voted for the first time. North Carolina joined the movement in August through a convention chosen by almost all of the counties. This body, as usual, agreed to economic retaliation against Britain and chose delegates to Congress. By that time Delaware had also acted, but without any political innovation except that the legislature met at the call of its Speaker (Caesar Rodney) before the usual date. As to Connecticut and Rhode Island, regular meetings of the legislatures in the summer and early fall made extralegal devices unnecessary.

Massachusetts, where all this excitement began, contributed no institutional innovation until September. But during the summer, since the Assembly was not in session, conventions met in almost all of the counties. These were usually more democratic bodies than the House, in that whereas many towns sent no representatives to Boston, most of them did so to these local gatherings. The Worcester County convention of August, for example, included 103 men against the 16 who attended the provincial legislature a decade earlier, and twice as many as traveled to Salem that fall. These conventions executed no decisions but recommended measures to the towns. The first colony-wide convention originated when Governor-General Gage called the General Court to meet in Salem on October 5—then changed his mind; whereupon the representatives gathered anyway, transformed themselves into a convention with Hancock as chairman, and adjourned to Concord on the 11th.

The first Provincial Congress of Massachusetts contained some novel materials. The membership of the General Court had remained stable, only a handful (15 per cent) of new men appearing each year. Despite the rapid growth of the western counties, the inland towns had only slightly increased their share. Representatives traditionally belonged to the top level of society, half having college degrees, and a disproportionate number being merchants and lawyers. Now, abruptly, a great number of previously unknown men attended, primarily from small farming communities, lacking formal education, often farmers, and of scarcely more than average property. Power had dramatically shifted outward and downward; the political spectrum expanded to include nearly everyone in the province. One cannot appreciate how stable and restricted Massachusetts politics had become until one contrasts the House to this Congress. The Provincial Congress proceeded now to seize sovereignty, moving past similar assemblies in other colonies. It arranged for the collection of taxes, appointed a new treasurer, took measures for defense, including the purchase of munitions, and endorsed a boycott of trade with Britain.

By October 1774, then, eight colonies had begun a process of political transformation accompanying the first stages of active resistance. These provincial congresses or conventions already pointed the direction, as yet tentative and reluctant, of the Revolutionary impulse. Essentially all were unicameral legislatures without an executive branch except as they established committees to pursue the policies agreed upon. They were democratic rather than Whiggish in that they lacked any checks or balances. They rested upon no legal foundation, depending for their existence upon a natural right to resist oppression, and deriving their authority not from the King or Parliament but from the electorate. That electorate had moreover been widened to include kinds of people or communities previously represented inadequately. More men participated in elections and more attended the conventions. Finally, these bodies began to choose officials who formerly would have been selected by the governor and council (the Massachusetts Congress appointed a treasurer). At the same time mass meetings allowed thousands of ordinary folk to express opinions, vote, and gain experience. These gatherings took place not only in the major towns but in smaller centers such as New Bern, Wilmington, Worcester, Stockbridge, Annapolis, Newark, and Savannah. In short, the colonies had taken significant and to many people dangerous steps toward political democracy. During the succeeding months these scattered steps became a stampede.

Developments in the various colonies after 1774 require individual treatment, but a general chronology will furnish some useful guideposts. Intercolonial cooperation bore fruit when the first Continental Congress assembled in Philadelphia during the fall. Delegates selected by the assembly or provincial conventions, depending on the local situation, adopted in October 1774 the Continental Association. This called upon the colonists to unite first against the importation of British goods and later, if the English remained adamant, in a complete boycott. Congress urged everyone to sign the Association and required each colony to set up machinery to punish nonsigners and enforce the boycott.

These decisions triggered a second series of conventions, for New Hampshire, Massachusetts, Pennsylvania, Virginia, and South Carolina all found special meetings necessary.

The battle of Lexington on April 18, 1775, and the need for electing delegates to the second Continental Congress stimulated still a third set of conventions, involving New Hampshire, Massachusetts, New Jersey, Maryland, Virginia, and North Carolina as well as colonies which had previously remained inactive—New York and Georgia. Thereafter provincial congresses convened depending upon the local situation, primarily to meet the continuing requirements of military operations and, in the spring and early summer of 1776, to debate independence.

New Hampshire's second Provincial Congress met in Exeter on January 25, 1775. Called by the Committee of Correspondence to implement the Continental Association and to appoint new delegates to the Continental Congress, it now included 144 members, over one hundred more than in the Assembly. We do not know their names or towns, but its successor, a smaller body, included representatives from all over the state, several rather small communities sending more than one. This and a third Provincial Congress, following hard upon the Battle of Lexington, began to usurp the functions of the regular colonial Assembly, which met only once more and then abdicated. The congresses at first simply recommended various measures: maintenance of order, organization of the militia, and presently the purchase of supplies. The fourth congress, in May, appropriated money, levied a tax of £3,000, then of £10,050, still later even more, and authorized the treasurer to issue notes (tax anticipation warrants) drawing 6 per cent interest. It also began to round up Tories, suggested that suits for debts be delayed, and in June recommended the adjournment of county courts. Moreover, it created executive agencies in the form of standing committees with broad discretionary powers. By fall the congress had taken over the government entirely.

The men who attended these sessions to some extent carried forward the colonial tradition. The presence of esquires, deacons, captains, colonels, and reverends indicate the persistence of the former elite, and anyone familiar with New Hampshire's colonial history would recognize some of the names. But nearly half the men clearly had no such roots. The trading centers near the Piscataqua, which under the Wentworths had controlled the assembly, now held only about one-fourth of the seats. If the practice continued of allowing every town no matter how small to send delegates, and if this all-powerful body continued to act as a sovereign government, New Hampshire would become a sort of absolute agrarian democracy. The provincial leaders therefore either drew back in alarm or tried as quickly as possible to organize a regular, less popular government.

Events in Massachusetts followed a similar course. During the fall of 1774 the first Provincial Congress had replaced the lawful institutions, resting its legitimacy upon natural rights. It created an army in which the men chose their company officers and these selected the field officers. The second congress, which held three sessions between February and May, was even larger than the first, and included more western than eastern delegates. It adopted essential military measures, borrowed £100,000 by issuing certificates payable in two years at 6 per cent, and advised local committees and selectmen to arrest potential enemies. The congress also empowered a committee of safety to supervise military affairs. The lack of any lawful basis for its activities probably influenced this committee to recommend the establishment of a new government, a step opposed by those still loyal to Britain but pressed both by the radicals and by men who feared chaos. A statement drawn by some members of the congress expressed alarm that the people were ceasing to respect property, and Elbridge Gerry urged the necessity of "subordination" because the people "feel rather too much their own importance." And, indeed, the people of Berkshire County were claiming the right to elect all of their officials, while throughout Massachusetts courts were ceasing to meet. Before 1774 the people quietly chose the traditional leaders and accepted with little complaint the decisions of the legislature and the courts. Now the leaders, the legislature, and the courts might end by obeying the people. A resumption of authority seemed as urgent to some as it was distasteful to others. In particular the eastern trading towns and their western allies faced a tidal wave from the agrarian communities which threatened fundamentally to alter the power structure and perhaps to democratize Massachusetts politics. Even before Independence, therefore, the colony plunged into a debate over the nature of its government.

The Revolutionary movement in New York did not produce a state-wide convention until after Lexington and Concord. Most of the merchants, lawyers, and great landowners who controlled the colony preferred peaceable, respectful protest rather than defiance. Through the DeLancey party they retained control of the Assembly, and they received support also from the prosperous farmers in the southern counties, especially the Dutch. They even succeeded in moderating the temper of mass meetings in New York City. In the absence of central direction, local committees organized resistance wherever public opinion allowed, which at first meant on Long Island and in the north. At this point moderates dominated even at the lower level of government. The first meeting in Tryon County on the Mohawk frontier, following the news of the Boston Port Act, set up a committee consisting of some of the area's most prominent men, and took no further action for nearly eight months.

What happened thereafter in Tryon may not be typical —we know little about these local committees—but it is suggestive. When we hear of it again, in May, three or four of the twelve members are obscure men, and later in the month more than half of a much larger membership are otherwise utterly unknown and several others, presently more prominent, appear for the first time on the revolutionary scene. This committee undertook to enforce the decisions of the Continental Congress in a region which, as they explained, "has for a series of Years been Ruled by one family"—the Johnsons, who had indeed dominated the Mohawk area but who now gave way to a mixture of respectable old settlers and upstarts. The committee now organized militia companies, made up lists of opponents, settled civil disputes, and elected delegates to the Provincial Congress.

The body naturally reflected the local power structure. In June 1775 only four of the eleven counties opposed the preparation of a plan of reconciliation with England, though a shift of one delegate from New York City would have narrowed the margin. At this point only the central counties of Orange, Ulster, and Dutchess, together with Suffolk, reflected the changed situation (Tryon as yet had not sent representatives), and New York continued to follow, not to lead, the Revolutionary movement. Yet the consequences of the movement were already clear.

New Jersey also proceeded very slowly, and changes in the structure of power remained minimal at this time. A second Provincial Congress met in January 1776. Governor William Franklin naturally did not attend, and the congress began to assume executive powers, granting military commissions upon the recommendation of local committees and electing various officers. The congress also received requests that taxes be levied on money at interest and that all taxpayers be allowed to vote. These petitions portended radical change, and the delegates took no action upon them. The West Jersey counties continued loyal or pacifistically neutral, and in East Jersey neither the Germans nor the Dutch showed any enthusiasm for resistance. The strong Presbyterian and New England influence of the latter section, which might have propelled the colony into revolution, suffered from the conservatism in New York, for New Jersey could not act without her neighbors' support. These powerful moderating forces restrained any impulse toward radicalism, and New Jersey's Revolutionary movement advanced cautiously.

In contrast, Pennsylvania's seems almost reckless. The Proprietary and Quaker parties, both counseling moderation, won the final elections to the Assembly. That body obviously would support the status quo. The Philadelphia committee therefore called a conference, selected by the other county committees, which met in June. Almost a hundred men assembled, and their political opinions are suggested by the fact that considerably more than half were militia officers. This assembly agreed that it was not sufficiently representative to seize political authority and decided instead that a provincial convention was necessary to form a new government. In effect they rejected a *coup d'état* and appealed to the sovereign people. The delegates would have liked to institutionalize a democratic shift of power by calling for each county to elect representatives in proportion to its taxables, but lacking information they decided to assume that each county and the city would have one vote, as in the conference. Thus each county was to choose eight delegates. The system assured a majority for the newer counties and since as matters turned out Philadelphia sent a "radical" delegation including several men of decidedly humble origin, the convention reflected a major change in the old order.

These developments contrasted sharply to events in neighboring Delaware, which took no action at all until after independence. In the two southern counties, Sussex and Kent, a majority opposed separation. An aggressive group of men, notably Caesar and Thomas Rodney, James Tilton, and Charles Ridgely, aided by pro-Whig sentiment in New Castle County, managed to keep the colony only slightly behind her sisters, but the people were dragged reluctantly into the Revolution and no shift of power occurred during the transition period.

In Maryland, on the other hand, Whigs had seized the initiative very early, and the proprietary government gave way to Revolutionary conventions in 1774. In November, after the Continental Congress had proposed the Continental Association, the colony's delegates called for new elections. In these, the freemen qualified to vote for representatives met at the courthouses where they chose committees of observation and deputies to another provincial convention. That body met in November and then, to obtain a fuller attendance, adjourned until the next month. The eighty-five members levied a tax, raised a militia, and fixed the profit of traders, allowing a 112 per cent advance for wholesalers and a maximum of 150 per cent to retailers selling on credit.

They also appointed a standing Committee of Correspondence and chose delegates to Congress.

In the following months local committees enforced the Association and carried out the decisions of the convention, assuming de facto power although the proprietor and his officials continued to exist and to carry out many functions unchallenged. After Lexington and Concord a third convention met with 141 members, three times as many as had sat in the old Assembly. To some extent this convention represented an effort by Maryland's traditional Whig leadership to regain the initiative from the committees and exercise a moderating influence. Opinion on the eastern shore and probably large sections of the western counties remained sympathetic to England, so that the convention still issued no challenge to the proprietor and stressed the need for maintaining order and respecting property. Circumstances, however, forced the delegates to act. They authorized bills of credit in August, created a Council of Safety as a new executive body, began to name new justices and sheriffs, and stopped suits for debt. That they intended no radical change in the status quo is suggested by their statement that they hoped to protect poor debtors but not to furnish any pretext for nonpayment to those able to pay debts. At the same time, in calling for still another convention, they specified that the franchise remain unchanged, and the procedure of voting by counties probably maximized the influence of the more loyal members.

The decisive shift came in the early summer of 1776, when Maryland's Revolutionary pendulum swung as far left as it was to go—which was not very far. Instead of voting by counties, now each individual voted, a step which encouraged expression of opinions by groups cutting across county lines, and may have maximized pro-independence sentiment. The ayes and nays would be recorded if a member desired, a colonial practice which had been suspended, and debates would normally be open to the public. Probably these steps increased the delegates' responsiveness to their constituents. The convention moreover allowed residents of Annapolis to vote if they owned a lot or £20 sterling in visible estate (against the usual fifty acres or £40), permitted both Annapolis and Baltimore to send representatives, increased the number of delegates from Frederick County in the west, and guarded against excessive military influence by excluding commissioned officers from civil posts. Temporarily, at least, Maryland's government consisted of a one-house legislature whose votes and debates were subject to public scrutiny, without a governor or council, and lacking any coercive power except that provided by local committees. While the men who had comprised the colony's "country party" still retained office, essentially the government rested upon popular acquiescence—a rather unstable foundation. Indeed, the leaders of the new state hastened to erect a more dependable scaffolding.

The actions of Maryland's convention suggest a somewhat recalcitrant electorate, probably in the loyalist centers, perhaps even among the rebel rank and file. Apparently Virginia did not produce such divisions. The well-to-do planters differed among themselves as to the pace and scope of resistance, but presented a united front to the British and to internal foes. Most Virginians followed their accustomed leaders willingly, and Burgesses merged into conventions without any sharp break. At the local level the committees consisted not of upstarts but of men such as Edmund Pendleton, Robert Carter Nicholas, Peyton Randolph, Landon Carter, Benjamin Harrison, and Richard Bland—names redolent of Family. The freeholders chose these at the county seats just as they had selected Burgesses. When courts ceased to meet, the local committees, including many of the same justices, took over their tasks. As a final illustration of continuity, when the Council of Safety replaced the governor as executive, it included primarily Tidewater planters of the colonial elite with Edmund Pendleton presiding. Theoretically, power would revert to the people if no legal government replaced the British when the colony declared its independence, but the planters hastily averted such a complication by drawing up a constitution at once.

None of the more Southern colonies enjoyed such a smooth transition from authority to authority. The first full convention in North Carolina met in August 1775. The freeholders of the counties had selected a variable number of men up to a high of eleven, and nine towns sent seventeen. The total of 184 was triple the normal membership, and its successor, though smaller, still greatly exceeded the colonial average. Sheer numbers therefore overwhelmed the men, mostly easterners, who had dominated the province. The Provincial Congress, as usual, adopted the Continental Association, began to raise troops, emitted £60,000 in bills of credit, arranged for the collection of taxes, chose a new treasurer and other officers, and among other activities dispatched ships to obtain military supplies. Most interestingly, the delegates as early as September 1775 prepared a plan for a new government. This recommended an annual congress consisting of from one to five men from every county and town. This body would in turn appoint a council to control the militia and spend money as necessary during recesses. No civil or military officer would be eligible. The congress would also appoint for each of six districts a committee of safety to direct military operations and supervise the activities of local committees. These last would consist of at least twenty-one freeholders in each country, or somewhat fewer in the towns, presumably chosen by popular vote, and conducting the principal functions of government at this local level. They would permit court actions and select the usual committees of observation. This un-Whiggish form of government, cumbersome and wholly lacking in checks, would certainly have involved far more people in the political process than had been the case previously, and would have been far more democratic than the pre-Revolutionary system.

The transitional years in South Carolina involved a lesser break with the past, but a clear diffusion of power did occur. By the winter of 1774–1775 the back-country people had learned of the new situation. No longer prohibited from sending representatives, they appeared in force. Each of the eastern parishes chose six representatives and Charleston sent thirty, while the westerners contributed a variable number amounting to 40 per cent of those present in November 1775. We do not know certainly how the delegates were chosen, but the Charleston committee which in November 1774 established the number which each district would send, allowed any white man paying a twenty-shilling tax to vote. During this period the back-country could not exert its full pressure because the friends of Britain there were as strong as her enemies, but in Charleston the artisans greatly increased their influence, gaining an equal weight with the merchants in selecting representatives. The great landowners, however, remained in control because the coastal parishes contained mostly large rice and indigo planters who, with few exceptions, joined in the resistance movement. Thus the Council of Safety consisted of some of the most prominent colonial leaders. The provincial congresses took the same measures as elsewhere, adopting the Association, appointing executive committees, and stopping suits for debt while nonexportation prevented men from earning money. By March 1776 the ardent Whigs passed a resolution for independence and proceeded hastily to legalize the new regime through a written constitution.

The Whigs in Georgia moved more slowly than those in South Carolina, opposed by a strong governor and a reluctant citizenry. An energetic minority, through a mass meeting in Savannah, called for a provincial congress in July 1775. More than a hundred members attended, most of whom lived within a few miles of the capitol. The congress consisted almost entirely of future rebels, and they adopted the same resolutions with which we are familiar, issuing certificates to be redeemed by future taxes. They widened the basis of representation by adding westerners as members of the next congress and allowing all taxpayers to vote. The usual local committees undertook to enforce the Association and a Council of Safety served as a central executive. These committees, composed of men who favored resistance, coerced the reluctant into obedience. The Savannah organization was a mixture of persons including an innkeeper, a Jewish merchant, and a blacksmith. By the fall of 1775 power had devolved on the committees, on a series of congresses, and on the Council of Safety composed of major leaders. With Governor Wright's departure in March, these bodies assumed complete control.

The two years between June 22, 1774, when Maryland's first convention assembled, and the decision for independence, witnessed a radical transformation of political institutions and in some colonies a significant shift in political power. The word revolution is not too strong. Indeed, the Whig leaders, who furnished much of the direction in every colony and the initiative in most of them, faced a serious dilemma. On the one hand they found themselves forced to oppose and then overthrow the legal government; on the other they believed in law, order, and authority. They had to obtain not simply the acquiescence but the active support of the common people, yet they opposed a participatory democracy. The dangers of this situation led many members of the ruling elite into loyalism, while others (such as John Jay, Robert Morris, James Duane, and John Dickinson) held back fearfully. The more enthusiastic "radicals" like John Adams, George Mason, and Charles Carroll of Carrollton pressed for new constitutions at the same time they advocated independence, not simply because the former logically accompanied the latter but because only through the simultaneous creation of new legal institutions could they maintain control.

The congresses and committees dangerously violated Whig political ideology because at the provincial level virtually all power rested with a popularly elected one-house legislature, and local governments consisted of irregular committees. The councils of safety did perform executive functions: they raised armies, collected taxes, punished loyalists, and even regulated trade, but they held power from and reported to the congresses, served at the pleasure of the delegates, exercised no veto, and in general had no independent existence. The various officials, such as tax collectors, military officers, and sheriffs, either held office simply by legislative appointment or—what was worse— by popular choice; as to the judiciary, it almost ceased to exist, with the congresses, or committees selected by the congresses, serving as a supreme court of appeals from decisions rendered as often as not by local committees of observation. The colonial councils of course vanished, and in most colonies no body replaced them. Thus the "aristocratic influence" had to compete with the "democratic" in a unicameral legislature. To be sure, the traditional leaders did often control that body, and the delegates in turn selected the elite to the committees and councils; yet, as we have seen, an alarming number of congresses became democratic assemblies, and no one could miss an almost universal tendency toward popular government, aided by a broadening of the suffrage and a greatly increased representation from the agricultural interior. The democratic element thus threatened to become omnipotent, at least with respect to the powers resting in the congresses.

For the congresses, devoid of legal basis, in reality exercised no power except that which the people permitted. Under British rule a variety of local officials carried out the decisions of the central authority, the people being compelled to pay taxes, submit to the courts, and obey any other orders. As British authority collapsed, the officials lost their ability to coerce the people and in some cases entirely ceased to exist. The committees of observation or correspondence derived their authority from popular approval. Moreover, during the Colonial period public officials had been selected by the Crown, rarely by the assemblies, but almost never by the people. Now the committees consisted either of volunteers or of men chosen in mass meetings of various sorts. This often meant that they were quite ordinary citizens, and it certainly meant that they owed their position to the electorate. In brief, the colonies were becoming democracies characterized by local sovereignty. The Whig word for this was anarchy.

This political revolution carried with it economic and social implications. Economically the people already displayed a reluctance to pay taxes or debts, and the increased influence of the farmers, perhaps also of the artisans, boded ill for traders and professional men. As the smaller property holders gained and the larger lost, an equalitarian trend would surely follow. Once accustomed to rule, men would lose the habit of deference. Thus the Bostonians' attack on Governor Hutchinson's house seemed to portend not simply a political upheaval but an assault on property and a challenge to social order. Faced with this truly revolutionary situation, the Whig leaders hastened toward a resumption of authority. They must at once form constitutions that incorporated the principle of checks and balances, transferred power from the locality to the state, restored law and order, created an independent judiciary, and maximized the influence of the better sort—the Whigs themselves. Even before Independence they had obtained constitutions in four states, and six more followed within a year.

## Chapter Five

# Conflicts over the Constitutions

MEN never can start from scratch. One may dream bliss-
fully of creating a new order and drawing ideal forms of
government for a perfect society, dream with Plato of his
Republic, with Thomas More of his Utopia or Locke with
his Carolina or Penn with his Pennsylvania, or with the
French *philosophes* before and after their revolution, the
radical Republicans planning a new South, the Mensheviki
and the Bolsheviki, or—getting down to business—with
John Adams and Thomas Jefferson. In reality, men do not
think *tabula rasa* because they inherit a body of thought and
passions. The Americans drew their political ideas not out
of thin air but from a complex ideological inheritance from
which they derived, as we have seen, notions of government
having at once broad similarities and sharp differences.
Moreover, men's theories reflect and respond to particular
circumstances. The Whigs found themselves intellectually

incapable of creating a strong, independent executive when for a generation they had been struggling against one; they could not except in a few states impose an aristocratic council in the absence of an acknowledged aristocracy; and they had to enlarge the ordinary voter's role beyond a mere choice among elite candidates. Whig thought seldom appeared in a pure form, and when put into practice the pull of democratic ideology distorted the blessed symmetry of a balanced government. In the same fashion, adherents of democracy, confronting both practical circumstances and a determined opposition, diluted their ideal with Whig accretions.

Events in New Hampshire illustrate these generalizations. That colony adopted a new constitution seven months before Independence. Governor Wentworth had departed in the summer of 1775, leaving the colony without an executive or a legal legislature. The members of the Committee of Safety and the president of the convention (Mesech Weare) asked the Continental Congress for advice. That body recommended a new temporary government, and the colony's delegates added their own suggestion, to postpone the question of an executive. The fifth Provincial Congress accordingly produced a "Form of Government," offering as justification the contest with Britain and the lack of a governor, a legislative body, or of courts. Therefore, "for the preservation of peace and good order, and for the security of the lives and properties of the inhabitants" the congress assumed the power of a house of representatives. They said nothing about its composition, but the fourth congress had agreed that every resident taxpayer could vote, instead of the previous requirement of a £50 ratable estate, and that the representative must be worth £200, reduced from £300. It had decided too that Portsmouth should send three men, five other towns two apiece, and the rest could choose one or join with others to select a delegate. The center of political power accordingly shifted westward, following the weight of population to the Merrimack Valley.

This house, more democratic than its predecessor yet bearing marks of the past, selected a council of twelve, apportioned among counties roughly by population, without any special qualifications. The councilors would serve only until the next December, after which, if the war continued, the people would choose them in a manner to be decided later. The council acted as an upper house equal in power to the lower except that all bills concerning money originated in the latter. The two combined to select most of the civil and military officials except company militia officers, who would be chosen by the men, and a treasurer and recorder of deeds, selected by the voters. The congress further specified annual elections and in September acknowledged the right of new towns to choose delegates.

The constitution probably was a compromise, and it lasted for almost nine years because its critics effectively counteracted one another. From the Whig point of view, the lack of an executive resulted in disorder and far less efficiency than desirable. And instead of executive, legislative, military, and judicial powers being separated, all found their center of gravity in the legislature, or "general court." New Hampshire, the Whigs believed, should abolish plural officeholding, deny all officials the right to sit in the legislature, and confirm the independence of judges through substantial salaries and long tenure. Portsmouth and other eastern towns complained that their population entitled them to more representatives, an argument based upon interest rather than theory.

Objections from the other side differed. Small western

towns claimed that each had the right to a representative, a system which of course would maximize the power of agricultural communities and therefore cannot be regarded as "democratic" doctrine. More interesting were the formal statements by "Spartanus," published in a newspaper, and the anonymous pamphlet entitled "The People the Best Governors." The former began by asserting that government should represent everyone, farmers and merchants, "people in high life" and "the poorer sort, who are perhaps nine tenths of the useful part of mankind." Reviewing the origin and various forms of government, the writer quickly dismissed monarchy, aristocracy, and the mixed type which had several branches, each checking the other, as in Great Britain. The best form was "a well regulated Democracy," in which "the people have all the power in themselves, who choose whom they please for their head for a time, and dismiss him when they please; make their own laws, choose all their own officers, and replace them at pleasure." He recommended a one-house legislature, frequent elections, rotation, and election of county officers by the people. The author of the second pamphlet also approved of democracy because the people "best know their wants and necessities and therefore are best able to govern themselves." He agreed that an upper house was useless, opposed an executive veto, and backed annual elections for judges. He favored an appeal from the decisions of the courts to the legislature. Finally, he joined the residents of many towns in criticizing property qualifications for voting or holding office because they favored the rich over the poor. Similarly, the town of New Ipswich in the south-central Souhegan Valley insisted that anyone owning a ratable freehold should be eligible for any office. Yeas and nays should by called and entered on the journal—which had not been the practice; no member of the legislature should hold executive office; and slavery should cease.

In the end, no change took place at all. Few liked the existing situation, which concentrated control in a few legislators, and a convention drew up a new constitution in 1778. Most of the delegates opposed the strong, independent executive desired by the Whigs but gave in to the eastern insistence upon more representatives. They forbade legislators from holding any important office and required that towns pay their representatives' salaries. This constitution failed because nobody liked it. Some easterners attacked the lack of an executive while westerners disapproved of it generally. Therefore matters continued in an uneasy balance.

Meanwhile, a very different constitution had been written in South Carolina. The low-country planters jumped the gun, if Edward Rutledge is typical of them, to "secure peace and good order" during the dispute with Britain. At this point the Provincial Congress contained only seventy members instead of more than two hundred, probably because the back-country delegates had gone home during the winter. The committee of eleven, entrusted with the task of framing a new government, contained no one except exceedingly wealthy planters, lawyer-planters, and merchant-planters, such as Henry Laurens, C. C. Pinckney, Rawlins Lowndes, and two Middletons. These drew up a document which did admit western representatives, an essential step if the colony were to unite against England, but otherwise enshrined the old order. The people had little influence other than to select members of the lower house, who must (as in colonial times) own outright at least five hundred acres and ten slaves, or other property worth £1,000 above any debts. Voters must own a hundred acres of land or an equivalent. Having thus assured the election of substantial men, even in the west, the congress added a Legislative Council chosen from the Assembly in order, as an observer later remarked, "that they might be composed of the wisest & learned men." An attempt to eliminate the second branch failed, 40 to 30. The two houses together selected a Privy Council with executive and judicial functions, and a president enjoying an absolute veto. The legislature chose the colony's officials. A majority of the lower house came from the eastern parishes, Charleston alone selecting almost half as many as the western districts combined, a fact which explains why ten of the thirteen councilors lived in the east.

We have little evidence of dissatisfaction with this constitution. A grand jury in the Cheraws, a back-country district, explicitly approved of it. Many westerners chose to support England rather than the new government, but that preference may have had nothing to do with the constitution. According to one source, some men criticized the presidential veto because it had thrown the state into anarchy and confusion, and the Council because it was dependent upon the Assembly. Perhaps the up-country people rejoiced in their ability to elect delegates for the first time, and saw in this government a great improvement on the old. In any event, the legislature produced a substitute two years later, which the president fruitlessly vetoed. This document incorporated several steps toward democracy. The executive lost his veto power and received little in exchange; plural officeholding was abolished; voters chose the Senate; the voter needed to own only fifty acres of land or to pay an equivalent tax; and any resident who could vote could serve in the house. None of these changes except the first violated Whig doctrine, and other aspects of the constitution refute any idea that the framers intended democracy. The governor and his privy councilors served for two years rather than one, must have resided in the state for ten years, and must own a plantation worth £10,000 free of debt, an extraordinary sum. Senators, also elected biennially, had to live in the state for five years and hold property worth £2,000 clear of debt. The low-country parishes contained an adequate supply of such men, but in districts lying a few miles from the coast not more than one man in ten would be worth such a sum and in the up-country scarcely one in a hundred. The Senate thus remained an aristocratic body.

The House of Representatives also reflected the dominance of the planter class. Its composition still discriminated against the west, which with three-fourths of the whites had only one-third of the seats. Qualifications for members remained the same at £1,000. The requirements for nonresidents were much higher than they were for other offices. A reapportionment was scheduled after seven years according to both numbers and property. Other aspects of the constitution also incorporated Whiggish rather than democratic ideas. Democrats would not celebrate the appointive power of the legislature, which extended to judges, justices of the peace, sheriffs, army and naval officers above the rank of captain, and other officials, those not mentioned being chosen by the governor. The justices, so important in the legal system, served "during pleasure." Finally, the constitution decreed adequate salaries. These provisions established the complete domination of the eastern elite.

In other respects the constitution reflected the Revolutionary atmosphere and testified to the changes that Independence made possible. No one could hold more than a single civil or military office except in the case of militia officers, nor could such men sit in the legislature unless especially re-elected. Judges and Continental officers could not serve in the Privy Council, nor could the father, son, or brother of the governors. Machinery for impeachment checked the governor, lieutenant governor, and other state officials. The governor no longer could adjourn, prorogue, or dissolve the legislature. Ministers, the framers felt, ought to devote full time to their important tasks, and therefore should not hold governmental posts. The constitution also established the outlines of a court system: a Court of Chancery (which decided on a basis of justice rather than law); ordinaries or probate courts, now one in each district instead of only in Charleston; a Court of Admiralty, the justices, and other judicial offices. The last served during good behavior but might be removed "on address of" the two houses. Certain officials, such as sheriffs, could not serve for more than four years. Several provisions testify that the constitution did not arise in a vacuum: thus all officeholders must take an oath of loyalty to the state and disavow obedience to the King. Voters must acknowledge one God and a hereafter, and state officials including legislators must be Protestants. The "Christian Protestant religion" became the established faith of the state, and societies of that faith could incorporate and hold property upon subscribing to five specified articles. People chose their ministers, in contrast to the colonial system in which the Anglican church imposed their clergy on the parishes. The constitution guaranteed the establishment of county courts, the lack of which had exasperated the inland districts. It also contained a brief list of rights, including trial by jury, freedom of the press, subordination of the military to the civil power, and a guarantee of less severe penal laws. Finally, any amendment required ninety days' notice and a majority of both houses.

Thus South Carolina's form of government recognized the new while perpetuating the old.

It is worth interrupting the chronology of constitution-making to introduce Pennsylvania, and thus to contrast its democratic constitution to the Whig document of South Carolina. The Pennsylvania constitution, completed in September, also reflected both history and current events, but these differed greatly in the one-time Quaker colony. The government had always been more popular, elected by a broader constituency with more local self-rule. Perhaps it had become less so by 1776, but in that year the war swept away both of the old "parties," leaving the field to a new coalition. The Presbyterians furnished its core. They produced leadership for the interior counties, drawing most of them into the revolution, as well as for Philadelphia's artisans and other small property owners who formed an eastern wing. This group pressed for a constitution not to maintain order but to aid in the struggle for independence and solidify their own control. They perpetuated the democratic aspects of the colonial government while moving far beyond it into the future.

Whence the framers derived their ideas we know only in part. Some Pennsylvanians were insisting that every soldier and every taxpayer should vote, and Thomas Paine, among others, advocated a popular form of government. The press carried attacks on the political influence of wealth. One full-dress pamphlet by "Demophilus" proposed a system which allowed the people to select many of the civil and military officials, but since he also wanted an upper house his influence is doubtful. The principal figures in the convention, on the democratic side, were James Cannon, a rather obscure college teacher; Timothy Matlack, a radical politician of little property; Dr. Thomas Young, a radical from New England; and David Rittenhouse, the scientist from an artisan background. Influential out of doors was a fiery Presbyterian lawyer, George Bryan, apparently a democrat by conviction. All of these were men of small property and humble origin.

The constitution which they produced placed most of the functions of government in a single legislative body. Such a concentration of power had its dangers, and therefore the people retained various checks. All free taxpayers and their sons of twenty-one chose their "General Assembly" annually. No one could serve for more than four years in seven, nor could he hold any other office except in the militia. Philadelphia and the counties sent delegates in proportion to their taxable inhabitants, to be freshly determined every seven years. Sessions of the Assembly would be open to the public except when secrecy seemed essential, ayes and nays were recorded when two members requested it, and the proceedings and votes were to be published weekly. Any delegate might insert into the minutes the reasons for his vote. The most interesting technique for assuring continuing public influence upon legislative proceedings was the requirement that all public bills be printed for the people's consideration before their last reading, and except for emergencies none could become law until the next session. The preambles should explain the reasons for such legislation. Thus the Assembly would function in a blaze of publicity and could not act unless public opinion approved. Prevented from doing harm, it might then be trusted with power to do good.

The representatives performed the legislative functions of government. The executive consisted of twelve men, with no special qualifications, chosen for three years by the voters. One-third left office every year and could not be re-elected, in order to avert "an inconvenient aristocracy." This Supreme Executive Council not only lacked the property requirements of South Carolina's Senate but played no part in making laws. It did, however, appoint high-ranking officials, carry out the desires of the Assembly, and perform other duties. Its presiding officer, Pennsylvania's "President," was chosen annually by the Assembly and Council.

The Constitution modified the existing court system. Supreme Court judges, chosen by the Council, held office for seven years. The Assembly could remove them at any time for misbehavior. Judges of the inferior courts, similarly chosen, apparently served indefinitely for an "adequate but moderate" salary and no extra fees. The voters nominated two justices of the peace of whom the councilors chose one (always the leading vote-getter, in practice). These men served for seven years and meanwhile could not sit in the Assembly. Other important local officials such as sheriffs and coroners were selected annually in the same way. All elections were by ballot. Thus whereas in South Carolina most officials served for four years and the rest for life, and held office from the legislature or governor, most of Pennsylvania's owed their positions to the people and served for limited periods.

The constitution-makers thought up another, and a unique, restriction on the unicameral legislature. A Council of Censors, chosen by the voters every seventh year, inquired into the conduct of public officials, investigated violations of the constitution, and (if two-thirds agreed) called a convention for its revision. The new plan also included several other unusual features designed to encourage popular participation and influence in government. Public service should earn compensation for the time involved, but offices of profit which might encourage "dependence and servility" should be avoided. The freemen chose their own militia officers as high as the rank of colonel. The legislature must establish schools in each county, paying salaries sufficiently high to enable the masters to instruct the youth at low cost. Finally, the constitution was preceded by a Declaration of Rights. It followed in many ways the much-copied Virginia clauses, but also encouraged the formation of new states where Virginia prohibited any such within her borders, added the people's right to assemble, to instruct their representatives, and to petition for redress of grievances, guaranteed the right to counsel, protected freedom of speech, and forbade forced military service of conscientious objectors. The Pennsylvanians wrote into the constitution proper the abolition of imprisonment for debt and a limitation of entails.

This document, signed on September 28, 1776, attracted prompt critical attention in Philadelphia. Whig ideas, as we have seen, differed radically. Even before the convention officially ratified its handiwork, a newspaper article asserted that mankind was prone to vice and error, and an excess of liberty led to anarchy and disorder. In the single Assembly the writer discovered "the most *unbounded* liberty, and yet no kind of barrier to prevent its degenerating into licentiousness" (the word meant unrestrained or lawless behavior). A council like that of South Carolina was essential to supply wisdom. A contributor signing himself "Farmer," apparently a lawyer, agreed. He felt that the people basically were monarchical because they had lived under such a government and because of "the great distinction of persons, and difference in their estates or property." He warned against lodging too much power with the people. His solution called for a governor chosen by the Continental Congress for three years, a council serving for the same period, and an annually elected assembly. The two houses would choose most officers for good behavior, the governor vetoing the appointments if he wished.

The major attack emanated from a meeting in Philadelphia on November 12, where the assembled citizens asserted that governments must recognize the weakness and depravity of human nature by guarding against both arbitrary power and popular licentiousness. They also opposed on principle any unnecessary change in the colonial system. Agreeing to the bill of rights, annual elections, and rotation in office, they advocated a two-house legislature, life terms for judges, an easier method of amendment, and submission of the constitution to the people. To this list critics would presently add a strong executive.

The constitution's defenders admitted none of these flaws. The only necessary check on the Assembly, they asserted, already existed in the ability of the people to restrain it, and those who preferred a council actually sought to perpetuate the aristocratic influence which the framers hoped to abolish. The convention, they felt, had been elected specifically to draw up a constitution. A referendum was unnecessary.

Whether most voters approved of the document we do not know: historians have argued on both sides. The only substantial body of evidence comes more than a year later, after a great deal of further debate. Then, in the winter of 1778–1779, the Assembly proposed a popular vote on whether to call a convention. Before the vote was taken, however, adverse petitions signed by more than 15,000 persons flooded in (the state contained at the time about 54,000 adult male inhabitants). A few men still argued that the people wanted reform, but all except seven out of fifty-four legislators thought differently and abandoned the plan. Pennsylvania's constitution survived further attacks until 1789, and exercised a profound influence upon such frontier states as Vermont and Kentucky.

Equally influential was the constitution already written by Virginians, which provided the precedent for Pennsylvania's Declaration of Rights. Virginia's convention resolved for independence in May 1776 and promptly selected a committee to draw up a constitution. The committee contained a fair representation geographically but consisted primarily, as one would expect, of lawyers and great landowners. More than half were decidedly wealthy. They certainly did not lack talent, with Madison, Henry, John Blair, George Mason, and Edmund Randolph the most prominent. Nor did they lack advice. John Adams's pamphlet *Thoughts on Government* circulated and pleased Patrick Henry, while from the Continental Congress Thomas Jefferson communicated some thoughts of his own.

Any right-wing Whigs who hoped to perpetuate the old order could cite a pamphlet written by Carter Braxton. This wealthy and conservative planter thought the English government, with its monarchy, Lords and Commons, ideal if one abolished the placemen and reformed the Commons to make it triennial and more representative. A monarchy could no longer exist, but Braxton warned against a simple democracy because it was hostile to "every thing that looks like elegance and refinement" and tended toward equal distribution of property. He recommended a lower house popularly elected every three years. The members, who could hold no other office of trust or profit, elected a governor and an upper house. Both served for life. The governor and a privy council appointed judges, military officers, and certain other officials during good behavior, while the lower house chose the rest. This plan did not win over the Virginians, although it may have encouraged some Marylanders.

George Mason produced a similar proposal which served as a basis for the committee's debate. A lower house, elected by the voters, would consist of men worth £1,000 each, the same as and perhaps inspired by the requirements for South Carolina's Assembly. The plan's crucial feature called for an aristocratic upper house of twenty-four members owning £2,000 worth of land apiece, and serving for four years. Each county would choose twelve "deputies" owning £500 each, and these in turn would select the senate. Apparently this means of guaranteeing rich men a veto over legislation enjoyed the support of Virginia's planter class: after all, Mason was no reactionary. Jefferson agreed with it, indeed proposing at first a senate chosen for life by the lower house, then shortening the term to nine years without re-eligibility. Still later he was to support an indirect choice by electors. Madison thought a six-year term would assure "system and steadiness." He, too, approved of an electoral college and advised special property requirements for the voters. The committee, probably aware that the convention would reject Mason's senate, modified his plan by eliminating the special property requirements for senators and substituting a one-year term, retaining however the "deputies" and their £500.

The convention accepted much of the committee's draft, but it would not agree to an aristocratic senate. Landon Carter asserted that the people sent delegates who would form such a government "that, by being independent of the rich men, every man would then be able to do as he pleased." Whether because of their own ideas or a knowl-

edge of public opinion, the majority eliminated the "deputies" and all special property requirements, so that the
senators were chosen directly by the voters. They would,
however, retain their office during four years without limit
as to the number of terms, so they might perhaps act independently up to a point. After this bow in the direction of
a balanced government, the convention then deprived the
Senate of the right to initiate laws or amend money bills.

The crucial branch, therefore, was the House of Delegates. Virginians did not go as far as Pennsylvanians in establishing popular controls over it, yet it showed many
characteristics of a democratic body. The freeholders of
each county annually selected two representatives and the
towns of Williamsburg and Norfolk one each. The delegates had no special property qualifications and could be re-
elected. The two houses chose, every year, a governor
without a veto to execute the laws. A Privy Council of eight
served for twelve years, two rotating every three years.
This stable, experienced group could not alter legislation
but helped to administer the government. The two houses
chose important civil officials, including judges for good
behavior. Justices, sheriffs, and coroners were nominated by
the county courts and appointed by the governor and
Council—a method which created a self-perpetuating oligarchy, made powerful by allowing justices to sit in the
legislature. We do not know whether the framers fully realized the consequences of this curious arrangement, which
seems to have partly counteracted the stated principle that
executive, judicial, and legislative powers should be separate,
and violated concepts of checks and balances. Mason's plan,
incidentally, had not called for nominations of the justices
by the county courts. The delegates exercised far more in-

fluence than any other branch, and would be organically connected with the major instrument of local government through the justices. Whether the government became an oligarchy or a democracy therefore depended entirely upon the composition of the delegates. The constitution somewhat tipped the scales toward oligarchy by denying the people any voice in the selection of county officials and by the provision that permanent salaries be granted to major state officeholders.

The convention's principal claim to fame was its adoption of Mason's "Declaration" of rights. This document asserted the ultimate sovereignty of the people, stated that government should benefit and protect them, and defended the right of a majority to reform or abolish it. Subsequent articles concerned rotation in office, trial by jury, search warrants, freedom of the press and of religion (but not of speech), and the militia as opposed to standing armies. At the same time the Declaration enshrined the republican and Christian virtues of temperance, frugality, love, and charity.

Virginia's Declaration of Rights, unlike her constitution, influenced members of conventions in other states. But those in New Jersey completed their work too soon to benefit, adjourning only three days later than the delegates in Williamsburg, and on the same day that Congress resolved in favor of independence. The New Jersey convention met on June 16, 1776, and spent most of its time organizing the war effort. It decided, the preamble noted, that "the preservation of good order," as well as unity, made a new government essential. The members then produced a constitution containing both Whiggish and democratic features. What influences affected them we do not know, for few letters have survived, the province lacked a newspaper at the time, and the convention paid little attention to the petitions it received (such as one asking for popular and annual elections of all civil officers).

The key to the government lay in a two-house legislature. The Legislative Council consisted of one man per county chosen annually by the voters, while the General Assembly contained three delegates per county. This provision diffused power throughout the state. New Jersey's counties did not differ nearly so much in population as did those of most states, and the two major sections had equal numbers. The crucial characteristic of the legislature was the property qualification of £1,000 in real and personal estate for councilors and £500 for assemblymen. Due to such stringent property requirements probably not over one Jerseyite in ten could sit in the upper house. Voting for the legislature was limited to "inhabitants" of "full age" owning £50 in clear estate, about average as far as property was concerned but so phrased as to include women, free Negroes, and non-Christians. The two houses together selected a governor every year. He received "full executive power," which presumably did not include the right to veto bills.

The constitution established a court system with the governor and Council at the top (as in colonial days), acting as final court of appeals. The two houses chose judges of the Supreme Court for seven years and the other judges for five, including justices of the peace—a relatively democratic provision. As to other officials, members of the militia selected company officers, and the voters chose sheriffs, coroners, constables, and men to hear complaints about unjust taxation. The legislature chose all other public officeholders. On the whole this aspect of New Jersey's government resembled Pennsylvania's rather than Virginia's and may indeed have influenced the former. The constitution did not contain a separate bill of rights, but it guaranteed the right to worship freely, forbade enforced taxes for religious purposes or any established church, excluded public officials other than justices from the legislature, and guaranteed trial by jury. The document was not submitted to the people but apparently no one protested, and indeed, apart from the property qualification for the Legislative Council, most voters had little to complain about.

Maryland's convention, by contrast, witnessed a struggle of which we know only the outlines, and produced a controversial document. Except for the lack of a strong executive it faithfully reflected Whig concepts of a balanced government and checks on the popular will. The convention assembled on August 14, 1776, and completed its work a month later. Two opposing groups quickly appeared. One reflected right-wing Whiggism. It included Charles Carroll of Carrollton, his relative Charles Carroll, "Barrister," William Paca, Matthew Tilghman, Thomas Johnson, Robert Goldsborough, George Plater, and Samuel Chase. All except perhaps the last belonged to the colonial elite and Chase, who had recently appeared in the role of a radical popular leader, shared his colleagues' aristocratic convictions. These men sought to limit popular participation through high property qualifications, long terms, and a centralized state government. They had the advantage of prestige, experience, and probably of ability, enabling them ultimately to succeed. On the other side were the representatives from Harford County, a small-farmer stronghold in the north which also contained many tenants of the proprietors, those from Montgomery County farther west, Rezin Hammond, Charles Ridgely, Cockey Deye, and John Stevenson of Baltimore, together with William Fitzhugh and John Mackall of Calvert and perhaps a few others. All came from the western shore, stronghold of the anti-proprietary party in colonial days. Although several owned sizable estates, in the years to come they would time and again vote on the side of the smaller land owners. Their ideas apparently found expression in a set of instructions signed by 855 freemen of Anne Arundel County, the recommendation published by the deputies of several battalions of militia in the same county, and in newspaper articles by a writer calling himself "Watchman." These argued for virtual manhood suffrage, annual election of both houses by the people, and popular choice of local officials including justices of the peace. They also favored levying taxes in proportion to one's property and postponing all law suits. In opposition, Carroll feared the prospect of "simple Democracies, of all governments the worst," and asserted that men of desperate fortune were trying to "introduce a levelling scheme." The convention entrusted the task of drawing up a proposal to a committee consisting almost entirely of Whigs. Chase and the Carrolls, upon receiving the instructions from Anne Arundel County, which demanded that they establish a democratic government, resigned and stood for re-election in order to avoid being bound by them. Chase later wrote that he had opposed popular election of the county officials and the notion that men without property should vote for delegates. A government, he asserted, must be "steady, firm and respectable." Chase and Carroll obtained seats and, freed from the obligation to create a democracy, resumed their work.

The committee presented a constitution which effectively guaranteed rule by the large property owners. Its crucial feature was a senate chosen by an electoral college much like that which Mason had proposed for Virginia. The voters would select two electors from each county plus one each from the towns of Annapolis and Baltimore, who must own property worth £500. These then convened and chose fifteen senators owning at least £1,000, nine from the western shore, six from the eastern. If a senator refused to serve, or when one died or resigned, the senate itself replaced him. This body would serve for seven years, a period which the convention reduced to five over the opposition of Chase, Paca, and Carroll. The senate might initiate all laws except money bills.

The convention shortened the committee's proposed three-year term for delegates to one year. Each county chose four, a system which discriminated against the more populous western areas. These men must own a £500 estate. Voters were required to own fifty acres of land or property worth £30—not a large sum, but the convention narrowly defeated a motion allowing all taxpayers to vote and another to fix the requirement at £5. The system therefore maximized the political power of the conservative eastern counties and tended to perpetuate the dominance of the large planters even in the lower house, to say nothing of the upper. Maryland's newly designed legislature attracted much favorable notice from lawmakers elsewhere, for example in the 1787 federal convention.

The executive branch, as in most revolutionary constitutions, featured a governor of "wisdom, experience, and virtue," chosen annually by the legislature. The property requirement of £5,000, of which £1,000 must be real estate, absolved all but wealthy Marylanders of the burden. He could serve only for three years. His Council contained five men worth £1,000 "in a freehold of lands and tenements."

High-ranking officials, including all judges and justices, held their posts for good behavior. Most of them were chosen by the governor and Council, who also selected all militia and other officers of the army and navy, together with nearly all the civil officials. The voters selected the sheriffs for a three-year term. Justices of the peace could sit in the legislature, from which other officials and army officers above the rank of captain were excluded. The system certainly permitted the people few checks, and the dangers received recognition in clauses warning against prejudice in appointments, bribery, and excessive profit-making on the part of the governor, council, and legislators. The Assembly could change the constitution by publishing the bill and awaiting the next election. But the eastern shore, which had strongly influenced the document, won the promise of no alterations affecting its position without a two-thirds vote of each house.

Maryland's Declaration of Rights exceeded Virginia's in length if not in style. The interesting articles included an attack on the poll tax and assessment of paupers and a statement that taxes ought to be levied proportionate to estates—to which the legislature paid little attention. The convention also inserted statements entitling judges to liberal salaries and favoring rotation in the executive departments. Another clause permitted a general tax for the support of the Christian religion but left the individual the right to decide whether the money should go to a particular church or to the poor. The Declaration also protected the aversion to oaths characteristic of Quakers and others. This part of the constitution, like similar declarations elsewhere, illustrates the liberal aspects of Whig thought, and contrasts to the rest of the document.

After the convention's approval in September, the constitution was published for consideration and ratified on November 11. Apparently no overwhelming adverse opinion developed. The eastern shore found its interests protected, and probably most people at this point preferred harmony and order to discord.

While Maryland's convention considered its committee's handiwork, a similar body in Delaware reached a similar conclusion. A vote for a convention, called by the last colonial Assembly, resulted in a loyalist victory everywhere except in New Castle County. Delaware's loyalism should not create in the reader's mind a picture of wealthy Boston Hutchinsons or New York DeLanceys adhering to Tory ideology and an aristocratic regime. These were farmers, a few rich, most not, who wanted to live without interference in a sort of rural conservatism reminiscent of Tory backbenchers in England and Dutch farmers in New York. They apparently saw no reason for radical change and trusted their traditional leaders. The convention selected a committee consisting, as one might expect, of such lawyers as attended and of men long prominent, notably George Read, Thomas McKean, Nicholas Van Dyke, and Richard Bassett. They presented the usual Declaration of Rights resembling those of Pennsylvania and Virginia. The Delawareans agreed with the Pennsylvanians that no one could be compelled to bear arms against his conscience if he paid an equivalent tax—important in a pacifistically inclined area. They also incorporated a restriction on the quartering of troops.

The core of the constitution acknowledged the new era while perpetuating the old. Though Delaware and Pennsylvania had been closely connected, their constitutions contrasted sharply. Delaware did not change the qualifications for voters. The lower house contained the traditional seven members from each county without special qualifications. The nine councilors, three per county, served for three years, and had powers equal to those of the Assembly except for money bills. The distinctive characteristics of a Whig senate—high property qualifications or indirect elections—did not appear in Delaware; indeed, the two houses did not differ. The president, chosen by the legislature, was given the usual minimum power and a Privy Council.

Although the voters could choose their delegates, they lacked direct control over public officials. The constitution established various courts, the judges being appointed by the legislature and serving for good behavior. The president and Council selected justices of the peace from a list nominated by the Assembly. They served for seven years. The people did have the right, as in Pennsylvania, to nominate sheriffs and coroners, the final selection being left to the governor and Council. These officials served for three years. The two houses together named all of the military officers. None of the civil officials except justices could sit in the legislature. The constitution also forbade the importation of slaves, the preference of any religious sect, and amendments without a majority of more than two-thirds of each house. The constitution certainly did not create a democracy, but it reflected the implications of independence, and we know of no opposition to it.

North Carolina's form of government aroused far more dispute because the men who had held power during colonial days found themselves unable to retain control. Why did the wealthy planters and their allies fail here while succeeding in neighboring Virginia and South Carolina? It was not a matter of numbers, since the small property owners formed a large majority in all three. Perhaps the inhabitants of South Carolina's back-country, divided as they were between Loyalists and rebels, could not exert their unified strength, and having been entirely denied representation before 1776 felt their new gains sufficient. Virginia's farmers were neither so divided nor so deprived, yet they too failed to achieve any radical shift of power. Probably the Virginia planters had governed with sufficient constraint that the people retained much of the old habit of deference, weakened enough to encourage some changes but strong enough to prevent an internal revolution. The North Carolina farmers, however, had already registered a decided lack of deference in the Regulator movement, and while they did not seek radical change they substantially augmented their political power. By the time the state's convention met, in November 1776, the delegates could consult not only what the Virginians had written but Pennsylvania's democratic constitution. They adopted Virginia's Declaration of Rights with minor changes, and then proceeded to form their own new government.

Some of the delegates brought with them instructions to create a democracy. The citizens of Orange County, in the heart of Regulator country, recommended two houses both responsible to the people and open to all voters. Any freeholder could vote for the upper house and all householders for the lower, provisions that would exclude only dependent workers. The people of Mecklenburg preferred "a simple Democracy or as near to it as possible," and advised their spokesmen to "oppose everything that leans to aristocracy or power in the hands of the rich and chief men exercised to the oppression of the poor." They opted for a one-house legislature and popular election of county officials. Both agreed that "the principal supreme power is possessed only by the people at large," and that elected officials were simply servants of the people. They also advocated other reforms, such as taxes levied in proportion to wealth, lower court costs, and salaries for justices instead of fees (which had been extortionate).

In the convention, however, democratic aspirations met opposition. William Hooper, who also communicated a proposal, preferred the historical ideal from which England had departed, wherein the "selected few" most able to govern would check the democratic impulse while they themselves were also checked. He insisted upon a senate "which may be a refinement of the first choice of the people at large," meaning an indirect election like that in Maryland, composed of men "selected for their Wisdom, remarkable Integrity, or that weight which arises from property and gives Independence and Impartiality to the human mind." He also urged the appointment of judges for good behavior so that they could be freed from dependence on the people. Another Whig theorist, Samuel Johnston, considered the major problem to be "how to establish a check on the representatives of the people." One suspects that supporters of the Orange and Mecklenburg view formed a majority among the people and very likely in the convention, but the outcome was a compromise.

The committee that drew up the constitution contained, as usual, the convention's best-educated and most experienced men, and that meant mostly Whigs. Three-fourths came from the eastern counties and towns; indeed, only three members of ability and prominence came from the vast agricultural interior. We do not know certainly, but probably most of the framers agreed with Hooper and Johnston: they voted on the same side during their later legislative careers. Yet they could not have everything their own way, for just as Virginia's convention had scrapped Mason's aristocratic senate, North Carolina's might very well reject any proposal from the committee which failed to embody the popular desire for a more responsive government. The lawyers and great landowners who produced the finished product accordingly combined Whiggish and democratic features with the latter, on the whole, more striking.

The legislature consisted of two houses. The House of Commons was composed of two delegates from each county and one from each of six towns. The selection of political units rather than population as the basis for representation followed both tradition and Virginia's example, and was more democratic than in Virginia because the population was more evenly distributed among the counties. Any taxpayer could vote, and anyone owning a hundred acres could stand for election. Freeholders with fifty acres could vote for senators, who must possess three hundred, a requirement much less restrictive than it sounds in a land where 250 was about average. Each county selected one senator, a distribution which located the geographical center of power one hundred miles from the coast. No regular army or navy officer or judge could sit in the legislature, but lesser officials, including justices, might become members.

The two houses jointly elected each year a governor, who might serve for three years out of six and must own a landed property of £1,000, a Whiggish requirement. He could not veto laws and had no power of appointment, but he did exercise the usual executive functions including the right to impose temporary embargoes and call out the militia. A Council of State, selected annually by the legislature, advised him.

The most democratic aspect of the constitution, aside from its lower house, was the method of selecting judges and other officials. The legislature chose judges, field officers of the militia and all regular army officers, treasurers, and justices of the peace, while the voters (by inference) elected sheriffs, constables, and coroners. Legislative choice of the judges aroused considerable opposition from the lawyers who argued that such men would attain their high positions through popularity rather than through learning or ability.

The constitution forbade state support of any particular church and the taxing of anyone for religious purposes, though only Protestants could hold office. It abolished imprisonment for debt if the debtor delivered his property, ordered the legislature to establish schools and prevent entails, and decreed that only the government could purchase land from the Indians. The legislature must publish its journals promptly and insert the yeas and nays on motions.

North Carolina's Declaration of Rights resembled that of Virginia, following the exact words in some cases but departing in others. North Carolinians added that the people had a right to assemble together, petition, and instruct their representatives. They forbade "perpetuities and monopolies" along with "hereditary emoluments, privileges, or honours." Although the Orange and Mecklenburg instructions asked for popular ratifications, the convention simply enacted their handiwork and left the question of amendments unsettled. The final product ratified the changes which independence required and in addition greatly enlarged the popular basis for government while still preserving for the elite a substantial share of power.

Georgia moved much further toward a democracy. We do not know the author of her constitution nor much about the convention that adopted it. It seems to have consisted of rather ordinary people, and the document itself contains awkward passages, suggesting a plebeian origin. The delegates abandoned the parish as the unit of local government and originated counties named not after local patriots, who had yet to achieve fame, but for English defenders of American rights such as Wilkes, Burke, and Chatham (William Pitt). This originality characterized the whole document, clearly a Georgia product.

The legislature consisted of a single house containing ten members apiece from five of the counties, fourteen from the largest one, one each from two others, four from Savannah, and two from the town of Sunbury. Any adult white male could vote if he owned property worth £10 or if he was a mechanic, but representatives must own 250 acres or property valued at £250, a higher figure than in North Carolina but admitting probably half the voters. This body had almost complete power. The constitution specified that no military officers or soldiers should appear at elections "in a military character," that voting be by ballot, and that anyone failing to vote must pay the heavy penalty of £5 unless he produced a "reasonable" excuse. No holder of an office of profit or military commission, except militia officers, could seek election. Justices of the peace, however, might serve.

The legislature selected each year a governor and an Executive Council, carefully deprived of power. The former, after his one year, must retire for two. He had no veto and no power of appointment except for vacancies. He did serve as commander of the militia. The Council reviewed all acts of the legislature but could only supply advice.

The constitution devised an interesting system of courts designed to bring them closer to the people. Small cases up to £10 continued to be tried in the "Court of Conscience," the local name for courts presided over by justices of the peace. Other cases were tried by superior courts, one in each county, in which jurors rendered the decision on the basis of both fact and law, requesting the judges only for advice. Anyone dissatisfied with the outcome might appeal, not to a supreme court but to a special jury. Court costs were limited to £3, and trials never could be continued longer than two terms. The judges, justices of the peace, and registers of probates received their appointments from the Assembly, but all other civil servants were elected annually by the voters.

The constitution lacked a separate Declaration of Rights, but the usual provisions were inserted briefly near the end. It flatly prohibited entails, stated that the state should pay for schools in every county, and forbade any tax for teachers of religion except by general consent. Petitions from a majority of counties could initiate amendments which would then be effected by a convention. This constitution, like almost all of the others, went into operation without a popular vote. More clearly than any of its rivals except in Pennsylvania and Vermont, it reflected the democratic impulse of the revolutionary years.

Just as the constitution of South Carolina contrasts to Georgia's, so does New York's new government with that written in Pennsylvania. The difference lay in the timing. Pennsylvania's more reluctant rebels, who might have dampened the democratic ardor of the framers, did not campaign for election to the convention because they hoped to block independence. Having defaulted, they could only watch helplessly. But in New York the issue of independence had been settled before that of a new government arose, and while the convention met many of the enthusiastic rebels, who might have pressed for major changes, had gone off to war or active civil service. The Whig leaders, including Robert R. Livingston, Gouverneur Morris, John Jay, and William Duer, seem deliberately to have delayed action for months while awaiting the most favorable circumstances to implement their political ideas.

The committee selected to draw up the constitution included, in addition to the above, Abraham and Robert Yates, Henry Wisner, John Morin Scott, Charles DeWitt, John Broome, James Duane, and William Smith of Suffolk. Duane, a distinguished lawyer, supported the Whig conservatives. DeWitt, a shopkeeper from Ulster County, Smith, a well-to-do farmer, and Robert Yates, an Albany lawyer, were political moderates. Abraham Yates, John Morin Scott, and Henry Wisner represented the agrarian-localist point of view, though none were primarily farmers. Apparently the only consistent proponent of major change was John Broome. The advantage of numbers, prestige, experience, and ability lay with the conservatives, who attended more faithfully and who evidently won over the moderates on critical issues. The major contributors included Duane, Livingston, Jay, Duer, Smith, DeWitt, the two Yateses, and Wisner.

The draft which the committee finally reported in April 1777 reflected a compromise which eliminated the most democratic aspirations of the time. The members proposed a governor selected for a four-year term by freeholders owning a £40 estate, with considerable power over appointments. The senate would be chosen for four years by men worth £100 (the idea of electors found some favor but eventually lost out).

The convention accepted the report with only minor changes. In what appears to be an agrarian effort to limit the influence of townspeople, the members diminished the potential electorate for the lower house by requiring a voter to own or rent some real estate. The convention reduced the governor's tenure from the proposed four years to three. It granted him a seat on a Council of Revision which could veto laws, but took away his control over appointments, transferring the power to a special Council of Appointment.

The constitution that finally emerged reflected more the Whig than the democratic philosophy of government. The Assembly was a genuinely democratic branch elected by small property holders, the members apportioned among the counties roughly according to population. The state was required to take a census after seven years, changing the representation as necessary. Voting by ballot would succeed *viva voce* voting as an experiment after the war. Voters for the Senate must own farms worth £100 clear of debt, a clause eliminating about seven out of ten men. The senators themselves came from four geographical districts, an arrangement which assured that the successful candidate would be well-known rather than obscure. Maryland may have furnished the model, though Connecticut achieved the same end by state-wide votes. The legislature should normally open its doors and publish its journal.

The governor would be elected every third year by those allowed to vote for senators. This is our first encounter with a popularly elected executive. One might assume, from our present knowledge, that the democratically inclined revolutionist would favor that method. But democrats feared that such a governor, once elected, might act without reference to the popular will, and the legislature could not control him because he was not responsible to it. They preferred, therefore, a president—a mere presiding officer—selected by and safely under the thumb of the Assembly. Besides, their experience taught them to fear a separate executive branch. New York's governor was not a democratic creation: the three-year term and restricted suffrage testify to that. Instead the Whigs, who had originally shared the general mistrust of a strong executive, were beginning to overcome that fear and to implement instead their concept of a balanced government with a governor chosen in such a way as to relieve him from any dependence on the legislature.

The constitution granted to the executive branch greater powers than was usual at the time. The governor himself commanded the militia and performed other functions including, incidentally, the preparation of recommendations to the legislature. Together with four senators he sat on a Council of Appointment which nominated almost all state officials for good behavior, including judges, sheriffs, and coroners. Justices of the peace, however, served for three-year terms. The people retained the right to select only such local officers as clerks, assessors, and constables. The governor also joined with the chancellor and judges of the Supreme Court to form a Council of Revision which could veto any law, communicating their objections to the legislature. Passage then required a two-thirds vote of each house. The Council must act within ten days or the bill became law. Thus while the governor himself could act only within a limited sphere, the executive branch of government enjoyed powers equal if not superior to the other branches.

The constitution included a few other features worth mentioning. It established a special court of impeachments which tried certain cases, and the representatives tried others. The constitution legalized all grants of land before October 14, 1775, protected the territorial rights of Indians, guaranteed freedom of religion, freed Quakers from militia duty upon payment of equivalent money, continued trial by jury, and provided for the naturalization of immigrants. It lacked a formal Declaration of Rights.

Considered as a whole, New York's new constitution ranks with those of South Carolina and Maryland as an embodiment of Whig ideology. The Senate may have been less aristocratic, lacking either a high property qualification or indirect elections, but the strong independent executive made up for that as did the independence of other state officials. It balanced democracy with aristocracy so carefully that, as John Jay observed, "another turn of the winch would have cracked the cord," and indeed it is surprising that the convention accepted its committee's report. Perhaps with the state under siege this was no time to quibble or to weaken the government; and probably those who sought a more popular form comprised a minority of the convention in April 1777.

New York's action came just in time to influence Vermonters—by furnishing them a horrible example. At this point they faced three choices: join New Hampshire, which claimed jurisdiction, unite with New York, which likewise asserted control, or seek independence. The leaders of the independence movement, convinced that the people wanted a "popular government," seized upon New York's constitution for proof that Vermonters must establish a separate state. They took as their model the constitution of Pennsylvania and produced, by the summer of 1777, a government that located power in the people.

The Vermonters established a one-house legislature chosen by freemen "of quiet and peaceable behavior." Towns with eighty taxables sent two representatives, the others one apiece. In 1777 no town contained enough to justify a larger number, so this system was, for the moment, fair. The legislators need not own property but must believe in Protestantism. As in Pennsylvania, the legislature's doors would remain open, its proceedings published, its votes recorded, and permanent acts printed for consideration before passage. A popularly elected governor and Supreme Executive Council paralleled the model, though in Vermont the Council reviewed and, as matters developed, even drafted bills. The freemen chose judges of the inferior courts, sheriffs, probate judges, and justices of the peace. Vermont's one major innovation was to establish a militia system in which the people chose all of the officers through the rank of colonel. Thus offered a democratic government and an army under popular control, how could Vermonters help but prefer independence from New York to subservience? And in fact they did. The towns considered the constitution during the next year, approved it with little dissent, and made good their claim to self-determination.

Unlike the states already discussed, Massachusetts did not lack a government after the downfall of the British regime: she fell back on her charter. This provided a lower house and a Council chosen by the lower. The Council simply assumed the full executive functions, assisted by the usual committees. It consisted primarily of east-coast merchants who protected the interests of their section and class, and after the election of May 1776 the balance of power in the House of Representatives also swung east. The demand for constitutional reform accordingly came from the interior, which hoped to increase its share of delegates and to abolish or at least democratize the Council. The eastern commercial group, including most of the prominent leaders and enjoying influential allies even in the west, blocked reform for many months.

The purpose of the reformers is suggested in petitions and

newspaper articles. The town of Ashfield wanted a one-house legislature annually elected, which must send proposed laws out to the towns for approval. Each town would select its own judges to settle disputes. Similarly, "An Old Roman" would abolish both the governor and Council. The popularly chosen representatives would select a presiding officer to act as moderator and exercise the executive power when the legislature recessed. The legislature chose judges, but the people would select all other officers. On the other side, "A Faithful Friend to his Country" warned that the state was contending against arbitrary power and oppression on one hand, and on the other "popular licentiousness, anarchy, and confusion." He argued that government came not from the people but from God. Men were selfish, savage, cruel, and fierce, and needed the restraints of a government; power should never reside in the hands of the people. He felt property restrictions on the right to vote were essential and praised the English constitution.

Most of the towns would have preferred a special convention to devise a new constitution. The eastern group, however, blocked this, and instead the legislature formed itself into a special body and proceeded, during the winter of 1777–1778, to contrive a proposal. The temper of the delegates may be inferred from their economic activities at the same time: they pushed through a deflationary monetary policy, imposed heavy taxes, repealed acts restricting prices, and raised the fees of public officials, all over opposition from the rural representatives. They could not, however, implement their complete political program. The committee report called for an executive veto and would have allotted extra seats to the more populous towns, but the whole body changed these features. Still, the resultant constitution reflected Whig aspirations rather than democratic views.

The constitution of 1778 continued the bicameral system. All free white male taxpayers of twenty-one years voted for representatives, who must own property worth £200. Every town could send one, towns with three hundred voters chose three, larger ones more. Each paid its own representative, which in practice meant that the poorer communities often would elect no one. Voters for senators must own £60 worth of property and the senators themselves £400. The convention adopted Connecticut's method which had proven effective in choosing the same prominent men year after year: elections in November furnished a list of nominees from whom the voters chose in May. The Senate enjoyed power equal to that of the lower house except for money bills. The governor, also popularly chosen like New York's executive, must own at least £1,000 in property. The governor and Senate chose most military and the higher-ranking civil officials (including justices of the peace), while the two houses selected lower-ranking state officers, the Senate holding a negative. The people chose none. The governor recommended measures to the legislature and could lay temporary embargoes. The document contained no Declaration of Rights except a guarantee of trial by jury and freedom of worship for Protestants.

The towns rejected this proposal overwhelmingly, scarcely one in five approving it. Most of the attack came from the democratic side, especially against the high qualifications for voting and for officeholding. No officer of any rank, asserted the town of Westminster, should be chosen except by popular vote. These critics seem not to have complained about the bicameral system, to which they were accustomed, but objected to the lack of popular influence upon the government generally. A different set of opponents, including the townspeople of Boston, did not complain of the lack of democracy but of the absence of a Declaration of Rights, the failure to call a special convention, and the system of representation which, they felt, should be proportionate to numbers or property or both. The famous "Essex Result" expressed this type of objection. The twelve towns which approved this pamphlet felt that more Whig ideas should be included. They too favored a Declaration of Rights. The executive, they believed, should be more clearly separated from the Senate, own even more property, and hold greater power. They sought to maximize eastern influence by increasing the number of representatives directly proportionate to population. The "Result" defended as essential a senate containing "gentlemen of education, fortune and leisure" and suggested indirect elections by county conventions. But this represented a minority view. A constitution, to succeed, must meet the criticisms from the left, not the right.

The General Court, recognizing the general wish for a constitution, now called upon the towns to vote whether they wanted a special convention. More than two-thirds voted in favor, so during the summer the people selected delegates who met in September. A committee to draft a proposal entrusted the major work to John Adams, James Bowdoin, and Samuel Adams, the first being primarily responsible for the finished product. Bowdoin, judging from his later career, advocated a strong executive power in an efficient government responsive to commercial and creditor interests. John Adams, of course, was an outstanding exponent of a balanced government based upon the ultimate sovereignty of the people and immediate rule by the elite. Sam Adams agreed with his cousin. The people, he explained to the French traveler Chastellux, were too subject to "passions and follies," so it was necessary to "moderate their first emotions." Therefore the committee, having provided a "purely democratical" lower house, added a governor and a senate to represent property. John Adams always regarded this constitution as a supreme example of the Whig ideal.

The constitution of 1780 differed from its unsuccessful predecessor in several ways. The qualifications of voters for the lower house were increased slightly so as to equal those for the other branches—an income of £3 annually from a freehold estate, or property worth £60. Qualifications for representatives remained the same, those for senators were slightly raised to £300 worth of land or £600 of personal estate. These changes certainly did not meet the criticisms. The system of representation remained substantially the same, allowing every town one delegate and larger ones more. The General Court now paid travel expenses but the towns still continued to bear costs of attendance. The method of selecting senators by two elections, one to nominate and one to select from the proposed list, gave way to a single vote by the people; but if some senators did not obtain a majority, as often happened, the legislature filled the vacancies. The executive became much stronger because he could veto bills, the legislature having the power to repass the bill by a two-thirds vote of each house. The new document lodged the power to appoint important civil officials in the governor, advised by a Council, instead of in the Senate together with the governor. Militia companies chose their own officers, and these in turn selected officers of higher rank. Both constitutions forbade plural officeholding and disqualified from the legislature army officers and certain other officials. That of 1780 guaranteed permanent and honorable salaries to the judges and the governor, a provision designed to free them from legislative discipline

(Adams called it undue influence or dependence). The argument that officials should be less independent of public opinion than formerly won only the slight concession that justices of the peace served for seven years instead of for life. The new document promised support to Harvard and for education generally. It did not deprive non-Christians of civil rights—probably an unpopular omission, and was preceded by a classic Declaration of Rights.

Whether this constitution was good or bad depended upon one's point of view. To Bowdoin, the Adamses, and the other merchants and lawyers and their supporters it seemed nearly perfect. Each branch was carefully separated and almost equal in power except that the governor had only a limited veto, which John Adams regarded as a flaw. Eastern, urban interests were protected in the lower house where the larger towns received additional seats. Property owners throughout the state were protected by the requirements for voting and holding office, through the method of selecting senators, and by the independent, permanent judiciary. Support came primarily from the towns on or near the coast. They detected imperfections: some felt that non-Protestants should not enjoy equal rights, and some, like the townspeople of Dorchester, next to Boston, believed that all taxpayers should have voting privileges so that they could protect themselves against oppression. But some forty towns found no cause for criticism, and sixty-five ratified with only minor objections.

Perhaps half the people, on the other hand, thought the constitution faulty. To them it seemed no improvement on the one just rejected. People with little or no property, however meritorious, were entirely excluded. Western towns objected to their lack of equality in the lower house. Others complained of the aristocratic Senate, the power of the executive, the life terms of the judges, and officials being appointed rather than elected. They wanted, in short, more democracy. These objections emanated primarily from the agricultural interior.

The three western counties of Berkshire, Hampshire, and Worcester voted almost three to one against ratification. Bristol opposed it two to one, and the inland villages of the eastern counties also tended to reject it. Perhaps the legislature ought to have declared the constitution defeated. But an eastern-dominated committee concluded, with some juggling and wishful thinking, that the people had approved. After all, the state had lacked a proper government other than the obsolete charter for five years, and in 1780 one seemed essential for survival. No one challenged the decision, but the struggle had driven a further wedge between the commercial and agricultural interests, between Whigs and democrats.

The remaining two states, Rhode Island and Connecticut, did not experiment with their colonial charters. Rhode Island enjoyed an exceptionally democratic form with £40 freeholders twice each year electing a lower house and once a year an upper, the "assistants." The governor was a member of the upper house with little power. The towns each sent two representatives regardless of population, except that Newport chose six and three other trading towns four each. The people regularly instructed their representatives and retired them promptly.

After Independence there was some talk about a reform, apparently emanating from the agricultural villages which hoped to reduce the extra seats of the commercial towns. In addition, the lower house probably responded to popular pressure when it voted to allow the militia to select their own officers. The town of Scituate urged that every new law be submitted to the towns and voted on by the people. In 1777 the legislature selected a committee of five to form a plan of government, but these men, who represented the merchant-lawyer interests of the major towns, never reported. Agitation continued into 1779, when the lower house attempted to equalize the representation. The upper house suggested an apportionment based upon both numbers and taxes paid, whereupon the two disagreed and accomplished nothing. In agricultural Rhode Island, then, the reform movement represented an attempt by the farmers to gain even more power. The trading centers succeeded in blocking these efforts but did not attempt to augment their own influence.

Connecticut's charter escaped without criticism until after the war. Since every town sent two representatives, the agricultural villages had little to complain of except for the upper house, controlled by the state's long-established leaders. The people nominated a colony-wide list in one election, and voted for the principal vote-getters in a run-off, the candidates' names being presented in an order based upon their numbers of votes. The system virtually guaranteed the selection year after year of the most widely known men, especially the incumbents, new men working their way slowly up the ladder. One newspaper writer did suggest a different method, but to no avail. In the absence of any general demand for change, the legislators remained content.

This survey of the conflict over the form of government reveals two opposing points of view. Each dominated in certain states, while in others the constitutions represented a compromise. Whig ideology found expression in the constitutions of South Carolina and Maryland, in that drawn up by Mason and presented to the Virginia convention, in the form recommended by the committee in New York, in Massachusetts' rejected constitution of 1778 and in less degree its successor, and in the defeated New Hampshire proposal of 1778. The opposing democratic point of view found expression in the constitutions of Georgia, Pennsylvania, Vermont, and to some extent North Carolina, as well as in the modifications made of the original plans in Virginia, New York, Massachusetts, and later New Hampshire. Whig convictions carried them in the direction of a stronger executive, to a senate representing the interests of large property owners, and toward indirect elections, relatively long terms of office, high property requirements, and the independence of public officials. Democratic ideology, on the other hand, continued to emphasize a weak executive subordinated to the legislature, either a unicameral system or an upper house just as responsible to public opinion as the lower, direct elections, short terms of office, low property qualifications, and the dependence of public officials on the popular will. In some states one or the other of these contesting ideologies clearly succeeded, but in most they compromised and the resultant moderate constitutions reflected therefore a kind of consensus, genuinely accepted by many Americans, incorporating ideas shared by Whigs and democrats alike, and recording the initial results of the Revolution.

# Chapter Six

# The New Governments

HISTORIANS of the Revolutionary era disagree over whether one should emphasize conflict or consensus. Some have seen not only a struggle between the British government and the colonists, but also internal controversies which, after Independence, move to the center of the political stage. They describe a people divided sharply over the form of government, the location of power, and a variety of economic, social, and cultural issues. These same writers stress the profound changes resulting from the whole Revolutionary movement. On the other side, equally learned historians regard these domestic differences as relatively minor compared with the broad underlying agreements of Americans. They interpret the Revolution as a struggle of the colonists to maintain their rights, not to acquire new ones; to make secure rather than to reform. They regard changes as fortuitous rather than deliberate, and as occurring within the framework of a continuing agreement over fundamentals, so that in the end the people simply substituted a new consensus for the old. "Consensus" historians trace a continuity of ideas and institutions, denying any fundamental disruption of old patterns, any abrupt shift of direction, any true revolution.

The conflict of opposing ideologies over the proper form of government, as detailed in the preceding chapter, should not obscure the existence of a large middle group of people who shared certain ideas of both protagonists, and the existence too of a common heritage of convictions held by almost all of the contestants. The elements common to the new constitutions become clear when we stand off a little and consider them in relation to pre-Revolutionary forms. Yet in examining this evidence for consensus we shall nevertheless not stress elements of continuity, for two reasons: first, because the new governments did in fact manifest important changes both in their institutional arrangements and in the distribution of political power; and second, because even when examples of change are less numerous than those of continuity, the changes themselves are more important: they are dynamic, pointing toward the future rather than to the past.

The innovative use of constitutional conventions in the years 1776–1780 illustrates the broad area of agreement. Most men, of whatever political conviction, agreed upon the necessity of written constitutions to secure liberty and define authority. These constitutions derived their validity in practice by general acceptance, and in theory because they were created by the people acting in their sovereign capacity. In 1776 and 1777 the new plans of government were produced by legislatures or their replacements, on the assumption that the peoples' chosen representatives had full authority not only to write constitutions but also to ratify them without further ado. The idea that the power to form new governments rested only in a special convention chosen explicitly for the purpose developed rather gradually. It assumed that the people as a whole, not just their representatives, possessed ultimate authority, a principle appealing more to the democrats than to the Whigs; and, indeed, the initial statements of the doctrine came from democratic spokesmen. The Whigs, however, wanted to elevate the constitutions beyond the reach of mere legislative enactment and beyond the scope of mass meetings or other extralegal gatherings, so they presently adopted the same view. Thus in Pennsylvania the "radicals" began by defending the product of their convention, while republicans soon were urging a revision by a new and specially chosen body. Meanwhile, in Massachusetts, eastern towns such as Boston and Concord joined western villages in demanding a convention to draft a constitution and a popular ratification of the proposed plan. This method, adopted also in New Hampshire, now became standard, and a major result of the Revolution therefore was the creation of new governments based on popular consent.

The new constitutions introduced or acknowledged major changes in the form of government and the distribution of power. The most obvious political casualty of the Revolution at the state level was the governor, who in four states lost even his name. Before 1776 he owed his appointment to the King and answered for his conduct to the Crown, not to the people or their representatives. After Independence his constituency became the legislatures, generally the two houses in joint session. Only Massachusetts, Vermont, and New York provided for the popular vote, which freed the executive from depending for his very existence on the legislative branch. Only New York, Delaware, and South Carolina chose their governors for more than one year, and the last two forbade his re-election, leaving New York as the sole state electing its executive biennially while at the same time permitting an indefinite number of terms. The framers of New York's constitution may have hoped for a comparatively strong and long-lasting governor as a result of their labors. If so, they succeeded, but it is symptomatic of the direction of change that the man who fulfilled that expectation, year after year, was no scion of the best families but a popular hero, General George Clinton.

Colonial governors usually had belonged to England's ruling families, and most people of the independent states probably anticipated that theirs too would come from the same stratum of society. The American social system, however, lacked any such clearly defined upper class. It did have an economic elite, and four of the states designed property requirements to ensure the selection of suitable candidates. Of these states three (South Carolina, Maryland, and Massachusetts) intended deliberately to exclude men of lesser economic status, and by implication those of lower social rank. But the other eight states imposed no such requirement. They referred vaguely to a "fit" person or omitted any description. Half the constitutions did not even specify a religious qualification. Most omitted an age minimum, and the highest was only thirty years. Six out of the twelve insisted that the governor must have resided in the state for a minimum period, generally only a few years, though Massachusetts required seven and South Carolina ten. All of these conditions, except the few requirements of large property, could be met by almost any free American.

What kind of man became chief executive under these

conditions? There were fifty-five in all states during the years 1776–1788, but the figure is deceptive. Ten of these are from Georgia, whose government remained highly unstable until after the war. Otherwise the thirteen states averaged less than four apiece, each of whom typically served nearly four years in office. George Clinton and William Livingston governed New York and New Jersey for the entire period. Massachusetts had only two governors—John Hancock and James Bowdoin—and Rhode Island only three. Mesech Weare of New Hampshire lasted for eight years, as did Jonathan Trumbull of Connecticut and William Greene of Rhode Island, while John Martin of North Carolina and John Rutledge of South Carolina each served five. The picture actually is one of stability, notably so in the North, and particularly where the governor was more than just a presiding officer. On the whole, the republican form of government recognized and rewarded men of great ability, regardless of how they were chosen: Clinton by the voters, Livingston by the legislature, Weare by a council.

The names Livingston, Bowdoin, Trumbull, Greene, and Rutledge suggest to the student of colonial history a continuity of the Revolutionary executives with the colonial past. The list also includes, to name a few more men, John Dickinson, Thomas Sim Lee, Samuel Johnston, Thomas Nelson, Thomas Pinckney, Edmund Randolph, and Nicholas VanDyke. Nearly half the governors did in fact belong to prominent families, inheriting large estates and enjoying cultural advantages, social prestige, and political experience. The obverse, of course, is that fully half did not, and the reader must decide for himself whether one normally expects the chief executives of the states to come from the top of the social ladder or some distance down it. The contrast to the royal governors, at any rate, seems clear. A dozen of the Revolutionary governors started at or near the bottom. To the name Benjamin Franklin we might add Richard Caswell, whose father failed in business, George Mathews, son of an Irish immigrant, John Sullivan, who began as a poor lad, and George Walton, an orphan who started as an apprentice. Another group of equal size grew up in average homes as did Thomas Johnson of Maryland and John Langdon of New Hampshire, both farm boys. Whatever their disadvantages of birth, the future leaders quickly demonstrated business ability, moved to the important towns, and entered politics. Again Franklin furnishes the obvious but also exceptional example, since these men usually became lawyers or merchants, not printers. In any event, they acquired large properties and represented their town or rich farming district in the legislature, characteristically attaining high office before the movement for independence began. Most of them would have been leaders without the Revolution, though certainly men such as Patrick Henry, George Clinton, James Sullivan, Thomas Burke, and George Walton made their mark only as popular leaders. Indeed, the single most significant development in the executive branch is probably the emergence of men who owed their position to broad public support, and who often as a result made their office far more influential than formal constitutional arrangements intended. The five men just named, together with Weare, Livingston, Caswell, and Rutledge, forecast the emergence of a strong executive in America.

The governors almost always had the help of and were checked by executive councils. These inherited some of the functions of the colonial councils and owed something also to the British Privy Council, several bearing the name. Ex-

cept in Vermont and Pennsylvania, where the voters chose
the councilors, they received their appointments from the
legislature, serving either annually or for a single term of
two to four years. Only Maryland and South Carolina introduced property or any other special requirements. These
councils, unlike their models, did not convey or permit
power but were entrusted with important functions. The
legislatures carefully selected some of the state's ablest
statesmen for office, forbade them to hold any conflicting
appointment, limited their terms, and within these con-
straints conferred certain powers.

The governor and his advisers primarily carried out the
desires of the legislative branch without initiating policies
on their own. The few exceptions underscore the generalization. The governor always commanded the militia, calling it
out when necessary but not always leading in person. Half
the constitutions allowed the executive to impose embargoes on trade when the legislature was adjourned, but
only for thirty days. Half allowed him to issue pardons, two
limited him to granting reprieves. Characteristically he
could not adjourn or prorogue the legislatures—the Southern states especially had experienced enough of that. His
most important activity, aside from implementing the legislature's decisions, consisted of appointing certain officials,
but only Massachusetts, Maryland, Delaware, and New
York granted substantial authority. In New York, a special
Council of Appointment, chosen by the legislature and in-
eligible for re-election, selected most officeholders, and in
Pennsylvania the popularly elected Supreme Executive
Council appointed a smaller number. In no case could the
governor create a political machine based upon his appointive powers. Indeed, in no case except perhaps in Massachusetts could a governor undertake effective action with-

out the assent of the peoples' representatives. Finally, while he and his council must submit to legislative supervision, they could not limit the power of the elected branch. Of these early constitutions only those of Massachusetts, New York, and (in 1776 only) South Carolina gave their executives a veto, which a two-thirds vote could then overcome. The governors could act, but they did not govern.

The events of the war demonstrated the necessity for a stronger executive branch, and for concentrating authority in a single governor rather than diffusing it in a council. But most people did not learn this lesson for many years. At first the congresses, conventions, and legislatures entrusted wide powers to councils of safety. These consisted of the state's outstanding Revolutionary leaders. At first they held office only when the parent body adjourned, but they presently became permanent. They raised and spent money, carried out the instructions of Congress, created and supplied armies, appointed officers, and summoned the legislature. Even after the new constitutions took effect, these councils sometimes continued. Since they lacked coercive power or any experienced officialdom to carry out their desires, and existed on a temporary, ad hoc basis, they depended upon the voluntary cooperation of the citizenry. Their effectiveness therefore varied and tended to diminish with time. Moreover, their duties proved so arduous, and the rewards either in prestige or money so small, that men became less willing to serve. Adequate in emergencies, they could not substitute for an effective, permanent executive.

The governors acted under equal disadvantages. Many served but a single term, most faced annual elections by the legislature, all received their pay from the representatives. Both political realities and constitutional restrictions made them servants rather than masters. Few brought to their office much executive experience, and fewer still had a chance to acquire any. They lacked skilled subordinates, and time did not permit the development of a faithful bureacracy. To overcome these handicaps required a combination of efficiency, self-sacrifice, and boldness that they rarely possessed. Thomas Jefferson, for example, could not bring himself to override legal restrictions in the face of an emergency, and failed to meet the British invasion effectively. His successor, Thomas Nelson, simply assumed power, authorizing impressments and seizures when necessary, and played a vital role in supplying the armies at Yorktown, reacting to a crisis without bothering about constitutional niceties.

Nelson's success showed what governors might do, and indeed a remarkable number overcame all their difficulties, contributing as much to victory as did the military leaders. As we have seen, some served for many years and became true heads of state. Jonathan Trumbull of Connecticut, Caesar Rodney of Delaware, Thomas Johnson and Thomas Sim Lee of Maryland, Mesech Weare of New Hampshire, William Livingston of New Jersey, George Clinton of New York, Richard Caswell of North Carolina, Joseph Reed of Pennsylvania, William Greene of Rhode Island, and John Rutledge of South Carolina, like Nelson, compare favorably with any list of American statesmen. By 1783 most people had perceived the perils of withholding essential executive powers and recognized the benefits that a strong governor could bestow. Enthusiasm for the principle of rotation in office diminished when constitutions forced six of the above twelve to retire. The revolutionary reaction against the monarchical principle had run its course, and would give way now to a resumption of authority.

The Revolution thus created a new kind of executive. The governors would in future recover some of their lost power, but not their independence. They became far more responsible to the people than their colonial predecessors and far more American in their experience, outlook, and careers. The same metamorphosis took place in the upper houses of the legislature: they became more representative bodies in both their composition and functions. They displayed in these respects great variation, for, as we have seen, men differed radically in their attitudes toward the senate; yet the same transition occurred everywhere in some degree.

All senators shared this basic characteristic: they no longer owed their office to the royal government but to fellow citizens, usually the same small property holders who chose the lower house (in the case of New York not quite so small, only in Maryland a quite separate group of men). Most constitutions made it clear, however, that the senates ought to contain a different sort of men than the houses of representatives: somewhat older (the word "senate" means a council of elders), a good deal more affluent, and presumably wiser. Most Americans thought of their senators as superior men, as a political elite, and justified the retention of an upper house in all but three of the states by assuming that it would improve the conduct of government. From this point of view a property qualification might be justified on the assumption of a high correlation between wealth and ability, or wealth and wisdom. Almost certainly, however, most citizens rejected this reasoning. Those who defended it believed that the senates, in addition to contributing wisdom, should also represent property, the two attitudes combining in the concept of an aristocracy house. This view triumphed only in three states: New Jersey and

Maryland, where the qualification of £1,000 would admit most men owning five hundred acres, for the time not a big estate, and South Carolina, with the much more restrictive £2,000. Elsewhere the property requirement eliminated few who would aspire to the senate, and four states imposed no such qualification at all. Nor did the term of office ensure the kind of body that admirers of the British system preferred. Maryland decreed five years, but nowhere else did senators enjoy that long an independence: indeed, in four of the ten states with bicameral legislatures, annual elections were the rule. Colonial councilors, of course, had served at pleasure.

The small numbers of senators and their large districts may have contributed more than these restrictions to their characteristics. Once again we must emphasize the considerable change in this respect, for before 1776 all councilors except in Massachusetts were selected "at large"—from any part of the colony, which in practice meant that they lived in or near the major towns. After 1776 every state except Maryland chose senators by districts, guaranteeing a comparatively even geographical distribution. In a few states, small counties each chose one, that the voters knew pretty well what manner of person they were selecting. In the rest, the large size of counties, or the combining of counties into districts, prevented voters from acquiring a personal acquaintance with the candidate, so the man of established public reputation won. Thus in a few instances the senates differed little in their composition from the assemblies, but generally they did contain more prominent men, while still not equalling, in this respect, the councilors. If we arranged these bodies along a scale starting, on the right, with those composed exclusively of the top 1 per cent of the people (by almost any definition) and on the left those who precisely mirrored the people's characteristics, we would locate the senators a bit to the right of center and the councilors near the right extreme.

Whether because of property restrictions, the method of selection, the conviction that senators should consist of the best men, or the habit of deference, the people did in fact elect exceptional, not typical men. About one out of four came from the established colonial elite, from the wealthy merchants, lawyers, and great landowners who joined the rebel side and retained power. New Hampshire's Senate, for example, contained three Wentworths, relatives of the royal governors, all rich men for the time. In New York's were James Duane, Sir James Jay, Philip Livingston, two Morrises, two Schuylers, two Ten Broecks, and a Van Cortlandt. Virginians returned to this high office more than a score of men with similar names—it would be hard to find a name familiar to colonial Virginians without relatives in the Senate. These men received excellent educations, had held various important offices, and probably exercised a disproportionate political influence in the legislature.

An even larger number belonged to the respectable middling families, the prosperous, reputable farmers, artisans, or professionals, and had acquired property and prestige in the law, trade, or commercial farming. New Jersey's Legislative Council is representative. Eighteen (about 30 per cent) of the members came from the colonial upper class. Another eighteen enjoyed no such advantages, but starting a little above the average became locally prominent. For example, John Cooper of Gloucester County, a substantial farmer, gave his name to a son who tripled his parent's estate, became a judge, and sat in the U.S. Congress. Joseph Hugg's father acquired a considerable property in trade but remained outside the colony's elite, while Joseph himself became wealthy and attained the rank of colonel. Men such as these might have succeeded in life without the Revolution, but, as we have seen earlier, they seized the chance and added power to their property.

A smaller but significant group of senators began their careers with no advantages except their own ability, and translated into reality the myth of the self-made man. James Caldwell, a farm boy, became one of New Jersey's famous ministers and rebel leaders; Robert Hoops appeared out of the blue to become a well-to-do Trenton merchant; William Paterson, son of a small entrepreneur, immigrated from Ireland to achieve immortality as a member of the federal convention; Colonel Mark Thompson moved from Pennsylvania, his family unknown, to acquire prominence and property as an iron manufacturer. Finally, an equally significant type of senator never accomplished such feats but remained an ordinary citizen, distinguished only by a brief appearance on this broader stage or some local office: Whitten Cripps, carpenter, farmer, and sheriff; Jonathan Hand, a miller; Abraham Kitchel, who started from scratch and remained a farmer, though politically active; Ephraim Martin, innkeeper and militia colonel. These men are important for two reasons: they never would have received an appointment to the colonial Council, and they supplied to the fashionably clad senators a suit of homespun. They symbolize, then, the democratizing effect of the Revolution and the transition of the upper houses from elitist to representative bodies.

Each senate, then, contained in some degree two attributes: a "democratic" element of ordinary citizens or men who spoke for the average voter, and an "aristocratic" element reflecting the ideas of the better sort. The former anticipated the future, the latter preserved the past. The former divided the senates into conflicting blocs, the latter ensured conservative control. As a result, the upper houses played three roles. Sometimes they became the scenes of lively legislative battles paralleling those of the representatives. At others they protected minority rights, most often the rights of large property owners and of the commercial interest. Finally, the senators reviewed, improved, and rejected laws that they considered imperfect or unwise. The first came as a surprise; we shall deal with it later. The second and third were expected, recognized as proper functions, and planned for.

The senators received powers equal to those of the representatives, with this exception: seven states denied the right to originate any bills at all. In compensation the upper house generally tried impeachments and shared in making appointments. Such equality signified a lessening of influence from prewar days, when the councils joined with the governor in his executive capacity and might sit as a supreme court. This mingling of legislative, executive, and judicial functions, common at the time, came under heavy attack from the Whigs because the council received—at least on paper— excessive power, and because the governor could influence legislation. Such a formidable combination of interlocking powers threatened the capacity of the representative body to protect the people against oppression, and violated Whig ideals of a balanced government. The constitution-makers therefore carefully separated the upper house from the executive, limiting the functions of both. But this process did not really weaken the senates, since in exchange for the loss of certain powers they became independent, no longer owing their existence to the governor but deriving their

authority from the voters. The Revolution thus truly transformed the senates both in their composition and in their
purpose.

The principal beneficiary from this redistribution of
powers was the house of representatives which became,
especially during the first years of statehood, the most important part of the government. Pennsylvania, Georgia, and
Vermont, indeed, lodged almost all authority in their unicameral legislatures. During the Colonial period most assemblies reflected the views primarily of the eastern men
of property; now they extended their constituencies geographically so as to comprehend if not all kinds of people at
least the majority. The senate represented primarily property and secondarily people; the house reversed that
priority.

This more democratic quality resulted from a series of
changes, none decisive individually but cumulative. Several
constitutions specified voting by ballot where *viva voce* had
been the rule, notably in Maryland, North Carolina, and
Georgia. During the Colonial period property requirements
for voting usually excluded the poorer farmers and artisans
together with most wage-workers. Some states continued
that restriction, but New Hampshire, Vermont, Pennsylvania, and North Carolina granted the franchise to all taxpayers, and several others (Maryland, New York, and
Georgia) reduced their requirement. Attempts to lower the
barriers even further lost by a narrow margin, as in Maryland and Massachusetts. Probably the number of new voters
increased by only a few percentage points overall, but the
trend was clear. Similarly, property requirements for officeholding excluded primarily those whose poverty and lack
of status would have prevented them from seeking the post

to begin with. Five states allowed any voter to become a delegate, and North Carolina's minimum of one hundred acres scarcely mattered. Only Maryland and New Jersey, both of which demanded £500 worth of property, and South Carolina, with an even higher requirement, excluded substantial numbers of potential legislators. In practice, delegates sometimes fell short of the minimum, and the houses seem never to have investigated their qualifications unless someone challenged them. The provisions regarding age (twenty-one), residence (one or two years), and belief in Christianity had no practical effect.

The distribution of seats did make a difference. Before Independence the inland towns and counties of several colonies exercised much less power than their population justified. New Hampshire, New York, Pennsylvania, and South Carolina all denied the interior communities adequate representation, while Massachusetts, Maryland, Virginia, North Carolina, and Georgia discriminated in lesser degree. To some extent the cause lay simply in the new districts growing so rapidly that legislation could not keep pace; but primarily the people of older areas disliked to share power with men whose interests diverged from their own. Of course, the western districts might have chosen the same kind of men as did the eastern, and these might have voted the same way. That did happen sometimes, but on the whole when the newer communities won the right they selected delegates of less education, status, and property, who voted on key issues differently than the representatives of the older area. To apportion seats by population commonly meant a shift of power westward, into the hands of farmers rather than townsmen, to men of lesser wealth, and into areas of limited contact with the outside world.

The only exception to this generalization occurred in those states where the agricultural villages already enjoyed full political participation, and any redistricting based on numbers would strengthen the populous trading towns.

The constitutions allocated seats in the lower house both by districts and by population, depending on the local situation, and granted the interior more power while guarding eastern rights. Five states continued the custom of a set number of delegates per county, and accommodated the westward movement by creating additional counties. Massachusetts and New Hampshire allowed the new settlements to send delegates, but until they reached a certain number of voters the towns had to combine, while the more populous centers received additional seats. New York, Pennsylvania, South Carolina, and Georgia assigned a variable number of representatives roughly in proportion to taxable inhabitants except in South Carolina, where the coastal parishes retained more on the theory that the legislature should reflect property as well as persons. The Southern states allocated special seats to their trading towns, which otherwise would have been deprived of a vote, twelve in all being singled out. In addition Charleston received thirty seats, while Philadelphia and New York also obtained special treatment. The total effect over the long haul would be to grant the rural districts an increasing share of the power.

The members of the lower house became more responsive to public opinion than before the war. Although the population had not doubled, the voters chose more than twice as many representatives and perhaps knew them better as a result. Elections became annual except in South Carolina, whereas many colonies had voted only once every three or four years. Four constitutions specified that the journals be published promptly, three, that sessions be opened to the public. Four required the recording of roll call votes, and in several others custom made the injunction superfluous. Indeed, only Connecticut, Rhode Island, and South Carolina failed quickly to adopt the practice, and the last began that practice in 1787. Six declarations of rights guaranteed the right of the people to assemble, petition, and instruct their representatives. Finally, Vermont and Pennsylvania required the publication of all bills for the people's consideration before final passage.

The relationship of the representative to his constituent also changed in response to a final factor: the tendency of the voter to select men of ordinary birth or circumstances instead of automatically choosing one of the local elite. This resulted from two simultaneous and interlocking developments: the declining prestige of the "better sort" and a rising confidence of the "middling sort" in their own ability. Probably both trends began long before Independence, and now accelerated.

Mobility helps to explain these changes. The demonstrated ability of ordinary folk to rise in status convinced them of their capabilities, while the presence among the elite of many men of humble origin reduced their pretensions to superiority. If, as seems probable, mobility decreased during the later Colonial period, it rose sharply after 1773. Several factors then enabled men to attain a higher position: a wider popular participation in political affairs, especially in the committees, conventions, and congresses; the opportunity to acquire fame and training in leadership through the army; and a better chance to make money afforded by wartime prosperity. At the same time the colonial elite, instead of agreeing on policies, divided, and people no longer trusted them so much as before. Within a few years every colony witnessed the humbling of once prominent leaders: thus in Charleston, spokesmen for the artisans ridiculed a Drayton; in Boston a mob wrecked Hutchinson's home; in Virginia the revelation that leading planters had appropriated to their own use the colony's money discredited the old leadership; in New Hampshire the Wentworths fell, in New York the DeLanceys. Illustrations could be multiplied. The people often turned to other more trusted members of the elite, but many times they followed new leaders—the Adamses, Searses, and Henrys.

The consequences of this process and the evidence for it appears in the composition of the Revolutionary houses of representatives. Everywhere the contrast between new and old is obvious. The western-most districts gained at the expense of the eastern, though the difference shows up less in percentages than in numbers—the frontier regions increasing sixfold. The proportion of merchants, lawyers, and large landowners, the colonial upper class, declined from roughly 60 percent to perhaps 35 per cent, while ordinary farmers and artisans made up 40 per cent of the new legislatures compared with 20 per cent before the war. Men from average families, of little education or political experience, became a majority, and the people's representatives owned only half as much property.

New York may serve as an example. Her 1769 Assembly of twenty-eight men included ten merchants, four lawyers, and five large landowners, probably worth £4,000 on the average, with only four or five prosperous middle-class farmers. The sole representatives from the frontier areas were a well-to-do Schenectady merchant and Philip Schuyler, one of the elite. By the 1780's the frontier was sending one-seventh of a larger Assembly, the middle class of farmers and artisans outnumbered the merchant-lawyer-planter group, and the mean wealth fell short of £2,000. Moreover, some of those with incomes above the average came from and reflected the views of small-farmer constituencies.

This shift of power within the lower house occurred simultaneously with the strengthening of its authority. The constitutions removed most of the restraints characteristic of pre-Revolutionary governments. The executives now merely carried out policy. Public officials exercised little influence upon and generally were excluded from the legislature. Only the senates limited the representatives' power, and even this check proved incomplete, for the lower houses over the long haul had their way. For example, during the agitation for inflation in the mid-1780's, only two senates blocked passage of a paper-money bill when a majority of the assembly clearly and persistently favored it. Three states, as we know, had no upper house to reject such a law, while the senates gave way in South Carolina, North Carolina, New Jersey, New York, and Rhode Island. The senatorial inability to originate and in several cases to amend money bills also permitted greater power to the lower house. Thus a major effect of the Revolution, although only a temporary one, was to locate primary authority in a body much more democratic in its composition and responsiveness to public opinion than the colonial assemblies.

Consider, for example, the progress of two hypothetical legislative bills before and after the Revolution. One would postpone the collection of debts for six months, the other would levy a general import tax. The first could scarcely have succeeded in any colonial assembly, dominated as they were by large property owners, and would certainly fail in the councils. The second might appeal to land owners as likely to relieve their tax burden, and many government supporters would approve of this revenue. If it succeeded in passing the lower house, it would encounter trouble in the upper, where the merchants were influential and where the governor would observe that any tax on British products infringed upon the royal prerogative and ran counter to Britain's interest. If the council passed it the governor probably would veto it, and if by some chance he did not it stood no chance of approval in England. After 1776 both laws would meet some opposition in the lower house, but during an economic slump either might pass. If so, in three states they would then be law. In the rest the senators would also divide. The anti-stay law and anti-import-tax forces were stronger there, yet both might succeed, and in every state but two they would then be law. In those two, governors had the power to veto laws, but they rarely did so and seldom succeeded in blocking a bill. In short, before the war a great many measures desired by the majority of voters could never have become law; after it they seldom failed.

The position of the judiciary also changed after 1776. During colonial times the judges received their appointments, technically, at pleasure from the King. The offices went to prominent colonials, usually acquainted with the law and ordinarily associated with the "court" party or its equivalent, that is, to men whom the government trusted. Once chosen they customarily held office for life, but they might legally be removed and this in fact did occur. In a few colonies appointments were political, and the profitable judgeships went to the most loyal men. Colonial judges tended to depend upon the executive rather than upon the people as the democrats preferred, or instead of being independent of both, as the Whigs wished. Moreover, the judges and other appointed officials had frequently sat in the legislatures. In several colonies they dominated the councils, creating the strong possibility that a vested interest would selfishly manipulate the legislative process. This threatened to duplicate the widespread political corruption that the colonial Whigs deplored in England. In New York seven of the sixteen councilors who held office after 1763 were also royal officials, in New Jersey nine of eighteen, in Maryland every one. A fair number turned up in the assemblies as well. Another grievance was the practice of plural officeholding which concentrated important positions and their financial rewards in a small number of men, tying them more firmly to the government. Most Americans agreed that judges and other public officials should be denied seats in the legislature, and that they ought to conduct their affairs free from executive interference. Probably most also agreed that the higher-ranking officials, such as judges of the state courts, ought not to be chosen by the people.

The new constitutions uniformly prohibited plural officeholding and commonly provided that men holding appointive offices of profit could not sit in the legislature. Justices of the peace generally were excepted on the ground that theirs was not an office of profit, and the number in the conventions and assemblies suggests that these important men retained their influence. Militia officers also could serve, perhaps for the same reason. Most of the constitutions allowed the judges to continue for good behavior, and set up machinery for removal by impeachment. Half further guaranteed their independence by specifying fixed and adequate salaries. The originial source of their power, however, varied. No state allowed the people to select judges except Vermont, where all but the supreme courts were popularly elected. The other states divided between those which granted the power of appointment to the executive and those which provided for a joint ballot of both houses of the legislature. Several constitutions established probate courts in the counties, but the methods of selection and terms of office showed no uniformity. The effect, however, was to decentralize some courts which had previously conducted business only in the capitals.

Justices of the peace occupied a peculiarly sensitive position because they could still serve in the legislature and because they performed many important functions in the local governments and courts. Although some constitutions defined them as not holding offices of profit, they did make money through fees and enjoyed great prestige. Before 1776 they usually held their posts from the Crown, at pleasure. Afterwards only Maryland granted the governor and council power to appoint justices for life. All the others limited their independence in some way. If the governor and council chose them, then they served for only a few years. Most often the legislature made the choice, while Vermont and Pennsylvania allowed the people to decide. As a further restraint, every state guaranteed trial by jury. In general, therefore, the new states freed their judges and justices from executive interference and either allowed them substantial independence or granted to the voters and their representatives ultimate control.

These institutional alterations did not cause any major change in the characteristics of the judges and justices themselves. Those who remained loyal lost their positions, of course, and such vacancies did sometimes open the door to men of lesser rank, especially if the voters or the legislature chose replacements. Those who became rebels usually retained their positions. Probably the only truly qualified men in any given community belonged to the local elite, who if they chose the right side maintained their reputations, aided by their influence in the legislatures.

Sheriffs, coroners, and other local officials more often were popularly elected for short terms. Only in Massachusetts did the governor and Council select them. In New York the Council of Appointment chose these officers annually. Maryland allowed the voters to nominate two sheriffs who must own £1,000 worth of property, the governor and Council selecting one and also choosing coroners. In Virginia, as we have seen, county courts—meaning the justices themselves—nominated men for both offices and the governor and Council approved. But in eight states the voters elected their local officials, usually every year. The same trend toward popular control occurred in the case of militia officers. Before 1776 the governor appointed most of them. This method continued in Maryland and New York (the Council of Appointment), but elsewhere either the legislature selected the officers or the companies themselves chose their own leaders. The most common system combined popular votes for ranks up through captain, with legislative election for field and general officers. This democratization of the citizens' army did not encourage efficiency, but there is no reason to believe that the soldiers risked their lives less bravely under officers of their own choice than among those imposed upon them—none of the militia facing death with any enthusiasm.

The constitutions also expressed other implications of the Revolution, ideals which the Americans now stated even when they did not always fully realize their implications. In eight states declarations (never "bills") of rights formally listed the ethos of society; another state soon added such a list, while others incorporated some of the same statements into their constitutions. These agreed in guaranteeing men's freedom to worship as they pleased, without compulsion, and most relieved the people of enforced taxation for religious purposes, though some continued to authorize the support of religious establishments. They generally opposed excessive fines, searches and seizures without warrants, and quartering of troops in private homes, while some promised freedom of speech and of the press, reform of the penal code, writs of habeas corpus, trial by jury, and the subordination of the military to civil authority. Yet these rights appeared only sporadically. The authors of the declarations proceeded with more high-minded idealism than attention to detail, and they included or omitted particular clauses capriciously. Thus Virginia's famous model omitted freedom of speech, whether inadvertently or deliberately. Some asserted the people's rights to assemble, to instruct their representatives, and to petition for the redress of grievances, yet the declarations of Delaware and Maryland contained no such provision and Virginia's acknowledged only the rights of individuals. Pennsylvania, North Carolina, Georgia, and the New England states promised to support inexpensive local schools, a commitment extending to universities in Massachusetts, Vermont, and North Carolina. The humanitarian impulse appeared in statements against imprisonment for debt in three of the most democratic constitutions (Vermont, Pennsylvania, and North Carolina), in provisions restricting private purchase of Indian lands (New York, Virginia, North Carolina), and in anti-slavery clauses (Vermont, Delaware). Other sections foreshadowed social and economic trends. Vermont, Pennsylvania, North Carolina, and Georgia—the four most democratic documents—opposed entails; Massachusetts, Maryland, and North Carolina condemned monopolies; Georgia limited the cost of suits in the Superior Court; while Maryland favored the abolition of poll taxes, the exemption of paupers from taxation, and assessments according to men's actual property. These provisions did not automatically create an ideal society, but they at least acknowledged the higher aspirations of the new country, which the people could never in future deny without guilt.

Considered as a whole, these constitutions transferred authority from a location somewhere between the colonial capitals and London, to a point a little west of the former, and from the next-to-top rung of the ladder to a position several steps down. Yet the framers rarely exposed their creation to a popular vote. In some instances they may have feared defeat, either from a combination of loyalists and opponents, as in Maryland and Delaware, or from a demand for still more popular government, as the referendums in New Hampshire and Massachusetts attested. The urgent need for a legal, effective government furnished whatever excuse was necessary for simply declaring the constitutions in force. Few of their framers could have assumed them final, and a majority of their handiworks contained explicit methods for amendment. These ranged from a simple act of both houses of the legislature or a convention called by the two houses in response to some demand, to a formal re-evaluation after a fixed period of years. The political effects of the Revolution did not halt merely because constitutions acknowledged them; they continued through and beyond the war years, gradually making the new governments obsolete. Constitutional reform, while it expressed a consensus, took place in the midst of conflict. Each new plan reflected only a transient political situation and embodied a momentary balance of power; another moment and each no longer reflected reality. The years after 1776 therefore saw further constitutional debates. These occurred either when people tried to democratize the political system even further, or when a countermovement attempted to reverse some of the trends toward popular sovereignty. The latter proved more successful during the postwar years.

Seven states heard almost nothing about constitutional change after 1776. The people of Connecticut and Rhode Island remained generally satisfied with their charters, while the inhabitants of New York, New Jersey, Delaware, Virginia and North Carolina also seemed content. All of these except Virginia and New York had established constitutions which reflected moderate majorities, though North Carolina leaned toward the democratic side. Those of New York and Virginia did not. Probably the success of the pro-farmer Clinton group reconciled his supporters to the status quo, as did the continued prestige and moderate policies of Virginia's planter class. South Carolina, Maryland, and Massachusetts all experienced attempts at reform by more democratic groups, while Whigs took the offensive in New Hampshire, Vermont, Pennsylvania, and Georgia.

Criticisms of the Whig constitutions concentrated on the senate, on underrepresentation of the newly settled areas, and on property qualifications for officeholders. In South Carolina the pressure for change came from the middle and up-country districts which, after the excitement of the war ended, petitioned for a constitutional convention, arguing that as matters stood "property is consulted and represented more than the number of free men." The reformers wanted a Declaration of Rights and hoped to abolish the Senate, which had been delaying action on popular economic legislation. The lower house favored the petitions but the Senate delayed, fearing for its life. A second attempt, in 1787, failed for the same reason. A vote taken in the Commons showed a clear sectional division, with the westerners picking up just enough support from those who, like a Charleston writer, agreed that the constitution was aristocratic; but the Senate continued to block change.

Not until 1790, after the adoption of the federal Constitution, did a convention finally assemble in South Carolina. It conceded only a little to the democratic impulse. Property qualifications remained, but now excluded fewer men from the Senate and governorship. On the other hand, the senators would serve for four years instead of two. South Carolinians resisted the general trend toward a stronger executive, denying him a veto, and the judges still owed their office to the legislatures. The most important change, which probably satisfied western leaders, granted the inland counties more delegates to equal, in power, the low country.

Opposition to Maryland's system of government also surfaced during the postwar years, again primarily as a reaction against the Senate's intransigence in defeating economic legislation. In this case the upper house rejected a paper-money bill, whereupon the advocates of a currency issue carried their case to the people. Essentially they argued that the Senate, no less than the lower house, must follow public opinion. The senators pointed out that if they were bound to the same master as the delegates, they no longer performed their function as a check. Instead they must act as they felt best for the public good, while acknowledging an ultimate sovereignty in the people. With the Senate adamant the critics could do little; indeed, we do not certainly know that the voters wanted major changes. Probably the pro-paper element among the powerful planter group sought fiscal reform without constitutional alterations.

Similarly, attacks on the form of government in Massachusetts developed during a crisis in 1786–1787. At that time judges and sheriffs, selected by the executive, were vigorously helping to collect debts and taxes, at considerable cost to debtors, while the Senate refused to support stay laws, valuation laws, paper money, tax reform, or other relief despite the actions of the lower house. Petitions adopted by town meetings and county conventions urged the abolition of inferior courts, transferring suits at that level to presumably more debtor-oriented justices, juries, or arbiters. Some also opposed the Senate. On the other hand, both the upper house and the courts found supporters who contended that the constitution was *too* democratic. Denied relief by legal means, the discontented exploded into Shays' Rebellion and suffered military defeat. Only a minority even among the reformers had advocated the abolition of the Senate, the dissatisfaction with the courts subsided when economic relief came in 1787–1788.

Thus the only serious democratic attempts at constitutional reform in the states during this period were directed against the senate. They occurred because of specific economic grievances during the depression years when the senates of South Carolina, Maryland, and Massachusetts opposed relief to debtors and a soft-money policy. Except on those occasions, the senates escaped attack, and never did a clear majority seek to establish a unicameral system or other important changes. Clearly the source of discontent during the postwar years lay in economic rather than in ideological factors.

The ratification of a Whig constitution in Massachusetts aided the movement for similar reform in New Hampshire. The document drawn up at Exeter early in 1776 had caused criticism from all sides, as we have seen, some seeking more

popular control, others a more careful division of powers
and increased efficiency. The failure of constitutional reform in 1778 silenced objections only temporarily. Massachusetts' decision, and the publication of the "Essex Result" motivated the eastern towns to try again, and the General Court called a convention in 1781. The failure of the
interior towns to participate permitted Portsmouth and its
neighbors to dominate the sessions and produce a document
characterized by strong checks on the democratic element.

The constitution of 1780 provided for a House of Representatives chosen not by the people but by indirect elections. The taxpayers of each town would elect one delegate
for every fifty taxables to meet in a county convention. The
delegates must own £200 worth of real property. The
county convention then chose the representatives: twenty
for Rockingham County, which included Portsmouth,
thirty proportioned among all the other counties—a fair
ratio. Voters for the Senate must be worth £100, the senators themselves £400, both figures being higher than before. The two houses had equal powers. The people also
balloted for a governor, and the legislature selected one
from among the four receiving the largest number of votes.
He must own property valued at £1,000 clear of debt, a
requirement that excluded practically everyone except the
eastern elite. The governor would have a permanent salary
and could veto laws, his veto nearly absolute because a
three-fourths vote of each house was needed to override
him. The governor and a special council appointed practically all officials, including even militia officers. The proposal compares favorably with the constitutions of South
Carolina and Maryland as a vehicle for protecting minority
rights.

The framers defended their handiwork in an address to

the people of New Hampshire, but the people in town meetings overwhelmingly rejected it, criticizing especially the system of choosing representatives, which deprived the voters of any direct influence and of the ability to instruct them how to vote. The reply that legislators should exercise their own better judgment did not convince the people. The same convention therefore tried again. It abandoned the idea of indirect elections, substituting a system whereby towns with 150 male polls could choose one representative, those with less combining, those with more selecting one more per each additional three hundred. Under this arrangement the three western counties would send well under half of the legislators unless some towns combined. Property qualifications for representatives were lowered to £100 and for senators to £200. All taxpayers could vote for them. The governor must own £500, not necessarily free of debt. Lesser militia officers would be chosen by their superiors rather than by the governor and council, though still not by the soldiers or towns. Otherwise the plan remained unchanged: the governor retained his veto, he and his Council still chose most officials, and the principle of property requirements for voting and officeholding continued.

The authors again accompanied their proposal with a defense, emphasizing the need for an independent executive. In the press, "A Republican" published a series of seven articles presenting the familiar Whig theories. He regarded the British government as falling short of perfection only because the King was too powerful. The constitution of 1776, he declared, concentrated all authority in the legislature, on which no check existed, even the judges being chosen by the representatives. He approved of the constitution's provisions throughout, remarking of the demand for popularly selected militia officers that not everyone had the necessary share of wisdom and patriotism: "we must take mankind as they are, and not as we could wish them to be." New Hampshire's species of mankind remained unimpressed. Most towns refused to ratify. Thus the Concord town meeting, in rejecting the constitution, demanded that executive powers be assigned to the legislature. Marlborough produced but one favorable vote, the majority proposing a series of changes including popular election of many officials. Obviously the convention must move further along the road to a popular government.

Accordingly, in June 1783 the convention introduced a new set of modifications. The "governor" became a "president" without a veto, and would depend for his salary upon annual grants. Perhaps equally important, the delegates ruled that a simple majority, instead of approval by two-thirds of the towns, would ratify the constitution. The concession and the change sufficed, and the new government took effect in 1784. In its amended form it closely resembled the Massachusetts model, with a Declaration of Rights, a democratically chosen lower house, a less democratic Senate, a separate but weak executive, appointments by the president and Council, and moderate property qualifications—fundamentally the Whig ideology with a bow in the direction of popular government.

At the other end of the country, a movement for constitutional reform in Georgia began in 1784. An article in a Savannah newspaper called for a two-house legislature in which county committees would choose representatives biennially. The legislature took no action, however, until after the ratification of the federal Constitution. It then recommended a senate elected every three years, consisting of men who owned £250 worth of property. A convention the following year incorporated this proposal into a new constitution. Georgia's government thus became bicameral with an upper house representing property owners. The state's governor must own five hundred acres and £1,000 besides. Chosen for two years by the legislature, he could veto laws, recommend legislation, and in general act effectively. In other respects, however, the new government remained faithful to that of 1777. Any adult white male taxpayer could vote, judges served for only three years, and a Declaration of Rights included the abolition of entails.

The most prolonged, intense, and interesting debate occurred in Pennsylvania. The "Republican Society" kept up a steady attack on the 1776 constitution. Critics opposed the required oath because it excluded Quakers and other conscientious objectors and because it demanded an allegiance to the very constitution they were working to overthrow. In recognition of this grievance, the legislature in 1778 allowed its members to add to their oath an explanation reserving their right to press for revision. Thereafter the reservation apparently was understood. From the start the Republicans, as the constitution's critics continued to call themselves, argued against the unicameral system. They stressed the dangerous potentiality of legislative supremacy. All men sought power, and the people must protect themselves against oppression by establishing checks. The Assembly, they pointed out, monopolized virtually all functions of government. Moreover, a single house made mistakes, and in just one session might reverse all the decisions of its predecessors. Evil laws would become permanent as selfish politicians consolidated their power while good ones proved temporary. A second branch would guard against both despotism and errors, and furnish stability besides. The Republicans recognized and lamented that the concentration of power in the democratic branch reflected a distrust of society's natural leaders, a feeling "among the unthinking *many*, that men of property, . . . experience and knowledge" should be avoided. The Republicans also argued that the popular election of justices and militia officers led to the selection of bad men, demagogues or "fools of faction," who would oppress the people. Similarly, judges who depended upon the legislature lacked the security essential to unbiased conduct. All officials should be independent. Increasingly too, as the war continued, Republicans saw the need for a strong executive.

The "Constitutional Society," forming an equally cohesive and determined party, denied any imperfections in their government. The people must retain power in their own hands and those of their immediate representatives. The Assembly's power, far from being absolute, was limited by the surest of checks: public opinion. Major laws were published for consideration before enactment; the people could read the Assembly's journals, study its votes, and retire any member annually. Officials ought not to be independent but responsible to the people. Constitutionalists suspected the Republicans of an aristocratic bias.

The meetings of the Council of Censors in 1783–1784 offered the Republicans a chance for major change, for the constitution authorized that body not only to investigate the conduct of the government but to recommend amendments. The Republican majority presented their usual criticisms, adding that rotation in office deprived men of incentive and the state of able servants. They wanted an upper house chosen for three years, a governor with a veto, and judges with fixed salaries serving for good behavior. The minority summarized this report from a very different point of view. "The grand objection to our present Constitution," they asserted, "is, that it retains too much power in the hands of the people, who do not know how to use it, so well as gentlemen of fortune, . . . and that it gives no advantage to the rich over the poor." They denied any flaws in their handiwork, and since positive action depended upon a two-thirds vote of the Censors, they succeeded in blocking change.

At the end of the decade the Republicans, with a majority in the legislature and the example of the federal Constitution, obtained a convention. Some members pressed for an aristocratic senate chosen by an electoral college and apportionment by wealth as well as by numbers. But other leaders bowed to the need for placating the Constitutionalists and probably the majority of voters. In the end they accepted popular elections but fixed the Senate's term at four years. At the same time they transformed the Supreme Executive Council into an efficient governor with a veto, and established an independent judiciary chosen by the governor. Pennsylvania's constitution thus became acceptable to the Whig theorists, yet defensible from a democratic point of view.

The only other state to adopt a new constitution during these years was Vermont, in 1786. It introduced no important change, retaining a unicameral legislature, almost universal suffrage, representation by towns, and popular checks on the House. Responding to a local political situation in which one group held too many offices, the right to elect judges of the inferior courts, justices of the peace, and sheriffs was transferred from the people to the representatives and councilors, but the militia officers, including colonels, remained under popular control. Other states also kept their existing forms except for occasional amendments through laws. In Rhode Island the agricultural villages tried vainly to reduce the number of representatives sent by the trading towns, but failed by a single vote. The impulse came not from theoretical commitment to equality, for of course the greater population of the commercial centers entitled them to more seats, but because the farmers wanted paper money. The legislature did exclude judges from sitting in the General Assembly. The same reform succeeded in Connecticut. In that state the upper house became temporarily unpopular because it approved of measures supporting Congress and the grant of half-pay for life to Continental army officers. An attack on plural officeholding in reality involved an attempt to change the composition of the Assistants. The attempt came to naught, as did a suggestion that votes should be published, salaries lowered, property qualifications abolished, and sheriffs selected by freemen.

Clearly the movement toward local control, toward pure democracy, had ceased soon after the constitutions of 1776. Advocates of complete popular sovereignty made almost no headway even against the relatively undemocratic governments of South Carolina and Maryland, nor did they succeed in maintaining their initial advantages elsewhere. Instead Whig ideas gained ground: the most democratic constitutions (those of Pennsylvania, Georgia, and New Hampshire) gave way to less democratic ones; Whig spokesmen scored a major victory in Massachusetts and repulsed criticism elsewhere. Essentially, the first year or two of constitution-making featured an important movement toward democracy and toward a weaker central government. After 1776 the pendulum swung back along both arcs, but it did not return to its colonial position. By the end of the era most constitutions reflected a compromise. Much of the old remained, modified by those Whig ideas that met general acceptance, notably the principle of checks and balances, and profoundly affected by the idea of popular sovereignty. The Revolution, independence, liberated the democratic impulse from its colonial shackles; but full realization lay far in the future.

# Chapter Seven

# *Economic Changes During the War*

THE British invasion of Massachusetts found the thirteen colonies fully capable of defending themselves. The people owned, in local money, £250 million in taxable property, yielding more than £10 million income annually. The quantity of money in circulation fell short of even normal requirements, but men had become accustomed to large credit transactions and to deficit financing in wartime. The economy furnished ample provisions, clothing, and other supplies for a large army, and what the people did not produce themselves they could purchase by the overseas sale of tobacco, rice, lumber, and other exports. The recognition of this strength gave men courage to challenge Britain: they thought that if worst came to worst they would win.

Pessimists, or the naturally cautious, pointed to some flaws. England's even greater strength would overwhelm resistance; her navy would block exports; the colonists

lived scattered over such distances that they could not concentrate their resources but would collapse piecemeal; above
all, far from presenting a united front, they disagreed radically among themselves. These Cassandras warned that
many colonials would not support a war, and that no rebellion could succeed without unity.

The argument had much merit. But for many months
after April 1775 practically everyone thought in terms of
a temporary emergency only, expecting that a spirited resistance would persuade the ministry to reverse its policy,
as it had backed off twice before. The hope that peace lay
just ahead, after one more campaign, yet one more sacrifice,
sustained the Americans year after year. In 1775 it em-
boldened them to oppose General Gage at Boston.

The news of the outbreak of war on April 18, 1775,
called into being a new set of provincial congresses. New
Englanders naturally reacted first, most decisively, and with
the least internal opposition. All four colonies borrowed
money during May in order to pay, feed, clothe, and arm
their militia. Massachusetts led the way by authorizing the
treasurer to issue 6 per cent notes for £100,000, payable in
two years, and urgently requested patriots to loan their
extra cash. This sum would support 13,600 troops. Rhode
Island also borrowed £30,000 at 2.5 per cent, while New
Hampshire issued £10,000 in tax anticipation warrants, accompanied by a tax of £3,000, and followed this with
similar notes and taxes. Connecticut also borrowed, expecting to repay the lenders out of the next tax collections.

The other colonies could not act so quickly, but during
June and July New Jersey, Maryland, Virginia, North
Carolina, and Georgia similarly issued treasurer's notes
secured (as they hoped) by future taxes. The war intensified that summer—the British took Bunker Hill on June 17

—so expenditures increased; Virginia prepared to spend £350,000. By August nine colonies had printed £750,000 in paper notes. South Carolina, far from the scene of conflict, would act soon. New York, Pennsylvania, and Delaware also delayed any contribution, but not because of distance: loyalists controlled all three, and the advocates of resistance there were depending upon help from the Continental Congress.

Congress had convened in May, and quickly undertook the direction of military operations, transforming the militia around Boston into a Continental Army and planning a military operation of its own into Canada. If Congress were to command an army for the common cause, it seemed reasonable that Congress finance its campaigns, apportioning the cost among the colonies. Indeed, only in this way could loyalist-dominated areas be forced to contribute. In New York, for example, the various committees could raise neither men nor supplies until money arrived from some outside source, yet the Canadian campaign depended heavily on New York. By providing its own money, Congress could call forth the energies of all the colonies, creating and supplying an army, concentrating the combined strength at key targets. But Congress lacked the authority to levy taxes or to collect them even if it dared to seize the power. Moreover, money from taxes would dribble into the treasury; Congress needed a flood. The only way to raise a lot of money in a hurry was to print tax anticipation notes and hope for the best. Accordingly Congress issued, by the end of the year, $6 million in paper bills, twice the combined contributions of the colonies. This sum the states would presumably repay, each in proportion to its population, over a four-year period beginning in 1779. The money consisted, then, of tax anticipation warrants, bearing no interest, and depending ultimately for their value upon whether the states collected taxes.

Congress's activities did not replace but only supplemented the efforts by the states. They continued to spend heavily, the outlay exceeding £1 million in moneys loaned by citizens, and more than £3 million in treasurers' notes by the end of 1776. Within another twelve months the total probably reached £7 million, in addition to which the states had levied a million in taxes. Thus every adult white man had already paid or promised to pay close to £20 into the state treasuries (and twice that sum to Congress). For this major effort on the part of the new governments there were several reasons. Although the Continental Army soon developed its own quartermaster and commissary departments, the states supplied much of the food, clothing, and transportation out of their own coffers, advancing money to Congress with the understanding that a general settlement of accounts would take place eventually. Second, the states engaged in various economic enterprises, financing, manufacturing, and trade. Most important, each state maintained its own army—the militia.

Officers of the Continental Army at the time, and many historians since, have scoffed at the state militias. They undoubtedly had their faults. The Continental troops consisted of voluteers, almost always young men from the poorer families who, if not in the army, would be working hard for low pay on the farm or in a shop. Probably a large proportion were younger sons without prospect of a good inheritance. As we have seen, the country produced many such boys. A few months' discipline turned them into regular soldiers, upon whom the officers could rely, and who would remain in service for several years. On the other hand, the militia naturally consisted of men who had not volunteered. Each community organized all of its able-bodied men (with very few exceptions, such as ministers) into companies. Most of the time they remained farmers and artisans, supporting their families and producing the provisions and clothing and other articles that the army and the country needed. Active service involved a considerable sacrifice because campaigns seldom occurred during the winter, when most men had free time, but during the busiest seasons. The militia lacked military training, discipline, and enthusiasm for the army. Their willingness to risk their lives—to act like Continental soldiers—varied directly with their perception of the need. Dispatched to some distant field, where their homes and friends were not at stake, ordered into some battle whose necessity seemed questionable, they departed on the least excuse. But on home ground, fighting with their friends for clearly understood, deeply felt objectives, they fought hard and effectively. Indeed, if one can argue that Continental soldiers won the war, one can just as easily argue that the militia did so. Gage and Burgoyne both lost to armies consisting primarily of militiamen.

Thus each state contributed men, money, and war materials to the Continental Army and supported its own military campaigns as well. Washington could never cope with all of the British incursions, but tried to meet those of the most general or serious concern. Each state, of course, pleaded for help whenever the British launched an attack, but always relied on the militia at first and sometimes exclusively. Each therefore waged an intermittent, often very expensive war. Massachusetts, for example, lost nearly £2 million in a disastrous attempt on a British port in Maine, an expedition which Congress refused to underwrite because it lacked general significance, while Rhode Island met unassisted the invasion of Newport in 1776.

Despite their individual efforts, the states failed to develop executive departments with men skilled in the business of supplying armies and navies. Instead the legislatures proceeded on an ad hoc basis, lurching from emergency to emergency, always hopeful that the next temporary arrangement would lead to victory. Especially during the first few years states did not plan strategic campaigns but merely reacted to emergencies with desperate, inefficient haste. Local militia officers would call out their companies, frequently purchasing essential equipment on their own credit until the government sent the means to pay, or issuing certificates exchangeable for money. Professional traders often took over the task. Urgently requesting funds, they rounded up cattle and bought other provisions from the farmers, purchased blankets, shoes, and others articles of clothing, hired wagons and horses or oxen, paid for all this as best they could, and added a commission. They then submitted a bill to the legislature hoping, of course, to obtain specie. The states presently learned to concentrate such functions in a few individuals, supplying them with paper money and relying on them to pay middlemen for supplies and services.

Rhode Island's experience illustrates the economic and military activities of the state governments during the first years of the war. Soon after Lexington and Concord, the General Court appointed a Committee of Safety to raise troops and provide them with £20,000 in legal-tender notes, redeemable after two years. Another £10,000 followed in June, at which time the deputies instructed the committee to equip two vessels for the protection of trade, and to collect saltpeter and brimstone for gunpowder from the towns. The committee also began to buy food and clothing for the troops. To assist that process the legislature forbade the exportation of provisions except for the use of the army. During 1776 the government emitted another £90,000 in legal-tender notes redeemable in five or six years. By mid-summer 1776 the first signs of depreciation appeared. The legislature tried to borrow money instead of issuing notes, but continued to spend in advance of revenue. Meanwhile, it passed a severe law requiring everyone to accept the money and to receive Continental money at par as well. During this period various individuals, especially members of the Committee of Safety and a commissary, had been spending as they felt the need, without any specific authorization, and billing the state afterwards. Then, in December, the realities of war came to Rhode Island with a shock: the British, who had already conquered southern New York, seized the island called Rhode Island, occupying one-third of the state, including Newport. The state could expect no help from Washington, who had his hands full, nor from New York, where the enemy had just taken Forts Washington and Lee. Moreover, growing inflation demonstrated the danger of continued deficit financing.

A convention of committees sent by the four New England states considered all this at Providence. They concluded that the legislatures should avoid further emissions of paper but instead should levy taxes and borrow money, offering up to 5 per cent interest. In case of emergency a state might again resort to paper notes, but these should bear interest. The states were to start calling in and destroying their bills so as to restrict their quantity and reassure everyone concerning their value. The delegates also suggested limits on prices, wages, and profits. They allowed for a moderate increase over prewar levels, recognizing the wartime demand for goods and services, but eliminating rises due solely to currency inflation. Importers could charge a maximum of two and a half times the wholesale cost of goods in Europe, and retailers could add 20 per cent. Rhode Island promptly enacted these recommendations and met her own military crisis by raising troops and borrowing money. Early the next year the state tallied its resources, discovering that its citizens owned more than £2 million in taxable property according to the current method of assessment, and therefore levied a modest tax of £16,000. In the first two years of war, the legislature borrowed £250,000 and received a like sum from Congress.

Up to this point, the war-induced demands had brought general prosperity to the thirteen newly independent states. The money issued during 1775 and 1776 furnished little more than what a healthy economy needed and had previously lacked. It quickened economic activity, which in turn stimulated the need for more money, helping to absorb the surplus. The total of perhaps £10 million equaled no more than a 5 per cent tax on the people's estates, or a year's income, certainly a reasonable debt. The depreciation which began late in 1776 probably reflected less excessive currency issues than a loss of confidence resulting from the occupation of New York City and the series of defeats administered to the Continental Army during the fall.

Except where the armies or Indians caused destruction, almost everyone prospered during these early months of war and independence. The embargo which began during 1774 naturally depressed the general level of agricultural prices. But the outbreak of war made exports imperative in order to obtain military supplies and earn profits. Prices then rose, stimulated by good markets in Europe and the West Indies and by the army's needs, until by the end of

1776 the farmers were receiving 150 per cent of their prices of five years earlier. Most of this was clear gain, since their costs did not rise as fast: they paid little more for labor and bought few manufactured goods. Many benefited also from a general moratorium on debts, and if they chose to pay, their higher money incomes made it easier. Tax collections in some states totally ceased for a time and in the rest remained at the low prewar levels. Tobacco and indigo planters, to be sure, could not at first ship their crops to Britain, and the latter lost their royal subsidy. But by mid-1776 the tobacco export trade reopened, now primarily to France, with excellent prices. At the same time the planters stopped the heavy importations which had threatened ruin to so many, and halted payments on their debts. They devoted increasing attention to raising livestock and food products. Even the British army, though it caused much damage, contributed to prosperity by large purchases. Indeed, the war demand took such enormous quantities of foodstuffs that local shortages were common.

Prosperity in the towns equaled that of the country. Before 1774 domestic manufacturing had not prospered. The British competed favorably both as to price and quality, and artisans also faced a shortage of capital and of skilled workers, primitive and expensive transportation, and lack of demand from a people who made things for themselves and had little purchasing power. Even after 1776 artisans continued to be handicapped by shortages of skilled workers and poor transportation, but beginning with the nonimportation agreements of 1774 they entered upon almost a decade of prosperity. British competition nearly ceased, and to buy American became patriotic. Even people of means began to dress in homespun, thereby rendering obsolescent the familiar upper-class costume that appears in the pictures of Revolutionary heroes. Some of the newly created wealth ended up in the hands of artisans, and state governments began to subsidize certain enterprises. Higher incomes enabled people to purchase a variety of nonessentials, and indeed the newspapers soon published criticisms of the demand for luxuries and lamented the penchant of conspicuous display. The army required shoes, other articles of clothing, carts, guns and gunpowder, barrels, blankets, rum, boats, and a great many other articles; it also hired various artificers such as blacksmiths, coopers, and carpenters. Milling, tanning, distilling, iron manufacturing, lumbering, and the making of gunpowder and salt flourished. Both the needs of the military and a profitable commerce stimulated shipbuilding.

Foreign trade was in the doldrums when the war began. The embargo ruined commerce, nonconsumption agreements prevented shopkeepers from selling British goods already on hand, and moratoria on debts closed still another source of revenue for merchants. In the spring of 1776, however, Congress opened trade with all nations except Britain and authorized privateers to seize English ships. Even more important, Congress and the states began to employ merchants to purchase supplies, putting into their hands large quantities of capital, some of which stuck to their fingers. One New Yorker, for example, spent £132,759 for the government during a six-month period before Independence, and General Philip Schuyler had sold the government nearly £5,000 worth of goods and services by the close of 1776. Men with foreign connections imported supplies for the army and goods for themselves, selling at inflated profits. Typical wartime shortages, especially of foreign products, forced up the price level, and merchants took full advantage of it. At the same time they resumed the export trade, especially selling tobacco from the Chesapeake, where Congress competed with private concerns in buying up and exporting that valuable commodity. As British and Scottish traders withdrew, and as loyalists abandoned their shops, native merchants moved in to lay the bases of a new trading class. The renewed commercial activity, together with the construction of continental and state navies, stimulated shipbuilding and brought full employment to sailors, innkeepers, retailers, artisans, and laborers and townspeople generally. Even small trading centers flourished during these first years of war.

Creditors suffered little during the early months unless they chose the wrong side. To be sure, suits for debt ceased temporarily: as long as the embargo prohibited exports, debtors could hardly be expected to pay, and then some time elapsed before the new governments re-established courts. But as the judicial system resumed normal operations these difficulties vanished. The legal tender quality of the new money did not at first injure creditors, because the bills remained near par, and the increase in circulation and supply made it easier for people to pay. Moreover, monied men, a category that included most creditors, enjoyed exceptional opportunities. Specie, of course, remained much in demand, and opportunities for investors with fluid capital multiplied. Perceptive business could easily anticipate shortages in provisions, salt, and imported luxuries; and investments in such articles or in privateering paid excellent dividends. Rather too excellent, in fact: by the end of 1776 the gentle, fertile rain of paper money threatened to become a downpour, and as inflation began to wash away profits, the people looked about them for the culprits.

For a good many Americans the winter of 1776–1777

marked an economic turning point, inaugurating a period of steady inflation and diminishing profits, culminating finally in a total change of policy during 1780 and 1781. Men made fortunes during these four years, but the collective economic account book now seemed to contain more debits than credits. This period of economic instability coincided with an increasingly gloomy military prospect and with political shifts of power.

Prices had been rising ever since the war began, but not until the fall of 1776 did people begin to worry about them. At this point New Englanders became sufficiently alarmed, as we have seen, to call a convention on the subject. During the succeeding years inflation spread, following in a general way the geographical course of the war, first into the mid-Atlantic states, then in the South. The British navy, operating always from New York and Halifax, from Savannah in 1779 and Charleston the next year, and occasionally from other bases in New England (especially Newport) and the Chesapeake Bay, disrupted commerce and caused local scarcities. Requirements of the Continental, state, and French forces sometimes exceeded the supply, and competition among purchasing agents forced up prices. Speculators took full advantage of their opportunities and created local monopolies, especially in such essentials as salt and wheat. Coveted imports from Europe and the West Indies became increasingly scarce, and the arrival of prize ships or merchant vessels, instead of reducing prices, allowed happy owners to multiply profits. Farmers contributed to inflation, selling to the highest bidder. A poorly developed interior system of transportation could not move surplus commodities to places where they were needed, and therefore caused local scarcities, while the British navy increased the cost of ocean voyages.

The major reason for higher prices, however, was currency inflation. Until late 1776, as we have seen, the additional money issued by Congress and the states did not exceed the quantity needed by an expanding economy. The country now began to perceive the necessity for prolonged heavy expenditures. Far from backing off as they had in 1766 and 1770, the British were exerting their full power to crush the rebels. They withdrew from Boston only to seize New York. A powerful navy blockaded the coast, and their army, strengthened by German mercenaries, loyalists, and Indian allies, prepared a wide offensive.

Tax anticipation warrants—paper money—depended for their value upon the credit of the governments, and the credit of Congress and the thirteen states depended first upon the progress of the war and second upon their ability to pay their debts promptly. When victory receded, repayment seemed less sure. Even after Washington's victory at Trenton, neutral observers were betting against the Americans. No foreign nation ventured to recognize their independence, though the French extended secret aid. Large numbers of Americans swore oaths of allegiance to the King as the British army marched by, and loyalists may actually have outnumbered rebels in the Middle states. A decline of confidence in victory inevitably meant loss of confidence in paper promises to pay. In addition, the government seldom provided adequately for repayment. Congress lacked power to do so, and though the states generally accompanied their emissions with a commitment to retire the money by taxes, few actually levied any such assessments, and these few called only for minor sums.

People reailzed clearly the consequences of this situation. Continuing price increases raised the cost of financing the war and impelled the governments to issue more paper notes, which they would be increasingly unable to support by taxes. The notes proceeded to decline in value, prices rose still further, requiring even more money with even less chance of redemption. Unless the spiral ended, no government would be able to pay troops or buy supplies. This prospective bankruptcy heartened the British and their supporters who contributed by counterfeiting Continental and state currency.

To forestall this impending disaster the states tried several expedients. All required a legislative majority of enthusiastic rebels and a popular majority willing to accept some sacrifices, both of which were often missing. These measures included anti-monopoly laws, restrictions on prices and wages, prohibitions on the export of necessities, laws requiring that everyone accept the paper bills as equal to gold and silver, the raising of money by loans, and the imposition of taxes. Taxes were especially important. Only they could furnish the sinews of war. With them the states need not issue so much paper money, and what they did issue would maintain its value because people could expect redemption. As the quantity and value of money stabilized, prices would cease to rise and the cost of war would level out. Theoretically these measures ought to have worked, but in practice each met opposition and no state could implement the entire set.

Americans shared a traditional dislike for monopolies which they had expressed at the time of the Tea Act and in declarations of rights. Everyone condemned the practices of forestalling—buying up local supplies of a desired commodity before it was brought to market—and engrossing—purchasing enough to control the price. But enforcement proved almost impossible, and in fact such obvious monopolistic activities seldom established prices. A few traders tried to corner the market in salt, and some shopowners held back other commodities longer than morality justified. These were caught and punished, yet prices did not drop because the overall demand remained high. Insofar as traders were responsible, the fault lay not in these conspicuous instances but in the almost universal fixing of prices just a little in advance of the current rate, as a hedge against inflation or to compensate for the hazards of business; and in the reluctance to accept paper money at par, which led traders to demand a higher price if one offered paper than if one bought with specie. To control such practices the people began to agitate for price-fixing laws.

Early in 1777 Congress recommended to the states the passage of restrictions on prices, profits, and wages, following the proposal of the Providence convention. Prewar prices and wages as they had stood before the nonimportation agreements, when presumably tradition plus the operations of a free market set fair exchange rates for all goods and services, would serve as standard. People recognized the customary relations so clearly that, in adjusting wages, one had only to specify a single example, usually the basic daily wage for rural laborer, and everyone could recognize the proportionate figure for all other workers. Commodities had varied more noticeably, but a given price for corn pretty well determined that for other grains. The legislatures (or sometimes executives or local committees) characteristically stated a few specific new prices and wages, allowing for a moderate increase, and for the rest permitted a general advance, for example 25 per cent. As to the price of imported goods, which Americans could not control at the source, new laws allowed the wholesalers to add costs of transportation and a stated markup for profit, while retailers could raise the price again. Supposedly the merchant would then make a fair income while cheating no one. Imported goods urgently needed for the armies, however, might be exempted, in order to stimulate the importers to a maximum effort.

This solution to the nation's problems, like anti-monopoly acts, possessed certain fatal flaws. Farmers disliked restrictions on the price of such crucial products as corn, wheat, beef, and pork because the profits from trading with the townspeople, the army, or British purchasers were too attractive to resist. Even if rural legislators gave in for the sake of patriotism, or to obtain restrictions on nonfarm prices, enforcement proved impossible. The country was too big, the governments too weak, and too many farmers violated the laws with impunity. Worst of all, the states did not cooperate. When during the winter of 1776–1777 the New England states adopted such regulations, New York, New Jersey, and Pennsylvania did not, nor had any of the Southern states. Similarly, traders and artisans, while complaining of high food costs, resisted limitations on the price of imported goods and domestic manufactures. Merchants argued that trade had become so hazardous that only a maximum profit on successful voyages would preserve men from bankruptcy and enable them to continue. Trade, like agriculture, must be encouraged, not restricted, for the mutual benefit and eventual victory. As early as the fall of 1776 antagonisms developed between town and country in the Boston and Portsmouth areas. A writer from the rural village of Needham, Massachusetts, accused Boston traders of adopting as their principle "Get what you can; no matter how, or who is oppressed and distressed thereby." They were destroying the poor, he claimed, and their exorbitant prices led farmers, manufacturers, and laborers to demand similar increases. On the other hand, a Portsmouth spokesman blamed the farmers who hoarded produce in their barns, doubling prices, while merchants lost their stock and could barely support their families. Price restrictions on commerce, he insisted, deprived traders of their property and punished men who were supporting the common cause by their economic enterprise and by paying taxes.

With opposition to price-fixing from every interested group, only simultaneous, firm action by all the states could succeed, and Congress recommended such action in January 1777. The failure of the Middle and Southern states to pass regulatory laws caused the New England states to repeal their acts, and prices resumed their climb. Later efforts also came to nothing.

A similar fate befell prohibitions on the export of scarce commodities. Both commercial farmers and merchants preferred to sell in the best market, foreign or domestic, and the country as a whole badly needed foreign exchange. Therefore the legislatures imposed such embargoes only in real emergencies, when serious shortages of provisions or other essentials caused suffering or deprived the army of necessary supplies. The law commonly authorized the executive to forbid exports for a few months or until the legislature met again. Neighboring states seldom cooperated; quite the contrary, they sometimes protested when they faced a shortage and a neighbor imposed an embargo. Thus this practice could not prevent inflation but only slowed price increases locally and temporarily.

Clauses requiring the universal acceptance of the paper notes on a par with specie accompanied the issuing of paper currency from the start. These at first lacked teeth, and many people refused to take paper money except at a discount, or—what amounted to the same thing—they raised the cost of goods or services when paper was offered.

Farmers, shopkeepers, artisans, professionals, men supplying or transporting the army, and, for that matter, legislators themselves preferred gold or silver which increased in value as that of paper declined. Creditors tried to avoid payment except in specie. And loyalists attempted to ruin the credit of the paper by refusing to accept it. Advocates of legal-tender laws therefore appealed to patriotism and gradually obtained stronger legislation. During 1776 and the first months of 1777 the states established heavy penalties for anyone failing to accept the mills when tendered in payment of goods, services, or debts. Governments also backed the money allowing citizens to pay taxes with the bills. Creditors in effect no longer dared sue for their debts lest they be discharged in paper.

What wrecked this solution to the financial crisis was the same defiance that defeated price restrictions: too many people disobeyed the law and the governments could not enforce it. Extensive loyalism, widespread neutralism when the American cause seemed doubtful, and the determination of a majority to profit, led people to discount state and Continental money. Those patriots who willingly accepted the bills at par, and they did exist, lost by their honesty. Their outraged protests became increasingly urgent during the next few years.

Tender laws stuck at the symptom, not the disease. The basic cause for continuing inflation lay in the increasing money supply itself. In December 1776, therefore, Congress urgently requested the states to stop issuing paper money. Instead they should rely on loans and taxes for current expenses, and maintain the value of the Continental dollar not only by enforcing legal tender laws but by providing for the prompt redemption of the tax anticipation notes as they fell due. For its part Congress opened loan offices, calling upon moneyed men to support the war and promising 6 per cent interest on the loan-office certificates. At the same time it tried, with temporary success, to reduce the issue of new paper notes.

The success of this policy depended upon the public's willingness to loan money to the government and to pay taxes. But for reasons already obvious a large segment of the population was not willing. A lender had little more prospect of recovering his interest and principal than did the owner of government notes, nor did 6 per cent seem especially attractive as an investment compared with, say, privateering. Many of the states really tried to follow Congress's proposal. The four New England states had already borrowed some £400,000 (we do not know the amount in Connecticut). They now contracted loans for another half a million pounds and stopped issuing paper money during the entire year. New Jersey had arranged for a substantial loan, and Pennsylvania opened a loan office. Virginia and both Carolinas also pleaded with their citizens to support the war; thus, when in December 1776 South Carolina authorized the issuing of £308,000 in legal tender bills, the state treasurer was instructed to try to obtain the money on loan instead, and in the summer of 1777 the state borrowed £1 million (local money, worth one-seventh of sterling). At the same time almost all of the states began to levy taxes, only New York, Delaware, and Georgia failing. The total sum assessed did not much exceed £1 million, far short of the need. The states generally spent far more money than they received from loans and taxes, and were forced either to issue paper currency or various forms of IOU's such as quartermaster certificates. The menace of Burgoyne's invasion and Howe's attack on Philadelphia required more funds than either the states or Congress could raise without resort to further paper.

Theoretically people ought to have been able to pay taxes in proportion to the general rise in prices, since the money in circulation was also increasing. But incomes rose very unevenly, some profiting considerably from wartime prosperity and others not at all, and the quantity of money varied from state to state. The tax structure might have been adjusted to accommodate this change, and to some extent that did happen. The real difficulty, and what caused the whole program of pay-as-you-go to collapse, was widespread reluctance to pay any taxes at all.

To some extent the dislike of taxes was habitual. Before 1776 the colonies imposed few. Ordinarily governments had required only a few thousand pounds per year, which in Pennsylvania, for example, the successful operation of a land bank completely underwrote. The French and Indian War had necessitated large expenditures, but the British reimbursed the colonials for much of it and within a few years tax levels returned to normal lows. Several colonies dispensed with taxes entirely except for customary levies on imposts or excises, and the rate elsewhere did not exceed 1 or 2 per cent of the assessed valuation, which of course was far below the real worth of people's property. Annual taxes, in fact, amounted to only a few pennies per person. Upon such a tradition, governments must step lightly if they wished to hold the people's loyalty.

Loyalty to the rebel governments, all too often, was tenuous or absent. Leaving details for the next chapter, we may simply assert that in the winter of 1776–1777 willing supporters of government formed a clear and reliable majority only in New England and Virginia. Elsewhere the rebels faced not only the open loyalists but the even more numerous fence-sitters, who were just as reluctant to pay taxes. The two groups combined often outnumbered the rebels. Therefore any government levying a tax faced the possibility of alienating a sufficient number of lukewarm patriots to foredoom the cause. The new legislators must fully establish their legitimacy and benevolence before they dared use force to compel loyalty and require contributions. The willingness of the fence-sitters to support the war varied with the local situation and the prospect of victory or defeat.

Prospects of victory during much of 1777 looked dim. Congress's plea that the states control prices and rely upon loans and taxes rather than paper notes reached the legislatures after Washington's victory at Trenton had considerably restored people's spirits. But neither New York nor New Jersey, both partly occupied, could contribute money for more than a year; on the contrary, they absorbed whatever the rest of the country could supply. The New England and Southern states began to respond well, but Burgoyne's gradual push southward toward Albany and Howe's capture of Philadelphia shook people's confidence. Taxes and loans produced money very slowly, and Congress was obliged to issue more paper. The value of Continental currency compared with specie, two to one at the beginning of the year, declined by 50 per cent, while prices doubled. This inflation temporarily halted with Burgoyne's surrender in October, the receipt of French aid culminating in a treaty (May 1778), and Howe's failure to accomplish anything while in Philadelphia. But these favorable omens brought no end to the war. On the contrary, American successes ended, and for three years—1778, 1779, and 1780

—the Continental armies suffered an almost unbroken series of defeats.

As a consequence, Congress's plan gradually collapsed. The states entered the war almost debt-free and prosperous enough to finance costly campaigns for more than three years without serious inflation—an excellent record. But during 1779 they began to face bankruptcy. Loans no longer brought in money, and the states north of Virginia ceased to issue tax anticipated notes. Instead they made a desperate effort to collect taxes, partly to draw paper currency out of circulation, partly to obtain cash. Thus Rhode Island, still face to face with the enemy, and accustomed to a budget of £4,000 annually, levied £96,000 in taxes during 1777, £94,000 the following year, and £433,000 by June 1779. Pennsylvania made up for a late start with taxes in 1778 and 1779 totaling nearly £5 million. The thirteen states combined imposed taxes of more than £25 million during those two years and more than £60 million in 1780. Meanwhile, Congress, which still could not obtain the necessary amounts from the states or by borrowing, reluctantly resumed issuing paper, first in diblets, then in a flood: only £8 million in 1777, but more than £20 million during 1778 and—the final blow— twice as much in 1779. By that time the paper currency had declined in value to the point that the purchasing power of the huge 1779 emissions fell below that of the comparatively modest 1777 issues. Inflation, increasing sharply during the winter of 1778–1779, raced far beyond the ability of the states to collect taxes or to borrow. The states' efforts deserve applause and probably would have succeeded but for two circumstances. First, they received almost nothing but paper money which they then destroyed. That reduced the debt but did not finance the war. Second, the intensification of the conflict in the South forced Virginia and the Carolinas to increase the money supply by £85 million, delivering a final blow to fiat currency.

Yet the war continued and the states must obtain supplies for the army. Both Congress and the states therefore resorted to quartermaster or commissary certificates. The military officials, or the civilian agents acting for the armed forces, paid out these notes whenever they lacked any other money. Thus an officer needing beef would pay the nearby farmers IOU's for their cattle. Increasingly, farmers became reluctant to sell because they might obtain a better price elsewhere and because the certificates, like all paper, declined in value. Moreover, the notes bore no interest. As early as December 1777 Congress asked the states to permit impressments. The states responded very reluctantly, for farmers were influential in most legislatures and no one liked the idea of impressment. Yet one after another they permitted the practice simply because they had no choice. Laws or executive orders then authorized purchasing agents to offer a fair price to a farmer who owned a surplus of the needed commodity above what his family required and to seize it if the farmer refused to sell. If the owner challenged the price, local disinterested arbiters were to decide. In practice, sympathetic agents paid higher prices than they ought in order to compensate the farmer for the loss he would suffer by the certificates' depreciation. The agents themselves preferred to receive their commission in loan-office certificates, which bore interest and retained their value fairly well. These certificates supposedly were reserved for men who actually paid money to the treasury, but increasingly governments handed them out to favored individuals. The states kept track of the notes issued by the loan offices, but not of the other certificates, which in an ever-increasing flood swelled the powerful inflationary tendencies. By the end of 1779 a dollar in silver would buy forty in Continental paper. Almost helpless, Congress was calling upon the states to save the nation.

During these long discouraging years the economic results of the war became bad instead of good. Inflation reversed the stimulating effect of the early expansion of currency because the quarter of a billion dollars which Congress issued shrank to only $6 million specie, and together with state money provided probably no more cash than before the war, which meant not enough. As usual in such cases, specie tended to disappear, and no foreign coin (except British) entered the country until after 1780. Thus the rise in prices counteracted any beneficial effect of a larger money supply. Real prices, taking those of 1771–1773 as the standard, and adjusting for currency inflation, rose seven or eight times by 1778. The profits of the first two years now vanished, and losses now equaled, if they did not exceed, the gains.

The principal losers were those living on fixed incomes or on wages that lagged behind prices, as they almost always did. Creditors dared not collect debts unless they arranged for payment in kind, an unusual situation, and they expected no interest. Soldiers lost most of their wages. Eventually, as the states took over the burden of war, legislatures authorized "depreciation notes" to compensate officers and enlisted men, but these benefited no one until after the war. Widows, orphans, ministers, salaried officials, skilled and unskilled laborers all found the cost of living greatly in excess of their incomes. Price restrictions injured artisans more than they did any other groups because the mechanics lacked sufficient political influence to prevent unjust decisions. The numerous farmers who produced only a small surplus gave up their crop for certificates the value of which then melted away in their hands, while the cost of necessities they must buy, such as salt, skyrocketed. They complained quite correctly that they must default on their taxes unless the government let them pay in paper money or certificates.

Commercial farmers benefited because they sold a large quantity of food as well as horses, oxen, wagons, and other products such as lumber to the townspeople, foreign markets, and the army. Provisions continued in such demand that embargoes occasionally proved necessary. Unlike the semisubsistence farmers, who simply did not sell enough to earn the money for both purchases and taxes, commercial farmers derived large incomes, enabling them to buy what they needed and pay war-levied taxes. Such advantages, however, were wiped out locally where the bayonets thrust into the economy. The British carried off thousands of slaves and created extensive damage in all the Southern states, especially after the fall of Charleston in May 1780, and raided the coastal areas. Many commercial farming areas therefore experienced losses equal to assets.

The years 1777 to 1780 brought mingled fortunes to the towns. The British occupation of New York affected adversely all the communities of the Long Island Sound and Hudson River regions. The enemy's long stay in Newport blocked Providence's access to the sea. British ships cruising in Chesapeake Bay and other Atlantic waters seized large numbers of ships. The high price of imported goods helped few besides the importers. Sporadic price regulations injured the mechanics, and townspeople suffered from the dearness of food, firewood, and clothing. Merchants and shopkeepers in traditional lines of trade found their profits melting away:

the times called for almost a radical adaptability to circumstance.

The war had its bright side for a few. Fortunate merchants, lucky privateers, and those who obtained army contracts flourished. In the summer of 1780 American privateers took nineteen or more ships of the Quebec convoy worth £20,000 each. Soon after Gates's defeat at Camden about the same time, a privateer arrived in North Carolina with two prizes rich in military stores worth, together, £150,000 sterling. The little Connecticut River towns alone sent out sixty-eight vessels to prey upon the British merchant marine, and by 1781 more than five hundred such ships were at sea. We do not know the total gain, but it certainly ran into millions of pounds—the privateers took 464 victims in 1777 alone. Economically this activity employed thousands who might otherwise have lacked jobs, including many fishermen, and more than compensated for maritime losses suffered from the British navy, bringing in quantities of essential military supplies. Some of the states' wealthiest men had gained their fortunes from privateering, including Stephen Higginson of Boston, who reputedly amassed $70,000, John Langdon of Portsmouth, and the Cabot family. Such profits helped to bring a measure of prosperity to towns along the north Atlantic coast.

Supplying the armies also enriched individuals and indirectly their neighbors. Congress and the states relied upon merchants to obtain military stores, allowing the customary commission ranging from 2.5 to 5 per cent. Very roughly a million pounds was up for grabs every year. Legislators or executive boards would appoint individuals to buy cattle, flour, rum, beef, salt, blankets, clothing, gunpowder, and other articles, furnishing them first with paper money, then more often with certificates. Ultimately, of course, these men were supposed to account for the funds entrusted to them, though they did not always do so. To the total sums they paid out as direct costs they added their own commission, being careful to retain for themselves the type of money possessed of the highest market value—specie first, then loan-office certificates, then other interest-bearing notes. In Rhode Island, for example, Stephen Mumford received from the treasury in cash (at this point the state was borrowing money from its citizens) £4,231, which he spent for purchases as a commissary, for a galley, his commissions, and "sundries." The state still owed him £95. Other men were spending for similar purposes and submitting similar reports. The Southern states never developed such tidy systems, indeed not until 1781 did the great state of Virginia begin to introduce any system at all, but the process differed little in the end. Basically the states relied upon the energy and ability of its Mumfords. The honest and patriotic servants received a fair return, which they then might lose by investing in loan-office certificates and watching them depreciate. The dishonest or unpatriotic used the public funds temporarily in their hands for private speculations. The conspicuous results of their success intensified social and political antagonisms.

Jeremiah Wadsworth acted on a far wider stage than did Mumford. He received an appointment from Connecticut at the very start of hostilities, in April 1773, and from his Hartford home built up a broad network of agents. Later that year he began to purchase supplies for the Continental as well as state troops. In 1778 he became the country's Commissary General, extracting .5 per cent of the entire sum received and spent by his department. After a year and a half he resigned under fire—a normal circumstance—perhaps because he could earn even more money as a private trader. Wadsworth continued to gather army supplies and invested in privateers. Even while in public office he continued private trade, and by 1780 he had sufficient influence to obtain a lucrative contract supplying the French army.

This profitable mixture of public and private business also characterized the career of Philadelphia's Robert Morris. In 1775 he occupied a key position as partner in the firm of William and Morris. At that time Congress's secret committee chose the partners to import military supplies, despite rumors, probably true, that they had already profited excessively from delivering powder. The choice was not fortuitous: both men served on the committee, which in fact consisted of fellow merchants. Morris then entered upon an Atlantic-wide trade, operating with William Bingham of Philadelphia in the West Indies, Silas Deane of Wethersfield in France, and various merchants and public officials in Amsterdam, Paris, Nantes, and other ports. Morris also engaged in privateering and organized a very profitable monopoly of the tobacco export trade to France. Even before his appointment as Financier of the United States he had developed extensive contacts with other American merchants while amassing a great fortune.

Such a crude mixture of public service with private profit was not illegal at the time, and most businessmen of the period did not consider it unethical. Walter Livingston observed to Philip Schuyler in 1775 that "Altho I was a Servant to the Public yet I have a right to work by night for myself," if the public did not suffer. Schuyler, who presently would extract so high a commission that even Robert Morris complained, doubtless agreed. Yet an increasingly widespread opinion condemned such activity as immoral profiteering. William Whipple of New Hampshire, himself a merchant, stated bluntly that anyone who increased his wealth during time of war was an enemy to his country. As the war continued and as some grew rich while many became poor, major conflicts developed over the states' economic policies. The controversy involved two primary questions: how to finance the war, and who should lose least by it.

The most intense debate occurred between the summer of 1779, when the final collapse of Continental currency began, and the summer of 1781, when a wholly new system took effect. All over the country, in newspapers, articles, letters, and petitions, men argued over what their legislatures ought to do. Two sharply opposed solutions appeared: one which advocated the continuation and enforcement of current policy, the other demanding an entire change. The first won the support of the less well-to-do, least market-involved people, primarily the small farmers. The other became the platform of the larger property owners, those in trade or the professions, the more substantial commercial farmers, creditors, and most public officials including a majority in Congress.

The course of events favored the viewpoint of the latter group. Continental currency began its final, fatal decline early in 1779. Beginning in mid-summer, a series of county and town conventions tried to stave off disastrous inflation by price-fixing agreements. Committees drew up proposed regulations which prominent citizens agreed to obey, and the legislatures in some cases ratified them. These efforts failed, and a new price rise followed. By the spring of 1780 the states were repealing the regulatory laws. Congress, unable now to continue issuing money, adopted a new technique: each of the states would furnish a quota of military stores and each would find funds to pay the troops. The state legislatures then engaged in a debate over how to discharge their obligation. In general they responded remarkably well by heavy taxes payable in army supplies ("specific taxes"), which they forwarded to the army, and in certificates, which they withdrew from circulation. They also tried to borrow money in order to pay the army, but with indifferent success.

In March 1780 Congress devised a further scheme. Each state would call in by taxes its proportion of the Continental money, now worth only a penny or two on the dollar, at a ratio of $40 Continental to one of silver. As the bills came into the treasury, they would be burnt, and the treasurer would issue instead a dollar's worth of certificates for every forty destroyed. Essentially the new certificates were the familiar tax anticipation warrants, but they were to bear interest. The plan called for their payment in gold and silver after five years in taxes levied for the purpose. Meanwhile the states would receive them for taxes, equal to gold and silver, and they would be legal tender for all payments. These provisions, together with a sharp decrease in the supply of money, would presumably maintain the value of the certificates.

The states responded nobly. Little Rhode Island, to continue our favorite example, had just announced taxes of £360,000, and now added £420,000, a sum totaling £15 for each person in the state. The United States, her legislature explained, had been driven into the war before the states could organize for the collection of taxes or arrange for the redemption of bills of credit which necessity forced them to issue. The bills, increasing in quantity beyond the amount needed for a circulating medium, and lacking funds for their redemption, sank in value. Now the states must reduce the quantity, calling in the bills gradually by taxes. The new bills, the legislators promised, would be paid in gold and silver by taxes beginning in 1786, and meanwhile would draw 5 per cent interest. By July all the states except South Carolina and Georgia, at that time fighting for their lives, had enacted similar stringent laws and were trying to collect the very large taxes.

What defeated the effort was not lack of desire but the continuing high cost of war together with unremitting inflation. The states were now responsible for paying the troops their bounties for re-enlistment along with their current and back wages, as well as replenishing their military equipment and supplies. Unable to collect sufficient tax money in time for the costly campaign of 1781, many of the states again resorted to currency emissions in the form of tax anticipation notes, supplemented by quartermaster and commissary certificates. In addition they issued to the soldiers bounty and depreciation certificates. By the beginning of 1781 not only Congress but the states too had exhausted both money and credit.

Public controversy over economic policy flared with each crisis. One line of argument defended deficit financing and blamed its apparent failure on poor enforcement. These writers asserted that the people lacked money to support the war by taxes, though over a period of prosperous, peaceful years a debt might be gradually retired. Meanwhile, the governments had no choice but to rely upon paper currency —upon tax anticipation warrants. Borrowing could not help because the government still must repay the loan; indeed, the burden of the war became heavier if interest was added to the total debt. The sole beneficiaries of loan-office certificates were rich men who could loan money and further enrich themselves at the expense of the taxpayers. Inflation, which threatened ruin to paper currency, did not result simply from an increased money supply and was not inevitable. Profiteers and speculators were primarily responsible. They selfishly raised prices and refused to accept Continental and state bills at par. The defenders of a paper system insisted that the governments must enforce tender acts and must strictly regulate prices, vigorously punishing all violators. As long as the paper remained legal tender, creditors could not oppress debtors, and people could easily pay taxes. With prices set by law at their original low levels, the cost of war would be minimized, the least amount of paper need be issued, the public debt limited. The states could deal with local shortages which forced up prices by preventing monopolistic practices, regulating the sale of goods, limiting the profits of traders, and perhaps even chartering state-owned privateers. In short, legal tender laws, price controls, government regulation, and taxes payable in paper money or certificates at par, would finance the war at least cost to the people. An alternative, recognizing the fact of inflation and the impossibility of maintaining the old money at par, called for letting money find its own value, regarding depreciation as a gradual tax, and issuing more as needed.

The opposing view appealed to what had already become a standard theory defending complete economic liberty, allowing natural laws to follow their benevolent and inevitable course. The "natural" quantity of money necessary in the new nation, they asserted, was around £10 million (the estimate varied). Any increase led inevitably to price increases in proportion to currency inflation. Tender acts violated natural laws and would fail, as experience demonstrated; the value of paper money always found its true level. Such laws were moreover not only uneconomic but immoral. They forced creditors to accept cheaper dollars than they loaned, paid soldiers and public servants with notes worth only a fraction of their reputed value, and defrauded poor widows, orphans, and laborers. The country, these theorists insisted, must return to specie.

They argued similarly that price regulations could not succeed because supply and demand, not legislation, determined prices. If the extraordinary requirements of the army or losses by trade forced up prices, people would exert themselves to benefit from the high price and by so doing increase the supply, thus reducing the price. By encouraging the profit-seeker, even the speculator, governments would alleviate temporary shortages. Economic liberty, not economic restrictions, would supply the army.

From these premises reformers concluded that governments must now start afresh. They found repudiation a hard pill to swallow, but once paper vanished the country could pay the interest on and maintain the value of interest-bearing notes, such as loan-office certificates, which these men possessed. They proposed that the governments publish a table showing the actual worth of the paper at various times—a "depreciation table"—and all business transactions, such as the payment of debts and the settlement of government accounts, would follow the table. For example, if on January 1, 1779, the Continental dollar stood at ten to one with specie, then a liability incurred on that date would be settled with one dollar in silver or ten in paper. In this fashion, the great mass of the nation's excessive money supply would vanish. Loan-office certificates and other interest-bearing notes which had depreciated only moderately would remain, and together with gold and silver would supply just about what currency the country needed.

How was the war to be financed in the future? According to the reformers, through current taxes and loans. Taxes levied in specie would create confidence in lenders, and people would rush to purchase loan-office certificates. With a strictly limited amount of currency in circulation, the value of such certificates would rise near par. Such taxes, collected over a period of ten years, would extinguish the debt. "An American," writing in Pennsylvania, recommended a land tax of $2 per hundred acres, a similar tax on every man capable of bearing arms, and a tax on farm animals, which combined would bring $3 million annually. A tax on houses at the rate of a dollar for each window over ten, a 5 per cent export tax, and an assessment of a dollar per ton on vessels of over ten tons would raise more than $4 million. He advised against taxes on specie or on money lent at interest, for the lender would simply pass on the cost to the borrower through high interest rates.

Whatever one may think about the economics of the question, there is no doubt who would benefit from the latter plan: anyone with money in hand. Governments would encourage them to trade without any restrictions, charging what they could get. They would loan most of the money to the government and recover every penny with interest, all the while paying only a small part of the taxes. A merchant earning $10,000 in foreign trade—which many did—would pay only $100 or so in taxes and, if he invested $5,000 in 5 per cent bonds, would recover $250 annually. By contrast, a farmer with three hundred acres would receive virtually nothing for any paper money or certificates he happened still to own, could not afford to invest in bonds, and would pay in taxes, following "An American's" proposal, about $20 plus his share of the export tax if he produced for export. Under this plan, too, creditors would have a marked advantage over debtors, as always during a period of currency deflation.

In order to carry out this policy, legislatures were advised to pass certain key laws. First, an act repealing all legal-tender clauses which required people and governments to accept at face value paper money or certificates. Second, the repeal of all laws regulating prices or other business activities. Third, a scale of depreciation establishing low rates for non-interest-bearing paper currency of all sorts. This would virtually wipe out the extant federal and state currency and prevent individuals or governments from discharging their obligations in cheap money. Fourth, once the states had returned to a specie basis, new financial programs could be instituted as already outlined. A crucial aspect of such a program would be long-term taxes to be collected either in specie, in certificates equal to specie, or in other money at its value set by the scale of depreciation. *Not* at its face value: that would enable holders to discharge taxes in cheap money, in effect evading taxes and depriving government of the revenue essential to the entire plan.

In state after state, during 1780 and 1781, the people's representatives struggled over this issue. Defenders of existing policies fought to save tender acts and regulatory laws, to maintain the value of paper currency and certificates, and to levy taxes payable in that currency at its par value, thereby calling it gradually out of circulation. They preferred to finance the war by yet more certificates and by selling loyalist property, forcing the country's enemies to bear the burden of the debt. The urgency of the legislative battles derived partly from the quantity of money at stake, and partly from the military situation which during much of the period seemed utterly desperate.

What happened in Massachusetts is illustrative. By 1780 the people of the commercial centers were vigorously pressing for a new economic policy. As early as 1777 interior farming communities had been protesting attempts to place the state on a hard-money basis: when the legislature responded to Congress's request not to issue more paper but to rely upon taxes and loans, thirty-one towns, every one of them in the interior, took the trouble to remonstrate against the act. In the early summer of 1780 a bill to repeal all legal-tender clauses and establish a depreciation table passed (54 to 51, on June 10) but when the Senate, which favored an even more drastic reform, amended the bill the lower house postponed it. In the fall the defenders of legal tender blocked another repeal, most of the negative votes coming from the interior while coastal towns favored the measure. In January, however, a series of close votes set up a scale of depreciation for government securities and provided for their gradual repayment. The state levied a heavy tax and arranged to borrow £400,000 at 6 per cent interest. Judges would determine the value of bills of credit for payments. Later in the year another law repealed all legal-tender clauses. The steps taken for maintaining the value of the new loan-office certificates pleased potential lenders, and men of property in general rallied to the support of the state. A series of votes on these measures revealed a sharp sectional division, with the coastal towns and the Connecticut Valley trading centers, traditionally allies of the Boston group, voting overwhelmingly for the new system while the inland communities, except only the Berkshire County towns, opposed by a two-to-one majority. Massachusetts maintained this pro-creditor, hard-money policy until agrarian discontent exploded in Shays' Rebellion.

Other states followed suit or balked, depending on their own economic situation and the balance of political power. Congress threw its weight on the side of fiscal reform. During 1780 the central government ceased to issue paper notes, which had already depreciated to virtually nothing, and relied primarily on the states to contribute supplies and pay soldiers for the duration of the war. Marking the demise of the old system, Congress recommended the repeal of legal tender laws and entrusted financial supervision to the mercantile community, notably Robert Morris. During the last year of major military operations, Morris had the great good fortune to receive more than £1 million from France, enabling him to purchase war materials, maintain American credit in Europe, and strengthen the home government. In 1782 and 1783 the French contributed more money, as did the Dutch, and domestically Morris began to receive significant amounts of specie from the states. This money he used to pay contractors for supplying the army, establish a bank, and pay some of the government's debts.

Meanwhile, the states, which enjoyed no such foreign aid, struggled to pay for the war without using tax anticipation notes. They began to raise considerable hard money by taxes payable only in specie (or certain certificates equal to specie), and by import taxes also payable in specie. But despite the gold and silver brought over by the French troops, imported by loans, and to some extent obtained by clandestine trade with the British, the supply of specie proved totally inadequate to finance the war. The hard money did enable the states to pay bounties to soldiers who promised to enlist for the duration, to meet equally critical changes, and to forward some specie to Morris. To obtain provisions the Northern states in particular levied taxes payable in military supplies, often proportioning the assessment among the towns and letting the local officials devise ways and means. Elsewhere, notably from Virginia south, the governments relied on a flood of certificates, authorizing procurement officers simply to seize what they needed and issue the notes at will. The desperate retreat through the

Carolinas in 1780 and the victorious campaigns of the following year were fought with certificates.

Cornwallis's surrender allowed an exhausted thirteen states to lick their battle wounds. Paper money had pulled them through five years of fighting. The basic wealth of the country, drawn forth by taxes, loans, and impressments, had secured victory. After Yorktown each state began to assess its losses, determine what it owed to its citizens, and arrange its finances for peacetime.

Ever since the collapse of tax warrants and continental bills in 1780, the advocates of currency reform had been gaining ground. In the North, where the armies remained quiescent, the states had repealed their legal-tender laws by the summer of 1781. The Southern states could not afford to do so because they continued to rely upon paper, either in the form of certificates for supplies or in further tax anticipation notes. Only when the end of fighting enabled them to cut costs did they return to a specie basis—in North Carolina and Georgia not until 1783. One by one, however, even these states adopted depreciation tables and began currency deflation. From these reforms followed several important consequences.

First, the wartime profits, such as they were, of thousands of small farmers and artisans almost disappeared. They had hoped to use these certificates for taxes, for the payment of debts, to buy more land, or for a higher standard of living. Petitions to the legislature pleaded that the government should protect, not destroy, the people's property. The legislatures attended to these complaints where such people exercised sufficient political clout. In some cases they allowed the payment of taxes in certificates, at the depreciated rate. Many states, sympathizing with the debtors, authorized the postponement of court suits for a time, especially for debts contracted before the war. In addition, legislatures received the certificates for land or for purchase of confiscated estates. Despite these concessions the ordinary holders benefited little from their wartime sacrifices. The soldiers who could keep their depreciation certificates form a partial exception, but most of them, returning impoverished, sold their notes at a discount.

Second, the postwar governments inherited a much smaller debt burden. Beginning in 1781 they began to consolidate and evaluate all of the multivarious notes, issuing new interest-bearing bonds. Anyone with a claim against the state submitted to the treasury his evidence, whatever that might be. The treasurer scrutinized it, reduced the claim according to the depreciation table, figured interest if any was due (as on loan-office certificates), and handed out the new certificate. The process continued for years, and nobody ever really knew or now knows the precise cost of the war, but according to the legislature's best estimates the readjusted state debt totaled about £9 million currency. To that must be added the federal debt of £30 million. Since the people owned six or seven times that amount of property, they certainly could finance such a sum eventually, and indeed it was a small price for so long a war.

Third, the men who owned interest-bearing notes, particularly loan-office certificates, benefited from the new policies. These debts remained a primary obligation of the states at their par value. Had the legislatures undertaken to redeem the entire mass of paper at par, the owners of loan-office and similar certificates would have formed a small part of a huge number of public creditors, all equally deserving. The states could not have collected enough specie even for interest charges, and to avoid bankruptcy would surely have discharged the debt by levying heavy taxes payable in the certificates. Now, however, the public creditors might hope for gold and silver, and could expect their notes ultimately to rise in value. These beneficiaries were the men of property who had loaned money to the government, the traders who took loan-office certificates rather than other types of notes for their commissions, and those who foresightedly had purchased or otherwise obtained the interest-bearing securities. Most of the public creditors lived in the towns rather than the country, were well-to-do rather than poor, and made their living through a nonfarming activity. In their own interest they now urged the governments to raise money for payments of interest and principal.

A final consequence of monetary reform, therefore, was the political implications of the redistribution of the debt. Large numbers of small property holders had held paper money, quartermaster certificates, and the like, had hoped to benefit financially from the war, and had looked to the government for payment; they had supported tax collections and in general approved of an effective government. Now, their view of the governments changed. Its functions had shifted from a patriotic support of a just war to an exploitive policy of extracting money for the profit of a well-to-do creditor class. Both the state governments and Congress derived their most enthusiastic support from these creditors—from an interested minority rather than from the people generally. The monetary changes of 1780–1781 divided the country while securing it.

Popular disillusionment made collection of taxes far more difficult than usual. The abrupt deflation created a serious money shortage, and the country's supply of currency was further depleted by an enthusiastic but ill-considered buying spree. Foreign, especially British goods, flooded into the country, yet exports never reached their prewar level until the end of the decade. By 1783, if not before, empty treasuries and widespread tax deficiencies became characteristic of most states. New Hampshire, for example, was able to balance her budget in 1782, and had at first collected a good deal of gold and silver. But by the fall of 1783 the brief commercial recovery had ceased, land prices collapsed, suits for debt became common, and tax deficiencies multiplied. Pennsylvania levied £792,000 specie between 1778 and 1783, but more than a third of this amount remained uncollected. Insurrections against tax collectors occurred in Virginia as early at 1781. South Carolina's treasury was empty in 1783, and the state had to sell confiscated property to meet even the smallest bills. Massachusetts, New York, New Jersey, Delaware, North Carolina, Georgia, and very likely others also could barely meet expenses in 1783 without borrowing money, to say nothing of furnishing money for Congress. The collection of taxes in specie proved impossible, and state after state bowed to public opinion, allowing payment in certificates and in kind. Even then arrearages grew steadily. The economic depression, exacerbated by the deliberate deflation, wiped out most of the peoples' wartime gains. Fortunately the country's basic capacity to produce quickly recovered, and by the end of the decade the states were retiring their debts and beginning to furnish significant sums to Congress.

The abolition of legal tender notes and the adoption of depreciation tables spelled hard times for debtors as well as for taxpayers. They now must pay in specie or its equivalent: that is, no longer could a debtor satisfy a demand against him with a certificate worth only part of the value of the debt. The virtual moratorium on collections gave way now to vigorous lawsuits for contracts dating long before 1776. Several types of creditors prosecuted suits: the state governments, which for example often sought payment for land bought from colonial predecessors; British firms or, if their property had been confiscated, whoever now held the debt, sometimes the states, sometimes individuals; loyalists, with the same conditions; and patriots, such as businessmen, now suing for long-standing book debts. Deflation left the debtors so vulnerable that state governments often took pity on them, especially with respect to British debts, for the public wasted little sympathy on British creditors. Pennsylvania, for example, in March 1783 postponed all suits for debts contracted before January 1, 1777. South Carolina accompanied her repeal of legal tender clauses, in 1782, by delaying suits until the next session when a further moratorium took effect. Georgia reopened her courts in 1782 but postponed debt proceedings for two years, and Maryland declared a two-year delay at the same time. Occasionally courts were enjoined to readjust claims on the basis of equity, and often the legislatures allowed no interest during the war years. Despite these concessions, creditors enjoyed a clear advantage as the war ended.

The final years of the war injured many and benefited few. The influx of specie stuck to the fingers primarily of men dealing with the French army or the American government. Robert Morris claimed that he could not pay the army, but he found hard money for his partners and their affiliates. The businessmen demanded and obtained interest-bearing certificates or other notes equal to specie; Morris himself hoarded specie while issuing personal notes based on his own credit. The states also issued notes, using as collateral the valuable loyalist property and the anticipated specie taxes. The state and federal debt enriched some men over the long haul, though these often remained paper fortunes for some years.

As the states funded their debts and took the first steps toward retirement, astute public creditors began to pick up bargains. The purchase of confiscated estates seldom required much cash but allowed the buyer to give bond. In this way men who in the course of business, public or private, came into possession of a little hard money (even though the specie really belonged to the government) made a down payment, planning to pay the rest out of their public certificates. A lenient, pro-debtor, or pliable legislature might later receive the state notes at their face value; and in fact loyalist property realized only a fraction of its real worth. Similarly, legislatures used state-held land to retire their debt, again allowing payment in certificates. Soldiers' notes in particular proved useful for picking up bargains in unoccupied land. Privates' pay was so meager that the common soldier disposed of his share quickly at a discount, while, on the other hand, high-ranking officers often acquired substantial farms, and speculators bought vast tracts. Finally, as the states tried to bring order out of financial chaos, they sometimes found it impossible to recover large sums undoubtedly due the state but for which evidence had vanished. The Southern states in particular never developed an efficient, businesslike method of accounting; indeed, they conducted the final campaigns in utter confusion. Most people suffered from this financial chaos, but a few prospered by it. These profits, it should be emphasized, existed only on paper, or depended for their ultimate realization upon the country's economic growth. As a result, the postwar depression destroyed many potential fortunes by wiping out paper gains or preventing speculators from completing their financial enterprises.

The concluding years of the war also brought great gains mixed with heavy losses in foreign trade. The British capture in February 1781 of the Dutch island of St. Eustatius in the West Indies decimated the American privateering fleet. The British haul included two thousand Americans and between £2 and £3 million sterling. The activities of the British fleet elsewhere cut privateering gains, one Boston firm claiming losses of £8,000 or £9,000 in two years. On the other hand, merchants pursued an expanded commerce with Europe and the West Indies, exporting tobacco and flour in return for a great variety of manufactures and products such as sugar, coffee, wine, salt, cloth, and, of course, military supplies. Beginning in the fall of 1782 heavy importations of British goods began. Even earlier a clandestine trade with the British, especially in New York and New Jersey, brought in scarce and expensive items, but the enormous hunger for such goods remained unsatisfied. With peace, shipments multiplied: South Carolina alone imported goods worth £320,471 during 1783, and purchased nearly £900,000 worth the following year compared with a prewar norm of around £300,000. Foreign ships conducted much of the import business, but American merchants profited through resale and they controlled much of the export trade.

The privateers captured marketable products at little cost to the country, but other such purchases must be paid for in specie. Clearly the balance of trade ran heavily against the states in these years. We have almost no data, but South Carolina exported, in return for the above goods, only £168,370 worth, and deficits also ran two to one the following year. At that rate, the country as a whole owed abroad about £800,000 during 1783 and £2.2 million more in 1784. Some of the wherewithal to pay came from French, Spanish, and Dutch loans, but American consumers came up with most of it. The country's temporary supply of specie was probably greater than before the war, but it quickly departed during 1782 and 1783. Merchants began to buy on credit, as during colonial times, relying on an expanding market to maintain payments, and then advanced credit to consumers. As early as the spring of 1783, English firms had advanced £150,000 worth of goods to Boston merchants alone. Such optimistic practices sowed the seeds of disaster. Americans wanted to buy but soon lost the ability to pay. The final years of the war thus enriched some merchants, ruined others, and left probably a great majority with potentially large but frozen—or at least cold—properties held in the form of public and private debts.

The farmers, many of whom had prospered until 1780, lost most of their war profits thereafter. British and French gold bought supplies in certain areas, but the armies caused much damage in the same districts as well as in extensive parts of the South. Federal and state army supplies skimmed off the surplus and left behind depreciating certificates. The British carried off thousands of slaves—possibly fifty thousand, causing a loss of £1.5 to £2 million. The resulting labor shortage limited the production of tobacco and rice, while indigo planters, deprived of their British subsidy, could not sell at a profit. Naval stores too no longer benefited from a bounty. Southern planters, who had backed resistance to Britain so enthusiastically, thus paid a heavy price for independence. Northern commercial farmers had gained in wealth by 1782, but so many splurged on imported goods that they wound up in the red, joining the more nearly subsistence farmers. Agricultural regions, characteristically short of credit, stood to lose the most by deflation and, as we have suggested, opposed the hard-money policy of the 1780's. Some farmers, like some traders, prospered, but most certainly made no money from the Revolution.

Manufacturing, which had boomed economically and won general applause as a patriotic enterprise, found with the return to peace an end both to profits and to honor. Since the army no longer needed supplies, and with foreign products flooding the market, artisans and mechanics lost their customers. Their savings evaporated with currency deflation, and the export of specie deprived everyone of purchasing power. The final period of fighting completed the destruction of the fishing and whaling fleets, and shipbuilding declined as trade slowed.

One major economic advance redeemed the final years of conflict and loss: the founding of successful private banks. Inspired by Robert Morris, the Bank of North America opened in 1781, primarily as a government institution, supported by a transfusion of French gold. During its early years it continued to serve the United States by loaning money to the government and to army contractors, using the Financier's specie as backing for notes. By carefully limiting the number of notes, Morris and his associates magnified their purchasing power. By mid-1782 merchants in other cities began to invest in bank stock, attracted by Morris's solid reputation and the prospect of high dividends.

The war had brought profits for some, but most people ruefully counted their losses. They had won: their economy had survived eight years at war. For their public and private debts and their deprivations they had exchanged independence, and only the future could reveal whether they had struck a good bargain. Socially and politically, too, the economic effects of the war created uncertainties. Men had, on the whole, united in the common cause, but they had divided bitterly over economic policy. Many people, probably including most large property owners, emerged with a permanent dislike for paper money, regulatory laws, and their advocates, while the rest traced their poverty to the deflationary policies of the final years. One could not predict, then, whether the war's legacy was a United States or a disunited people.

# Chapter Eight

# Loyalism in the Thirteen States

AN important part of the people in the thirteen United States remained aloof from or hostile to the struggle for independence. They made up a heterogeneous mass labeled "Tory" by the patriots who sought, and failed, to win them over. Probably one in six Americans cheered for a British victory, and a much larger number did not care who won, asking only to be left alone. Efforts at repression, lawful or otherwise, took three forms: identifying these presumed enemies in order to prevent them from impeding the war effort, imposing various penalties and restrictions on them, and confiscating their property. After the fighting ended, many "patriots" tried to block the loyalists from recovering their former privileges and estates.

Who were the "loyalists"? They included many types, but we can distinguish several major groups. First, a large segment belonged to the urban elite, primarily merchants, lawyers, and high-ranking officials, but including some well-to-do owners of real estate, Anglican ministers, doctors, and a very few manufacturers. These are the most conspicuous of the loyalists, the best educated and most articulate, who published most of the arguments before 1776 and apologia afterwards. Their ideas are familiar, their names recognizable. Their strongholds were in Boston, Newport, New York City, and Philadelphia, while a subspecies, consisting primarily of merchants and recent immigrants not yet fully Americanized, lived in the Southern seaports. Lesser towns also contained representatives of the same type, especially the provincial capitals such as Portsmouth, Annapolis, and New Bern.

Most of these men were quite rich. After the war some five thousand loyalists claimed reimbursement for losses of £8 million sterling. A small percentage of claimants worth £2,000 or more apiece requested most of this. They probably exaggerated their wealth, but the total, whatever it was, made a captivating sum, and the states eventually captured it. They did not seize the estates of the overwhelming majority of loyalists, whose wealth scarcely deserved notice, but of this particular species. The money involved, perhaps £5 million sterling, was also worth fighting for from the loyalist point of view, and they and their friends tried to recover it.

Because these men belonged to the colonial elite, they enjoyed the active sympathy of rebel members of the elite. Both came from the same families, and they knew one another socially. The upper-class leaders on both sides shared the same fundamental ideas, the same Whig ideology. Few of them trusted the majority or worked for a pure democracy; all preferred rule by themselves. They disliked leveling principles or "agrarian" laws which would make men equal. All agreed in protecting the rights of large property owners. Few had greeted independence enthusiastically, nor did they ever seek revolutionary change. In striving to preserve the status quo, their quarrel was over means rather than ends. The loyalist members of the elite had more faith in the rectitude of the British government, perhaps less in popular sovereignty, considerably more respect for England's military power, less confidence in colonial strength. Once their point was won, the rebel segment rallied to the support of their loyalist friends, trying to protect them from punishment and to save their property from confiscation. After the war the same sympathizers worked to repeal anti-loyalist legislation, partly no doubt from principle but not least because the two groups, reunited, would again work together politically to re-establish their hegemony. The other side of the coin is, of course, that many people in the thirteen states regarded the well-to-do loyalist as an enemy for reasons quite apart from loyalism.

The second kind of loyalism was primarily rural rather than urban and consisted of small property owners rather than large. They resembled therefore the great mass of patriots in most of their attributes and, like them, ranged from the enthusiasts who fought for the King to passive neutrals who did not really care much which side won, and who expressed their lack of enthusiasm for the rebel cause by a reluctance to swear oaths of allegiance, pay taxes, contribute supplies, or serve in the militia. They included several distinct groups.

Some loyalists of lesser means did live in the towns. These were principally English immigrants who had attached themselves to leading loyalists, joining, for example, the proprietary party in Philadelphia, the DeLancey faction in New York, the Wentworth family group in Portsmouth, and Governor Bull and his supporters in Charleston. Savannah, Norfolk, and Newport produced numbers of such men. They caused a good deal of trouble during the early stages of the Revolutionary movement and helped the British armies during their occupation of various ports. Probably they account for most of the fifty thousand or so loyalists who left with the British fleet at the end of the war.

Another important component of middle-class loyalism, perhaps more accurately designated neutrals, lived in areas so exposed to attack by the British navy that they dared not challenge England, while others looked to Britain for protection against Indian raids. The residents of Cape Cod proved most reluctant rebels, and the Otis family in Barnstable struggled against a hostile majority. The people of Nantucket, who relied upon whaling, considered themselves too vulnerable to support a rebellion. Other islanders and men of the fishing villages felt the same way, as did the people along the shores of the "Delmarva" peninsula—the eastern shores of Virginia and Maryland together with southern Delaware. Georgians depended so heavily upon British aid and protection that many remained loyal, and other parts of the frontier witnessed Tory uprisings. Examples include the Carolina back-country, parts of what is now West Virginia, western Maryland, western Pennsylvania, and the Mohawk Valley in New York. These people had various motives for their attitude, but common to all was their belief that England did not threaten their liberties but protected them.

The largest subspecies of loyalists, broadly defined, consisted of those farmers who simply refused to help the patriots unless forced to do so—if then. Many, perhaps two thousand, lived in Connecticut. Most of the farmers in southern New York, especially in Kings, Queens, Richmond, and

Westchester counties, belonged to this type of loyalist or neutralist, as did a strong plurality if not a majority in New Jersey, particularly Bergen and Sussex counties in the north and the counties of the southwest. Most of the farmers of southeastern Pennsylvania shared the same opinion. Loyalism or neutralism in the Delmarva peninsula flourished not only along the coast but throughout Kent and Suffolk counties in Delaware, as well as in Somerset, Worcester, and other Maryland counties. In Virginia, Princess Anne and Norfolk counties, together with Accomac and Northampton on the eastern shore, proved centers of loyalist influence. Farther south, the small-farmer areas of the Carolinas, in contrast to the coastal region, contained numerous Tories. We are not simply enumerating communities where a significant fraction of the people refused to support the Revolution but are indicating those in which a probable majority became loyalists or neutralists. In addition, people of like mind swore allegiance to the Crown in the South Carolina low-country when the British arrived, and substantial groups of the same sort turned up elsewhere: apparently the planter leadership throughout Virginia quickly suppressed at the very outset a potentially powerful resistance to the Revolution.

An explanation for the attitude of these people lies beyond, or prior to, the scope of our narrative, but a few generalizations about them are important. First, some belonged to national groups which did not feel any sympathy with or understanding of the principles for which the rebels fought Recent immigrants from the Scottish highlands remained faithful to their chiefs and to the King; most Dutch farmers in New York and New Jersey held aloof from the conflict, as did many Germans there and in Pennsylvania, Maryland, and North Carolina. Second, some of these men belonged to pacifistic sects which were inclined to blame the advocates of resistance for causing all the furor and who refused to support the war in any way. Patriots regarded them as lending aid and comfort to the enemy. They exercised the most influence in West Jersey, the Philadelphia area, northern Maryland, and back-country North Carolina. Third, others among them inherited continuing antagonisms from colonial days, most often involving hostilities of farmers to the rebel Whig leadership, as in the tenant revolt on Livingston Manor (1777) and the extensive loyalism among South Carolina Regulators. Echoes or slightly similar instances occurred in frontier New England among the Berkshire (Massachusetts) "Constitutionalists," in western New Hampshire, and in Vermont. Finally, the largest number of loyalists and neutralists simply saw no reason to become involved. Content to run their own local affairs under their own trusted local leaders, they resented outside interference. They did not wish to serve in the army or pay taxes or accept paper money, and they preferred to sell in the best market. British economic policy did not injure them. The threat to their autonomy came, it seemed to them, more from fellow Americans than from the British. These people were so numerous that, as we have seen, they profoundly affected economic and political policies. Attitudes similar to theirs, moreover, can be found in the ideas of many Americans who chose, often by a narrow margin, the rebel side; so that just as the loyalist elite found sympathizers among a patriot equivalent, so also the neutralist rank-and-file were protected from persecution by their neighbors. A few among these thousands actively aided the British and fled the country. Most sat out the war and stayed put. Forming a majority in their locality, they remained little touched by all the ruckus and no one forced them to leave. That is why Delaware, the most loyal of states, furnished the smallest number of refugees.

Anti-loyalist laws followed a rough chronology. In 1776
and the first part of 1777 the patriots concentrated on smoking out the loyalists and neutralizing them. The laws became increasingly severe during the next two years as legislatures punished the openly disaffected by banishment,
quarantine, and seizure of property. Finally, the need for
money led to the sale of confiscated estates. Hostility after
the war persisted, and many states continued to deny civil
rights, to reject applications for readmission, and to sell loyalist property. Throughout the period these policies aroused
controversy. Most Americans approved of bills which prevented the Tories from doing harm to the rebels, but laws
doing harm to loyalists also met considerable opposition
from groups sympathetic with them, and such legislation
continued to be a major source of dispute during and after
the war.

The first anti-loyalist activity occurred in 1775 with the
organization of committees to enforce the Continental Association. These committees tried to persuade everyone to
sign an agreement, as Congress put it, "to associate for the
defense of American liberty." The subscribers bound themselves to execute the decisions of Congress and provincial assemblies, and to regard nonassociators as enemies to the liberties of the people. As we have seen, most members of
these local committees enthusiastically promoted the resistance movement, and they proceeded with more vigor than
restraint. The use of force to compel conformity gained acceptance during the Stamp Act crisis, and the associators
simply extended the principle to entire counties, where
necessary. Thus when the residents of Wilmington, North
Carolina, proved reluctant to sign, John B. Ashe at the head

of a few hundred soldiers compelled them to do so. Since they lacked any legal basis, the committees could not systematically eliminate the opposition, but they forced the more convinced loyalists out into the open and either hounded them out of the country or cowed them into submission. In some areas the rebels failed in their objectives because public opinion prevented them. They often succeeded, however, even against a majority, through superior organization, initiative, and firm conviction of their right.

A common type of anti-loyalist activity at this early stage destroyed the power of the "River Gods" in western Massachusetts. When Colonel Israel Williams of Hatfield made a feast day out of a Fast Day, and reputedly was corresponding with Gage, a mob smoked him all night in a smokehouse until he agreed to condemn the Intolerable Acts. The once-deferential people similarly compelled other leaders, such as John Worthington of Springfield, John Murray of Rutland, Timothy Paine of Worcester, and Abijah Willard of Lancaster, all members of the Council, either to flee or to give up their offices and retire. Comparable techniques sufficed where the recalcitrants formed only a small minority. At the other extreme, several counties of North Carolina produced a loyalist army of sixteen hundred men. In that case militia from the more rebellious areas marched against the Tories and defeated them, thus crushing North Carolina loyalism. By these various efforts the associators obtained the upper hand in most, though by no means all, of the states even before the decision for independence and before any laws required conformity.

Beginning in 1776 the informal, unsystematic, and illegal methods of the committees gave way to an organized, well-considered campaign by the states. In March the Continental Congress recommended the disarming of all those "notoriously disaffected to the cause of America." As the state legislatures convened they began to pass laws which distinguished friend from foe and neutralized the latter by depriving them not only of arms but also of the right to vote, hold office, and speak freely, and forbade a wide spectrum of other activities. The process by which the Whigs gradually captured the state governments, first in New England, Virginia, and the Carolinas, last in New York, Pennsylvania, Delaware, Maryland, and Georgia, appears clearly in the progressive passage of laws requiring loyalty oaths ("Test Laws"), defining treason, and imposing penalties on the recalcitrant. Subsequent treatment of the Tories, while conforming to a general pattern, varied significantly from state to state depending upon the strength of the loyalists, military developments, and other local factors.

New Hampshire's loyalists posed no threat to the struggle for independence. The association test and petitions indicate only scattered opposition in the central and western sections, for example in Claremont, an Anglican stronghold. Loyalism centered in Portsmouth and its satellite towns, where the Wentworths had dominated, but even in the capital city only fifty-nine men supported the governor's own counter-"association." Of his supporters fully two-thirds came from the town elite, especially merchants, officials, and relatives of the in-group. Considering the prestige of the signers and the presence of two British ships, Wentworth's inability to win even 10 per cent of the men proves the rebels' overwhelming strength. The governor and his closest supporters fled six months later, removing any internal threat and rendering unnecessary any severely punitive legislation.

Not until January 1777 did the New Hampshire legislature take any action, by which time local committees had averted all danger. It then established penalties ranging from death for waging war or for other treasonable activities, to small fines for speaking against the common cause, discouraging enlistments, and the like. Careful legal procedures prevented injustice. Later in the year the state rather belatedly excluded British sympathizers from holding office or practicing law (though not from voting or engaging in business) through an oath of allegiance. A subsequent act allowed nonjurors to take the oath without penalty.

The earliest law provided for the forfeiture for life of the loyalists' property at the discretion of the court. This provision led to the premature sale or to the misuse of such estates, so the government soon forbade any transfers and arranged for the securing of all such property pending further action. The fall of 1778 brought additional steps. These resulted not from any military danger, since the state remained safe from invasion, but partly to prevent Tories from returning to the state and largely to replenish an empty treasury. Two acts named seventy-eight exiles forbidden to return and confiscated the property of twenty-five individuals including John Wentworth. For the moment only the personal estate was to be sold, and that only after an inventory was taken and provision made for the families. A subsequent act of June 26, 1779, included real property but postponed all sales until the settlement of claims against the estates. Apparently the latter provision, while satisfying to creditors, prevented the treasury from realizing any profit whatever, so it was repealed in 1780. The need for money continued, especially after the spring of 1781 when New Hampshire, like other states, tried to finance the war on a pay-as-you-go basis. The legislature therefore tried to hasten the sale of the property and confiscated, in broad language, all estates of the absentees, of

British subjects, and (in 1782) of anyone guilty of aiding the enemy.

In the end, the state punished only a handful of men. It never imposed any special taxes on recalcitrant citizens, and executed nobody. Early in 1777 the legislature allowed whoever wished to leave the state to depart and to sell their possessions. Thus only the most conspicuous loyalists suffered because of their politics. The government had seized about £70,000 worth of property. It realized no return from these estates until the war ended and very little thereafter: as late as 1789 sales in one country had brought only £300 specie out of £9,000. By the mid-1780's New Hampshire had removed all penalties, and former loyalists were gradually recovering their influence and offices.

Loyalism in Massachusetts paralleled that of her northern neighbor. Prominent men of some interior towns, especially in the Connecticut Valley, and a few religious minority groups such as the Baptists of Ashfield, opposed independence but posed no threat to the war effort. The longer seacoast and numerous exposed islands produced many Tories or neutrals, but they were physically isolated and the course of events simply bypassed them. Boston contained a number of very prominent, influential loyalists, yet even in the capital they numbered not more than a thousand, most of whom were immigrants and mariners. They sailed with Gage in 1776, thereby decapitating their party in Massachusetts. Thereafter the people had no reason to fear loyalism, so that anti-Tory laws in Massachusetts reflected enmity, jealousy, or economic motives.

The patriots completed their task even before Independence. Local committees took over loyalist estates, prevented suspected Tories from voting or holding office, and forced prominent nonconformists to flee. An act of 1777 merely recognized the existing situation. Thus it authorized the selectmen of each town to publish the names of men suspected of inimical disposition, a list which the voters might extend or amend. Justices of the peace would arrest the suspects, who then stood trial in a court and if found guilty were exiled. They were allowed to remove their personal estates and collect debts. The representatives took no further step for more than a year, imposing no special taxes or other penalties, relying on local initiative to cope with any problem.

When in November 1777 Congress suggested that the states confiscate and sell loyalist property, the Massachusetts legislature at first delayed until it could identify the estates in question. At this point no compelling economic need existed, and many legislators from the eastern towns opposed such an extreme step, which might imperil property in England. On the other hand, a probable majority of the voters, if not of their representatives, hated the Tories and wanted to punish traitors. Moreover, creditors of the loyalists hoped to collect their debts, which was impossible without appropriate legislation, and other men surely anticipated a nice profit from the purchase of valuable property for less than its true worth—perhaps for a trifle. Temporarily, however, the legislature merely forbade the return of a long list of exiles.

The change of policy during 1779 probably reflected the worsening financial crisis. After an overwhelming majority passed a basic confiscation act, the legislature authorized the immediate auction of some major estates, after debts had been settled and families provided for. This brought a considerable profit—in Essex County alone more than £130,000 —but not all of this was in cash. Late in 1780, when the legislature was struggling to raise money for military bounties, it authorized a loan of £60,000 in specie, and as a further revenue measure ordered immediate auction of all confiscated property.

The state benefited little from the sale, which ought to have returned hundreds of thousands of pounds. The legislature permitted the creditors to skim off such specie as the sale produced. Auctions took place when few people could afford to purchase, after the deflation of 1781. The government also lost money by allowing payment in various types of paper. Such policies transferred the property of a few hundred men into the hands of a somewhat larger number of persons who were already large property owners, with little advantage either to the government or to the rest of the people.

As the war drew to a close, some of the exiles returned to their native land. Certain towns accepted them without fuss if they held their tongues and won support from Whig leaders, as did Henry Van Schaak when his old friend Theodore Sedgwick sheltered him. By the end of the decade Van Schaak even won election to the legislature. The debate swirled mainly around the conspicuous Boston elite, whose homecoming was angrily opposed by a Boston town meeting, newspaper articles, and petitions to the legislature. But the urban merchants and professionals defended them, and their spokesmen in the House of Representatives joined with men from the coastal towns to urge readmission. Most of the interior communities blocked the attempt, and not until the fall of 1785 did the lower house pass a bill to repeal all anti-loyalist legislation. Even then the Senate rejected the measure, according to one account because certain senators had plundered confiscated estates. Thereafter opposition subsided. It seems clear that the Tories never threatened the success of the Revolution, once it had fairly begun. The punitive laws stemmed from emotional antipathy, avarice, and the financial crisis.

Unlike northern New England, the Long Island Sound area saw altogether too much of the British after 1776. Connecticut, though unoccupied, suffered sporadic raids, while British troops held one-third of Rhode Island for many months. In neither state, however, did the loyalists threaten the governments, which therefore followed policies similar to those of Massachusetts and New Hampshire.

Rhode Island's legislature could react quickly to emergencies because it met frequently and no superior power could delay decisions. It therefore managed to take over loyalist property before enthusiastic patriots could waste it. As early as October 1775 the government authorized the seizure of several valuable estates, to be rented for the colony's benefit. The next month an act punished by death or forfeiture of property anyone found guilty of traitorous correspondence or military activities. Within a few months the "nonjurors," who refused to sign a loyalty oath, were forbidden to vote or sue in courts; town officers were disqualified unless they would "subscribe the Test." In 1777 several men who had cooperated with the British were sent to towns in the interior, though not to Connecticut as the deputies first recommended. No further punishment followed, and instead the legislature relieved Quakers and other pacifists from military duty. When too many people took advantage of this leniency, the legislature merely required such men to hire sufficient substitutes in order to raise the necessary soldiers. In 1778 an act enabled all previous nonjurors to subscribe to the test without penalty; later in the year even those who still refused were allowed full use of the courts. In 1784 the test act was repealed. Such liberality, especially in view of the prolonged occupation of Newport, speaks well for the people and their leaders. It appears that all but a handful of Rhode Islanders lived without penalty regardless of their political views.

The exceptions resided in Newport, which from the start harbored pro-British officials and merchants. The exposed position of the city probably won for these men some local support among the people, and loyalism also existed in other towns on the island. Yet even in Newport only 10 per cent of the people left with the British evacuation. These few included some owners of large estates, and since several wealthy Bostonians held extensive farms there, the legislature determined to mix punishment with profit.

At first Rhode Island merely "sequestered" loyalist property, renting several rich farms but selling none. This brought some hundreds of pounds into the treasury annually but did not contribute significantly to the war effort. When Congress recommended confiscation and sale Rhode Island delayed, and indeed was one of the last states to act. A law of October 1779 began the process by defining as aliens all who had actively aided the enemy or left the state. The Superior Court was to hold sessions in every county, with juries, and only after conclusive evidence would the alien's estates become forfeit. This act included no provision for the sale of the property. In September 1780, however, the legislature tried to use certain confiscated estates to maintain the value of some specie bills and in general support the state's failing credit. This produced a few thousand pounds. Further sales resulted from the British destruction of Newport, which caused an estimated loss of £125,000 specie, thoroughly angered the people, and furnished the legislature with an excuse to use loyalist estates for the army's wages. Unlike the situation in Massachusetts, where the interest of creditors formed an important motive for sale, the proceedings in Rhode Island stemmed from the state's need for money plus the desire for revenge. Not until 1783 did an act secure the claims of creditors.

Sales continued slowly, and the state also received small sums from rentals. The beneficiaries, aside perhaps from certain creditors, were a handful of individuals. Thus the valuable "Point Judith" farm sold for £10,000 to three men, apparently all merchants. On the whole, loyalism in Rhode Island proved neither a curse nor a blessing to the patriot cause.

Connecticut's loyalists formed a larger proportion of the population than in the other New England states and involved many more towns. The greatest concentration occurred in southwestern Fairfield County and in New Haven, both Anglican strongholds. In the former they may even have predominated, but loyalism there took a neutralist form rather than active support of the British. Popular action suppressed resistance during 1775, and by the spring of 1776 even the Fairfield loyalists had been silenced. In December, for example, several hundred militia marched into New Town, seized the Anglican minister, the selectmen, and other prominent citizens, disarmed them, and forced them to submit. They then invaded five other towns, jailing some of the most stubborn residents. At the same time the legislature identified as treasonable various activities which, after a trial, might lead to the forfeiture of property and imprisonment. The act also prevented critics of the government from holding office and established such penalties as fines and disfranchisement. Another clause legalized the local committees' activities. In the fall of 1776 a test oath deprived the loyalists of voting privileges and enacted the death penalty for treason, under which clause, in fact, a few Tories lost their lives. These laws reacted to the strength of loyalism in the southwest. Finally, in February 1781 the state passed a harsh law, probably because of British raids, prescribing the death penalty for anyone who regarded the King as ruler of Connecticut.

During the spring of 1776 the legislature confiscated loyalist property, holding it for the benefit of the state while paying creditors. Apparently little of it was sold until 1782, when another act provided for the rapid settlement of claims against the estates and their sale for specie or notes given to the soldiers of the "Continental line." According to loyalist claimants, the state seized property worth a quarter of a million pounds, but we do not know how much the government actually received.

After the war anti-Tory feeling quickly subsided, and all but the most extreme loyalists returned. An article in a New London paper observed that the loyalists would "give Energy and Stability to all the Measures of a *democratical* state," while the influence of the Anglican—now Episcopalian—church ensured support for tolerance. By 1784 ex-Tories won nearly half the offices in New Haven, and loyalism ceased to be an issue in Connecticut.

The most recent careful student of loyalism in New York concluded that a majority of Yorkers supported independence. The Tories, however, formed so powerful a minority that the state confronted problems unknown in New England. Until late in 1775 the provincial congress relied upon local committees to control nonassociators. That fall, while emphasizing its regard for freedom of speech, rights of conscience, and personal liberty, it concluded that the public safety required the imprisonment, banishment, or disarmament of anyone opposing the congresses or the committees. Unable to enforce this decree in much of southern New York, the delegates requested the aid of Continental troops. In May the congress published a long list of men considered hostile and set up machinery for arresting, trying, and punishing Tories. During the following months the government arrested hundreds of men, banishing some of them to jails in other states. Meanwhile, the local committees had begun to seize and even to sell the personal property of those who had joined the British, a step legitimized by the Provincial Convention in the spring of 1777. Shortly thereafter the state constitution disfranchised anyone refusing to take an oath of loyalty, and an act the following year exiled and levied a special tax upon the estates of men considered a threat to the government.

Not until 1780 did New York begin to sell the real estate. Agitation for confiscation began earlier and, as we have seen, local committees early seized some property. An appeal to the legislature in 1778 argued that a general forfeiture and sale were necessary "to support the credit of our paper currency, and to the preservation of the state." Governor Clinton and his supporters favored such a step, but the state's most prominent leaders, such as the great landholders Robert Livingston, Richard Morris, and Abraham Ten Broeck, together with many merchants and lawyers, opposed such an attack on property. They also hoped to minimize the number of persons penalized and warned that the British might destroy New York City in revenge.

In March 1779 the legislature passed a general confiscation act which was vetoed by the Council of Revision. That body thought the bill unjust, pointing especially to the lack of trial by jury and the illiberality of seizing real estate belonging to British subjects who had not committed any crime. The Senate sustained the veto, and not until October did a new and more carefully drawn bill pass into law. This act, which named fifty-nine men most of whom were wealthy and prominent, passed because of the support of Clintonians from upstate rural districts. The next spring, coincident with the financial crisis and an effort to obtain money without issuing paper, the Clinton group introduced a bill calling for the immediate sale of the property. Opponents of the measure succeeded in excluding from the act most land in the occupied counties, and in using the money only for paying the Continental troops. They pushed through the Senate a clause requiring an effort to raise money on loan before selling the property—a policy corresponding with the concurrent reform efforts of hard-money men—but the Assembly rejected this amendment. The division formed along sectional lines, anticipating post-war political alignments. Men from New York City, several of whom now represented other districts, together with most of those from other southern counties, tried to modify the bill. The Council of Revision objected again, this time because the property would sell for less than its true value, and because few farmers or soldiers could buy so that only speculators would gain. Moreover, the Council argued, several months must elapse before the state received any money whereas the troops must be paid at once. Both houses passed the bill over this veto.

During the next few years the state did in fact receive little money. The most valuable property remained under British control, and since the legislature permitted payment in certificates and granted extensions of the period for pay, the treasury took in far less specie than it had hoped. The enemy's withdrawal in 1783 enabled the state to seize the property in the southern district. Continued anti-loyalist feeling together with the need for money to pay the state debt led to the introduction of a bill in March 1784 which called for the immediate sale of all forfeited estates worth

[287]

£20,000 or more. A more extensive one became law in May over the opposition of the anti-Clinton group. This act, like its predecessor, permitted the purchaser to use various certificates and required only a one-third down-payment. Subsequent acts further postponed the day of reckoning. Under these laws the state ultimately collected more than $3 million for property whose true market value was much more than this, and received no benefit from these sales until long after the financial crisis had passed.

The state's Tories continued to suffer in other ways, for the long occupation and civil war left a bitterness unmatched in New England. Men such as Alexander Hamilton, John Jay, Philip Schuyler, James Duane, and the Livingstons, supported by delegates from the southern counties and the town of Albany, worked to restore the loyalists' liberties, but they faced determined opposition. The legislature continued to deprive former enemies of the right to vote, and as late as 1787 passed an act preventing them from holding office. Double taxation continued until the end of the war, and the Clinton group stubbornly opposed readmitting the Tories or paying debts to them. The famous case of *Rutgers vs. Waddington* became a *cause célèbre* in 1784. Mrs. Rutgers, under a New York law, sued Waddington, a loyalist merchant, for damages to her New York City property which he had occupied. Hamilton pleaded that the Treaty of Peace rendered the law invalid, and the decision, rendered by Mayor James Duane, allowed Waddington to escape costs from 1780 on because he was then acting under military orders. A majority in the legislature bitterly condemned this outcome, the votes clearly showing the alignment already described. Public opinion sided with the Clinton party. A meeting in Westchester County agreed that treaties could not override the wishes of a popular majority.

Tories, the people asserted, favored an aristocracy and might subvert the government. The passage of time, of course, favored the loyalists as enmities subsided. In New York City they soon recovered their influence, and the legislators allowed them to vote in 1786. Hamilton won election to the legislature the next year (for the first and last time) despite his unpopular legal position, and by 1788, as one historian has put it, the Tories were "almost completely emancipated."

New Jersey, as we have seen, lay exposed to two influences handicapping her war effort: the loyalist stronghold on her eastern boundary, and Pennsylvania's pacifism in the west. In consequence, as her statesman William Paterson observed, loyalism developed extensively. While he mentioned Sussex and Hunterdon as particular strongholds, he added that "the other Counties in the State are more or less pestered with them." Bergen County, next to New York, produced a great many Tories or neutrals, while from Monmouth, Essex, and Middlesex, also in the eastern part, many prominent men fled to the British lines and presently led aggressive raids. This section of the state therefore was so torn by civil war that enthusiastic eastern Whigs pushed hard for anti-loyalist legislation. Western delegates agreed in condemning clearly traitorous activity, but coming from a pacifistic region where active Tories were rare and neutrals formed the majority, they opposed any law that punished those who withheld active support from the war.

Unlike many other states, therefore, New Jersey did not punish nonjurors but only thoroughgoing Tories. The ordinance passed in the spring of 1776 allowed anyone whose religious principles forbade them to bear arms or sign the general Association, to follow their signature on the association with the words "as far as the same is consistent with my religious principles." They were supposed to surrender their arms and give security for good behavior, but otherwise were left alone. An act passed that fall requiring an affirmation of allegiance to New Jersey's government applied only to civil and military officials, not to voters. A year later the legislature extended its provisions to lawyers, jurors, and teachers. Not until December 1778 did loyalists lose the right to vote, and then only the more conspicuous were disfranchised. The only important restriction on the great majority of neutrals and inactive loyalists forbade them to trade with the British. A series of such laws testified to the futility of this prohibition.

The confiscation of loyalist estates began in August 1776, when New Jersey's convention authorized local committees to seize the property of all those who had fled to the enemy, to sell perishables, and to secure the rest. In the following year the legislature, while pardoning the repentant, took over the personal estates of the obdurant, and presently began to sell these and to lease the loyalists' land. A more vigorous act passed in 1778 set forth procedures for jury trial, secured the debts owed to the estates, and ordered general sale of the real property. During the following months the state took in more than a million pounds, primarily from East Jersey. The West Jersey neutrals refrained from the overt activities that would have classified them as loyalists, and retained their property. The treasury obtained only a small amount of specie, and far less of any sort of money than it hoped. Apparently speculators plundered this rich property. At one point the Assembly voted 21 to 4 that certain commissioners in charge of selling confiscated land had abused their offices, and later it agreed to impeach Hunterdon County's commissioners. In 1781, therefore, the legislature suspended sales. Economic need probably accounts

for their resumption in December 1783 over the strong opposition of the West Jersey group. A clause allowing the
use of state loan-office certificates resulted in so much fraud
that the act was again suspended less than a year later, the
delay eventually lasting until the mid-summer of 1786. Once
more the legislature agreed to accept almost every kind of
note, and probably received little hard money. In all, the
state sold off property supposedly worth £1.5 million for
only about £45,000 specie.

Within a few years after the war the loyalist problem in
New Jersey ceased. In 1786 men who had refused to take
the oath of allegiance could once again vote, and even before that time several counties had elected known or suspected Tories to the legislature. The most conspicuous loyalists went into exile, but most stayed and soon regained
their rights.

Pennsylvania's situation resembled New Jersey's in that
she contained a large number of people—perhaps one-third
—who refused to support independence because of religious
principles. Their presence exasperated more warlike citizens
who refused to admit the morality of pacifism when liberty
was imperiled; the pacifists also exasperated the British, who
occupied Philadelphia expecting to stimulate a general uprising of loyalists. It is not easy for us today to distinguish between the Tory whose aid to the British merited penalties
and the neutralist whose pacifism might be tolerated. At the
time, many rebels denied any distinction at all. Considering
the strength of pacifism in Pennsylvania, which threw the
whole burden of war on what may well have been a minority, anti-loyalist legislation seems lenient rather than harsh.

The Provincial Convention took the first steps in the summer of 1776, ordering the militia to disarm nonassociators.
Voting was restricted to those who took an oath not to sup-

port the King nor to oppose the new government. Later, nonjurors were fined for refusal to serve in the militia and required to pay an additional tax. At its first session in June 1777 the legislature obliged all white male inhabitants to take an oath of allegiance. Those who refused lost their citizenship, could not sue for debts or engage in real estate transactions, and were disarmed. Subsequently a double tax was imposed. Howe's occupation of Philadelphia in the fall of 1777 brought further measures, notably the removal, in advance of Howe's conquest, of certain prominent Quakers whose loyalty the government doubted. The government unceremoniously rounded up these men and exiled them all the way to the Shenandoah Valley in Virginia.

The first confiscation act was passed in March 1778, probably as a result of the damage done to Philadelphia during the British occupation, estimated at nearly £200,000. The government was short of money as well. During the next three years the Supreme Executive Council identified as traitors 453 persons, including such prominent men as Tench and Daniel Coxe, Joseph Galloway, William and John Allen, and Samuel Shoemaker, though not all of these lost their property. By this time the state no longer suffered from or feared invasion and could afford greater leniency toward pacifists and other neutral groups. The legislature repealed the double tax on nonjurors early in 1779 and over-whelmingly refused to renew it that fall.

As we have seen, the Republican Society had opposed from the first the loyalty or "Test" oath, and consistently defended the pacifists. The state's financial difficulties combined with war weariness to place the Republicans in power after 1780. During the succeeding years the legislature debated the reduction or removal of restrictions. The Quakers' adamant stand did not help their cause. Thus they refused to celebrate the victory at Yorktown, arguing that they opposed shedding of blood and could not rejoice in the advantages gained from it. The effort of loyalists to return in 1783 also excited a determination to maintain the wartime restrictions and to restore no confiscated property. By the fall of 1784 a majority in the legislature favored repeal of the Test law, but Constitutionalists stayed away in sufficient numbers to prevent a quorum. When that party won the next election, its members stubbornly opposed change. They insisted that men who for years had refused to attach themselves to the community and to obey its laws, demonstrated that they were either British subjects, enemies to liberty and the rights of mankind, or cowards. Yet these men remained impenitent, arrogantly claiming a grievance. How could they expect to enjoy privileges equal to those who had risked their lives and sacrificed their property? Public opinion was changing nevertheless. The following spring the Constitutionalists reluctantly allowed former nonjurors to recover all their privileges if they transferred their allegiance from the King to the state, and a year later a Republican majority omitted mention of the King entirely.

Meanwhile, the sale of confiscated estates continued, with what results we do not know. The state took over the Penns' land, agreeing to pay them £130,000 sterling for it, while leaving them their personal possessions and some private real estate. In all, the value of the confiscated land may have reached £400,000, including several large properties. The amount available, however, was reduced by sizable claims against the loyalists, which the state as usual undertook to pay out of the estates. From the beginning purchasers could use state money and notes, and in 1780 all the estates were appropriated for the redemption of soldiers'

depreciation certificates. Sales therefore brought in no ex-
pendable revenue at all, but only helped to retire the debt.
Wealthy Philadelphians seem to have bought these certificates and obtained much of the property. The state still retained "a considerable amount" in 1785, which was so en-
cumbered by debt that it played a very minor role in the
state's budget.

Delaware's Whigs controlled only one of the state's three
counties and struggled throughout the war to cope with the
Tories and neutrals. In June 1777 a committee reported to
the legislature that residents of Sussex County were furnishing information and supplies to the British navy, yet the
Assembly refused to act. A year later uprisings in both Sussex and Kent counties required help from other states. The
delegations from those areas, and a majority of the Council,
persistently dragged their feet on taking effective action.

The constitution required from all civil officers an oath
of allegiance but did not restrict the right to vote. The first
law punishing treason merely levied a fine, unless one were
convicted of actually waging war, which was unlikely since
the judges were Tory sympathizers. Early in 1777 a more
extensive bill led to a long debate between the two houses,
with the Legislative Council vigorously defending their
own version which, they declared, "preserves freedom of
speech and privilege of freemen" whereas the Assembly's
"will encourage a race of informers, the pest of society, and
who always were the engines of tyrants in every State. It
is to be hoped," they added, "that the just cause in which all
America is embarked is not to be injured by the speeches
of rash, foolish or wicked individuals, or at least they are
not to be so much apprehended as the effects of so dangerous a precedent in the infancy of our Government." The
two houses finally agreed to require an oath of loyalty, for

voting, holding office, or serving on juries. Conscientious objectors were excused from militia service upon payment of a fine. From this point on the Whigs retained control of the government, but they carefully refrained from wholesale persecutions.

The uprisings that resulted in this act also led to a law forfeiting the estates of those who levied war against it. The legislature listed forty-six individuals, most of whom were obscure. Altogether the state took over estates worth around £20,000—half as much as the damage caused by a British raid into New Castle County. The property sold for £150,000 in inflated currency. The confiscation probably was punitive rather than economic and had little effect on the state's finances or society. The loyalist issue disappeared soon after the war. The Assembly passed a bill in 1783 which would have deprived nonjurors of civil rights for six years, but the Council defeated it. Few Delawareans left the state—in much of it they did not need to flee a hostile population but remained with loyalist-inclined friends. The exiles, including the richest of them, returned without incident.

The treatment of Maryland's loyalists developed into a major controversy between the conservative Senate and the House of Delegates. From the start a large amount of property was at issue, including about 375,000 acres of proprietary lands and several other large estates, the whole amounting to well over half a million pounds sterling. Also involved were the large number of loyalists or neutrals in the northernmost counties (Baltimore and Harford), the eastern shore, especially Somerset and Worcester, and the far west.

An uprising on the eastern shore early in 1777 provoked the first important anti-loyalist laws. Most of the people there may have participated in this movement, in which they refused to support the militia or to pay taxes while attempting to gain control of the peninsula with the co-operation of the British navy. The legislature prepared to send in two regiments of Continental troops, but some of the state's militia and a detachment from Virginia quelled the insurrection. Trouble continued, however, coinciding early the next year with the similar movement in Delaware, and during 1780 the government dispatched militia to compel the payment of taxes.

Therefore in April 1777 the House of Delegates introduced a strong measure requiring an oath of loyalty from all voters and officials, punishing treason with death and forfeiture of property, and levying fines up to £10,000 or imprisonment up to five years for various activities. The governor and Council could exercise emergency powers during invasion. The Senate attempted, with some success, to modify the measure, in particular eliminating a much more extensive test oath and protecting the interests of men who had left the state.

The debate continued when the ardent Whigs introduced a stronger militia bill providing for the energetic collection of heavy fines for men who refused to serve and requiring another test oath. Those in favor of this policy wanted to force anyone whom a judge or justice considered suspicious to subscribe to an oath of fidelity. Nonsubscribers could not preach, engage in trade, practice medicine, or take part in politics. Apparently anyone, such as the local committees, could turn in a suspect to the judicial authorities. Absentees, defined as whoever who had left the colony after August 14, 1775, must take the oath within twelve months or lose their rights and property. The senators objected because the state ought not to deprive people of their political rights,

property, and their very ability to earn a living merely because they dissented from the majority's opinion. To punish
for active opposition was justified, but for mere neutrality
was not. Oaths do not prevent revolutions, they insisted,
and governments had no right to delve into the secret
thoughts of their subjects. On the contrary, governments
should protect freedom of communication. "Tests of this
nature, it is true, have been imposed by our ancestors, but
we wish to imitate their wise, not impolitic institutions."
When the delegates refused to give in, the Senate vetoed
the act. No doubt the senators were thinking, in the
troubled summer of 1777, that the absentees might soon be
returning triumphant; a man of property might well exercise some caution.

The delegates reintroduced the bill in the fall. By that
time Burgoyne had surrendered and very likely a public
anti-loyalist opinion had solidified. Some idea of the legislative alignment is conveyed by the delegates' 30 to 17 vote
favoring a general test oath: the opposition came primarily
from the centers of loyalist or neutralist strength—Somerset, Dorchester, Baltimore, Harford, and Washington counties. The Senate eliminated the confiscation and sale of
nonjurors' property, but otherwise the act represented an
extreme anti-loyalist measure. A preamble asserted that in a
state, allegiance and protection were reciprocal: no one was
entitled to the benefit of one if he refused the other. Every
person should attest his attachment and fidelity to the government. The law required a universal oath of allegiance.
Nonjurors would pay a treble tax for life, and could not sue
in court, engage in trade, practice any profession, hold office, or vote. Traitors, if found guilty by law, lost their
property.

Roughly two-thirds of the men took the oath. The local

proportion varied with the energy of the justices, of course, but primarily with the people's attitude toward the war. The outcome revealed continuing loyalism in the areas already noted, and stimulated additional measures, including acts which granted the executive emergency powers. During succeeding months the legislature received numerous petitions from nonjurors, begging relief from the treble tax on such grounds as ignorance, religious scruples, or even service in the militia. The legislature rejected these but in 1779 suspended the tax temporarily. Subsequent legislatures extended the suspensions, gradually began to relieve some individuals, and finally repealed the tax entirely in the fall of 1782.

An even more prolonged contest involved the confiscation of estates. Debate began in 1777 when the lower house attempted to confiscate the property of nonjurors and narrowly defeated an act seizing proprietary lands. The major effort, however, started in December 1779. It arose, as the delegates frankly stated, from the urgent need for money. When the Senate pleaded lack of time for considering what it called an extraordinary measure, the delegates replied that the state could not continue the war without the property. The people simply lacked money to meet Congress's requests, and paper would not serve because of depreciation. It was better, they asserted, to seize the property of one's enemies than to force loyal citizens to sell their possessions for taxes.

The Senate, in its reply vetoing the bill, advised that if the people lacked money for taxes, neither could they purchase the estates. The war might be financed through the sale of back lands, by borrowing, and by taxes, which really were less burdensome than the House believed. Finally, the Senate questioned the legality and justice of so extreme a step. Essentially the two bodies were expounding two familiar opposing economic policies, while also including moral pronouncements.

During the following months the newspapers printed some fifty articles on the subject, evenly divided. The Senate based its argument partly on legal grounds, but it also warned that Maryland might lose the war, and that in any event such sales would benefit only a few speculators while the state would realize little money. Men would lose their property for no crime but absence from the state. The right to acquire and hold property, the senators believed, was a necessary consequence of civil society and ought not to be taken away unless as the result of a violation of some known law, or unless it was incompatible with the safety of the society. The solution to the financial crisis, they asserted, lay in return to a hard-money basis and a repeal of tender laws, after which men would willingly loan money to the state. The lower house continued to insist that the state must obtain the money. The delegates promised to limit confiscation only to enemies, to pay debts due to Maryland citizens, while arguing that the measure was both just and legal.

The Senate surrendered in October 1780, apparently because of several new factors, including the British confiscation of American property, their refusal to allow the state to draw on its Bank of England stock, and damage inflicted by the British navy. Two related acts safeguarded the interests of creditors, allowed the purchasers to pay in depreciation certificates, and permitted tenants to buy over a period of years at a price one-tenth below the true value of the land. British debts were excluded at the Senate's insistence. Apparently the legislature had not contemplated the sale of all the property, but the army's urgent demands the following year removed any scruples. By the end of 1781 the state had realized nearly £140,000 from the sales, mostly in paper money, and by 1785 the balance stood at nearly £500,000. The treasury, however, received less than a tenth of this in specie or specie equivalents. Obviously the expected financial gain did not materialize, though its promise may have helped during 1781 and 1782.

Sales continued through the 1780's, but in other respects anti-loyalist measures ceased. In 1781 the legislature removed the prohibition on trading, preaching, and the use of courts. Anyone taking a new oath in 1780 escaped the treble tax, which ended entirely in 1782. By 1786 ex-loyalists could vote and hold office if they took a new oath, and refugees were returning to the state without difficulty.

In sharp contrast to Maryland, Virginia contained relatively few loyalists. The planter leadership suppressed tendencies in that direction before 1776 everywhere except in the southeasternmost area near Norfolk, on the eastern shore, and in Middlesex County. Riots against a draft law occurred in scattered counties during 1781, but posed no danger. The most prominent group of loyalists, and that which created the most difficulty, consisted of the British merchants residing primarily in Norfolk, Portsmouth, and Williamsburg.

The anti-loyalist campaign began with committee actions during 1774. The Assembly presently authorized these committees to seize the estates of anyone who had aided the enemy and refused to take an oath of allegiance on demand. A strong act of May 1776 required confiscation and imprisonment. This measure led to the exodus of scores, if not hundreds, of men, including most of the merchants. The first legislature after Independence incorporated these penalties into a new law which also prescribed death for treason and heavy fines for lesser offenses. But not until May 1777 did the legislature require a universal test oath. This act deprived nonjurors of the right to hold office, serve on juries, sue for debt, or buy land, though evidently they might vote. The state did not exempt Quakers or Mennonites until May 1783. A later act in 1777 took away the right to vote and imposed a double tax, which was tripled the next year. Evidently most Vriginians took the oath.

Beginning in 1777 the legislature turned its attention to the economic aspects of loyalism. The British merchants held two important kinds of property: land and debts. An act of October 1777 enabled Virginians to pay into the state's loan office, for the use of the treasury, debts owing to British subjects. Since the sum at stake exceeded £2 million sterling, and since the debtor could use state currency, a good deal of money was involved. The gradual decline in the value of Virginia's paper, the small sums actually received by the loan office, and moral qualms brought a repeal of the act in May 1780. Meanwhile, about five hundred Virginians paid in £273,544 worth of paper, the sterling equivalent of which was only £15,044. Thus, even if the former figure be accepted as the amount discharged, Virginians had reduced the principle by only one-eighth or thereabouts, not counting interest. These debts remained to plague the people after the war ended.

Virginia did not at first confiscate the remaining British property but administered it for the benefit of the state. The state's finances and the desire of the citizens to profit at the expense of the loyalists led to confiscation in December 1779, the lower house approving by the close vote of 44 to 42. The legislature expected to receive £1.5 million, which it proposed (perhaps as a salve to some consciences) to reserve for Congress. The act applied to British subjects absent from the United States on April 19, 1775 (the day of Lexington and Concord), unless they demonstrated allegiance, to others who left the country, and to those openly aiding the enemy. Sales began at once, the largest sums coming from Norfolk County. By 1783 the state had collected £3 million, but virtually all of this was in paper money. If the ratio of currency to actual specie collected was the same as that for debts, the treasury obtained only £160,000. Sales therefore contributed little to financing the war and failed to maintain the value of the state currency. Almost all of this property consisted of lots, buildings, and land belonging to British merchants, not Virginia planters. The latter, unless they actually joined the enemy, were allowed to sit out the war unharmed. Thus the state did not seize the five-million-acre Fairfax estate as long as Thomas, Lord Fairfax remained alive, though he was a nonjuror. His nephew, an Englishman, successfully inherited one-sixth of the land, and only after a long court battle did the state succeed in transferring title to the major part of the estate from the Fairfax heirs to the settlers.

After the war the exiled merchants returned to resume trade and, ominously, to collect debts. The legislature considered a bill to readmit them, but first postponed and then rejected it. The people expressed their opinion both by petitions and by force, and the treatment of the exiles remained an issue, together with the question of British debts, for some years. In the end they were admitted with few restrictions (1786) and the debts were paid, much later, by the United States government in accordance with Jay's Treaty.

Loyalism in North Carolina also involved many British merchants, but it was far stronger and more complex than in Virginia. A significant group of Scottish immigrants, comparable in some ways to the Johnson followers in New York, remained faithful to the King. The pietistic sects adopted their usual neutralism. A part of the officeholding and planter elite joined the British, and, finally, a considerable number of farmers in the western third of the state favored the royal cause. In sharp contrast to the situation in the Old Dominion, as many men opposed the rebellion as joined it. This situation led to civil war beginning with the loyalists' defeat at Moore's Creek Bridge in 1775 and culminating with their capture of the governor and Council in 1781. Both sides murdered and ruthlessly destroyed property, creating bitterness which lasted long after the war.

North Carolina's rebels needed no legislation to commit their share of atrocities, but the government furnished legal foundations and took punitive action itself. At first the Provincial Congress allowed the Tories who had fought at Moore's Creek Bridge to sell their property before being exiled, but within a month it declared that anyone aiding the enemy forfeited his estates. Already it had authorized the local committees to extract an oath of allegiance from suspects. The first legislature decreed death and forfeiture for treason, and partial forfeiture and imprisonment for other unfriendly actions. Everyone must swear allegiance to the state, Quakers and others taking an affirmation which did not acknowledge an obligation of military service. County courts might require anyone refusing to take the oath to leave the state. In the fall of 1776 another act deprived nonjurors of the right to vote, hold office, sue, acquire land, or keep arms. At the same time the state confiscated the property of those who had sided with the enemy or departed unless they became citizens within a year. The Senate vote of 12 to 9 on this act is very revealing: those favoring the bill came primarily from the northeast, those opposed were from the west. Support for confiscation was coming from the interior, and western delegates were protesting an act which merely started the process because it made no provision for the sale of the property. An act in 1778 amplified these measures, ordering commissions to record all loyalist property and enabling them to sell the personal and rent the real estate after settlement of debts and provision for the family. At the same time the legislature offered nonjurors another chance and again provided a special form for pacifists. This leniency coincided with a lull in the civil war.

Public opinion, however, demanded more decisive measures, and the North Carolina's financial needs presently led to the introduction of a bill listing men whose property was to be confiscated and sharply limiting the rights of the family. The bill authorized the state to sell both the land and the personal property. At first, in January 1779, the bill lost by a two to one margin, the easterners continuing to oppose strong measures. A petition from Mecklenburg County, in the west, remonstrated that their enemies continued to enjoy the profits of the real estate and urged immediate sale both to punish transgressors and help the treasury. The legislature gave in that fall. An angry dissent by conservative representatives from the northeast protested the punishment of women and children and the injustice to innocent merchants. A subsequent measure, passed after the British invasion, together with enthusiastic enforcement, filled the jails with prisoners and resulted in miscellaneous seizures of property. The real estate sold at minimum prices to the great benefit of the purchasers.

Such experiences called for the exercise of some restraint. The legislature suspended sales until it could devise a method that would protect the inoffensive yet realize a return to the treasury. Government-appointed commissioners took over the property in trust. In 1781 a law directed the rental of land and slaves to the highest bidders and punishment of trespassers, and another act gave nonjurors a second chance, fining and threatening further punishment to those who still refused the oath. This moderate policy may have owed something to the British troops, who perhaps frightened some legislators into a less extreme position for fear of reprisal. But the times certainly prevented the state from selling the property at a profit, and the delay was well advised. The lower house would have preferred more drastic measures, but the Senate vetoed two such bills.

North Carolina's policy after 1781 moderated the wartime punishments only gradually. An act of pardon and oblivion in 1783 erased past crimes but excepted those named in the confiscation acts, those who had fought with the British, or those who refused to return within two months. At the same time the legislature repealed the special twofold tax on pacifistic sects, though anyone who refused to take an oath within six months must pay the extra charge. Laws passed in 1783 and 1784 denied to any British adherent the right to vote or to hold civil or military office. The state resumed sales of confiscated property in 1782. The estates supposedly sold at their sterling price, and purchasers could use state certificates only at their specie value. The buyer need not pay for five years, but must give bond with security worth double the value of the property. In 1784 the state rather too generously allowed payment in soldiers' certificates—a clause supported by the western bloc. The eastern delegates, among whom were many Tory friends and sympathizers, persistently tried to moderate the laws and exempt certain individuals, with indifferent success. Laws penalizing the loyalists remained in effect until the end of the decade.

The sale of loyalist estates, typically, brought more benefit to purchasers than to the state. Since the legislature also confiscated debts, the debtors discharged these in depreciated money; such prominent men as William Blount, Willie Jones, and Governor Abner Nash did so. During the earliest period of sales, 1779–1780, North Carolina collected such small sums for personal property that confiscation contributed nothing to financing the war. Sales resumed in 1783 and eventually totaled £600,000. The property may have been worth two-thirds of that sum, but since the buyers paid in paper, the state gained little of actual value. Had this property sold for specie, the state debt might have been reduced by more than a third. The taxpayers might well resent a policy which punished some for the cupidity of others.

South Carolina's loyalism took two quite opposite forms. The back-country, particularly the section around Camden and the district west of the Broad River called Ninety-Six, contained many farmers who had participated earlier in their own Regulator movement and were either pro-British or indifferent. Many of these were recent immigrants. At the other end of the state, Charleston, like other Southern cities, produced loyalist merchants, officials, and their followers. The nearby planters, rebel in sympathies, could not always resist the temptation to swear allegiance to the King in order to save their property. Had the British captured Charleston at the outset of the war, as they did Boston, they might well have won over a majority of the inhabitants. But they did not succeed until 1780, by which time many of

the capital's Tories had long since fled and the interior loyalists dispersed.

The state took energetic action against the internal threat
in April 1776. A law required a loyalty oath of officials and
of anyone suspected of being unfriendly, depriving nonjurors of their right to hold office and property. The government also confiscated the estates of those who left the state,
though no sales took place. Another law levied a double
tax on those who refused the oath and presently on absentees. These laws at first did not extend to the great majority
of citizens, who took no oath yet continued to vote. Growing wartime animosities gradually led to more severe measures. In March 1778 everyone was required to swear allegiance to the state, and later in the year an act empowered
not only justices of the peace but militia officers to administer the oath. Nonjurors now were compelled, under penalty of death, to sell their property and leave the state. In
1778 the legislature granted emergency powers to the governor, enabling him to arrest and jail potential enemies in
case of invasion—an authority which Governor Rutledge
found very useful.

The British conquest of 1780 threw the state into anarchy
and prevented further measures for many months. During
this period many Carolinians, especially in the low-country,
joined the British or accepted British protection. When the
legislature finally reassembled in February 1782, it took vigorous punitive action. Anyone who had withdrawn allegiance to the state or showed pro-British tendencies lost the
right to vote. More than two hundred men were deprived
of their estates which, by law, would be sold in relatively
small tracts of two hundred to five hundred acres in order
to stimulate immigration, improve agriculture, and discour-

age monopolies. An even larger number suffered an amercement ranging from 12 to 30 per cent. During the first two years of sales the government sold £18,000 worth of slaves to obtain money for legislators, judges, and soldiers. Returns from the sale of land fell far short of expectations, and also of their real value, partly because claims of creditors ate up much of the cash, and because the treasury accepted bonds without any security. On paper the sales totaled £700,000 or even more, but the cash value to the state was far lower. Certainly they came too late to help finance the war.

Scarcely had the confiscation act passed than efforts began to relieve individual loyalists from penalties. Friends and relatives of the principal sufferers rallied to their support and succeeded in reducing many penalties from total confiscation to amercement and from amercement to entire forgiveness. British merchants and others who had remained in Charleston during the occupation, and who had taken oaths of loyalty to the King at that time, were amerced but allowed to remain in the city, at first temporarily, then permanently. An outburst of public hostility reached a climax in riots during 1784, but the city's elite quickly suppressed them. By March 1787 the delegates from Charleston and the low-country parishes succeeded in passing a law which allowed ex-Governor William Bull to return, and the next year they succeeded in restoring such confiscated estates as remained unsold. Western representatives continued adamantly opposed to moderation, which now had won the support of practically all the delegates from eastern South Carolina.

Georgia's loyalism resembled that of her neighbor. An important group of merchants and officials, including the older leaders of the colony, supported the Crown as did miscellaneous residents of the interior, consisting of German and other immigrants, Quakers, and some frontiersmen. The loyalist problem therefore resolved into two separate conflicts. In the back-country a civil war led to severe personal punishments but seldom to confiscation of property. On the coast the antagonists clashed over the seizure of valuable estates.

The constitution of February 1777 required a loyalty oath for voting and holding office, and a law later in the year expelled the state's enemies. On March 1, 1778, the legislature confiscated, and provided for the prompt sale of, property belonging to 117 named as traitors. To this was added an act in November ordering all nonresidents to return upon pain of confiscation. The British conquest of Savannah in December halted sales, and until 1782 the state engaged in civil war. Beginning in January of that year a series of acts seized the property of an even larger group, levied amercements on some, and expedited sales. At the same time many of the exiles were forbidden to return. Should they re-enter the state after being expelled they were subject to the death penalty.

The acts of 1782 arose from mingled revenge and hope for gain. The state had no money and desperately needed cash. Sales therefore proceeded rapidly and in six months totaled about £345,000, almost none of which brought in any hard money but transferred valuable property at a fraction of its value to politically influential Georgians. The results were so unfair, and the confusion so great, that the legislature suspended operations in 1783, presently instituting better controls and requiring half the payment in specie. All told the state disposed of more than £400,000 worth but actually received little except bonds. The government did, however, obtain a limited revenue from selling personal property, especially slaves, and it settled some debts and obligations by giving away land. The government's mismanagement of a considerable resource became a political issue in later years.

Meanwhile, anti-Tory feeling gradually subsided. Men once banished began to return in 1783, as did British traders, despite the usual outcry of protest. In 1785 the legislature granted almost full rights to aliens. As in South Carolina, confiscations were reduced to amercements and amercements forgiven, until in the end only a few hundred men had suffered any major loss of property.

The loyalist question appeared in every state in much the same light, though varying greatly in intensity, and it followed everywhere a similar sequential pattern subject to the fortunes of war and finance. The first problem confronting the patriots on the home front was to identify the loyalists in order to repress them. Loyalty oaths served as the instrument in the hands of local committees or officials. At first only an individual suspected of pro-British sentiments might face the demand that he swear allegiance to the rebel cause, but as the Revolutionary movement polarized the entire people, everyone was forced to declare his position. Those who were not for the War for Independence must be against it. The new governments therefore formally required each citizen to pledge allegiance to the state and disown the King.

Next came the punishment of nonjurors. From the first they lost the right to hold civil or military office. Then they were denied the right to vote. These penalties, imposed during 1776 and the first months of 1777, eliminated both open loyalists and neutralists from the political process without discriminating between them. The latter escaped with two further penalties. Service in the militia became obligatory, and anyone who held religious prejudices against force or who otherwise refused to enlist was compelled to pay a fine. In addition, many states levied special taxes on nonjurors, so that every member of the community contributed to the war effort whether he would or not. The actual enforcement of these laws, however, varied considerably, and despite the states' growing need for money they often forgave the additional tax. A few legislatures imposed further penalties on the inoffensive nonjurors, such as forbidding them to engage in trade or practice a profession, but ordinarily they merely paid a fine of some sort, lost their political rights, and then lived in peace.

When, however, the British threatened actual invasion, even peaceable neutrals might suffer restrictions because of the fear that they might sell supplies to the enemy, give information, or even turn into active loyalists. Enough such cases occurred to underline the danger. Therefore the governor and council made use of emergency powers to seize and hold or exile potential enemies. The removal of Quaker leaders from Philadelphia into Virginia is the most dramatic example, but many others were temporarily jailed or sent to a remote place. A certain amount of suffering and loss of property accompanied these actions, but they did not last long and caused no loss of life.

The open loyalist, who aided the enemy or sought British protection, received less lenient treatment. State legislatures early defined acts of treason and other less heinous crimes. Offenders were variously disarmed, deprived of their property, occasionally imprisoned, sometimes banished, and very rarely put to death, while also of course suffering the penalties shared by neutrals. Usually the open loyalist could not sue in court, buy or sell land, or practice law. In a few instances Tories were denied the right to engage in medicine, the ministry, or trade, but such prohibitions were rare and brief. The severity of the laws differed from state to state, being mildest in New England and Virginia, where the loyalists posed the minimum danger, and in New Jersey and Delaware, where they held much political power; and their enforcement also varied with the military danger. In general, the British adherent who wished to remain in the states enjoyed no freedom of speech, no political rights, and suffered considerable practical, if not legal, economic disabilities.

Those who exposed themselves as traitors risked everything. Actual loss of life rarely occurred except, of course, when the loyalists engaged in military operations. In such states as New York, New Jersey, and the Carolinas, loyalists waged a guerrilla warfare with the inevitable result. Since neither side abided by the customary rules, and since the distinction between military and civilian blurred or vanished, the line between combat death and murder also disappeared. Each side justified its own atrocities and condemned those of the other. These circumstances existed only locally and occasionally even in the states mentioned. Elsewhere almost no loyalist lost his life except for crimes deemed capital in peace as well as in war, or except as a result of some hardship, accidental rather than deliberate.

Property losses necessarily accompanied exile. The refugees took their personal belongings with them where they could, but much remained behind, notably debts owed to them and slaves. In some instances the legislatures or their predecessors allowed those who wished to depart to sell such property. As time went on, however, laws stiffened, and the exiles left everything behind. Land and houses, of course, remained where they were. At first the government "sequestered" most of such holdings—preserved them and tried to make money from them but did not sell them, except for perishables. But some legislatures took title to—confiscated—the property of the more obnoxious enemies.

Pressure for extensive confiscation followed by universal sale began at once and ultimately proved irresistible in every state. The motives were various. The legislatures argued that the British government, having started the whole affair, bore ultimate responsibility, and anyone adhering to the Crown shared the blame for the enormous cost involved. Therefore why should not the British pay for the war? Furthermore, the royal army and navy, often aided by loyalists, destroyed vast amounts of property, for example in the burning of Newport and during the occupation of Pennsylvania. Estimating losses suffered in the most notorious cases, one could easily obtain a figure of several million pounds sterling and, if the total cost of the war be included, several times that sum. Confiscation acts in Maryland and South Carolina, as well as in Rhode Island and Pennsylvania, resulted immediately from this factor. This argument justified the seizure not simply of loyalist property but that of all British citizens. As time passed and wartime emotions intensified, revenge became increasingly important as a motive, for example in Delaware and South Carolina.

Pressure also came from creditors who wished to recover their debts from loyalists or from British subjects. As long as property remained in the possession of its owners, their chances were nil, but once the government secured it the creditor could apply to the treasury, or to the proper officials, with excellent prospects. These men comprised a small but quite influential group, important in certain states such as Massachusetts.

On the other hand, debtors to loyalists or British firms sought a similar solution to their problems. They escaped prosecution as long as the war continued but faced the certainty of suits thereafter. If, however, the government confiscated these debts, it would certainly make a more lenient creditor, perhaps even allowing payment in depreciated money. As we have seen, the legislatures of both Maryland and Virginia considered this question with opposite results.

Other men also strove for personal profit—those who hoped to buy valuable property for a fraction of its value. They did not publicize their motives, but three kinds of evidence reveal them at work: first, contemporaries stated that the advocates of confiscation intended this result; second, the laws permitted purchase in depreciated money finally, we know that speculators actually did obtain large tracts. Georgia furnishes the most obvious illustration, but, as a further example, fraud also forced New Jersey and North Carolina to suspend sales.

Last but very important among the motives behind confiscation, the states hoped to receive badly needed money from the sale of this property. During the early years of the war the states seldom touched these estates except for the sale of perishables and for rentals of land, buildings, and slaves. Confiscation laws transferring title came in 1777 and 1778, though three states waited until 1779. But even then the legislatures usually delayed before extensive sales. This final step almost invariably coincided with the financial crisis of 1779–1780, or with a later emergency. Legislatures sometimes anticipated the receipt of cash for current expenses, especially payments of enlistment bounties to soldiers and salaries to key officials. They also expected that the estates, considered as a resource, would provide security for paper money, thus shoring up the depreciating currency of 1779–1780. Advocates of deficit financing, opposed to a system based on taxes and loans, hoped to avert the collapse of their system. Later, confiscated loyalist property served as collateral for the loans of 1781–1782. Still later, governments began to retire their debt by allowing the people to purchase the estates with certificates, especially soldiers' depreciation notes. Virtually every state opened such sales with high hopes of profit. Pressure for this action therefore came not only from the least loyalist areas (for example, northern Delaware rather than southern, east Jersey rather than west) but from regions or peoples most anxious to lighten the tax burden and reduce the debt painlessly, such as the New York Clintonians and the settlers in the Carolina uplands.

In the end the states took over property worth around £5 million sterling, but the treasuries and the taxpayers realized little benefit. Practically no specie exchanged hands, and the payment of certificates reduced the specie debt not by £5 million but by a far smaller sum, possibly only a tenth of that amount. A useful trickle during the last years of the war helped with specie expenditures, and the potential of a much larger income probably did help maintain the credit of some states. But the principal beneficiaries were the purchasers, who secured valuable property for a fraction of its true worth.

As the fighting ended, defenders of the loyalists tried to remove the disabilities. They had always considered harsh measures unnecessary and unfair, and could point to many instances of injustice. Now that the United States faced no danger to its security, the laws lost their principal moral justification. The treaty with England undermined their legality by the clause calling upon (though not actually requiring) the states to repeal all anti-Tory legislation. Friends and relatives of refugees supported their readmission, the restoration of such property as remained unsold, and the remission of fines. They favored an end to discriminatory oaths and the granting of full citizenship to all but the most active Tories. Gradually they succeeded in all their objectives.

The return of the refugees became an issue in every state during 1783–1785. Communities of all sorts expressed horror that enemies to liberty should return, perhaps to conspire against the new governments. The principal excitement, however, appeared in the towns where in some instances mobs arose again to torment the enemy. These outbursts expressed the usual hostility plus an economic motive, for many townsmen had bought loyalist estates, others had moved into positions vacated by the exiles, and some owed money to loyalists. Few of the prominent Tories ever returned, though some of the more inconspicuous crept back. Prejudices lingered for years, but by the mid-1780's legal restrictions were vanishing.

Similarly, the legislatures modified test oaths so that a former loyalist might subscribe without qualm. Opposition took no systematic form except in Pennsylvania where the repeal became a party issue. Special fines and taxes ceased with the fighting. The restoration of estates remained controversial for some years, especially where sectional and class antagonisms merged with the economic and emotional. Thus in the Carolinas western farmers resisted the attempt of eastern merchants, lawyers, and great landholders to halt sales. By the late 1780's the exchange of property was almost completed and the question became academic.

On the whole, the treatment of the loyalists seems both lenient and justifiable. They seriously threatened the success of the Revolution. Thousands fought for the British; other thousands fed information or supplies to the invaders; the rest resisted taxes, helped to depreciate the currency, refused military service, or sullenly withheld support from the struggle for independence. No people fighting for survival can act with more restraint against internal enemies. The wonder is not that some loyalists suffered but that so few civilian loyalists lost their lives. Only a small percentage fled the country and of these, no more than five thousand claimed loss of property, scarcely one twenty-fifth of those men who hoped for a British victory. The legislatures delayed confiscation until several years of hard fighting had nearly bankrupted the states, when it seemed that without additional resource their cause was lost, and after the British had already inflicted great damage to property. Only then did the states act.

There is indeed another side. In some states the absence of harsh measures is attributable to fear of alienating the neutrals rather than to restraint, while in other states the loyalists posed no threat. Injustices did occur. Individuals committed crimes against the persons and property of loyalists. Confiscation acts transferred valuable estates from one set of individuals to another with little profit to the state, and the exile or imprisonment of Tories often caused needless hardship. On the whole, however, the victors had suppressed dissent with little bloodshed—extracted pounds rather than flesh. Unlike some other revolutionaries, they won their freedom without destroying liberty.

# Chapter Nine

# Social Changes
## in the Revolutionary Era

FOUR circumstances growing out of the Revolution altered American society during the years after 1776. First, the departure of the loyalists and the confiscation of their property as well as of the estates belonging to the Crown, the proprietors, and other British citizens, enabled many men to acquire or enhance their wealth and prestige. Second, the removal of various restrictions on westward expansion permitted a rapid movement of population into new territory, a development that increased the people's mobility and the nation's prosperity. Third, the humanitarian impulse implicit in Revolutionary ideology led to a movement to emancipate the slaves and, less successfully, to encourage greater economic and social equality. Finally, the same equalitarian impulse combined with other factors to accelerate the decline of deferential attitudes and of a social order based on consensus, in favor of a more individualistic point of view.

Historians have long debated the results of the confiscation and sale of loyalist estates. Some have perceived a division of large holdings into smaller ones as contributing to an economic democracy, while others have discovered only a substitution of one group of well-to-do men for another equally prosperous. These conflicting interpretations grow out of microscopic studies of events in particular states or even counties. Reviewing these studies as a whole, it seems clear that the "substitution" interpretation applies to the valuable properties owned by wealthy loyalists in the towns and commercial farming regions, and that the democratization involved primarily the extensive, lightly populated tracts of the interior. Purchase of the most desirable estates, the highly developed farms, the town houses and lots, and the slaves, required what only men of means possessed: cash or credit. Had the states deliberately set out to assist people of little or no property, they would have been obliged to forgo any quick profit and to arrange appropriate credit facilities. But the states rarely expressed such intent, wanted cash badly, and restricted credit to purchasers with good security. Most of the property sold, therefore, to men with cash, credit, or influence.

A survey of our rather spotty knowledge about the disposition of loyalist property will illustrate the process. New Hampshire confiscated about £70,000 worth, very roughly 10 per cent of the state's total value. Widows and children retained some of it (they were entitled to a third), creditors claimed another share, and the rest sold for a fraction of its value, apparently accompanied by a good deal of fraud.

The important loyalists lived in Portsmouth, and though they owned land all over the state, the principal beneficiaries of their losses probably were Portsmouth men. The people as a whole certainly improved their prospects by ridding themselves of Governor Wentworth, whose practice of granting land to himself and his favorites, together with his monopoly over the mast business, had already milked the colony of considerable wealth. But the transfer of estates probably had little direct effect on society.

The rich loyalists of Massachusetts who suffered confiscation also lived in the trading centers, primarily along the coast. In 1779 the legislature authorized the sale by public auction of the most important properties, including those of Thomas Hutchinson. These realized £132,410 in Essex County, £464,814 in Suffolk, and additional sums elsewhere, but the figures are in depreciated currency and the state received little hard cash. After an interval, sales resumed in 1781. Although Massachusetts' money system was now based on specie, the treasury again gained little, much of the potential cash being reserved for widows, children, and creditors who in fact gave their permission for every sale and reaped most of the proceeds. The state realized only £57,768.

The only existing study of confiscation in Massachusetts deals entirely with Suffolk. There only a small fraction of the property lay outside Boston, where it involved less than 1 per cent of the land. Sales in Boston amounted to about 11 per cent of the value of the city's real estate, but the transfer did not change the pattern of ownership. On the contrary, the early auctions sold the estates of eight men to twenty-six, and later ninety-two men bought the property of forty-six loyalists. Nearly all the property passed into the hands of rising entrepreneurs, some of whom had moved into the town after the British evacuated, and almost none of whom had been prominent earlier. A couple of dozen artisans and mariners did seize this chance to increase their property at bargain rates, but fundamentally the process transferred city real estate from part of the old colonial elite to a segment of the new upper class, who thereby stabilized their position.

No such detailed study exists for Rhode Island, but it matters little, for confiscation affected only a few individuals. Some of the larger properties taken over by the state belonged to Bostonians such as Thomas Hutchinson, his close associate Andrew Oliver, and the Merchant John Borland who owned the thousand-acre Point Judith farm at the entrance to Narragansett Bay. The displacement of such absentee proprietors by resident owners may register a social gain of sorts, but since the Point Judith farm was sold to three other merchants the social impact was negligible. The other loyalists came from Newport; their departure, like the exodus from Boston, doubtless affected the people there but caused scarcely a ripple in the rest of the state.

Lack of information prevents us from reaching any conclusions about the social effects of confiscation in Connecticut. The original owners, the wealthiest of whom had been merchants, lived primarily along the coast, so the sales did not affect the great mass of the farmers. The loyalists later claimed losses of a quarter of a million pounds, of which three-fourths consisted of properties worth at least £2,000 and up. The redistribution may have resulted in some social leveling in the coastal areas, but in the state as a whole not more than 1 per cent of the total changed hands, and according to one historian too few loyalists lost property to affect the distribution of property.

New York's case differed fundamentally from that of

Connecticut because the state had confiscated some huge properties, including, for example, the Johnson lands along the Mohawk and those of Oliver DeLancey, Beverly Robinson, Roger Morris, Frederick Phillipse, and John Watts in the south. Thirty-nine of these men later claimed losses of more than £10,000 each; the state ought to have added £1.5 million to the treasury. As much as 10 per cent of the state's wealth may have changed hands. Authorities differ concerning the effects of this vast transferral, some arguing that the land merely passed from one elite to another, others perceiving a trend toward wider ownership.

Sales in the north and west involved over 160,000 acres which sold for £172,559, at least on paper. Although the original act specified that no one could buy more than five hundred acres and that tenants should be given priority in the bidding, actually during the first few years the moneyed men in the area bought most of the land. After the war ended, however, thousands of settlers moved into the area and competed with the more well-to-do. Some tenants also began to buy, and early purchasers began to sell their holdings, often at a considerable profit. This process continued for several decades. Ultimately nearly three hundred individuals bought the land of forty-five men through initial sales, and resales further broadened the class of new owners. Still, considering that not hundreds but thousands of settlers flooded onto New York's lands, the expansion of ownership from this particular process appears minor. The major change in the upstate region occurred not because of the sale of loyalist land but as a result of the removal of the Iroquois and the exile of the Johnsons, whose great properties along the Mohawk had blocked westward expansion except for their tenants.

In southern New York, too, some tenants gained freehold

status, as did nearly two hundred on the fifty-thousand-acre Phillipse estate in Westchester County. Dutchess County, immediately to the north, contained two enormous manors belonging to Beverly Robinson and Roger Morris, which now passed into the hands of more than four hundred individuals, half of whom obtained property they had once rented. Some of these eventually lost their farms through inability to complete payments to the state, but other small purchasers benefited from later resales. A large part of this property, however, came into the possession of men already well-off. Successful Whig business and professional men, both newcomers and members of established families, profited by the displacement of wealthy loyalists.

The net effects of confiscation in New York varied greatly. New York City and the nearby areas experienced little net social change. But in the upstate counties hundreds of families became independent farmers on land once owned by Tory magnates. Thus New York's loyalists had unwillingly contributed their mite toward a more democratic society.

The loyalists in New Jersey lost only a third as much property as those in New York, nor did they own quite such large tracts of land. Daniel Coxe claimed to have lost £40,000, David Ogden about £20,000, and six others held, or pretended to have owned, estates in excess of £10,000. Nine-tenths lay in East Jersey, almost half in the two counties of Bergen and Middlesex.

The only detailed account of the loyalist sale applies to Bergen County. Unfortunately it covers only the first few years when transfers there were relatively minor. This study indicates that property belonging to forty-eight men fell into the hands of fifty persons among whom only a few were tenants. Other evidence strongly suggests that the state's commissioners in charge of the sales, and their friends, bought most of the land, using depreciated money worth between two and fifteen cents on the dollar. Two of the major beneficiaries were Frederick Frelinghuysen, a commissioner, eminent lawyer, patriot, member of Congress, and future United States Senator, and his ally William Paterson, also a lawyer, Senator-to-be, currently the state's attorney general, and eventually its governor. Although these men probably bought on speculation, no one has traced the process. Whatever the results, they were limited primarily to the area near New York.

Pennsylvania took over two types of property. First, the state acquired the proprietary land, paying the Penns £130,000 sterling. Since the Penns themselves had been selling this property before the Revolution, the state's acquisition had but a limited effect. If the state sold the land for less than the Penns, the purchasers would benefit, but of course the government would receive less money and might be forced to impose taxes in order to pay off the Penns. The people saved money by being relieved of quit-rents, but that did not affect the distribution of wealth. Besides the purchase of the Penns' lands, the government confiscated and sold the properties of more than four hundred individuals, primarily in the populous southeast, including, as usual, wealthy men such as the Quaker merchant Samuel Shoemaker and the lawyer Joseph Galloway. Their combined wealth, however, did not exceed 2 per cent of the total property in the state, since most of the upper class retained their estates. As far as we know, the sales simply enabled members of the same class to increase their property.

Delawareans inherited no such windfall as their neighbors, for only forty-six men acted so openly as to expose themselves to confiscation. Their total wealth did not exceed £20,000 within the state, though at least one also owned land elsewhere. This sum represents an insignificant proportion of the state's total property. New Castle County contained most of it, which sold for £150,000 in the inflated currency of those years. We do not know who bought it, but so small an exchange could effect only a negligible result.

By contrast Maryland, like Pennsylvania, took over the proprietary estates and other property. Henry Harford, heir to the Calverts' princely grant, owned more than 250,000 acres in the settled part of the state and 125,000 in the west, which he considered worth £327,441 and which certainly would bring more than £200,000. In addition, the sale of the Principio Company, a British-owned ironworks, enriched the treasury by £87,000. The government also realized £21,000 from another British firm and £83,000 from the estate of Daniel Dulany. All together the state confiscated the estates of more than 150 individuals and companies, eleven of which exceeded £10,000 in value, totaling more than £600,000.

With the exception of the proprietary holdings, this property passed into the hands of Maryland's economic upper class. In Baltimore, for example, twenty-four men bought twenty-five estates, paying an average of some £1,500, and the Dulany lots and houses in Annapolis went to eleven men for well over £1,000 each. These purchasers were primarily merchants and lawyers (including such prominent men as Samuel Chase, Luther Martin, Daniel Carroll, and William Paca). Baltimore businessmen bought the Principio Company's valuable property. Essentially, then, the wealth of British and loyalist entrepreneurs benefited patriotic businessmen.

On the other hand, Henry Harford's land and a few other extensive rural tracts did benefit some small property holders. The usual interpretation celebrates the opportunity for Harford's tenants to obtain title to their rented farms. The law did allow them a 10 per cent reduction in price, but apparently many of the tenants simply could not raise enough cash, even in certificates. Often the men who actually bought the farms already owned land and the tenants stayed on, continuing to pay rent. The sales therefore did not make tenants into freeholders but often resulted only in enhancing the possessions of men who were already property owners. The replacement of the proprietor did enable some tenants to acquire land, but it cannot be called a social revolution.

Some social gains also accrued to the three thousand ex-soldiers and the pioneers who obtained as bounties or for a low price the 125,000 acres Harford owned in the west. The proprietors would have disposed of this land eventually, but their asking price of a pound per acre in the settled areas and seven shillings sixpence in the west was too steep; the state charged half or a third as much. Some democratization of landholding may have occurred later on too, when certain speculative purchasers who had given bond for payment at a future date defaulted, as often happened, or resold the land on credit to others, providing the means to buy land where the state had not.

In Virginia also, the government seized one huge property and many smaller estates held mostly by British firms. Few among the native-born elite suffered any loss; John Randolph, Thomas and Richard Corbin, Jr., and William Byrd Page were exceptions. British merchants who had invested heavily in real estate accounted for most of the total, Norfolk County alone containing one-third. These properties sold for £3 million, but the figures are enormously inflated because sales took place mostly in 1779 and 1780. Thus one and a half acres and a building in Norfolk brought £50,000, probably forty times their sterling value. Evidently (for we lack precise data) Virginians with considerable extra cash bought most of this, so that property passed from Britishers to Americans without other social consequences.

The single great holding belonged to the Fairfax family, who had leased much of their grant between the Rappahannock and the Potomac but still claimed over five million acres. In 1776 this belonged to Thomas, Lord Fairfax, a Virginian who did not take the oath of allegiance but remained unmolested, blithely renting land until his death late in 1781. When he died he left most of this tremendous estate to a brother and one-sixth to a nephew, Denny Martin Fairfax. The latter remained in possession of his 220,000 acres, but Virginia confiscated the rest in 1782. Both the Fairfax family and the government now proceeded to sell land; at issue also were the rents collected by the Fairfaxes from their tenants. Ultimately, in 1796, the land that had been granted passed into possession of the settlers, the rest going to the state. To some extent therefore the Revolution in Virginia helped to free tenants from their inferior economic status and transferred what was left of the Fairfax grant from the English lords to the public.

North Carolina confiscated about the same number of properties as did the Old Dominion, and except for the Fairfax estate the results differed little. The only really large tract belonged to the Earl of Granville's heirs. He, like Fairfax, had obtained title to a big slice of northern Carolina, for which the trustees claimed £365,749. The state added this property to the general public domain. Henry

McCulloch valued his sixty thousand acres at £54,265. This land lay in the central and western part of the state and sold in plots averaging two hundred acres to more than a hundred purchasers, some of whom picked up a number of sections. The next largest property belonged to a mercantile firm which lost debts rather than land, several prominent politicians paying obligations in paper. Except for the Granville trace, the sale of these estates could not have significantly affected the state's society. The loss of some large holdings are balanced by purchases of nearly equal size, and while some men bought small tracts others forfeited them. Since almost all of the great landowners sided with the rebels, the native upper class emerged untouched, while the rest of the people gained or lost with little net change.

The loyalists of South Carolina, like those of the other Southern states, consisted primarily of British merchants, officials, and numerous small farmers. The estates of the latter, insofar as they formed part of the confiscated property, contributed little to social mobility because they merely passed into the hands of other men of equal status, a few perhaps poorer, others richer, the net effect doubtful. In South Carolina we may therefore ignore more than a third of the men who lost their posesssions and who lived in the back-country.

The crucial group consisted mostly of Charlestonians. These men claimed losses of around a million pounds sterling, doubtless an exaggerated estimate. The treasury sold this property after the currency devaluation for at least £700,000, though the state did not actually obtain any such sum. Therefore between 5 and 7 per cent of the total wealth of the state changed hands. Although the people generally gained no direct benefit except, no doubt, some satisfaction at seeing their enemies suffer, those living in Charleston witnessed the transfer of a significant proportion of that city's property. Unfortunately we do not know the details of the sales. The law required that the land be divided into tracts smaller than five hundred acres, but the commissioners were authorized to dispose of larger blocs if the requirement threatened "great and manifest prejudice" to the sale. The purchaser buying on credit must offer security in land, which effectively prevented any landless person, and probably any poor person, from buying at all. It seems likely that in practice, well-to-do men, with the necessary credit, picked up most of this windfall, giving in payment bonds rather than cash.

The probability of this guess increases from a study of the confiscation in Georgia. The amount at stake was somewhere between the £400,000 received by the state and the £600,000 claimed by the loyalists, the former figure being more likely. The property belonged mostly to well-to-do merchants and officials in Savannah, the exceptions contributing nothing toward social change. Most of these holdings were sold during the first few months after the passage of the act, the purchasers giving bonds of doubtful value. In the end only 188 men bought the property of 166 loyalists, of whom the most notable were ex-Governor James Wright and the wealthy merchant and planter, Councilor John Graham. Beneficiaries included Generals Nathanael Greene, who received a beautiful estate worth more than £4,000 once belonging to Graham, and Anthony Wayne, to whom the state gave one of Wrights' plantations. Twelve men bought more than one-seventh of the state's total. These, like the other large purchasers, represented a mixture of well-established families who simply augmented their wealth, and some men only now risen to prominence. The exchange of loyalist properties thus aided some of the Whig leaders to replace the Tory elite but did not affect the rest of the people.

An assessment of the social consequences of confiscation must distinguish between the transfer of loyalist property generally and that of a few very large holdings. The men who submitted claims to the British government estimated their losses at £8 million sterling, which most observers, aided by logic, consider exaggerated. The uncertain value of state certificates precludes an exact estimate of what the states would have received had they obtained specie from the sale, but £5 million sterling seems close. This figure then stands as a reasonable guess within an error of 20 per cent.

What portion of the country's wealth did this represent? Connecticut's assessment list, upon which the state based its taxes, came to nearly £2 million (local money), which an informed observer considered one-twelfth of the true figure, or slightly more than £100 per person. Pennsylvania's list was £40 million, also just over £100 per person. Assessment lists for other states, while unreliable, indicate a similar average, which in sterling would vary from £50 to £67, and £150 million or more for the whole country.

This rough estimate seems reasonable if we examine the value of probated estates. One small sample for the middle states, which omits money and debts receivable, yields a figure of £48 sterling per head, slightly lower than that obtained from a much larger number of inventories in New Hampshire, Massachusetts, New Jersey, Virginia and South Carolina. This data suggests a total value for the nation's real and personal property of very nearly £150,000 sterling. Thus less than 4 per cent of the nation's real and personal estates changed hands.

Even had the states wrested every bit of this from the

hands of rich men and redistributed it among the poor, the distribution of wealth would have remained essentially unchanged except in certain areas. Actually our survey, though incomplete, shows conclusively that at least three-fourths if not more of the total property enriched the well-to-do traders, professionals, and speculators who alone commanded the capital or credit to buy it. Some of these men descended from old families, others were of humble birth. In either case, loyalist property did not make them wealthy, did not by itself create social change, but rather ratified and solidified a process already completed in which the new elite displaced part of an old one.

When we consider the great proprietary and similar tracts, however, we reach a different conclusion. In New York the great properties of the Johnsons, the Penn and Harford lands in Pennsylvania and Maryland, the Fairfax grant in Virginia, and that of the Granvilles in North Carolina totaled millions of acres. Had the Revolution never occurred, these properties would have continued to enrich their lordly owners. Moreover, the British government and their American governors had displayed an alarming tendency toward granting more such magnificent estates. Some of this property now became the outright possession of former tenants, either by purchase from the commissioners in charge of sales or by free grant of the state. The rest was bought by a mixture of new settlers, local farmers, and speculators. Unoccupied lands became public property, and though the states eventually sold much of it to large purchasers, some went to small farmers. In either case the owners held the land as freeholders, not as renters. In addition, the states gave large tracts to soldiers as a reward for their services, or sold land to them cheaply for their certificates. Whereas previously the Penns, Calverts, Fairfaxes, and others had extracted thousands of pounds in the form of quit-rents, now the farmers retained for their own use the land's returns, except what they paid for taxes. Much of this land did enable men to improve their status from tenant or even propertyless to landowner, and did democratize the rural class structure in certain areas.

More important than any of these individual transfers of property, the states came into possession of all the western territory held by the British government, particularly the whole Ohio region. Thus Georgia's huge back-country, which at this point extended to the Mississippi, belonged to the people, whose representatives could dispose of it, just as the land of Tennessee belonged to North Carolina and the vast territory now Kentucky and West Virginia to Virginia. Perhaps the British government would have encouraged purchase by small freeholders rather than by speculators or great landholders, but the trend seems to have been the other way. Whatever the demerits of the policies followed by the state governments, they were, after all, the work of local representatives.

Another circumstance favored a major expansion of settlers into much of this new territory: the decline of the Indians' military strength. The Iroquois no longer postponed the white occupation of western New York and Pennsylvania, and in Kentucky, though sporadic attacks continued, white settlers poured through the mountain passes. Indians still blocked expansion farther south, but Carolinians could exploit large tracts of vacant land just as New Englanders could move into the mountain valleys of New Hampshire and Vermont.

Historians disagree about the effects of this westward movement, but an agricultural society confined to a limited geographical area surely affords less opportunity to the man who begins life without land, than one that permits almost unrestricted migration onto fertile, comparatively cheap soil. The former situation tends to freeze the social order, the latter animates it. In all probability, then, it was not the estates of loyalists that encouraged social mobility among the people of the thirteen states but the opening up of the West. During the half-dozen years after the war, 200,000 people occupied the fresh lands from the Mohawk to the Georgia frontier. While some of these may have been merely moving from one farm to another, many must have found opportunities in the West denied them at home. Perhaps in this way, then, those poor boys and ex-servants and younger sons of farmers who had fought the British for depreciated money may have at last gleaned their reward.

Those most in need of fundamental social change were, of course, the slaves. Several circumstances delayed or prevented laws granting them equal opportunities. First, most whites regarded the blacks, free or servile, as inferior rather than equal. Second, whites in areas of heavy slave population feared that emancipation would lead to a great many evils, including attacks on life and property. Third, the whites believed slavery to be profitable—the price of slaves remained high, responding to a continuing demand. These factors minimized the slaves' chances for freedom. On the other hand, for many years major forces had worked toward emancipation. The victims themselves tried to obtain their freedom by whatever means offered: revolts, which proved counterproductive because they led to death penalties and more stringent laws; running away, which freed the lucky or the hardy but brought repression to those left behind; exceptional services to the whites, such as enlistment in the army; and in the North by court suits. These activities affected the slave population as a whole only slightly, for the number of slave births and of importations greatly exceeded the number of liberated blacks. Still, such continual signs of discontent proved to any impartial observer that the slaves desperately wished to be free, a conviction urged by the freed negroes who constantly pressed for total abolition. More decisively, a growing proportion of whites became convinced that slavery was evil, sometimes through their own personal experiences, occasionally as a result of Enlightenment ideas about the equality of man and the right of the individual to freedom, most often through religious conviction. In particular, the Quakers and other pietistic sects, including many Baptists, led the way. Their doctrine taught the existence of an inner light through which God spoke to all men equally. Most Quakers had freed their slaves before 1776. An evolving New England Congregationalism too, insofar as it began to stress salvation instead of damnation, the goodness of man rather than his depravity, and equality instead of election, could not tolerate slavery. The Methodists also favored emancipation at this time. On the other hand, old-fashioned Calvinists, including many Presbyterians, members of the Dutch Reformed church, and some Congregationalists, believed that only a few would be saved and the many condemned to hell. They had no difficulty in identifying themselves with good and all others, including blacks, with sin and punishment. The Anglicans, stressing the hierarchical nature of society in which some men had authority through high rank while those in lowly station obeyed, also could justify slavery. Thus many Americans lacked any compelling religious motive for abolition. They needed a new reason; the Revolution provided one.

We have already seen that the Whig emphasis on liberty, in its political application, contributed to the democratic demand for a popular government. The doctrine of ultimate sovereignty led to notions of immediate sovereignty: if, as a statement from the Carolina back-country argued, England could not tax without the consent of the people, then the local governments also required the consent of the people. But if the people now were to participate equally in politics, did they not also share economic and social rights? Just as the Pietists, starting with the notion that all men were equal in the eyes of God, tended to infer an equality in every other way and to end with a communitarian ideal, so the advocates of liberty and equality in the political realm perceived a more general application. State constitutions and numerous writers echoed the words of the Declaration of Independence. But whether men acknowledged the logic of this theoretical position depended upon the strength of counteracting forces. In the same way that the possession of power and the acquisition of wealth inhibited many Quakers from following the radical implications of their creed, so the ownership of slaves, racial prejudice, or the fear of social upheaval deterred most whites from pursuing emancipation as a desirable goal. Thus the slaves and the free Negroes gained ground during the Revolution in a degree inversely proportionate to their numbers.

The war itself afforded an opportunity for emancipation through enlistment, especially when the Continental line's shortage of troops became critical. At first, however, only Connecticut and Rhode Island allowed volunteering, and most states forbade any blacks, free or slave, to join the army. Later the New England states sanctioned enlistments, in part because Negroes accepted low bounties, and by the end of the war the states as far south as Virginia were drafting free blacks, but not slaves. Whites generally regarded slaves with guns as more dangerous to their masters than to the enemy, and moreover a dead or maimed black represented a substantial money loss. In addition, Southern whites refused to serve on an equal basis with members of the inferior race, so that blacks could be used only in menial capacities, not as soldiers. Few slaves gained by volunteering.

New Englanders, with the fewest slaves, had the least excuse for delay. They achieved emancipation almost furtively, with no public comment and certainly no self-praise. Indeed, we have absolutely no idea how slavery ended in New Hampshire. The legislature passed no law and the courts rendered no known decision, but there were 656 slaves in 1775 and only 157 in 1790. Not until 1857 did the state explicitly forbid slavery. The process in Massachusetts was almost as well-disguised. Some towns passed resolutions to free the slaves, but most of the active pressure on the legislature came from certain ministers and the negroes themselves. The legislators considered an abolition bill but ultimately referred the question to the Continental Congress, where it died. The proposed constitution of 1778 explicitly recognized slavery, and the voters, in rejecting it, did not protest that clause. Its successor, ratified in 1780, contained nothing on the subject except the usual statement concerning freedom and equality in the declaration of rights. The lower house did pass a bill in 1783 stating that slavery had never been legal in Massachusetts, but the Senate killed it. Some slaves successfully sued for their freedom in the courts, and during the following years apparently all the rest of the blacks thereupon assumed a free status without contest.

Connecticut's slaves won their freedom in a similarly indirect fashion. An initial act encouraged emancipation by relieving masters of responsibility for maintaining slaves after their liberation, also enabling slaveowners to enlist their

Negroes in the army and so escape service themselves. The military motive seems to have outweighed all others, including the ethical. The legislature rejected a measure for outright abolition in 1779 and again in 1780. Then (according to one account) in 1784 Roger Sherman and Richard Law, engaged in revising the statutes, quietly inserted a previously unknown clause freeing all children born in slavery when they reached the age of twenty-five. Since the legislators adopted the entire code with neither amendment nor comment, we have no idea whether they had acted intentionally or accidentally. Another account of the affair states that the legislature itself had added the pertinent clause. In either case there certainly was no fanfare. Thus three New England states abolished slavery without any clear statement of intent.

Rhode Island and Vermont proceeded more openly. Rhode Island had freed slaves who enlisted, but this lasted only briefly despite the excellent military record of the two black battalions. The legislature indicated its ultimate intent by prohibiting, in 1779, the sale of slaves out of the state "until some favourable Occasion may offer" for abolition. Why the present occasion was unfavorable the delegates did not say, but the presence of nearly four thousand blacks (6.5 per cent of the population) may explain it. The legislature delayed, defeated bills fulfilling its promise, and finally granted only a gradual emancipation, freeing children born after passage of the law but allowing owners to retain their current slaves. As late as 1810 more than a hundred remained in bondage. The prize for forthright action therefore belongs, without a contest, to Vermont, whose democratic constitution of 1777 abolished slavery outright. The clause may have freed a few score persons.

If New Englanders did not celebrate their generosity at

least they did not speak out against abolition. In the other Northern states, however, the slaves gained their freedom against open opposition. In New York this lowest class formed a third of the population in King's County, one-fifth in Queens and Richmond, and more than one-tenth in New York City, Ulster, Westchester, and Suffolk. During the war the legislature freed such slaves as enlisted in the army but took no other action. The impetus for further steps came from the Quakers, together with a New York City society founded in 1785, and upstate idealists such as Ephraim Paine, a Connecticut-born sometime preacher and activist democrat who introduced an abolition bill into the Senate. The major contest took place during 1785 in the Assembly, where the southern slaveowners, many of them Dutch, tried to defeat the measure to further postpone the evil day and to deprive free Negroes of various civil rights such as voting, holding office, or bearing witness against a white. They also attempted to levy a £100 fine on any Negro marrying a white. The emancipation act which passed contained only the prohibition against voting, but the Council of Revision vetoed the entire bill ostensibly because of the suffrage restriction. In all probability the councilors used the clause as an excuse to block a measure they fundamentally opposed. The pro-slavery group in the Assembly upheld the veto.

The outcome proved most unfortunate for the slaves, for it prevented the abolition movement from achieving its goal during a period when the legislature favored it. Indeed, the passage of the bill and then the many years' delay that followed suggest the reality of a humanitarian spirit accompanying the Revolution and its decline afterwards. The legislature did halt importations, made emancipation easier, and required trial by jury for slaves accused of capital crimes, but more than a decade would elapse before New Yorkers re-entered the struggle to end slavery completely.

Slaves in New Jersey also made little progress. The state contained fewer of them than did New York, most of whom lived in East Jersey, especially among the Dutch. The initiative toward reform began with the Quakers, who tried unsuccessfully just before the Revolution to obtain a duty on imports and a bill to encourage emancipation. During 1780 and 1781, after the legislature had simply filed away abolitionist petitions, the newspapers carried a series of articles attacking and defending the institution. Adherents insisted that members of this inferior race fared better when cared for by their masters than if they were free, and defended the rights of property. Not until 1785 could the anti-slavery legislators even obtain a committee, and that only to prevent further importations. The same act relieved masters of the requirement that they support their Negroes after emancipation, a measure of dubious benefit to the slaves. In 1790 the state still contained more than eleven thousand slaves and only about two thousand free blacks.

Pennsylvanians had never owned many slaves, and thanks to the Quakers emancipation had begun well before 1776. The Friends, who included a large part of the wealthy residents, held most of the slaves, and their decision to expel slaveowners from the Society meant the enforced manumission of several thousand in the Philadelphia area. Pressure on the legislature, however, diminished after the Quakers lost political power. Fortunately, some leaders of the Constitutionalist party also opposed the institution, and in 1779 they produced a bill which, in conformity with the constitution, the Assembly published for the people's approval. Whites generally agreed that lack of education and experience unfitted mature slaves for freedom, so the act (like that of

Rhode Island) freed only children born after the act's passage and then only after they had served as indentured servants until maturity. White opinion also found expression in clauses outlawing interracial marriages and indenturing freedmen if they did not support themselves. A subsequent version lengthened the term of servitude but eliminated other restrictions. Early in 1780 the legislature passed this measure 34 to 21, the opposition coming from some Presbyterians and Germans who crossed party lines.

The slaveowners did not accept this decision meekly but resorted to delaying tactics. Technically everyone was supposed to register his slaves, and those not so registered went free. Numerous petitions now asked for an extension of time and the reinslavement of those Negroes freed by the failure to register them. Newspaper articles appearing at this juncture justified slavery on the familiar grounds. A majority in the assembly, including men of all sorts, resisted this pressure, and by 1790 the number of slaves had declined to fewer than four thousand.

On the whole the Northern slaves had gained substantially during the Revolution. Probably twenty thousand had won their freedom by 1790, and of the nearly twice that number who remained in yoke, one-fourth would soon gain their liberty. On the other hand, thirty thousand others had no immediate prospects. The whites almost everywhere had conceded limited freedom ungraciously, often accompanied by clauses emphasizing the Negroes' separateness. New York and New Jersey had failed to act at all. Moreover, the improvement in status, when it came, brought few tangible benefits, nor could the Negroes expect any until the whites genuinely accepted the idea that all men are equal.

Most of Delaware's slaves lived on the farms of Sussex

County. New Castle County, northern not only in its geo-graphical location but in its attributes, and Kent in the center, contained relatively few Negroes, and in the latter a large number of black freedmen testified to the institution's decline. In Sussex, on the other hand, the first reliable census—that of 1790—indicates that slaves composed one-fifth of the population. The residents of that area, far from approving manumission, petitioned the legislature for stricter regulation of free Negroes and to prohibit slaves freed in other states from living in Delaware. The state did forbid the importation of slaves in 1787, and special permission was required for exporting them, apparently to prevent the break-up of slave families. The same act allowed the manu-mission of the Negroes but confined them to the nether world of the social order: they could not vote, hold office, testify against whites, nor enjoy any other rights of freed-men except owning property and obtaining redress at law for injury to themselves or to their property.

This law probably copied one passed four years earlier in Maryland. The proportion of slaves there greatly exceeded that in Delaware, remaining at one-third of the population during the Revolutionary era. The eastern shore contained the average number, the northern counties far fewer, and the west even less, but in the southern part of the western shore the number of blacks equaled that of the whites. This last area had early become the center of tobacco culture and of business enterprise, and the predominantly Anglican and Catholic planters had accumulated great wealth. Other sections of the state, more diversified religiously and eco-nomically, either had acquired fewer slaves or, as on the eastern shore, may have found slavery less profitable for stock-raising, lumbering, and the production of grains than it had been for tobacco. The structure of power in Maryland placed decisions concerning emancipation in the hands of the great planters.

As a result, Maryland allowed her slaves no better chance for freedom than did Delaware. Maryland forbade further importation in 1783, but we do not know whether this represented moral disapproval or economic choice. The law also denied the freedmen full equality as in Delaware's later act. Another law allowed slaveowners to hire out their slaves under restrictive circumstances, which an act of 1787 further narrowed. The significant development was the delegates' rejection by a 32 to 22 majority of petitions, probably originating with Quakers, for immediate or gradual abolition. The alignment seems to have been primarily sectional, reflecting geographical patterns of slave ownership. The minority, who agreed to receive the petitions, came mainly from the eastern shore with help from the west and the towns. The center of opposition was located on the western shore among the prosperous tobacco planters. This defeat completely stopped the anti-slavery forces, who never even obtained a vote, nor did private manumissions increase to any extent. Maryland's Negroes gained nothing in the Revolution.

Blacks were even more numerous in Virginia, comprising 40 per cent of the people in 1790. The largest number lived in the counties neither along the coast nor in the west but midway in between. In the eastern part of the state and in the Northern Neck, landowners were trying to abandon tobacco culture and diversify into other crops for which the ownership of slaves may have been more burden than asset. The center of tobacco culture was shifting southward and westward onto fresh lands. Slavery was therefore increasing in the Piedmont at a time when it stagnated farther east. The counties west of the Blue Ridge contained few slaves, and the people (except in Kentucky) wanted none.

In 1782 the House of Delegates authorized the manumission of slaves, requiring only that the master guarantee support for his Negroes if they could not provide for themselves. The same relatively liberal spirit, which one finds expressed by some of the larger planters, won a law limiting the time for which indentured servants could be bound and requiring the master to feed, lodge, and clothe them adequately. The former act aroused considerable protest primarily from the south-central area, reflecting the whites' desire for tobacco hands. These pro-slavery spokesmen stressed the property rights of the owners, recited the biblical justification for the institution, and warned against the evil social effects of emancipation, including possible attacks on whites. Indeed, it is curious that the people where slavery was new became much more frightened than those where slavery had long existed. Counterpetitions extolling liberty as "the Birthright of Mankind, the right of every rational Creature without exception," insisted that arguments based on racial differences were "beneath the Man of Sense, much more the Christian," and dismissed fears of attack. In 1785 the delegates voted that a petition to repeal the act encouraging manumission was reasonable, but then defeated such a bill, 35 to 52. Another bill executing a will which freed the testator's slaves carried 67 to 40, and the humanitarian element defeated a measure that would have required all freedmen to leave the state within a year upon pain of re-enslavement. The legislature thus defended the limited concessions it had granted to black laborers but did not move further toward general emancipation.

The major pressure for manumission in Virginia came from the relatively slaveless west, from religious groups such as the Baptists, and from some of the large planters. The opposition was found all over eastern Virginia but centered especially in the Southside. Curiously, the alignment parallels very closely that on economic and political issues, which we shall presently describe. The most rural, localist representatives defended slavery, so that one is tempted to postulate a relationship. But since the alignment was reversed in New York, apparently the particular situation in each state affected men's views. In Virginia's case, then, the division of opinion primarily reflected the current status of slavery in a given area. Slavery's most extreme defenders lived where it was just developing, not (as a rule) where the institution had reached or passed maturity, nor where it did not exist at all.

The situation in North Carolina was quite similar. A single vote, recorded by the Senate, shows a willingness to allow emancipation by owners in the longest-settled section of the state, the northeastern counties, while opinion elsewhere divided. But opinions, unless backed by action, did not allow much hope for the slaves. An act did levy a duty on imported slaves because the trade was "productive of evil consequences, and highly impolitic," but it was not forbidden, and the Senate rejected a bill allowing men having conscientious objections to slavery to free their Negroes. The "evil consequences" probably referred to the money paid out for Negroes, not slave feelings.

White pocketbooks clearly settled the issue in South Carolina and in Georgia. Despite the efforts of the highly respected merchant Henry Laurens and his son John, and of other anti-slavery spokesmen such as David Ramsay, South Carolina's legislature would not consider emancipation even when the British invasion created a desperate need for manpower. The representatives did not think about limiting the importation of blacks until September 1785, after the planters had saddled themselves with a quarter of a million pounds sterling in debts for the purchase of five thousand slaves. Unable to pay, they then debated a temporary embargo as one of several expedients, including paper money and shutting up the courts, to bail out the slaveowners. John Laurens's tragic death in one of the war's last skirmishes symbolized the hopelessness of the anti-slavery movement in the two southernmost states.

This survey shows that the slaves gained little in the Southern states where the overwhelming majority lived. Some sought freedom by escaping to the British, a few by serving in the American army, and a few were liberated by their masters, but most by far remained in servitude. Even in the North the states with the largest black population began only gradual emancipation. Clearly the whites, with few exceptions, agreed to abolish slavery only where it played little economic role—where it scarcely existed or where the owners did not derive from it a crucial part of the incomes. In such areas, where the institution had never flourished, the efforts of humanitarians and especially of Quakers succeeded in launching the emancipation process. It is impossible to detect any enthusiasm among the great body of whites. They agreed apathetically, at the same time taking good care that the freed Negroes would remain near the bottom of, and in some ways outcasts from, white society.

Although the Southern states failed to help the blacks, slave or free, they did display some attachment to ideas of equality among whites. Symbolic of the equalitarian ideal, for whites anyway, was the repeal of laws encouraging entail and primogeniture. By the former, a landowner could require that his real property remain intact: his descendants could not sell it or even give it away. By the latter, the estate would pass only to the eldest son. Thus the thousand acres of a great tobacco planter would continue in the possession of one man, who might add to it but could not subtract from it, tending to create a hereditary aristocracy which gradually increased its wealth. No one else, including the younger sons, could ever share this property, but must divide what land remained. As long as the supply of available land was increasing, which fortunately had been true throughout most of the South, these excluded ones might still acquire riches of their own, but when inevitably no more empty land remained, then rural society would crystallize into two classes: the landowners and the landless. And power would follow property.

To prevent this the legislatures one after another repealed the laws that had encouraged these practices, North Carolina leading the way by forbidding entails in its constitution. The practical effect of the prohibition remains doubtful. Apparently few estates had ever been entailed. Men had consolidated and broken up great plantations before 1776 and would do so afterwards. Passage of these laws, however, repudiated as a desirable social goal an aristocracy based on inheritance.

We find, then, indications of social change during the Revolutionary period at the top and bottom of society. The flight of well-to-do loyalists and the confiscation of their property left an economic and social (as well as a political) vacuum into which moved some men who had not previously been part of the upper class. At the same time a few thousand slaves became freedmen, tenants won title to their land and escaped quit-rents, soldiers and other men without property obtained farms, especially in the West, and conceivably a few younger sons, formerly disinherited, now received their share of the parental estate.

Is there any concrete evidence that these developments changed the distribution of property or the prestige order within the society? Not much, but a little. Thus in New York City, Boston, and Philadelphia the successful merchants included more self-made men after the Revolution than before it. The colonial towns had always offered excellent opportunities, and one is tempted to attribute the leavening process to the opportunities of the war rather than to a displacement of loyalists, in which case it was, of course, only temporary phenomenon. We need more information before we can speak with confidence.

On another count, the share of the nation's wealth owned by the richest tenth of the population probably declined slightly between 1770 and 1788. An examination of nearly six thousand inventories of estates shows that only in Massachusetts did the larger property owners acquire more of the property; in New Hampshire, New Jersey, Virginia, and South Carolina they owned less. We may speculate that only Massachusetts lacked ready access to cheap unoccupied land, and we have some evidence that the distribution of property in that state had stabilized before 1776. The overall net decline of 2 per cent is not very impressive, given the usual margin of error in such data, but it does suggest a tendency. If so, the war years apparently saw the temporary reversal of a long-range trend toward the concentration of wealth.

A final circumstance affecting the social order was the continued decline of deference—the acceptance by ordinary men that certain individuals merited respect and obedience. What one well-to-do Yankee called a "due subordination" of the mass of mankind to their betters had already been diminishing before the war, probably for many decades, and the Revolution accelerated the process. The "better sort of people" lost face in many areas by their reluctance to support the Revolution, by widespread and notorious speculation, and by their failure to adopt policies that most ordinary folk regarded as beneficial, especially concerning economic questions. For their part, the small property holders began to take equalitarian ideas literally. They engaged in military service, sometimes as elected officers, helped form interim governments and constitutions, selected men of their own sort to represent them, rejected or modified the ideas of their superiors, made money in trade, and now began to demand the respect that they once accorded to others. Their minds, as John Langdon wrote fearfully, had been poisoned with a "levelling spirit."

All of this might have taken place without a revolution, and we cannot measure precisely the degree of change. Most historians agree that before the war American society was becoming somewhat more rigid, imposing barriers on the prospects of the poor, preserving the wealth of the rich, and limiting the opportunities of the small property holders, at the same time that in opposition to these trends people increasingly valued individualism over subordination, equality over deference. The Revolution contributed to the decline of deference, increased mobility, delayed the trend toward an economic and social aristocracy, and momentarily reversed the growing concentration of wealth. Whether intended or not, and whether permanent or ephemeral, these changes registered a clear gain for social democracy.

# Chapter Ten

# *Northern Politics During the War*

THE experience of the Revolutionary War served in many ways to unify the thirteen states. All faced the same problems: forming their newly independent governments, raising and supplying armies, resolving social and cultural issues, devising means of financing the war, suppressing loyalists, encouraging economic growth, and conducting external affairs among themselves and with the central government. At the same time, however, each state struggled with its own unique difficulties, or devised peculiar means of resolving common problems; each state had its own history. We must therefore attend to each independently before we can risk further generalizations.

New Hampshire, as we have seen, established a temporary constitution early in 1776 which provided only a rough framework for a government. An executive branch scarcely existed, and the legislature proved unable to act with dispatch. The members of the two houses argued interminably among themselves, leaving important tasks undone. The failure resulted partly from poor transportation to Exeter, the capital, and the town's lack not only of housing facilities but of social and cultural attractions. As time went on, the best-qualified men lost interest. The pay was low, and after the first exciting years the delegates had finished apportioning the political plums. The office seemed burdensome rather than attractive, and towns began to rotate the job among various citizens. Increasingly rapid turnover and absenteeism characterized the legislature. Other states, however, shared these handicaps without similar results. The major reason for New Hampshire's political difficulties probably lay in her colonial history, when the Wentworths and their associates ran the government and most of the towns chose no representatives. As a consequence New Hampshire, like Georgia, never developed a large class of men with broad political experience at the provincial level. Moreover, an unusually large proportion of her trained public officials left as loyalists in 1775.

Fortunately the state did contain a few able, experienced men who stepped into the political vacuum, and fortunately the people and their representatives had sense enough to let them run the government independently of restrictive constitutional arrangements. These men generally came from inland eastern towns: Mesech Weare, the perennial president, from Hampton, Matthew Thornton from Londonderry, Josiah Bartlett from Kingston, Nathaniel Folsom from Exeter, Ebenezer Thompson from Durham, and John Dudley from Raymond. Only William Whipple and John Langdon, during these years, carried on the Portsmouth tradition of leadership, and Langdon proved inefficient. The Committee of Safety became the instrument by which these men governed the state during the crucial years of the war, and through it they supplied what the constitution had failed to establish: strong executive leadership.

Luckily New Hampshire's struggling leaders did not face an invasion. The state sent forth its militia on only two important occasions after the first year of war: in 1777 during the Burgoyne campaign, and a year later to meet the British threat in Rhode Island. Still, she had to maintain a militia organization and fulfill her federal commitments. The task became increasingly difficult, but New Hampshire contributed a larger share of her male citizens to the Continental Army than any state except Massachusetts and Connecticut.

The new state had limited economic resources. The profitable prewar lumber trade declined and the commerce of the coastal towns suffered severely. One town even found itself unable to afford a representative, while Portsmouth experienced serious unemployment. Individual merchants, notably John Langdon, prospered from fortunate privateering ventures and through government contracts, but the mercantile community as a whole lost money. Agriculture proved the peoples' salvation, and the state exported great quantities of livestock and grain. As prices rose with the wartime demand, farmers prospered. Continental and state money flowed richly into the countryside.

From the government's point of view, as we have seen, the best method of financing the war was first to issue paper currency and then, as the money passed into the people's hands, to levy taxes drawing into the treasury enough to prevent depreciation. In theory the government could perfect a delicate balance between revenue and expenditures which would furnish enough money for the war without raising costs through inflation and without imposing an excess burden—putting money into circulation just a little faster than it was withdrawn, the difference constituting a debt which postwar taxes could easily finance. Presumably the confidence of the people in the government's ability to tax, and in the success of the war, would maintain the value of the paper during the period between its first issuance and its retirement. As we know, the states could not apply this procedure. The legislature could neither levy nor collect sufficient taxes, and unexpectedly heavy expenses ran far ahead of receipts. New Hampshire therefore shared the universal experience of inflation and a sharpening conflict over fiscal policies.

The legislature began well, levying a series of taxes during 1775 totaling more than £24,000 to cover tax anticipation notes. By colonial standards that was a respectable sum. In 1776, however, the treasury found itself compelled to issue £80,000 in legal tender bills. Alarmed, the legislature tried to borrow £20,000 at 6 per cent interest "inasmuch as Emitting money at this time on the Credit of this State might be Attended with Great inconvenience and the Public Suffer in a Deprecian [sic] of their Currency." Meanwhile, in order to raise troops, the treasurer issued another £30,000 worth of notes. The citizens loaned only half as much as the representatives hoped, compelling them to extract by force what they could not by persuasion. Therefore in November 1777 they courageously levied a tax of £40,000. At the same time they proposed to call in such bills of credit as did not bear interest, replacing them with 6 per cent notes. The delegates tried to adjust the tax structure according to the principle "that every Person may be compelled to pay in proportion to his Income" for, in addition to the universal contribution of a poll tax, farmers were assessed for improved land and livestock and traders paid for stock in trade and money at interest. Further to combat inflation, a law required everyone to accept paper notes equal to gold and silver, even for debts; and another act fixed prices at a level somewhat above prewar rates, at the same time limiting wages and the profits of traders. Early in 1778 the legislature accompanied a new issue of paper with yet another tax.

It is hard to see what else the New Hampshire legislature could have done, but their efforts neither prevented inflation nor provided enough money. During the summer of 1778 the government was compelled to call on the towns for help in supplying men and money. In this exigency, and not until then, the state confiscated loyalist estates and imposed a tax on unimproved land, both of which measures injured primarily the Portsmouth elite. These actions did bring in additional income, and a renewed effort to limit prices by popular support rather than by government fiat enabled the treasury to avoid disaster during 1779 and 1780. The ultimate failure of this policy was not New Hampshire's fault: she had carefully limited her issues of paper, levied extraordinary taxes—more than £3 million by the end of 1780—collected almost nine-tenths of it, and strained to contain prices. She could not insulate her economy at the borders, however. The quantity of Continental paper and the general inflation simply overwhelmed the state, and the legislature found itself compelled to adjust to a national crisis.

Pressure for a change of monetary policy came from the eastern trading centers, following action by Massachusetts. The legislature passed an act depriving paper money of its legal-tender quality and fixing it at a low value, which placed the state on a specie basis. This act carried by the narrow margin of 22 to 21, with most of the interior representatives absent. The biggest block of favorable votes came from within the area around Portsmouth, while more distant towns actively opposed the bill. Further measures extended the familiar hard-money policy, including the imposition of even heavier taxes. During the last year of the war the state assessed and collected from the towns quantities of military supplies and specie. By 1783 the state government enjoyed financial security. The public debt apparently was about £65,000, less than a pound per capita—a reward for financial virtue. Expenses, except for servicing the debt, almost ceased, and trade had begun to revive after Yorktown. This apparent prosperity, however, had been achieved at the expense of the farmers. The state had confiscated their paper money and seized their gold and silver. Deprived of their earlier wartime profits, they would be unable to withstand a new economic crisis.

New Hampshire faced no serious social or cultural problems during the war years, but confronted a dangerous separatist movement on her western frontier as well as discontent in the east. The towns along the Connecticut River found several reasons for dissatisfaction with the Exeter government. Their settlers had come up from Connecticut rather than from eastern New Hampshire, as had most of their neighbors in what was to become Vermont. Miles of hills divided them from the Exeter-Portsmouth area. Thus from a geographical, economic, and cultural point of view the Connecticut River towns ought to have formed one state, incorporating the two westernmost counties of New Hampshire with the eastern part of Vermont, then claimed by New York. Politically the western towns felt themselves excluded from New Hampshire's government by an eastern oligarchy, and in fact, as we have seen, power had passed from Portsmouth only as far west as the Merrimac Valley. Moreover, the constitutional arrangement by which the least populous villages were bunched together to elect delegates prevented the small western towns from sending a representative apiece. These facts suggested to the dissidents that the legislature would ignore the Valley's interests. Town meetings and pamphlets also complained of property qualifications, the existence of an upper house, and the constitution's lack of a Declaration of Rights. Finally, the faculty of Dartmouth College, who furnished intellectual leadership for the region, feared the loss of financial support from the eastern government.

During 1777 and 1778 this region acted independently, refusing to pay taxes or send representatives to Exeter; and in 1778 many of the towns formally joined Vermont. But some counteracting forces now blocked the separatists. Vermont's powerful Allen party feared that if Vermont included these additional towns, the center of power would shift from the Bennington area near New York, where they held sway, to the Connecticut River. They therefore began to cooperate with New Hampshire leaders to avert the union. The towns of the valley would really have preferred to form their own state, leaving western Vermont to its fate, but Congress opposed this. Faced with the choice of joining a government controlled by the Allens in far-off Bennington or continuing the historical allegiance with New Hampshire, many westerners preferred the latter. Thus when in 1781 the Allens, in order to strengthen their new government, decided to admit the two counties and appointed officials, many of the towns refused to join. The New Hampshire legislature, roused to decisive action by the secession, resolved to send troops. Fortunately the Vermont legislature, hoping to curry favor with Congress, hastily abandoned its claim to the disputed area, and by 1783 almost all of the towns had rejoined the old state.

The other area of discontent centered in Portsmouth. The town's leaders remained lukewarm toward the Revolutionary government and inclined to protect loyalists. The town suffered economically, with the exception of a few lucky opportunists such as John Langdon who obtained offices and profitable concessions from the legislature. During the early years of the war the interior towns directed economic policy. Creditors fared poorly as they always do in wartime, laws restricting prices injured the trading interest more than the agricultural, and intermittent embargoes on trade hurt commerce. Portsmouth residents also felt the tax structure unfair, and its richer citizens resented the assessments on unimproved land when they were finally made. They also opposed confiscation of loyalist property. Perhaps most of all they resented the shift of political power that deprived the colonial capital of its former importance and influence. Events after 1780, however, reconciled them. The new monetary and pro-creditor policies met their approval. Economic prosperity returned, at least temporarily. Finally, the outlook for better political arrangements seemed hopeful: a new state constitution was in sight, and most merchants applauded New Hampshire's grant of a tax power to Congress (the "impost"), which forecast a stronger national government.

The period ended with New Hampshire apparently prosperous and united. The state had surmounted its economic difficulties, defeated the enemy, thwarted a secession without the use of force, and organized a new government which fairly reflected the various elements in its population. Two flaws, however, mar this picture. Deflation deprived most of the people of their wartime gains and disabled them from paying the state debt, small though it was: tax deficiencies were mounting. Second, the controversies of the years had tended to alienate the Portsmouth trading area from the agricultural towns. These cleavages would lead to major controversies in the postwar years.

Massachusetts also experienced economic and sectional controversies, but she resolved smoothly from colony into state without major change in leadership or loss of experience in government. Like New Hampshire, she remained free from invasion after Gage's evacuation of Boston in 1776. Bay State militia, however, took an active part in military operations, including the Canada expedition and the campaign against Burgoyne, and conducted a disastrous attack on British posts in the Penobscot region which cost the state a million pounds in 1779. Massachusetts furnished more troops to the Continental Army than any other two states combined.

During the first years of the war the people strained to support it through taxes and loans. Almost free of loyalists, and safe from an invasion which might create a pro-British force, the legislature did not hesitate to adopt conservative fiscal policies. Forced to issue tax anticipation notes during 1775 and 1776, the state actually imposed more taxes than it spent—at least on paper—in the following two years. In September 1778 a legislative committee could report that no further supply of money was needed until December, and the treasury paid more than a quarter of a million pounds to Congress.

The first price increases reflected factors other than currency inflation. Successive military defeats eroded confidence in the government's money. Shortages created by military demands and a decline of foreign trade, plus the usual cases of profiteering, contributed too. The legislature imposed sporadic embargoes on the export of provisions and in 1777 passed a "Regulatory Act" setting prices and wages at a level 50 per cent higher than that of 1774. The law failed to prevent further increases and stimulated a debate between the trading and the farming towns. A Boston town meeting instructed its representatives to seek a repeal. The law, the people asserted, and was unenforceable and created animosity between town and country. Free trade, with unlimited imports, would reduce prices: restraints on commerce always proved injurious. Moreover, the act put law-abiding traders out of business, benefiting only speculators. And it cast doubt upon the value of the state's currency, thereby injuring it. On the other hand, a convention of the Plymouth County committees of correspondence called for the better enforcement of the act, condemning avarice and extortion. Thus some men blamed farmers for excessive profit-taking while others criticized traders. In the legislature, Boston's representatives found themselves unable to fulfill their instructions. Instead, the country members defeated an attempt to repeal the act, 112 to 31.

Two circumstances, evidently, soon nullified the policy of government price- and wage-fixing. First, the state neglected to set up agencies for enforcing the law, relying entirely on voluntary compliance. But too many men refused to obey it, justifying their conduct on the ground that others were violating it, or that it was wrong on principle. Second, to the basic causes for inflation another and even more powerful was added: the enormous increase and consequent depreciation of paper money. This decline in the value of money became serious in 1779. Massachusetts' fiscal policy certainly cannot be held responsible, for the state levied more than £6.5 million in taxes during the year. At the same time the people made a further and, as it proved, final attempt at price regulation. Government action having failed, private efforts might succeed. A series of conventions, supported even by the Bostonians, set maximum prices. The merchants of the great port agreed to sell only for paper money, not specie, and urged cooperation from towns everywhere. The legislature decreed another embargo on the export of provisions to help alleviate the distress of the townspeople. These efforts continued throughout the summer and into the fall, but ended in failure and mutual recrimination. A nationwide inflation due to the heavy demands of war and the flood of Continental currency was primarily responsible, but the farmers blamed the trading interest and the traders blamed them. Thereafter an increasingly powerful attack developed on the entire paper-money system, led by the Bostonians and resisted by the country folk.

Until this point the eastern group, while not entirely happy with the state's policy, had refrained from major criticism. As long as the value of money remained reasonably stable, creditors gladly accepted the payments which prosperity made possible, while traders and artisans both profited. Price rises compensated for heavier taxes; indeed, the mercantile community, acting through the Council, supported taxes as a means of maintaining the credit of the paper. Probably they were responsible for the resolution, adopted by the House in September 1777, "that the future Expenses of the State in carrying on the War be supported by Taxation only," followed by an act for retiring the state's paper, a decision that provoked an angry flood of remonstrances from inland farming towns. Most of the commonwealth's prominent leaders continued to oppose legal-tender laws and deficit financing, and by 1780 they grew insistent. But the inland towns stuck to their guns. Their answer to increased military expenses remained the issuance of tax anticipation notes, the values of which was supported by regulatory acts, legal tender clauses, and taxes payable in the paper.

The contest lasted for more than a year. An act of April 1780 lowered the value of Continental money to 40:1, but since it had declined still further, creditors dared not bring suit for debts. In June the House passed a bill repealing all legal tender acts, setting up a scale of depreciation which nonetheless continued to peg the value of paper money at no less than 40:1. By a narrow vote the representatives postponed for six months the execution of judgments on court actions brought as a result of the bill. When the Council sought to attach amendments more favorable to creditors, the lower house postponed the entire measure.

During November the lower house defeated a pro-creditor bill, but in January the decisive act passed, putting Massachusetts on a hard-money basis. All paper notes were liquidated to their real current value, which judges of the Supreme Court would periodically determine. The state now undertook to resume payment of interest on public securities and, in the manner already described, provided for a combination of taxes and loans in hard money or paper equivalents. The votes on this bill probably exceeded in importance any others during the entire period of the war, for Massachusetts was the first state to repeal her legal tender clauses, and she thus inaugurated the victory of the hard-money party throughout the country. Delegates from the eastern towns voted solidly in favor of the act, those located on the coast being almost unanimous. The inland agricultural towns opposed the change overwhelmingly. The Worcester County delegates, for example, voted against it by three to one.

Far from being reconciled to the new economic system, western towns protested vigorously and won a majority in the lower house that summer, when a vote to reconsider the repeal of legal tender provisions carried 76 to 47, only to be defeated in the Senate. But subsequent acts reaffirmed the new policy. The state now doggedly attempted to pay its creditors everything they could wish. The legislature passed an excise act to provide funds for payments of interest on the state debt, and the government energetically pressed the collection of back taxes as well as a heavy new tax on polls and estates. At this point the public debt stood at more than a million pounds, which the legislature increased, during 1781, by contracting a loan of £400,000. An additional loan provided for the payment of the Continental line.

Massachusetts' economic situation at the close of the war was mixed. Heavy taxes in specie were draining the rural communities of hard money. The sharp deflation further deprived them of their cash, and with prices returning to normal levels, neither savings nor incomes could make up the loss. Artisans, like the small farmers, saw their wartime profits melt away during the war. On the other hand, a temporary resumption of commerce helped traders, and the commercial farmers who, like the merchants, had prospered during the war seem to have held their own financially. The state as a whole ended with a debt of £1.5 million and, in July 1783, a temporarily empty treasury; it could expect little income from sales of loyalist property or vacant land. Still, a population of 320,000 might reasonably expect to finance such a debt and contribute its share to Congress, assuming a return to prewar levels of prosperity.

Massachusetts politics during the war years were characterized by fundamental internal divisions, primarily sectional, and were based upon the opposition of the eastern trading interest to the interior agricultural communities. The traders attracted support from nearby farming areas and certain western towns, notably along the Connecticut River, and especially among traders, lawyers, and other professionals. These men, providing leadership for the state as they had for the colony, struggled to obtain a congenial form of government, as we have seen. They also tried, at first unsuccessfully, to devise a sound economic system based upon hard money and to create an environment beneficial to creditors and entrepreneurs. By 1782 they had succeeded, crowning one part of their efforts by establishing Courts of Common Pleas of which the judges, appointed by the governor, would hear all civil cases involving more than £2.

At the opposite end of the state, Massachusetts had her equivalent of the Dartmouth College secessionists in the Berkshire "Constitutionalists," who also agitated for a more democratic form of government and who as late as 1780 threatened to secede. Discontent spread eastward late in the war. During 1782, when the new economic policy was fully implemented, the legislature received numerous petitions complaining of tax collections and suits for debt. A sizable convention in Worcester County, paralleling similar gatherings in Berkshire and Hampshire, called for an investigation of the state's finances to uncover frauds, protested the high incomes of officials and lawyers, recommended that actions involving less than £40 be settled by local justices, and asked for payment of taxes in produce. A series of mob outbreaks against tax collectors and sheriffs punctuated the years 1782 and 1783, resulting in an act temporarily suspending the writ of habeas corpus, which pleased the easterners, and an evaluation law, which did not.

One might suppose that the many interior towns would overwhelm the eastern group. In fact they did form a ma-

jority in the House of Representatives if enough sent delegates to begin with and if the delegates attended faithfully—
neither of which happened. Anyone from the coast could
reach Boston quite easily, for but interior representatives
the trip was long, arduous, and expensive. The easterners
passed most of their bills during the winter months. Distant
towns persistently pressed for an interior site and voted in
June 1781 not to reconvene in Boston; but they rejected
Andover and failed to agree on a substitute, so the campaign
collapsed. The easterners' political power was enhanced by
their superior capacity for leadership. Most of the state's
experienced and respected men came from the trading centers, and they generally controlled the Assembly's committees. Their prestige, together with a similarity of viewpoints,
always won over some of the westerners, including most
of the important men. Still another advantage of the eastern group lay in their control of the upper house which on
a number of occasions intervened successfully. The constitution of 1780, as we have seen, helped to solidify this structure of power, and its ratification doubtless contributed to
the political revolution of the following months.

By the end of the war, therefore, the Massachusetts legislature contained two clearly defined groups reflecting fundamental divisions in society. The series of votes during the
years 1780 to 1783 revealed the division. One set, as we
have seen, settled the state's fiscal policy. Another set established the system of taxation based largely on polls and
estates. Several votes relating to the return of the loyalists
shows precisely the same alignment, as does one on granting
the governor a permanent rather than an annual salary,
which the eastern group favored. The evaluation act of 1782
passed over the unanimous opposition of five Bostonians
and was supported by two delegates from Salem and one

each from Dorchester, Hingham, Cohasset, Beverly, Lynn, and Medford; in all, eastern towns voted against it 7 to 16 while westerners favored it 54 to 18. Despite these dissensions, however, the people had retained a basic unity. They had reorganized their government, conquered the British, successfully solved difficult financial problems, and emerged, on the whole, with excellent prospects.

Alone among the New England states, Rhode Island endured a long occupation by British troops and an even longer blockade by the British navy. An almost continual emergency forced the people to unite and delayed the emergence of those inevitable controversies that characterized the wartime policies of New Hampshire and Massachusetts. And Rhode Island, like Connecticut, persisted contentedly in her colonial institution, nor do we find any movements toward secession or even mild reform until the fighting ceased.

The small group of Rhode Island loyalists and neutrals included only a fraction of the state's leaders, so that their withdrawal affected neither the structure of power nor the quality of leadership. Before the Revolution the colony's exceptionally democratic system led to hard-fought electoral contests between the Ward and Hopkins factions. These now disappeared, both groups agreeing on basic policies, and no new divisions replaced them until the military danger ceased. Elections proceeded without contest except between local rivals; changes in the membership of the legislature did not herald shifts of policy.

From the start, Rhode Islanders enthusiastically supported the war. The University of Rhode Island, for example, contributed its entire endowment, more than £4,000 in specie, asking only interest. The state produced more Continental soldiers per capita than any other and led the way in levying taxes during the first years. She had no easy time of it. The British invaded the island of Rhode Island in December 1776, occupying Newport, Middletown, Jamestown, and Portsmouth and blockading New Shoreham and Bristol on the mainland. The enemy thereby closed the outlet of Narragansett Bay, utterly destroying the shipping and commerce from which the colony had derived its prosperity, and controlled directly or indirectly one-third of the state's wealth. The legislature responded by placing emergency executive powers in a Council of War, which efficiently raised and supported the army thereafter. The military demands placed upon the small population induced the legislature to raise a battalion of slaves, promising them freedom as well as bounties, and compensating their masters. Only six delegates dissented from this remarkable step, and they objected entirely on theoretical grounds. The state prepared an attack on the British in the summer of 1778, with aid from her neighbors, but it proved a failure and depleted her resources. The enemy remained until October 1779, and the state did not feel secure until the French arrived in July 1780. During these years Rhode Island scarcely could feed her population and suffered heavy economic losses. Newport was destroyed, and the other commercial towns, Warwick and Providence, experienced an almost continual depression because of the British navy. During the last years of the war the people fortunately averted the threatened collapse. Trade reopened under French protection, and French gold bought agricultural produce. The ensuing boom promised a complete recovery.

From the start Rhode Island relied upon the usual tax anticipation notes to finance the war. During the first two years the legislature issued £140,000 in legal tender notes payable after five or six years. Since the state's assessed value barely exceeded £2 million (though the real figure was doubtless higher) the burden would be considerable unless trade flourished. On the contrary, the British stopped exports while their presence removed from reach property worth a quarter of a million pounds. The four New England states considered the inflation in December 1776, agreeing in a convention to avoid further paper issues except in absolute emergencies, but instead to rely upon taxes and borrowing for short periods at a maximum rate of 5 per cent. Rhode Island accordingly borrowed, that winter, £120,000, and followed this with further loans of £73,000 during the next year. In 1777 the legislature levied taxes of £96,000, adding even more in 1778. The same convention had recommended laws regulating prices, and Rhode Island preceded her sister states in implementing this decision. The scarcity of provisions resulting from the blockade, together with the people's own needs, forced the legislature to abandon price-fixing agreements and to lay an embargo on exports; indeed, the state had to buy provisions from Massachusetts and Connecticut.

Rhode Island's courageous attempt to maintain a hard-money policy in the midst of a war began to founder during 1779, just after she had set about to call in all her bills of credit and just as she was expecting to collect back taxes from Newport County sufficient to balance the budget. The British reoccupation of Newport forced the legislature to raise twelve hundred men, to retain money destined for Congress, and to issue £40,000 in promissory notes. Conventions that summer, paralleling similar meetings in other states, tried to reverse the rise in prices and wages. The legislature continued stubbornly to levy taxes but could collect little except paper, which now began its final decline. The deputies therefore fell back on assessing the towns for specific articles. Fortunately the rich agricultural land of the southern towns remained safe from the British, and during the last two years of campaigning they furnished essential provisions. By June 1780 tax delinquencies became serious, levies of more than a million pounds being simply too much for the people to pay even in notes and supplies. The state found the treasury bare, and to supply the army again retained £60,000 intended for Congress. In this emergency the legislature once again resorted to paper notes, this time bearing 6 per cent interest and based upon the security of confiscated loyalist property. The arrival of the French that fall, bringing money to pay for supplies, encouraged taxes in gold and silver and aroused hope for financial salvation.

Despite Rhode Island's historical reputation for fiscal irresponsibility, the government throughout this period had followed relatively conservative financial practices. The merchants, though few in number, clearly exercised great influence. In March 1780, when the paper money began its final collapse, the legislature suspended the legal tender act for prewar debts and a committee set to work determining a scale of depreciation. By May 1781 a general repeal of legal tender clauses enabled creditors to recover their debts at once, the value of state money being set by courts and that of Congress by the legislature. The merchants, as well as other Rhode Islanders, undoubtedly concurred with the governor when he explained to Robert Morris that fall that his state could not possibly pay to Congress the sum requested. Rhode Island, he pointed out, had supplied the Continental Army with some £250,000 worth of supplies, had paid large sums in requisitions, and was trying to reimburse the soldiers for their back wages. The state's specie had been exhausted by 1780 when the last gold and silver went to pay the army. The money then issued, funded on the confiscated estates, had been entirely spent, and the state was compelled to collect provisions from the people. A final effort to raise troops in 1781 had succeeded, but the state was now exhausted.

The governor's statement, while intended to justify Rhode Island's refusal, appears accurate. New taxes brought in no more money, and the treasurer had to borrow in order to pay the Rhode Island line. During 1782 the legislature was forced to postpone tax collections because many town treasurers were in jail for previous delinquencies. Deficiencies continued and forced further postponements for many months. Not until the state levied an import tax did she find a firm path through the financial morass.

In 1783 Rhode Island's debt stood at £123,830, consisting primarily of soldiers' notes, commissary and other certificates, and lawful money loans varying from 4 to 6 per cent. Considering the assessed valuation, still around £2 million (and surely underestimated), the outlook certainly seemed favorable. The state's economic prospects depended upon the merchants' ability to re-establish prewar trade routes and to find markets for an agricultural surplus. Their profits then would finance the purchase of imports and payments on the debt. The people of the trading towns, who as usual conducted their business on credit, regarded a hard-money policy as essential to economic stability. The farmers disagreed. Emerging from the war with little cash, and that mortgaged to the tax collector, they preferred a monetary policy that would enable them to buy what they wanted and pay their debts. The different objectives of these two major interest groups were already apparent by 1783.

The political controversy that occurred near the close of the war seems at first glance entirely political: the apportionment system by which Newport chose six deputies and three other towns selected four each, while the rest sent two apiece, came under attack as unequal. But several circumstances indicate deeper roots. The towns that protested the status quo were agricultural, the four in favor were commercial. The campaign for reform was preceded by a newspaper attack on lawyers and ministers and followed the repeal of the legal tender acts and the sharp deflation that followed. It seems likely that during the war Rhode Islanders of all sorts united to meet the common enemy, and the blockade prevented the traders from earning those profits that elsewhere had excited jealousy. The extraordinary financial record, characterized by unusual restraint in the issuance of paper money and an exceptional willingness to levy taxes, demonstrates that the country deputies assented to policies that one ordinarily associates with merchants, and indeed merchants occupied key posts in the government. But by 1782 the farmers apparently were becoming disillusioned. With paper currency disowned, specie scarce, and taxes high, they might well prefer a policy based upon an expanded money supply and lower taxes. In 1783, however, serious political strife lay in the future. The state faced the postwar world with an empty treasury but basically solvent and united under an unusually democratic government.

Little has been written about Connecticut during the years 1776–1783 because few records survive. The newspapers shed little light on internal political, economic, or social affairs, a fact that implies a lack of discord until 1784, when there emerged sharp disagreements over several issues. People had divided during the Colonial period over religion, expansion into northern Pennsylvania, and the question of resistance to British measures; but these issues either vanished or were submerged by the war. Long before 1775 anyone with loyalist leanings had been forced out of power, and Connecticut entered the war relatively united.

This unity strengthened the conservative tendencies within the state and inhibited important political changes. The members of the upper house and the principal officials continued in office without interruption or challenge. These were mostly lawyers from Connecticut's leading commercial, professional, and large landowning families, who therefore exercised great influence on policies. The lower house consisted, perhaps even more than before, of farmers, so that the purely agricultural interest shared in political power, but the superior prestige of the Assistants (the upper house) predominated until the very end of the war.

Another factor contributing to unity was the presence of British troops on the north shore of Long Island, across the Sound. Several thousand refugees fled to Connecticut from Suffolk County and kept up a constant communication with and occasional raids on their home towns. The British also raided Connecticut, burning New London on one occasion. These activities kept the people fully involved in the war even though the state suffered no major invasion.

Despite her small population, ranking seventh among the states, Connecticut stood second only to Massachusetts in the size of her Continental Army. She raised money and obtained supplies in much the same manner as Rhode Island, but with less strain because she could draw on greater resources. At first the legislature authorized tax anticipation notes and declared them legal tender. After a final issue in December 1776 the state obeyed the decision of the Providence convention, relying upon a series of loans during the following months and levying considerable taxes. During the first years of the war Connecticut conscientiously accompanied every issue of paper money with a tax bill.

In 1780 Connecticut moved very rapidly to deal with the general financial crisis, assessing £3.6 million in taxes (payable in Continental money), borrowing £1 million to retire Continental bills, devaluating all previous paper issues so as to protect creditors, and securing new tax anticipation warrants by allowing interest and imposing still another tax. From this point forward she relied upon taxes in specie and specifics—a typical sound-money policy. This procedure apparently won the support, at least temporarily, not only of the commercial towns but of the agricultural communities. While some traders such as Jeremiah Wadsworth had become very wealthy, the benefits of the wartime prosperity spread more evenly over the state than was usual elsewhere, especially in the commerical farming areas, because Connecticut's farmers supplied exceptionally large quantities of produce for the army. They succeeded, in 1779, in enlarging the tax base so as to shift some of the burden onto the town dwellers. The system that continued throughout the war established a basic assessment list of about £2 million, which observers considered one-twelfth of the actual wealth. The legislature tried to estimate the average annual value of all property and the income from people's economic activities. Some newspaper critics felt that the list underrated trades and manufacturers, but spokesmen for the traders complained of excessive taxes on money, trading stock, and debts.

Apparently Connecticut survived the war in good financial condition despite an unusually high per capita state debt, a result of unusual patriotism. But the farmers were becoming dissatisfied with her spartan policies by 1782. In that year they obtained a valuation law enabling them to pay private debts in a great variety of property appraised by three freeholders. They also changed the method of assessing nonfarm occupations, in effect raising the taxes of traders, professional men, artisans, and millers. By the fall of 1783, if not earlier, some people began to attack the upper house, trying, according to one account, "to drop every man of ability, of liberal and independent sentiments." This attempt seems to have originated less from internal differences than from opposition to Congress's request for power to levy an import tax and to a grant of half-pay to officers. These proposals won support from the governor and Council, but a majority of the lower house opposed them. One of the legislature's very rare votes, recorded in 1784, reveals a sectional alignment, with the opposition concentrated in the agricultural towns. These instances of internal division were so few as to suggest that on the whole Connecticut escaped the conflicts that disturbed other states.

New York did not, and conflicts characterized her history during much of the Revolutionary period. Both the northern and southern sections suffered almost continual invasion and extensive property damage. In the north, the Mohawk Valley area lay exposed to sporadic Indian raids and to several important British campaigns, the more destructive because Tories avenged themselves on former neighbors. Even after Burgoyne's defeat in 1777, fighting continued on the western frontier. Tryon County, now roughly all that area west of Schenectady, lost two-thirds of its population and seven hundred buildings, leaving twelve thousand farms uncultivated. The enemy occupied New York City during August 1776 and remained until November 1783. During this period the British controlled and established military posts in Richmond, Queens, and Suffolk counties (Staten and Long islands) and extended their influence north into the Bronx. These long-established and prosperous counties had furnished over half the colony's taxes before the war. Moreover, the rest of the state had no outlet to the sea except by wagon roads along the west bank of the Hudson and far down into New Jersey, or by crossing Westchester County to reach the north coast of Long Island Sound. Fishkill, in Dutchess County, served as the focus for communications. That part of the state not in enemy hands consisted of a rather thin ribbon of settlement along the Hudson from just north of Albany down to near Yonkers, a distance of 150 miles. Fortunately, the ribbon included some excellent farmland and numerous mills, so that Revolutionary New York could raise its own food and subsist even when isolated.

The greatly reduced state compensated in some degree for its loss of population by more cohesion among those who remained, and the patriotic majority also gained by the rebellious spirits who fled from New York City and Long Island. Events thus imposed a comparative unity which lasted until the end of the war. This situation also had political side-effects. The more enthusiastic rebels held a greater degree of power than was to be expected in view of the heavily neutralist sentiments in the state. Although the prewar elite retained positions of influence and dominated the committee that wrote the constitution, they lost control of the Assembly. Their decline resulted partly from the convention's decision that incumbent delegates from the south would remain in office until elections could be held, which proved to be until 1784. These delegates reflected the "radical" rebel element, more likely to cooperate with the upstate leaders than to differ with them. The sectional controversies that surfaced after the state was reunified during the mid-1780's therefore scarcely appeared. In addition, some of the southern delegates ceased to attend regularly, though in compensation a few city men represented other counties. Thus in the lower house the trading interests of the state became less powerful than the agricultural. The Senate's membership, on the other hand, continued to favor the prominent old families. It included, along with some farmers and men of moderate property, many members of the state's economic upper class, who engaged in trade, law, or large-scale agriculture.

New York, like New Hampshire, formed a new government in the midst of the war, indeed in the midst of invasion. The hiatus reduced her effectiveness, but she seems to have inherited enough experienced men from the old regime to supply able leadership. Men such as John Jay, James Duane, Ezra L'Hommedieu, Philip Schuyler, John Morris Scott, and the Livingstons furnished a nucleus which relative newcomers like George Clinton greatly strengthened.

An aspect peculiar to New York's politics deserves mention. The movement of New Englanders into the state continued steadily throughout the war. They already had settled Suffolk County on Long Island and eastern Westchester. The eastern sections of present-day Putnam, Dutchess, Columbia, and Rensselaer counties now became New England strongholds, as did all of Washington County, which adjoins Vermont; delegates from the latter also attended as representatives of "Charlotte" County. The immigrants were enthusiastic rebels and expressed an unusually democratic, agrarian viewpoint. Their arrival counterbalanced the Dutch, who tended to be more moderate in their political ideas and conservative economically. The British occupation of Dutch strongholds on Manhattan and Staten

Island and in Brooklyn minimized their influence during this period.

The various groups active in New York politics submerged most of their differences during the war, for the British invasions absorbed every energy. The first legislature under the new constitution did not meet until September 1777. Meanwhile, the provincial congresses and the convention had existed virtually without money, for the colony had been collecting no specie except from imports, excises, and interest on loans. The delegates dared not impose new assessments, for they had neither the authority nor the popular support. They first appealed to Congress for funds and presently printed £300,000 in paper bills on the credit of the state. When early in 1777 Congress urged an end to paper money, New York technically complied, but in order to obtain troops and supplies issued certificates. Not until March 1778 did the legislature, in its second sitting, devise a tax measure. This established a rate of three pence in the pound on real property and half as much on personal estates—a curious ratio for an agricultural state. We do not know what sum the legislature expected to collect, but until this point Yorkers probably had escaped with lower taxes than the people of any Northern state.

New York's isolation compounded her economic difficulties. Although her citizens were creditors for large sums to men in other states, especially Connecticut and New Jersey, they could not collect, and in the absence of an export trade New York soon ran a heavy adverse balance. Nor could she afford to sell farm products to New Jersey or Connecticut because she was fighting for her life at home. Scarcity reinforced the inflationary effect of paper currency. The government, however, hesitated to impose price restrictions or to prevent exports of military supplies because the state's major supporters, the politically powerful commercial farmers, army contractors, and merchants, profited thereby. Thus when early in 1777 the executives of both Massachusetts and Connecticut urged New York's constitutional convention to join in stringent price controls, the Committee of Safety refused to do so. On the contrary the committee, dominated by traders and large landowners, presented a typical hard-money theory advocating free trade and taxes, while apologizing for New York's inability to levy taxes because she lacked a government.

When the legislature met early in 1778 it confronted a crisis despite Burgoyne's surrender. The delegates set prices and wages at a 75 per cent advance over 1774 rates and allowed traders a 25 per cent profit. A bill to prohibit the export of provisions, however, failed. The first tax law, in March, called for the payment of $200,000 to Congress. In addition to the tax on land and personal property, traders and manufacturers bore a special assessment of 5 per cent on their profits since September 1776. The legislature balked at further taxes, and despite the governor's urgings the year passed with no more legislation. The failure resulted in part from a legislative deadlock, but it contrasts to the much more decisive action of other states. Not until October 1779 did the state begin to levy the really large sums necessary for carrying on the war. Collections lagged, and army requirements forced continued use of impressments and certificates.

By the spring of 1781 the people were so tired of the war and showed such alarming signs of discontent that the legislature published a lengthy address. They agreed that the people had every right to complain, and repeated the causes: heavy taxes, harsh measures undertaken to control the loyal-

ists, forcible impressment of supplies for the army, calls
upon the militia for active duty which forced them to leave
their farms, and the destruction along the frontiers. They
pointed out, however, that the legislature could not lessen
the burden of these taken collectively, nor of any one
without increasing others. Lower taxes, for example, would
require more drastic impressments; reduction of the militia
would leave the frontier unprotected. They were trying
to persuade Congress to request less money from the state
and had granted further time for the collection of the last
tax, but really the people ought not to expect lower taxes.
The war had been carried on for several years without any
taxes at all, and a large sum was coming due in order to
redeem the various notes.

In order to support the Continental Army during what
fortunately proved the final campaign, the legislature resorted to the immediate sale of confiscated estates, a step
opposed by the Senate, which preferred to raise money
from loans, and by the urban representatives from Albany
and the New York City area. Taxes were imposed on unimproved land owned by absentees, including those in occupied
territories. The representatives authorized further impressments and required the collection of additional taxes payable
in wheat and flour. At the same time the government, including the future anti-federalist Governor Clinton, urged
the grant of greater powers to Congress. The sale of confiscated estates did bring in some essential cash, but the
most valuable remained under British control and could
not be touched until 1784.

A letter written by the wealthy New York lawyer and
ardent nationalist James Duane conveys some idea of the
state's difficulties. He himself had drafted an address recommending the calling of a convention to amend the Articles

of Confederation, yet he defended New York's refusal to comply with the requisitions of Congress. The state, he wrote, was impoverished, and needed assurance of a better spirit and greater exertions on the part of other states than hitherto.

After Cornwallis's surrender the state could breathe again. The British remained in New York City, gradually contracting their operations. A certain amount of trade developed involving the sale of supplies to the British and of luxuries to the Americans, in which the latter probably lost money. When the British withdrew they took with them thousands of loyalists and several million pounds' worth of property. Only then could the legislature begin to replace wartime losses by the sale of confiscated property in the southern district, the levy of a special £100,000 specie tax on the people there, and income from the resumption of trade. The recovery of the northern counties proceeded much more rapidly. Immigrants were pouring across the border from New England, and with the Indian barrier down, land-hungry settlers exploded into the rich farm land north and west of Albany. Even so, as late as December 1785 these upstate counties still owed the state treasury £172,608 in back taxes.

New York's politics during the war bore little resemblance to the colonial situation and anticipated postwar developments only on a few issues. Many disagreements in the wartime legislature required roll-call votes, but these usually show the legislators dividing in a miscellaneous fashion, reflecting individual opinions. The divergent sectional interests that characterized peacetime New York were submerged because everyone cooperated on common problems, and because one side was bottled up by the British occupation.

They did, however, appear on two questions: taxes and the confiscation of loyalist property.

Representatives from northern New York steadily opposed higher taxes and tried to increase the rate on personal as opposed to real estate. That section suffered more loss of property, and since much of it was a frontier area it contained less taxable wealth, the people owning small amounts of personal property and the land, on the average, being less valuable. Moreover, since the southern districts could not be assessed while they were under British rule, the burden fell entirely on the unoccupied counties. Much better, then, to minimize or even postpone collections until New York City and its neighbors could pay their share—or a little more! As a substitute the northern delegates pressed for the sale of confiscated property as a means of financing the war. Fundamentally they adhered to a system of finance based upon paper, the value of which would be maintained by confiscated estates as collateral and the promise of future taxes. They tried also to reduce government costs wherever possible. On the other side were representatives of the southern districts, supported by some of the men from the central counties. These were generally traders, lawyers, and others following nonfarm occupations, plus a few large landowners—men of means for the most part, whereas the northern party consisted principally of farmers, few of whom owned large properties. The division primarily reflected sectional views, though on particular issues other alignments emerged. Thus a vote concerning a proposed special tax on those who had acquired wealth as a result of the war, and another tax on wrought plate, separated the representatives along the lines of economic class. But these conflicts remained muted until after the British withdrawal. New York emerged from the Revolution seriously injured by the war, yet with prospects for rapid economic growth as foreign trade recovered and immigrants increased agricultural production.

New York's success in overcoming her enemies without complete collapse was attributable not only to the fundamental wealth of the land but to the determination of her people and the energy of the able Governor George Clinton. New Jersey, too, found a governor who could summon forth and concentrate the efforts of a heterogeneous people. Also like New York, she faced invasions and internal dissent.

After the British captured New York City in the late summer of 1776, they conquered all of New Jersey by wintertime. Even after Washington's victory at Trenton forced them to abandon the western part, they retained control of the eastern section until July. From that point until the close of the war, British and loyalist troops conducted occasional raids into the East Jersey counties and blocked their outlet to the sea, for Elizabeth and Perth Amboy send their ships across lower New York Bay and through the narrows between Sandy Hook and Long Island. Since the Dutch and Germans in the northern counties of Bergen and Sussex were unenthusiastic about the war, and the latter suffered Indian attacks, East Jersey fought under great difficulties. The rest of the state—historically "West Jersey"—escaped these handicaps. Except when the British occupied Philadelphia, the western counties remained free from invasion after 1776. They exported through Philadelphia or their own small ports, and their rich soil produced essential provisions. The people prospered greatly, but their material well-being did not aid the war effort as much as might be expected because of their pacifistic attitude. Thus the aggressively rebel half of the state was willing but less able to support the contest than the abler but reluctant west. Fortunately the latter, though not participating enthusiastically, did pay taxes and furnish supplies, and representatives in the legislature from the west usually belonged to the more militant elements.

During the first years of crisis the New Jersey government performed rather poorly. Her political system had never produced leaders who could unite the state under an efficient administration. No group emerged to equal the New Yorkers. Probably one source of the trouble lay in the diffused nature of the state's politics, society, and economy, for instead of a single major city to act as a focus and produce wealth, New Jersey contained several widely separated small towns. West and East Jersey leaders followed different paths. They did not intermarry, looked to Philadelphia or New York City rather than at one another, and argued more than they cooperated. The legislature symbolically met alternately in Burlington and Perth Amboy, during colonial days, in Trenton or Princeton after Independence. Every state faced serious difficulties in developing a skilled group of officials who could surmount the wartime problems; in New Jersey the process took longer. Her ultimate success, dating from mid-1778, owed something to improved morale after military successes and the French alliance, but much to William Livingston. Elected governor annually from 1776 to 1790, he furnished continuity and ability.

The Provincial Congress, which governed until October 1776, struggled against a general reluctance to support the war financially or to enlist enough men, especially among the West Jersey people. It issued £50,000 in bills of credit and ordered a tax of £10,000 annually, which it could not collect. The congress did not dare to implement anti-loyalist legislation. The first legislature borrowed £125,000 and passed a legal tender act but defeated a tax bill and took no effective action against loyalists, nor did it implement price regulations. The British invasion and occupation then brought the government almost to a standstill. Many citizens sought British protection, and for a year and a half New Jersey's government passed little important legislation. A Council of Safety supplied the only effective government, the militia law did not meet the state's needs, and corruption compounded problems of supply. Lacking specie, New Jersey, like her neighbors, resorted to certificates. They proved no match for British gold in purchasing provisions and teams for transportation. Burgoyne's defeat barely compensated for Howe's capture of Philadelphia, a conquest which meant that New Jersey lay open to the British on both sides, while the American army wintered at distant Valley Forge. Relief came at last with Howe's departure from Philadelphia in June 1778. After the drawn battle at Monmouth the British withdrew into New York, leaving the state finally rid of invaders.

From that point on, matters improved. The legislature had passed a small tax in March, followed this with a larger one in December, and during 1779 imposed levies of £4,-375,000, part of which was earmarked for Congress. More to the point, tax collections became effective. In December 1778 the legislature authorized the immediate sale of confiscated estates, preceding the other states in that method of raising money. The prolonged invasion, while injurious to the government and some individuals, had deposited large amounts of money in the hands of New Jersey's farmers: certificates and Continental dollars from the Americans, and gold and silver from the British. The legislature now actually received petitions recommending higher taxes, and it sent to Congress a message urging uniform price restrictions. By November 1779 the treasury had received nearly £400,-000 from the sale of confiscated estates, a figure which rose to £1,350,000 two years later. By that time, moreover, taxes were at last being paid. In May 1780 the state was able to furnish nearly $2 million to Congress and to the Continental Army. The Assembly complained that unless Congress paid for the large quantity of goods bought from Jersey citizens in something other than promises, the state faced bankruptcy, yet at the same time the House agreed, with only one dissenting vote, not to receive quartermaster and commissary certificates for state taxes because the state had plenty of money in the treasury, not counting the sums in the hands of tax collectors! Again in December the Assembly discovered such a satisfactory financial situation that it voted not to introduce a tax bill. The reform fiscal program of 1781 carried through both houses with little difficulty. Of the £100,000 tax levied in 1778, the state collected virtually all; of the £4,375,000 in 1779, it collected seven-eighths, and of the £470,000 specie taxes during 1781–1783, it had received, by the end of the last year, all but 16 per cent. Considering the state's many problems, the record is remarkable.

During its first sessions the legislature did not reflect divisions among the people because, as we have observed, all but a very small minority of the delegates aggressively supported the war. As time went on, however, roll calls began to reveal sectional conflicts. These concerned two major and two lesser issues, all relating to the financing and conduct of the war. The West Jersey "party," using the term in its contemporary loose sense, opposed the confiscation of loyalist estates. Its members had not, with some exceptions, resisted the passage of anti-Tory laws despite the neutralist sentiment among their constituents, having for example supported a clause depriving nonjurors of the right to vote, nor had they objected to the original confiscation act and the first sales. Once the fighting ceased and the state no longer desperately needed money, however, opinions changed: the East Jersey delegates continued to press for immediate sale and the West Jersey group opposed this almost unanimously. Most of the property lay in the eastern counties and was being purchased by eastern politicians. It seems likely that the East Jersey group, bitterly anti-loyalist, sought revenge for wartime damages and wanted money to pay for the certificates that their constituents held, at the same time satisfying prominent colleagues. The westerners shared none of these motives and probably felt a humane sympathy for the loyalists.

The question of taxes also divided the legislature along sectional lines. Again legislators agreed during those early years when the taxes burdened no one. The first division occurred in the fall of 1779, when the delegates from those counties least enthusiastic about the war limited the new assessment to $9 million. Subsequently the East Jersey bloc took the lead in levying taxes and implementing Congress's proposal of 1780, all the more because the "new emission" bills would pay the cost of war. The plethora of certificates in East Jersey led its spokesmen to defend payment of the debt at par, and to advocate the sale of confiscated property for that purpose. The West Jersey bloc advocated repudiation, which would render confiscation unnecessary. When the war ended the latter reversed its stand and began to support heavier assessments.

The passage of acts regulating business, prices, and wages also separated the two legislative blocs. The first bill passed without a division, and a suspension, in 1777, failed by a nonpartisan vote. Beginning in the fall of 1779, however, West Jersey delegates voted against such acts. A more significant division appeared late in the period on votes concerning the energetic prosecution of military operations. In the spring session of 1780, West Jersey representatives opposed the appointment of a council of safety with extensive power and voted against granting the governor authority to declare martial law. They also opposed impressments of hay and teams later that year, and objected to measures strengthening the militia. Indeed, not until January 1781 did the legislature pass an adequate militia law. The distaste for fighting centered in the northernmost counties and in the area of Quaker strength, and explain why New Jersey contributed less than her share of men to the Continental Army.

Considering the state's political disadvantages, her lack of commerce, the extent of neutralism, and the damage caused by troops, New Jersey had performed reasonably well. She had contributed large quantities of supplies, if not of men, and closed the war in excellent financial condition. Her legislature displayed an unexpected degree of unity, for not until the outcome of the war was no longer in doubt did the fundamental differences between the two Jerseys become divisive. The loyalists presented no problem as the war came to a close; she faced no secessions, her constitution aroused no hostility; she continued to benefit from Livingston's strong leadership; and her citizens might well anticipate both peace and prosperity.

The Revolutionary history of Pennsylvania is varied enough to support almost any thesis, but sufficiently complex to refute all of them. Divisions on the basis of religion, national origin, section, class, and occupation are all significant, and the people differed with respect to several key questions. During the late Colonial period a distinct alignment had developed, and another would characterize the politics of the postwar years. The period 1776 to 1783 represents a transition between old and new, with some peculiar features of its own.

Three major religious groups influenced the government. Adherents of the Church of England had generally opposed extreme measures of resistance, preferring to remain within the empire if at all possible. Many did not lose hope until long after July 1776. Influential in the Philadelphia area, and occupying important positions, they did not wish to rock the boat. When it took from their point of view a dangerous port tack, they sought to recover the helm. Thus Reverend William Smith, Tom Paine's protagonist in the dispute over independence, struggled to retain the presidency of the College of Philadelphia, under him an Anglican stronghold, against Presbyterian efforts to expel him. Episcopalians such as the ironmasters Thomas Bull and Robert Coleman, together with the merchants George Clymer and Robert Morris, became leaders of the "Republican" party.

The Presbyterians, on the other hand, enthusiastically supported independence and worked to minimize the Episcopalian influence. A small group from Scotland, including the doctor Benjamin Rush and the lawyer James Wilson, settled in the southeast and, once the issue of independence had been decided, tended to support their Episcopalian and Quaker neighbors. The great majority, especially those from Ireland, lived some distance inland, where they furnished political leadership to the western, "radical" party, sympathizing with a democratic political system and farmer-oriented economic policies.

Finally, the Quakers and other religious groups of similar origin and convictions, including many Germans, occupied a unique position. As pacifists they of course opposed the war or paying taxes for the war. While they included all sorts of people, the Quakers in particular had prospered, so that they produced far more men of wealth than the Presbyterians. Most of them lived in the Philadelphia area and were influenced by that great commercial and cultural center. A few Quakers of the artisan class broke with their brethren to become enthusiastic rebels and radicals, like Timothy Matlack. More characteristically, the militant segment adhered, in other respects, to the ideas of the pacifist leaders. Thus the wealthy merchants Samuel Meredith and Thomas Mifflin, who had previously left the church, acted politically with George Logan and Samuel Morris, who remained members. Very likely in so doing they reflected the ideas less of their religion than of their section and class.

The Germans preferred to avoid politics entirely, hoping to escape both military service and taxation, which led them to support the Quaker leaders. After 1776, in the absence of an effective Quaker party, they found neither of the two major blocs particularly to their liking and divided irregularly, depending on the issue. During the war years they tended to support the Republicans, who were less associated with militant action and restrictions on voting, but thereafter they began to change, reacting to economic issues. A solid German vote never emerged.

Pennsylvania's population in 1776 extended along the southern part of the state in an elongated right triangle, the base running along the Delaware River and the apex near Pittsburgh. Most of the land remained empty. Quaker and Anglican immigrants from England and Wales had settled near Philadelphia along the Delaware and its tributaries such as the Schuylkill. This rich farmland produced a large surplus for export or, during the war, for the armies. The region also contained important manufacturing establishments and supported a profitable foreign trade. It was therefore highly commercialized, and its inhabitants were cultured, cosmopolitan, and contented. In Philadelphia, however, class differences had developed, and the increasingly self-conscious and articulate artisans challenged the domination of the merchants, professionals, and large landowners. The artisans may properly be called radical in that they sought major political changes and did not hesitate to use force. This militancy put them at sharp odds with the Quakers, whose radicalism never involved coercion, and with the Anglicans who tended, like many Quaker leaders, to prefer the existing arrangements.

West and northwest the people became more polyglot, German and Scottish-Irish settlements adjoining the English. The land continued generally rich and accessible to transportation, yet the people's attention focused more exclusively upon agriculture because they seldom traveled to Philadelphia nor did they follow the Susquehannah down to Baltimore—though their surplus might take that route to market. The commercial towns of York, Lancaster, and Reading, together with the presence of some prosperous traders, lawyers, and larger farmers, supplied a cosmopolitan element, so that this was in every way a transitional region. Still farther inland the counties of Cumberland, Franklin, Bedford, and Westmoreland in the west and Northumberland in the north remained frontier regions, as was Northampton in the northeast. These last four, for example, received tax relief because of Indian raids. Scottish-Irish and English settlers furnished leadership for the farmers, who tended to maintain extreme agrarian views. Separated from eastern Pennsylvania by mountains, poor roads, and rivers running the other way, the people differed in their goals and in their ideas from the Philadelphians.

The division of opinion concerning independence, as we have seen, made possible a political revolution symbolized by the state's democratic constitution. A struggle for independence requires the united energies of the people and is a dangerous time for political reform. Nevertheless, Philadelphia's radical leaders seized their chance, and perhaps the town artisans and the inland farmers, whose political influence grew, fought better under the new government than if the framers had entrusted power to the traditional rulers. On the other hand, the latter, many of whom were unenthusiastic about the Revolution anyway, either withdrew from politics entirely or fought, as it were, with only one hand. The state's serious financial problems during much of the war, and the uncertain quality of her leadership, stem from this division. The rancorous debate continued through and beyond the war years, separating the people along class lines and contributing to the development of political parties.

The Quakers and their pacifistic allies also contributed to the state's lack of unity. Pennsylvania was not alone in requiring an oath of allegiance which effectively disenfranchised pacifists, but the consequences there became doubly important because the nonjurors were so numerous and influential, and because the issue was related to support of the constitution. The Constitutionalists defined as enemies of the country not only those who were lukewarm about independence but critics of their government, and punished the Quakers on both grounds so that the opposition Republicans easily won over the Quakers. Although both parties agreed in penalizing outright loyalists, the treatment of neutrals remained controversial. As the war drew to a close the Republicans sought to modify anti-Tory legislation. Thus in June 1781 they unsuccessfully opposed an act requiring all nonjurors or anyone who had not served in the militia to pay taxes entirely in specie. So also they almost unanimously defended a loyalist's petition for a trial which might remove his burden. Ultimately the Republicans did repeal the test oath and other restrictive laws.

The widespread distaste for the war in the richest part of the state and among some of its wealthiest inhabitants prevented Pennsylvania from exerting her full financial strength until late in the contest. The Constitutionalist leaders, who occupied the key positions of authority, drew their support from artisans and farmers, not the financial elite, and they themselves owned modest properties: George Bryan, Charles Wilson Peale, David Rittenhouse, and Benjamin Workmen were able lawyers, artists, scientists, and pamphleteers, but they were better at drafting constitutions than raising money. They were able at first to draw on a surplus in the treasury which tided them over until March 1777. At that point the government issued £200,000 in legal-tender tax anticipation notes secured by a rather small tax of one and a half shillings in the pound (7.5 per cent) on the yearly value of the state's property, which would presumably return the £200,000 just printed. A revision that fall tripled the rate because of inflation. In March 1778 the legislature imposed a higher assessment but still lagged far behind most other Northern states, forcing the Supreme Executive Council to borrow from Congress. Moreover, the people paid taxes very slowly and reluctantly.

The state, of course, had suffered from the British occupation of Philadelphia and destructive raids in the west, but some of the delinquent counties lacked any such excuse. Indeed, the state must have prospered. British purchases of supplies and services probably offset the damage they caused, while American armies bought large quantities of provisions. Philadelphia merchants profited more than those of any other city, and the federal loan office depended primarily on them and other northern traders. The process by which Pennsylvanians acquired a large share of the federal debt began during these years. The rapid increase of money in Philadelphia also meant that inflation proceeded most rapidly there.

The Constitutionalists, lacking the confidence of the business community and confronting almost insurmountable financial problems, took the blame for the inflation and lost the election of November 1780. Even before that they had shifted their financial policies. A hard core clung to paper money and legal-tender laws, but early in 1780 the Philadelphia leaders agreed to suspend the tender act, carrying with them enough scattered rural votes to pass the measure. The Republicans, led by Robert Morris, provided not only votes but some of the major statements in favor of the new policy which Morris himself implemented as treasurer. The embarrassed Constitutionalists, still unable to raise enough money by taxes, were obliged to authorize Morris in June 1781 to buy necessary supplies and draw up to £500,000 in notes. Morris agreed because, though he disliked putting more money into circulation, he desperately needed supplies. At the same time the legislature levied a tax payable entirely in specie, abolished legal tender acts, established a new scale of depreciation satisfactory to the merchants, arranged for the sale of state-owned Philadelphia property, and pledged the arrearages for prewar land grants as collateral for the new bills. The state's financial problems continued. In the spring of 1782 the legislature authorized the government to borrow money for the defense of the frontier, which fortunately proved unnecessary. That fall the treasurer borrowed £5,000 from the Bank of North America and in the spring, with the treasury again empty, Governor John Dickinson offered £1,000 (at interest) to enlist men in the army.

Pennsylvania's record, however, was not entirely bad. She had levied, between 1778 and 1783, £21 million in continental money, £367,000 in state money, and £745,000 specie, receiving most of the first two but only about a third of the last. Her debt in 1784 stood at £540,280, exclusive of £216,667 owed to the Penns and her share of the federal debt, estimated at £124,000 annually. On the credit side, she held extensive vacant lands expected to bring in £28,000 annually, plus a like sum from miscellaneous licenses and fines, perhaps £90,000 from import duties and an excise tax on liquor, and whatever she could collect from taxes on real and personal estates, valued at £30 or £40 million. The legislature estimated annual expenditures at around £210,000 so that an assessment of a little more than two-tenths of 1 per cent of the taxable property, or about 4.5 per cent of the annual income, would easily balance the budget. Indeed, the collection of back taxes would pay the domestic debt. Everything depended, of course, on the resumption of prosperity.

Raising and supplying the army proved difficult in Pennsylvania because so many people opposed military service and because Indian pressure on the frontier kept western militia units pinned down. The Constitutionalists pushed through a basic and fairly effective militia bill in March 1777. This enrolled all white men between eighteen and fifty-three, with a few exceptions, into companies, allowing the soldiers to elect all their officers even up to colonels. Each company would contain eight classes, which the Supreme Executive Council might call into service in rotation. Anyone could find a substitute. A subsequent law added exceptions, relieved any two persons who procured a recruit for the Continental Army, and imposed heavy fines for non-service. Subsequently the state promised to volunteers tracts of land ranging from two hundred acres for privates up to two thousand acres for major generals. This combination of rewards and punishments enabled Pennsylvania to furnish her share of Continentals.

The Assembly and Congress both depended upon this rich state for supplies, with indifferent success. The suffering at Valley Forge finally compelled the legislature, meeting almost as a government-in-exile at Lancaster, to authorize impressments, a practice which subsequent assemblies continued. As customary, the commissioners paid current prices as set by neighbors for whatever the family did not need. In 1780 the legislature began to impose taxes payable in provisions, salt, and rum. These measures, belatedly enforced, seem to have succeeded. But efforts to regulate prices failed. The Assembly passed a regulatory act in March 1778, trailing most of the other Northern states by some months, but suspended it the next session. Sharp price increases and rumors of profiteering by speculators led to widespread demands for a strict law. A legislative committee recommended such a bill, and during 1779 various town committees undertook to enforce price restrictions. The trading interests, however, strongly opposed any general policy, as we have seen, and fought it off successfully. The Assembly did prohibit the exportation of provisions, but when the Republicans gained power in 1781 they repealed the law. The debate over this question helped to divide the people politically.

Several issues which became even more important after 1783 also divided the Pennsylvanians during the war years. Robert Morris and other merchants obtained a charter for their Bank of North America in 1782. The Constitutionalists from the outset suspected anything Morris approved. The bank's usefulness prevented them from entirely opposing the charter, but they did seek unsuccessfully to restrict its power, attempting to deprive it of the right to own land and to require reconsideration of the charter after seven years. The votes on these clauses divided the two parties very sharply. The Constitutionalists also indicated their political point of view by protecting the interests of debtors, first through advocacy of legal tender acts and then by other legislation after the repeal of those acts. Both parties worked to collect taxes during the war years, but with the cessation of military need the Constitutionalists began to express the rural reluctance to pay the government debt, voting in December 1782 to suspend the collection of a tax intended for Congress. The different composition of the two parties is also indicated by an Assembly roll call on whether to levy a tax on ready money, which the Philadelphia Republicans and their supporters blocked; the division clearly reflected the relative wealth of the legislators. The two groups also opposed one another on the College of Philadelphia's charter. In 1779 the Constitutionalists succeeded in repealing the charter so as to abolish the trustees, the Anglican President William Smith, and his faculty, replacing them with a new, pro-rebel, Presbyterian set. The alignment on the abolition of slaves also followed party lines in a general way, but it was partly sectional and primarily cultural.

Although the full flowering of Pennsylvania's two-party system came after the war, the contending groups had actively struggled for power ever since the writing of the state constitution. Both ran "tickets" in various counties, got out the vote, and attacked each other in the press. One Philadelphian explained to a Rhode Island correspondent that the Republicans who succeeded in the election of 1780 were "whigs of a more moderate and deliberate cast, of more property and more respectable capacities—Many of them old hands in the legislature—Many Quaker Whigs." The Constitutionalist view of the same men differed only in words. To them, the political existence of the Republicans demonstrated that the rich were more corrupt than the poor, and less favorable to independence: "Very wealthy men have seldom been patriots, either in ancient or modern times." The Republicans, moreover, sought to "exchange a free Constitution for a System of aristocratick or monarchical Despotism." Behind the rhetoric lay real issues: the treatment of pacifists, the nature of the constitution, monetary policy and other economic questions, the bank, the college, and control of the government. The Republicans derived their leadership from the state's economic and social elite, from the Philadelphia business and professional men. They drew support from Episcopalians, Quakers, southeastern farmers, and men of the same interests everywhere. The Constitutionalist spokesmen generally owned less property, often engaged in farming, and drew their votes from the rural areas and less reliably from the Philadelphia artisans. In both, political ideology, religious conviction, sectional objectives, and economic interest mingled in a typically American political amalgam.

# Chapter Eleven

# Southern Politics During the War

THE states from Delaware to Georgia, considered collectively, faced even more serious difficulties during the war than did those to the north. They were handicapped just as much by loyalists and even more by a shortage of liquid capital. The extensive settlements from Virginia south created vexing problems of transportation. The virtual absence of experienced native traders deprived the governments of financial ability and the armies of efficient supply officers. Finally, the Southern labor force furnished relatively few soldiers because it consisted mostly of slaves. These ingredients varied, of course, from state to state. Delaware, fortunately, escaped all but one, though the exception at first almost took her out of the war.

Loyalism in Delaware, as we have seen, took the form of sullen reluctance to aid the war in any way. From the beginning Sussex County strongly opposed radical action, and the two sides were equally matched in Kent. After the Declaration of Independence, opponents of the decision remained powerful, winning the November elections in Sussex. The legislature sent moderates to replace Caesar Rodney and Thomas McKean in Congress because they had voted for independence, retaining George Read, who had opposed it. Under President John McKinley the state dragged its heels. That fall the legislature issued a small number of bills secured by future taxes and agreed to raise a battalion, but took no effective action against loyalists and levied no taxes for more than a year. The Sussex delegates to the legislature rarely bothered to attend during 1776 and 1777. Uprisings continued there in 1777 and again in 1778. These disturbances and the general state of public opinion reduced the state's effectiveness throughout the war. She contributed fewer men to the army than did any other state: Rhode Island, for example, with only a slightly larger population, furnished two and a half times more Continentals. Fortunately for Delaware, most of the fighting took place elsewhere.

The Whigs finally gained control of the government in the late autumn of 1777. The British invasion in September, during which they occupied Wilmington, aroused the patriots to greater efforts, while many of their opponents disfranchised themselves by refusing to take the oath of allegiance.

Once the Whigs commanded the legislature they could take more effective action. The New Castle County delegates generally could count on support from Kent County, and the Legislative Council contained some able, though moderate, leaders. The government assessed steadily increasing taxes and succeeded in borrowing money to pay the militia and provide supplies for the Continental troops. A June 1778 law prevented the export of provisions, though

Delaware refused to regulate prices despite pleas from Congress and private agreements by prominent New Castle citizens (indeed, Pennsylvania used Delaware's failure as an excuse to rescind her own law). Also in 1778, the legislature first offered nonjurors a chance to reconsider, then confiscated the estates of forty-six men. By the end of another year, sales in New Castle County furnished more than £10,000 toward the war effort.

Delaware had to contend with the same inflation as did the other states. She seemed, however, not to contribute to it except by her refusal to enact price restrictions. The state issued relatively little paper money, relying instead upon loans and taxes. The legislature never authorized the avalanche of certificates that plagued other states, but obtained supplies by taxes payable in flour, hay, corn, beef, pork, wheat, oats, rye, beans, peas, and salt. Her leaders refrained from exacting those sacrifices that full participation in the war demanded, for fear that the people would not tolerate it. Her per capita taxes, however, compared favorably with those of other states, and she experienced no serious financial problem until after the 1781 deflation.

In the closing years of the war public opinion forced some easing of the financial burden. The legislature followed its repeal of legal-tender clauses with a reduction of taxes and a stay law on suits for debt. In the spring of 1783 the Council recommended that the people pay £39,000 specie in order to meet all demands, but the Assembly would permit only £26,250. At that time the taxpayers were defaulting on earlier hard-money assessments, and it seemed more to the point to press for the collection of old taxes than to multiply burdens. A year later the budget, including all state expenses and Congress's requisition, came to £23,625, a reasonable figure for a population of 45,000. Even the Legislative Council's estimate of £39,000, derived from a more pessimistic view of the adjusted debt, would not have been excessive, assuming continued prosperity.

Delaware's legislature during the war reflected persistent sectional divisions within the state. New Castle County contained almost all of the manufacturing and the principal commercial centers. Most of the people there were farmers, but men with nonfarm occupations dominated the economy and sent business or professional men to the legislature. This area, growing rapidly in wealth, was the dynamic, cosmopolitan region. Its representatives favored energetic prosecution of the war, support of Congress, efficient collection of taxes, and measures benefiting their county. Their opposites in the legislature came from agricultural Sussex County, whose people lacked a good port and remained isolated from the outside world. They were more ready to repel interference than to cooperate with their neighbors. After 1777 Sussex delegates supported the war despite their constituents' neutralism. On other grounds, however, they frequently opposed New Castle's representations. Kent County, the central county, was divided. This north-south alignment continued after the war.

On the whole, Delaware's legislators had carried out the wishes of their constituents. They had supported the war, but not with enthusiasm, had allowed all but a few loyalists to live in peace, used force only against insurrection, had limited expenses, avoided impressments, permitted the less martial to hire substitutes, imposed moderate taxes, and kept united a badly divided state.

Marylanders also divided over independence and internal issues, but loyalist areas in the state were scattered and weaker. The southernmost counties of the eastern shore, as we know, had to be kept in line by force, and that section generally produced only halfhearted rebels. Almost all of the people there farmed for a living, producing livestock and miscellaneous food products rather than tobacco. The area was isolated, containing few schools or towns and no newspapers, and few inhabitants ever traveled across the bay. Leadership came from a few principal families, whom the people habitually chose to office and who, like the English country squire, usually supported the King rather than his critics during the Colonial period. They entered upon independence reluctantly, producing few outright loyalists but few ardent rebels. It was perhaps fortunate for the Revolution in Maryland that geography reduced the political influence of the eastern shore. The capital was situated across the bay, so the more distant delegates arrived late, left early, and sometimes never attended at all. Such behavior characterized all the eastern shore, but the degree was roughly proportionate to the remoteness of the community.

The three northernmost counties of Baltimore, Harford, and Cecil also contained many nonjurors, produced little tobacco, and consisted principally of small farmers. They differed, however, in other respects. Except for a fringe along the coast near Baltimore, where some large landowners lived, there were few slaves. The farmers worked the land themselves, concentrating on generalized agriculture with a surplus of grain and perhaps pork. The area was only recently settled, and the dominant point of view was a rural radicalism reminiscent of that in many Northern communities or of the Carolina Piedmont. The town of Baltimore had not yet become influential, and it seems to have been politically cut off from the countryside. Why so many of the farmers in the area failed to support the revolution remains unclear. Perhaps the presence of Quakers had something to do with it. Moreover, in Maryland, large-scale tobacco planters and townspeople led the movement for independence, and the northern farmers may have regarded them as natural opponents rather than as trustworthy allies, a conviction which the state constitution would confirm. Their refusal to swear allegiance to the Revolutionary government probably reflected less a loyalism to the old regime than a suspicion of the new one.

The same factors contributed to neutralism farther west. Here also were many small farms, relatively few slaves, diversified agriculture, recent settlements, and political opposition to the tobacco planters. In addition, German and Scottish-Irish settlers moving south from Pennsylvania had little in common with the easterners and tried to avoid militia duty. Representatives from Montgomery, Frederick, and Washington counties joined with those from the north to form the axis of a minority party in the legislature.

The politically dominant section of Maryland consisted of the five counties between the lower Potomac River and the Chesapeake Bay and the two major towns, Annapolis and Baltimore. Here lived the great tobacco planters who, as the "country party," fought proprietary rule before 1776 and led the Revolutionary movement. Indeed, resistance to England seems, in Maryland, to have been causally connected with the tobacco economy. Until 1776 the tobacco planters took the opposite side on many issues from the urban merchants and lawyers and the eastern shore planters, but after that date they tended to unite behind the conservative, elitist constitution, forming a coalition of essentially like-minded men who differed only on certain sectional issues. The alliance dominated Maryland throughout the war.

Maryland's government benefited from the services of most of the colony's experienced leaders. Only a handful, such as the Delanys, left the state, while able men like Charles Carroll, Richard Barnes, Daniel of St. Thomas Jenifer, George Plater, John Smith (the Baltimore merchant), and Thomas Stone brought business as well as political acumen to their high offices. After the first few years the executive departments, under Thomas Johnson and Thomas Sim Lee, operated efficiently.

The state escaped any important invasion of British troops and suffered little physical damage during the war except from the naval blockade of the Chesapeake. British troop activities, the temporary closing of overseas markets, and the English seizure of Maryland property in Britain caused economic losses, but the French were soon buying tobacco and the West Indies absorbing whatever supplies the American army did not purchase. The state began the war in excellent financial condition and emerged wounded but basically strong. Loyalists created little trouble. Brief riots in the west expressed only temporary resentment against forced military service, and the uprisings on the eastern shore ceased after 1777.

Despite her relative freedom from strife, Maryland contributed only an average share of men and supplies to the war effort, and so may serve as a typical example. All of the states south of populous New England encountered great difficulty in filling their Continental battalions. Relative to the supply of productive land, New England had an abundance of labor, but farther south the farm boys either remained on their more profitable farms supervising their slaves or sought the attractive vacant land. Maryland throughout the war struggled with indifferent success to recruit enough soldiers. The legislature early supplemented Congress's bounty with further inducements. An act of 1777 enabled citizens to escape military duty for three years if they furnished a soldier for the American army. They could not, however, enlist an artisan or pay anyone more than $30. This proving inadequate to fill its quota, the legislature enacted a draft law. High-ranking officers formed all eligible men into "classes," or groups, equal in number to the soldiers needed. Each class then either found a volunteer or drafted one of its members. The threat of a draft, the payment of bounties, and early enthusiasm for the war enabled Maryland to supply its quota of men during 1777 and 1778. After that year the supply of volunteers decreased, probably due to a mixture of war-weariness, depreciation of the soldiers' pay, and a closer acquaintance with army life. The legislature attempted to avoid a forced draft by exempting any two men who supplied a third. A general revision in 1780 tried to meet the criticism that rich men escaped by buying the service of the poor. Now the county lieutenant formed the classes out of the tax assessment rolls, each class containing men worth, collectively, £16,000, mixing the well-to-do men with others having little property or none. Each class then supplied a recruit. If a class failed, someone was drafted by lot, all of the others paying a fine of which the draftee received one-fourth and the state the rest. In addition, the recruit earned a Continental bounty, clothes, fifty acres of land, and a tax exemption during his service and for four years thereafter. The delegates countered the obstacle raised by the soldiers' inadequate pay by pledging loyalist property, after its confiscation, for the redemption of the certificates. Maryland also, like other states, issued depreciation certificates for the difference between the intended and real value of the soldiers' notes. In October 1780 the legislature permitted slaves to obtain their freedom by enlistment, reimbursing the owner for his loss. This step reflected the military crisis of that year; other slave states avoided it. At the same time the delegates again threatened to draft men if the propertied members of the "classes" could not bribe a substitute. Apparently the state's line filled for the first time in two years. As a rule Maryland fell short of her quota, and she stood halfway down the list in Continentals per capita.

The state also organized militia units beginning in 1775. The basic law, two years later, enrolled all able-bodied whites aged sixteen to fifty except members of the Council, the chancellor, judges, ministers, and indentured servants. Every company was divided into eight classes which the governor could call into service. One of the more interesting votes of the period limited the militia's service outside the state to two months. Another in 1783 excused from militia duty members of the legislature and delegates to Congress. Opponents of the exemption argued that these men, as gentlemen of the first character and fortune, should set an example to the people; but those favoring it replied that persons who had such qualities would surely step forward voluntarily if needed, with even better effect.

Maryland, unlike Delaware, passed effective laws to obtain supplies for the army. Beginning in June 1777 the legislature regulated prices and profits and placed embargoes on the export of provisions which she renewed every session until March 1781. For more than a year the government prohibited the distilling of liquor from grain. The legislature authorized the impressment of clothing as early as the fall of 1777. Especially chosen purchasers gave certificates, the value being determined by agreement or by some reputable person, and if the owner refused to sell, two or three neighbors would decide what he could spare without distress. The governor and Council received extensive emergency powers including the purchase of provisions and control over the militia. The legislature always limited the duration of these laws very strictly but renewed them every session until 1781. Early in 1778, when the Continental Army was encamped at Valley Forge, the Council authorized purchasers to seize cattle if the owners refused to sell, leaving enough for the family and paying a fixed price. They also allowed the impressment of wagons, teams, drivers, boats, and laborers. When Chesapeake Bay froze in November 1779, causing a serious local shortage of food for the army, the legislature empowered committees to search out surplus grain and flour and to impress boats, wagons, and storehouses, paying in interest-bearing certificates. The same exceptional powers were granted again in July 1780, being finally revoked after Yorktown. A report of the House in December 1781 conveys some notion of the results. An act of the previous year to obtain provisions had raised £69,941 of the required £82,706, or nearly 85 per cent. These efforts seldom met Congress's requisitions but did furnish enough supplies for the Yorktown campaign.

Considering the difficulties, Maryland's record was commendable. Almost from the start the rise in prices made farmers reluctant to sell for state-determined prices, even if they favored the rebel cause, which many did not. They viewed the quartermaster certificates with no more enthusiasm than they did Continental and state money. Even when the commissioners did obtain livestock and flour, a scarcity of salt or barrels could prevent slaughtering and packing, while inadequate transportation might further dam up the supplies. Bad weather, insects, profiteers, and the British navy multiplied the difficulties as they did throughout the thirteen states.

Maryland's relative success in obtaining supplies was due to her exceptional financial strength. At the beginning of

the war the treasury showed a surplus of more than £200,-
000, primarily in bonds loaned by the colony and stock in
the Bank of England. This capital had enabled the proprietary government to issue an equivalent sum in paper notes
which served as currency. The assessment list of about £12
million encouraged the convention to issue £400,000 in
tax anticipation notes. The first tax, in February 1777, imposed a rate of ten shillings per £100, or about .5 per cent,
plus assessments on the profits from trade and professional
activities. A year later the legislature, finding the auditors'
books in a mess, reorganized the financial system. It reported
no money in the treasury and levied a further tax, which
together with loans furnished enough money so that a house
committee discovered, in November, "a sufficient sum in
the treasury to answer any demand thereon that is likely
soon to be made."

This happy situation changed over the winter, and in
March the government found it necessary to issue £300,000
in legal-tender notes backed by another tax of roughly that
amount. Efforts to assess even more were defeated in the
lower house. By 1779 the tax rate had jumped to nearly 10
per cent, and the state had imposed half a million pounds in
two years. In November the lower house concluded that
the people could no longer bear property taxes sufficient
to meet Congress's requisitions and the state's needs. The
debt had reached nearly a million pounds and Congress
needed still more. Moreover, collections were lagging and
the auditors had not yet created an orderly system. The
delegates were willing to impose another tax but insisted
upon the confiscation of British property as an essential war
measure.

The crisis excited the usual financial debate, with the Senate fighting against confiscation and proposing even higher

taxes together with a return to a specie basis. The delegates agreed to further taxes payable not in specie but in provisions, tobacco transfer notes, and certificates, adding also levies on tobacco exported and on imported goods. As they gradually moved toward currency deflation the delegates protected debtors by prohibiting suits for prewar 1776 debts. The Senate ultimately agreed to this and accepted confiscation, while on their part the delegates in the fall of 1780 adopted a hard-money policy, borrowed funds at 6 per cent interest using the loyalist estates for security, and imposed another new tax. At this point a revised estimate of the annual cost of the war stood at about £300,000 specie to be raised from a tax base of £16 million, not an impossible burden in itself but heavy on top of back taxes and the necessity of paying interest on the debt. Unable to raise sufficient money from the people, the legislature again resorted to issuing £200,000 worth of tax anticipation notes, tried to borrow money by offering a bonus of 8 per cent, began to sell confiscated land, and reassured the state's creditors by starting a thorough adjustment of claims. Fortunately this program met the approval of the conservative Senate and of the Annapolis and Baltimore townspeople. County committees of prominent planters also agreed to support the new bills.

These measures pulled the state through the final year of fighting but left the treasury exhausted. A finance committee reported in November 1782 that the annual cost of government, including Continental requisitions and current state charges, would exceed £200,000. The tax base had declined to £12 million, necessitating a rate of 1/60, or one-third of the annual income as people usually estimated it. It seems likely, however, that the actual value of the state's property was about double that of the assessment list. The committee believed that the state's coin did not exceed £100,000. It recommended that the needed tax be made payable in certificates of debt, tobacco, pork, wheat, or notes of the Bank of North America. They further recommended the prompt sale of confiscated estates. On paper, then, Maryland's budget balanced, and a report the following May found the state's assets equal to her liabilities. The assets, however, included a large sum in uncollected taxes, a problem compounded because the treasury always lost by payments in produce. The prospect, therefore, depended upon the people's ability to pay their very considerable private debts and still meet the state's demands. A report in 1787 estimated that all of these obligations, including the prewar British debt, totaled nearly £2.5 million owed by the people to public and private creditors. Only a high level of prosperity would enable Maryland to solve her financial problems.

During the war years Marylanders divided not only over resistance to England but on many other issues. One group of delegates reflected the views of the farmers in the northern and western counties, while another represented the dominant opinion of the eastern shore and the southern counties on the western shore. Whether the voters agreed with their spokesmen is hard to say, but probably they did except on the eastern shore, where the legislators, chosen from the planter elite, supported the war regardless of the loyalist spirit among the ordinary folk. Of these two parties, the eastern shore-southern Chesapeake bloc invariably controlled the Senate and usually, but not always, the lower house.

Since almost all of the delegates either had favored independence or supported that step after the fact, policies toward the loyalists did not divide men along "party" lines but according to individual opinions. The Senate proved more protective of liberty and property while the representatives passed harsher restrictive laws and backed confiscation. Similarly, the vote on ratifying the Articles of Confederation and on many lesser questions revealed no consistent alignment.

Problems relating to support of the war, however, other than disciplining Tories, found the two groups opposed. The northern and western bloc disliked energetic or expensive measures which might injure small property holders. They voted against the forcible collection of blankets, the strict draft law, and prolonged militia service out of the state. They also disapproved exempting high civil officials from military service, a step which would of course throw a corresponding burden on the rest of the people. They disliked high taxes, whether intended for Congress or the state. They objected to assessing farm products, trying instead to shift the burden to nonfarm property such as carriages and mercantile paper and the profits of professionals and traders. These delegates tried to avoid payment of taxes in coin, preferring certificates or farm products.

The same group sought to reduce expenses wherever possible. They favored low salaries or fees for public officials—except members of the legislature. In the latter case, they argued, recompense should be high enough to enable ordinary folk to leave their farms and represent their neighbors, otherwise government would fall by default into the hands of the rich. Their opponents replied that profitable salaries might attract demagogues or profiteers instead of gentlemen who, lacking any base pecuniary motive, would govern impartially. The northern and western men also reflected their economic interests by supporting high prices for beef and pork but a low rate for tobacco. Similarly, they displayed an anti-business bias, as when they tried to reduce the profits of retailers below 30 per cent and prevented officials from engaging in trade. They backed low land prices for soldiers and favored debtors over creditors. Their fiscal policy relied upon continued issues of legal-tender paper money, and they fought the financial reforms of 1780–1781. We can judge something of their social and cultural ideas from their opposition to a theater in Annapolis.

These votes together with the geographical distribution of the opposing groups indicates their principal characteristics. The eastern shore–southern Chesapeake bloc, which also included the Annapolis and Baltimore delegates, contained most of the traders and professional men, who indeed made up five-eighths of their total. Even the great landowners among them often had some other economic interest, as did Henry Dennis of Worcester, a privateer. These were men of large property, often well-educated, who came from Maryland's more prominent families and enjoyed considerably more political experience than their antagonists. Those men of reputation who sat in the lower house belonged to this group, including Samuel Chase, John Smith, Richard Barnes, Nicholas Maccubin, and the two Hindmans. The northern and western bloc boasted no such well-known names. It included almost no one except farmers and few men of wealth, education, or experience. It was the rural party, the party of localists, rather narrow, yet much closer to the people. It remained a minority throughout the period.

In 1776 Virginia exceeded every other state in the number of her people and the extent of her territory. Most of the people and almost all of the slaves, however, lived in that part of the state east of the Blue Ridge and in the Shenandoah Valley just beyond. The most productive counties were now some distance inland. The old coastal counties had long since begun to feel the twofold effects of soil exhaustion and debts. The large planters, who still dominated the east politically and socially, attempted to restore their declining fortunes by shifting from tobacco to grain or livestock, but many found themselves chained to tobacco culture. Some historians have seen in economic discontent a motive toward separation from England, and it is true that many prominent rebels had debts while some conspicuous loyalists did not. Certainly loyalism centered in the coastal counties, where tobacco was becoming less profitable rather than in the newer, more fertile tobacco lands.

The successful planters had rapidly moved up the major river valleys. One of their strongholds was the "Northern Neck," a scene of vast speculative activity between the Potomac and the Rappahannock, now filled with great landholders, some small farmers, numerous tenants, and many slaves. A similar development, though with fewer tenants, took place along the James. The area south of that river—the "Southside"—like the counties of the west-central region, had been settled during the generation just before the war. Although some big tobacco planters had quickly moved in and the number of slaves was increasing rapidly, small farmers predominated, setting the economic, social, and cultural tone. Virginia east of the Blue Ridge was a rich agricultural state, exporting an impressive surplus. Unfortunately her people's appetite for imported goods consumed the income from exports, and her failure to develop a strong native merchant class proved costly. Thus she entered the war with little liquid capital.

Another rapidly expanding area lay in the Shenandoah River valley beyond the Blue Ridge, where independent small farmers produced excellent wheat and livestock. Farther west, however, the war halted the movement of people into what are now West Virginia and Kentucky. The westerners engaged in a long sporadic Indian war, with the usual indiscriminate slaughter on both sides. The legislature did appropriate money for their relief, but the pioneers never obtained what they wanted and needed: men and supplies for a truly decisive campaign. They grew increasingly bitter, and we find them reluctant to pay taxes or otherwise support the easterners' war. Secession sentiment smouldered throughout the period.

The war also created, discontent at the other end of the state, where the two detached counties of the eastern shore and the region near the mouth of the James lay open to British raids. Norfolk had been burned, its hinterland invaded, and naval activities in Chesapeake Bay continued to injure commerce. Fortunately the rest of the state remained untouched until early in 1781, when Benedict Arnold landed in the James Valley and for several months controlled that rich area as far west as Richmond. Cornwallis arrived in May and at one point sent a detachment to Jefferson's home in the foothills of the mountains. Not until June was the state safe again. The people of the southeastern counties lost much property from these operations, especially in slaves, but most Virginians escaped entirely. On the whole they got off lightly.

Virginia's government during these years remained under the control of the large landowners. Unlike Maryland's legislature, the House of Delegates contained only a handful of members in trade, and practically all representatives and senators were farmers at least some of the time. The agricultural interest therefore ruled with little help from businessmen—not a desirable situation during a war. Ordinary farmers, as opposed to large planters, increased their influence as a result of independence, a change applauded by some observers and deplored by others, but the degree of change can easily be exaggerated; most representatives still were men of considerable property, and the more important committees consisted of the same sort of person who had earlier controlled the Burgesses. They solidified their power, as we have seen, by increasing the influence of county justices and then making them almost an oligarchy. These leaders possessed intelligence, political experience, and good educations along with their property; whether these qualities sufficed for waging a war remained to be seen.

At first sight Virginia appears fully capable of sustaining a prolonged conflict. Both her population and her tax base considerably exceeded Maryland's, and her exports, especially of tobacco, were nearly twice as great. But she had several weaknesses. She relied too heavily upon tobacco as a cash crop. Although she did contain some iron manufactories, few industries had developed and, like most Southern states, she depended upon imports for many necessities. Her wealth lay primarily in land and slaves, not easily converted into the sinews of war. Unlike Maryland she had never generated much of her own capital but depended upon Britain, partly because her trade remained almost entirely in the hands of English and Scottish merchants. Rather, instead of accumulating capital, Virginians acquired debts. Instead of a nest egg in the Bank of England, the Virginia treasury contained almost nothing, a situation partly created by Treasurer Robinson's loaning provincial funds to his friends on inadequate security. Some planters, like Washington, prospered by careful attention to profits and losses and by diversifying their investments, but most of them seemed unaware of business methods, operating at a net loss, spending freely, and running deeper into debt without maintaining their credit by payments. Deficit financing became almost a way of life, justified perhaps by the exploitation of great natural resources, but conducted through accident rather than by policy. As a result, Virginians proved less prepared than their northern neighbors to surmount the economic obstacles of war.

The state began wholeheartedly with a prohibition on the export of provisions in 1775 and an act raising soldiers for the Continental Army. But Maryland's failure to follow suit led to a repeal of the embargo, which was not reimposed until the seige of Yorktown. Efforts to fill the Continental line lagged from the outset because the treasury lacked money for bounties and volunteers did not appear in the necessary numbers. The legislature never overcame these difficulties. The refusal to enlist slaves deprived the army of one potential source of recruits, though freedmen could serve. Farmers proved reluctant to leave their homes for prolonged periods, even when more well-to-do men raised money to hire substitutes. Toward the end of the fighting the legislature drafted militia units into the regular army, but public opinion, as expected, condemned this "odious, unequal and oppressive" method which "has always met the aversion of the people, and they have dreaded it as one of the greatest calamities that could befal them." In the end Virginia contributed somewhat less than her share of Continentals and fewer than Connecticut.

The government's reluctance to use coercion and to centralize control of the war effort seriously hindered efforts to supply the army. The state never developed an efficient quartermaster corps but relied upon ad hoc arrangements; as late as March 1781 a permanent organization remained only a subject for discussion. Not until the fall of 1780 did the legislature pass a law establishing a fixed system for county quotas for clothing, provisions, and wagons, paid for by receipts. Long before this, depreciation had led many farmers to insist upon specie. Not until the British invaded the state did the legislature authorize the executive to impose embargoes and impress provisions, and not until Cornwallis surrendered were the sheriffs subjected to heavy fines for failure to furnish horses and wagons. These belated measures promptly aroused protest. A petition from Prince William County termed them unconstitutional and complained of robbery and tyranny; a militia colonel felt that seizures "soured" the minds of the people and discouraged industry. Enforcement under Governor Thomas Nelson, a merchant and a general, helped greatly to supply Washington's victorious troops, after which the government backtracked and the troops suffered.

Although some states acted with greater decision and efficiency, many of Virginia's troubles existed everywhere. Certainly her financial difficulties were far from unique, though her lack of liquid capital compounded the problem. As usual, Virginia at first resorted to tax anticipation notes to pay for her armies, issuing more than £1.1 million during the first two years. Not until the end of 1777 did the legislature come to grips with the financial realities of a long war, providing for interest-bearing loans and levying taxes which were expected to realize £250,000 annually. This assessment, following that of Maryland earlier in the year, amounted to .5 per cent on the value of land, slaves, horses, money, the income from salaries, and a few other items, together with a general poll tax, an export tax on tobacco of roughly 5 per cent, and an excise on liquor. The delegates rejected a proposed tax on dogs. The following year the government tried unsuccessfully to borrow money in France, but did draw £300,000 on loan from her own citizens and about half as much in taxes, leaving a deficit of £445,000 paid out in the form of treasurer's notes. The state's financial record to this point compares unfavorably with that of her Northern allies, in that she had issued far more paper and obtained relatively less from loans and taxes.

In the spring of 1779 the legislature tried to speed up tax collections by two reforms. First, it recognized the unequal distribution of property by evaluating the land of each county separately. Second, it levied a special tax payable in wheat, corn, rye, barley, oats, hemp, or tobacco. It then increased the tax rate, to such good effect that the people paid twice as much as before. The treasury succeeded in borrowing more too, but ended by again issuing some £1.2 million in notes. Virginia thus contributed £3 million to the inflation which became serious that year, and which private price-fixing agreements failed to halt. The practice followed by some sheriffs of privately loaning out moneys to their friends, though it had excellent precedent in Virginia, did not help matters: thus the state received nothing from Prince William County, all the money going to the high sheriff himself and to the state's attorney, Cuthbert Bullett, both of whom bought land with government funds.

Forced again to borrow money, well aware of inflation, yet unwilling further to burden the politically powerful planters, the delegates sought other sources of revenue to provide security for loans and money for Congress. In the fall session of 1779 they began the sale of loyalist property, increased the poll tax, introduced a 2.5 per cent tariff, and assessed the same rate on all of the retailers' stock, making this part of the act retroactive to the first of the year. They then added subsequently a .5 per cent tax on other property and included cattle on the assessment list. The taxes on trade aroused strong protests from the merchants and shopkeepers, but they could be ignored. More worrisome were petitions from farming communities pleading lack of funds.

During the final two years of the war, Virginia, like her sister states, barely eluded bankruptcy. Supplies for the campaigns in the west and around Yorktown came largely from seizures and the use of certificates; paper money gradually lost its value and ceased to circulate. Sales of public land helped a little, and the treasury received about £20 million (in depreciated currency) from taxes, sales of loyalist property, loans, and lesser sources. Nevertheless the government had to anticipate taxes by more than twice that sum. Clearly, Virginia's citizens, even after extensive issues of money, lacked the financial capacity necessary to adopt a fiscal system based on hard money, until the fighting ended. What pulled the state through was her immense wealth in public lands, pledged as collateral for the final issues of paper, and as inducements to soldiers. In December 1781 the legislature finally risked popular displeasure, already evident in anti-tax riots, by repealing legal-tender laws and imposing taxes payable in specie, specie equivalents, tobacco, hemp, and flour. The people's answer seems to have been refusal to pay except in commodities and little even of that, forcing the delegates to postpone collections. By April 1783 no less than forty-three counties, scattered all over the state but located especially in the west and south, owed £56,386. The liquidated state debt in 1785 exceeded £2 million, one of the country's highest per capita.

The Virginia planter class inherited from these economic problems a permanent horror of paper money, curious in a people who had experienced its benefits before the war and most unusual in a largely agricultural society. But they fully appreciated one effect of the Revolution: the new composition of the legislature. It was one thing for a planter-dominated House of Burgesses to issue paper money and quite another for the post-1776 House of Delegates to do so.

Thus the principal leaders were converted to a gold and silver standard. Not everyone adopted the hard-money view: petitions from the Southside stated forcibly that debtors would suffer and that taxpayers could not endure a monetary system depending upon specie.

As we look back on it, Virginia could have followed no other course during the war but deficit financing, relying upon the ultimate productivity of her land to pay the cost of victory. Her failure to draw forth her full resources, if we have properly assessed the situation, seems due to the planters' reluctance to employ forceful, energetic measures —to use coercion, a reluctance evident in her slowness to enact embargoes, price-fixing laws and taxes, and to authorize decisive action by her executives. The major exception, a willingness to confiscate British debts and prolong the life of legal-tender laws, flowed from the same economic difficulties that plagued Virginians throughout the war.

The initiative for confiscation acts and legal tender clauses came not from the eastern planter leadership but from men of the south and west. While most Virginians agreed in their determination to win the war, scattered votes in the House of Delegates reveal a persistent opposition between the men of the eastern conuties and the Potomac Valley on the one hand and those from the more newly settled areas on the other. The former area, while including many small farmers, also contained, as we have noted, scores of large planters together with most of the towns. The latter consisted of far fewer great landowners, practically no towns, and thousands of small farmers. The older regions sent to the legislature members of the social and cultural elite, Virginia's first families, with an occasional small planter; the newer counties elected men of less property, education, and experience, with a few of the upper class. Neither cast unanimous votes in the legislature, but they did reflect different views of the world and revealed distinctive voting patterns even at this early date.

The delegates from the Southside and their allies opposed acts subjecting the militia to a sterner discipline, favored removing the capital from Williamsburg to Richmond, tried to restrict the executive's emergency powers, and in a series of votes supported low taxes, the postponement of collections, and the tender acts. This group included almost no one of prominence except for a few of the Shenandoah Valley leaders, who would be shifting sides soon, and an occasional maverick such as Patrick Henry and General Joseph Jones of Dinwiddie. The big names—George Mason, Mann Page, Jr., William Fitzhugh, Richard Henry Lee, John Tyler, Robert Wormeley Carter, and Thomas Nelson, Jr.— pressed opposite policies on behalf of the Northern Neck and eastern counties. Sons of the planter-lawyer elite who had dominated colonial Virginia, they had obtained a constitution which, though far from their ideal, enabled them to retain much of their former power, and in 1781 they finally succeeded in enacting their political and economic program. The contrast with Maryland is striking. There the same kind of men established dominance at once through the constitution and preceded the Virginians throughout the war: in stabilizing state finances, setting prices, authorizing impressments, protecting creditors, repealing legal tender clauses, and delaying the sale of loyalist property. The comparison can be pushed too far, but Maryland seems the more business-minded, the more "Northern" of the two states.

North Carolina's disadvantages greatly exceeded those of Virginia or Maryland. From the first the state contained a large loyalist and neutralist element, located in the trading centers and throughout the extensive interior, and powerful

enough to nullify, at times, the assistance rendered by patriotic back-countrymen to the rebel cause. The movement
for resistance began both in the Piedmont (such as in Mecklenburg, home of a famous, much investigated Declaration
of Independence) and the coastal counties, but the tobacco
planters provided the decisive impulse as they did both in
Maryland and Virginia. In those two states the planters kept
the dissidents under control except for sporadic riots on the
eastern shore, but North Carolina's rebel leaders encountered
more difficulty. Old antagonisms together with primitive
transportation and communication facilities prevented the
government from rallying the people, so that the war in
North Carolina proceeded atomistically. The state contributed fewer men per capita to the Continental Army
than did any other, even Delaware, and contests fought on
North Carolina soil involved out-of-state armies or miscellaneous, ad hoc militia units; it was primarily a guerrilla and
a civil war.

During the first few years of conflict North Carolina
escaped invasion, though the government faced loyalist uprisings from 1776 until late in 1777 and again in the summer
of 1779. She had of course contributed to campaigns elsewhere, supplying two regiments to the Continental Army
which, with a thousand of her militia, were captured at
Charleston; but for a state containing nearly 200,000 whites
her effort fell far short. The government tried without
success to recruit many more. The British capture of
Charleston and the interior posts of Ninety-Six, Cheraw,
and Camden laid the state open to invasion by June 1780,
beginning another series of engagements between loyalists
and patriots. Some twelve hundred militia turned out to help
General Gates (fewer than New Hampshire furnished her
General Stark at Bennington), most of whom Gates lost at

Camden in August. At this point North Carolina raised enough men to defeat decisively the loyalists under Ferguson and to harass, though not to repulse, Cornwallis. Continued loyalist activities kept many militia units at home, and their failure to oppose the British regulars allowed Cornwallis to rest his troops in Wilmington and to march without hindrance north into Virginia. During the long months of early 1781, despite occasional American victories, North Carolina offered more hope for the British than to the Americans; a loyalist force even captured Governor Burke and his Council in September. Fighting continued until May 1782. The Tar Heel state's small contribution to Washington's army, then, resulted partly from the British invasion of 1780–1781 but primarily from her exceptional number of militant loyalists who not only refused to volunteer themselves but kept militia units pinned down.

Under these circumstances the legislature could not expect to enforce tax collections or compel contributions of supplies. Compulsion might create even more tories, and the power of the central government, which diminished rapidly as it left the locus of authority until it vanished among swamp and forest, nearly ceased during the invasion. The people raised plenty of food, but between lack of funds to buy it and inability to transport it, the troops often had to live off the country. The brief statement in the records of February 28, 1777, that there was no money in the treasury, signified the beginning of a prolonged crisis.

In response to this information the legislature, in its first session, imposed a tax of one-half penny in the pound, or about .2 per cent, on most kinds of taxable property, with a poll tax of four shillings on men owning less than £100— when they would pay that sum—and a double tax on anyone refusing to pay on demand. Probably the state's tax base was

£10 million, so the legislature planned to raise £20,000. Meanwhile the treasurer had to draw upon the Continental Congress for funds. The representatives also tried to borrow money and quickly levied another tax of the same amount, which they quadrupled in the fall. These measures fell far short of the need, and by August 1778 the treasury was empty again. Probably the people possessed too little specie at this point to contribute much more.

The new emergency forced the government to depend upon deficit financing. It therefore emitted £850,000 in tax anticipation notes, some of which was spent in retiring earlier bills of credit and the rest for outstanding debts. At the same time it hopefully levied a tax based upon a re-evaluation which took a seven- or tenfold inflation into account and might raise a comparable sum. But expenditures continued far ahead of income, and North Carolina had no choice but to contribute to the inflation by further issues of paper. Aware of the danger, the legislature during 1780 made a new attempt to pay for the war through loans, secured in part by confiscated property (which it ceased temporarily to sell), and by further taxes amounting to more than £4 million, much inflated. Simultaneously the delegates passed a strict anti-monopoly law. These measures failed. The legislators repealed the last measure, acknowledging that it had merely impeded commerce without producing the expected advantages. At the same time, in the fall of 1780, they levied a special tax payable in grains or meat in order to supply the army, just now reviving. The same act authorized officials to seize these products from anyone who refused and to hire or, if necessary, impress wagons, horses, teams, and boats. This measure worked so well that the state renewed it until the fighting ended. Successive legislatures continued to impose heavy taxes payable in paper money and certificates, but apparently the treasury had to rely primarily upon issuing various types of notes, and the soldiers received, in lieu of specie, the familiar depreciation certificates.

North Carolina never returned to a specie basis until long after the war had ended, in 1783. To some extent her soft-money position reflected the dominance of farmers in the legislature. Even the Senate consisted primarily of substantial planters, not great landowners, merchants, or lawyers; indeed, it sometimes proved more pro-farmer than the House. The legislature throughout the war treated debtors tenderly, authorizing local justices to settle most suits and passing a stay law when it repealed the legal-tender clauses in 1783. An economic policy relying upon specie taxes and loans would not work in North Carolina: the people lacked hard money. Deficit financing and payments in military supplies suited the state's abilities. The gradual depreciation of widely held certificates injured men roughly in proportion to their property, except perhaps in the case of the soldiers' depreciation certificates, which the legislature did try to handle separately. At the end of the war the public debt stood at about £10 million, or, if reduced to specie according to its current value, at £1.6 million. This imposed a per capita burden greater than that of any other states except Massachusetts, Connecticut, and perhaps South Carolina, but North Carolina's immense resources in land would relieve the taxpayers. Considering the number of loyalists, the primitive transportation facilities, and the lack of liquid capital, North Carolina's record was respectable.

These policies did not receive the united support of all the people. A division appeared on several issues, separating the eastern delegates, especially those from the Albemarle district, from the western. The former was the oldest part of the state, with many slaves, and the people often chose

traders or professional men from the towns as their representatives. The newer area naturally had fewer slaves and
almost no towns. Both chose patriots, but the easterners
opposed regulatory acts, anti-monopoly laws, and legal-
tender clauses whereas the inland legislators favored all three.
Both houses contained these two sides, which reflected
fundamental sectional differences in the state.

Similar sectional differences characterized South Carolina.
As in other Southern states, the revolutionary impulse came
from the men producing a staple crop, in this case rice,
not from those engaged in diversified farming who often
opposed the movement. As we know, the economic, social,
and political interests of the low-country planters centered
in Charleston, from which they had ruled the colony and
now governed the state. They did not need to worry about
a small-farmer opposition in their own parishes because
such men scarcely existed. In 1790 the parishes near Charleston had only about eighteen hundred white men owning
43,000 slaves, or twenty-four blacks apiece. Accordingly,
these parishes returned exclusively great landowners.
Charleston itself differed in that the ratio of slaves to white
men did not exceed three and a half to one, and many artisans, shopkeepers, sailors, and laborers were challenging the
city's merchant and professional upper class. The mechanics,
seizing the initiative in opposition to British measures, found
themselves allied with the great planters; moreover, some of
the "radical" merchants and lawyers provided leadership for
them. Thus, instead of engaging in a class conflict with the
local power elite, the artisans joined with their wealthiest
neighbors. The Revolutionary movement in South Carolina
therefore succeeded under the direction of such men as Peter
Timothy, printer, Christopher Gadsden, wealthy merchant,
and Charles Pinckney, lawyer-planter.

In the Chesapeake Bay region the eastern planters had pushed upstream, extending their economic and social order into the interior. Those near Cape Fear and in South Carolina's low-country had not done so, tending instead to sidle along the coast into Georgia or to enter trade and the law. The up-country derived its population from a movement of pioneers southward through the Piedmont and a migration also of low-country white farmers unable to buy land and slaves in the east. The people of the interior found themselves separated from the coastal planters not only by their social origin but by geography, for a belt of pine forest characterized by poor soil divided the two sections. And, lacking a staple crop (for cotton culture lay in the future), the westerners practiced a generalized agriculture. A few Joseph Kershaws and John Chesnuts were beginning to make their fortunes, but back-country Carolina remained a society of small farmers. They had almost nothing in common with the eastern leaders, and probably a majority opposed independence. The new government assigned them only an inferior position in the state's power structure.

South Carolina's losses during the war exceeded those of all the other states except perhaps New York's and Georgia's. Like North Carolina, the back-country became involved in a civil war and furnished men for both sides throughout the contest. After the British occupied Savannah they began to raid northward, seizing slaves and destroying property. They captured Charleston in May 1780, forcing many residents of the city and adjacent parishes to take an oath of allegiance. They then shattered the Continental Army at Camden, in the northern part of the state, and the militia at Fishing Creek, some thirty miles to the northwest, in mid-August. The enemy remained dominant throughout the interior for the rest of the year and did not retreat until summer. Moreover, they held Charleston for another year and a half, withdrawing only in December 1782. Thus the state's principal port was blocked for the better part of three years, and the redcoats, with their loyalist allies, preyed upon the whole state for a year. When the British finally departed they carried off thousands of slaves. The total loss to their former owners exceeded £1 million sterling.

Fortunately this destruction occurred late in the war. After the repulse of a British attack on Charleston and the defeat of the Indians along the frontier in the summer of 1776, the state enjoyed three years of peace. During that period the loyalists remained quiet and the central government, under Edward Rutledge's able leadership, consolidated its control. It placated the back-country by granting representation in the legislature, provided it with a court system and its own local officials, appointed some of its leaders to important posts, and attended to other western needs, for example, by setting the price of agricultural products at a reasonable level and halting suits for debt. The government also began vigorously to support the war.

When hostilities began the state was in excellent financial condition even though the treasury lacked specie. In November 1775 the provincial congress issued £1 million in local money notes (about £140,000 sterling) backed by bonds currently owed to the treasury and the presumed credit of the state. By the next spring it had authorized the expenditure of some £270,000 sterling, at the same time urging the citizens to lend money to the state. The first legislature, meeting in the winter of 1776–1777, allowed the treasurer to issue $308,000 in legal-tender bills (about £68,-300) and backed this by a tax of 1 per cent on slaves and land and half that rate on the profits from trade, manufacturers, and the professions. No further tax bill followed for a year, but South Carolina did obey Congress's plea to avoid further paper issues by borrowing more than £ 200,-000 at 7 per cent. Perhaps surprisingly, the people must have loaned some such amount. Encouraged, the legislature levied a tax in March 1778 ten times higher than the previous rate, doubled it for absentees, and called upon the executive to borrow even more. By the end of 1779 apparently the South Carolinians had loaned roughly £ 1.8 million sterling at 7 to 10 per cent interest and had presumably paid £ 1 million in taxes. More loans and another tax followed in the early spring just before the British attacked Charleston, by which time her citizens had contributed more money through loans and taxes, per person, than the people of any other state.

For almost two years thereafter the legislature could take no effective action, and the energetic Governor Rutledge, with a few aides, led a wandering, hand-to-mouth existence. Congress supported the Continental troops, and both they and the militia paid for supplies in certificates to an unknown sum. A good deal of the provisions and transportation came from other states, and since the militia often lived off the land, these activities seem not to have cost the treasury much money, though the people paid in other ways. When the legislature reassembled in January 1782, the British still controlled part of the state. We know little about this session because few records remain. During the invasion a considerable number of Charlestonians, some of them wealthy, and various prominent planters had signed a congratulatory address to the British conqueror while others had taken an oath of allegiance. They thus unintentionally disclosed an excellent source of funds. The delegates, in a vengeful humor anyway, promptly confiscated more than two hundred estates and imposed a special tax on the property of less heinous offenders. Since almost all of her sister states had repealed their legal-tender laws, South Carolina followed suit, reopening the courts for action, but in view of the small amount of hard money in circulation the legislature postponed suits for debt until the next session. It also passed a law to pay Congress the state's quota, but did not accompany this with a tax measure.

The sale of confiscated property, whatever its ethics, brought in essential money. The governor told the legislators at their next sitting, in February 1783, that he had no money even for them, and a committee reported none in sight except from confiscated slaves, whereupon the anxious representatives authorized the sale of eighty blacks. Later in the session they paid the judges and the delegates to Congress by selling two hundred more. The legislature also passed a tax law—the first in two years—to raise the £100,000 needed for the year.

Considering the large loyalist minority and the long British occupation, together with the heavy slave population which kept the coastal planters at home, South Carolina's record was honorable. She furnished considerably less than her share of men to the Continental Army, but her militia contributed much to victory. Her financial record until the moment of the British conquest excites admiration. At the end of the war her debt stood at nearly a million pounds sterling, half of which she would collect from bonds given primarily for purchases of confiscated estates. An annual tax of £91,000, less than she had imposed early in 1777, and certainly less than 1 per cent of her prewar tax base, would balance the budget. On the other hand, her taxable property had diminished by as much as one-fifth due to the loss of slaves, property carried away by loyalists, and general destruction. And she no longer would receive subsidies for indigo and naval stores. In compensation her people would continue to expand into the up-country, borrow to replenish their supply of slaves, re-establish foreign markets, and within a few years nearly double their prewar wealth.

Georgia also would expand after 1783, but the war left her exhausted. Internally divided, economically weak, and politically disunited, she could not withstand the shock of the long British occupation. South Carolina took full advantage of a four-year period to strengthen herself, but Georgia could not do this. Her available fighting force of four thousand men in 1776 had to guard four times that number of slaves and faced Indian attacks; they could hardly hope to repel a British invasion. Many in fact welcomed that event. Georgia supplied fewer men to the Continental Army than any state except Delaware, but one wonders how she could find even 2,700. The colonial government had depended upon a British subsidy, and though some of her citizens had accumulated large properties, many of those with ready cash remained loyal. Under these circumstances, Georgia depended from the first upon outside assistance both of money and of men.

Governor Wright's departure in March 1776 left the local Tories without support and allowed the rebels to form a new government, as we have seen. Unfortunately, they did not organize an efficient political system. Archibald Bulloch, the first president, might have succeeded, but he died suddenly and no strong leader replaced him. Power rested in the Assembly, which divided into competing factions. The disappearance of legislative records prevents the historian from reconstructing the events of these years, but apparently the state levied taxes, issued some paper money, organized a militia, created courts, and granted land. Whereas South Carolina collected many thousands of pounds through taxes and loans, Georgia failed to remain solvent but went bankrupt by mid-1777, and from that point forward depended upon handouts from Congress. Partly in an effort to restore its credit the legislature confiscated loyalist property in 1778, but sales did not bring in sufficient money at that time to make much difference.

During these early years Georgia remained on the periphery of the war, but hers was an exciting backwater. She launched three unsuccessful attacks on St. Augustine, endured an occasional naval blockade, and utterly failed to halt persistent raids from Florida. Georgia's farmers may have benefited by supplying these troops, but they lost property from the raids and probably inflation took the rest of their profit. The Indian frontier escaped large-scale war, but occasional skirmishes and the constant threat of hostilities prevented expansion. Between the Indians and the British, the Georgians found themselves hemmed in.

In December 1778 the British took Savannah and completed the conquest of the coastal district during the next few weeks. The up-country remained under Whig control, experiencing civil war for several years. The state government retreated to the frontier county of Wilkes, but could rally only enough resistance to survive. The enemy remained dominant until they lost Augusta in June 1781, after which they continued to occupy Savannah, the state's only port, until July 1782. When the British finally departed, they carried off more than three thousand Negroes.

Throughout the period Georgia remained ineffectual. Until 1780 two different groups tried to assert political authority, one led primarily by easterners, another by men sympathetic with the up-country. In that year a legislature controlled by the latter met briefly and passed an act encouraging expansion of the frontier. Another assembly held a five-day session during August 1781, reorganized the government and the militia, and the renewed state laws. It also began to process actions against suspected loyalists. Since it passed no economic legislation the state remained penniless and existed by impressments or buying on credit at enormous advances.

The first effective Assembly, representing every county, met in January 1782. By that time military operations had almost ceased, and the delegates needed to issue only £22,-100 worth of certificates to finance the final campaign against Savannah. Confiscated property served as collateral, and slaves were sold for other immediate expenses. The legislature still imposed no tax, nor did that which assembled later in the spring; instead it passed a new confiscation act. Basically, until 1783 Georgia relied upon $2.5 million voted by Congress, furnishing only some supplies and a minimum of troops.

When the British withdrew they left behind some specie, but the slaves who accompanied them and the personal property belonging to the loyalists balanced this. A large number of refugees, driven from place to place during the occupation, further drained money from those who had some, while the trail of certificates which marked the passage of armies depreciated too rapidly to benefit anyone. When the state began to sell confiscated estates it proved necessary to accept certificates for half the purchase price and bonds for the rest, realizing in consequence very little specie. Apparently the only Georgians who acquired any property during these years were some merchants in Savannah who battened off the British and stayed on after the evacuation, together with a few profiteers who picked off rich tory estates, paying in cheap certificates and bonds on which they then reneged, or who in other cases used depreciated money to buy excellent land. The average citizen escaped taxes, but in every other way he was fortunate simply to survive.

The government's finances remained chaotic for several years. Not until 1786 could the governor submit a tentative balance sheet. He estimated that previous to January 1784 the state had owed £354,010, of which, however, £156,544 worth of certificates had been paid in and destroyed, probably for confiscated property and land, leaving a debt of roughly £200,000, higher per capita than that of most states. Purchasers of confiscated estates, however, owed enough to retire the whole deficit if the state could collect, which it could not. For the moment the people lacked the money to pay the interest on such a sum, nor could they pay Georgia's share of the federal debt; but of course no state with such extensive vacant land needed to worry for very long.

When we take a retrospective view, as the people at the time would have said, we are impressed with their ability to overcome great difficulties and defend their claim to independence through seven years of war. Most of their handicaps were not of their making. They could not prevent the British from occupying large sections of the country, invading and raiding other areas, and blockading long stretches of coastline. The enemy controlled southern New York for seven years, most of Georgia for three and a half, eastern South Carolina for two and a half, a third of Rhode Island for more than two. In addition, all of Georgia, most of South Carolina, western North Carolina, northern New York, and parts of Virginia, Pennsylvania, and New Jersey experienced invasions lasting some months, while even Connecticut, Delaware, and Maryland were raided. Indian attacks afflicted New York, New Jersey, Pennsylvania, Virginia, North Carolina, and Georgia, forcing expenditures of money, commitment of troops, and loss of considerable property.

[432]

Loyalists also created problems which ranged from the merely annoying to the almost insuperable. Opposition to the war prevented several states from contributing their share to the army, delayed the imposition and collection of taxes, and restricted the gathering and transporting of supplies. Delaware, Georgia, and North Carolina virtually ceased fighting for various periods. Loyalism and neutralism in New Jersey, South Carolina, New York, and Pennsylvania also reduced the contribution of those states, while even Virginia and Maryland had to cope with internal dissension.

The states' geography made organizing, supplying, and transporting a continental army difficult, though it did favor local militia campaigns. The great distances discouraged the governments of Virginia and North Carolina in their war effort. Separatist movements arising at least in part from geography worried New Hampshire and Massachusetts, while long-standing sectional controversies divided the people of New Jersey, Delaware, Pennsylvania, Maryland, and the Carolinas. To these may be added the differences between the commercial and agricultural towns which impeded united action in states such as New Hampshire, Massachusetts, and Pennsylvania.

Problems growing out of the transition from colony to statehood also handicapped the governments. A delay in forming new constitutions prevented New York from levying taxes for many months, kept the executive department of New Hampshire weak, and caused dissension both there and in Massachusetts. Pennsylvania's constitution increased opposition to the Revolutionary government while Georgia's failed, perhaps inevitably, to provide a strong authority. Both Georgia and New Hampshire were deprived of trained leadership, and the states south of Maryland, except for South Carolina, lacked experienced businessmen to organize their finances. All needed more specie than they had, but Virginia, North Carolina, and Georgia especially found themselves short of hard money. Instead only the New England states, Pennsylvania, South Carolina, and Maryland clearly contributed a per capita surplus in taxes and loans beyond their own defense. Georgia, Virginia, North Carolina, and probably New York just as clearly subtracted from the general stock.

Fortunately the thirteen states possessed some important assets. A majority of the people undoubtedly supported the war, and among the men who believed in the rebel cause almost every one served in the army sometime or other. New Hampshire, Massachusetts, and Connecticut scarcely saw a British soldier after 1776, leaving them free to send, out of their rocky hills, enough surplus farm boys to fill half the Continental battalions. Pennsylvania, Virginia, and Maryland, free from invasion most of the time, added nearly 30 per cent. The Southern states in general furnished far fewer men in proportion to their white population than did the Northern—less than 5 per cent versus 13 per cent—probably because the majority of the Southern labor force were forbidden to serve and perhaps because the Northern lads had no better prospects during the war. Many states entered the war in excellent financial condition, enabling them to contribute their share and compensate for their less fortunate allies: Maryland, Pennsylvania, Massachusetts, South Carolina, Connecticut, and Rhode Island seem to have been especially strong. South Carolina far excelled all other states in her ability to borrow money.

The men who held power under the new government proved adept at solving most of the problems confronting them. Constitutional changes usually allayed fears, and a mixture of coercion and toleration minimized the loyalist threat. Especially able executives and other capable officials appeared in such states as New York, New Jersey, Massachusetts, Pennsylvania, Maryland, and South Carolina; no state suffered a complete lack of leadership. Combined with the military men they did in fact constitute an extraordinary group. Supplementing their work, merchants supplied the business acumen that, if it could never really solve the problems of money and supply, at least prevented collapse.

Every state followed a different road to victory, but they all faced and overcame, or bypassed, certain common obstacles. The vehicle which got them into, around, or out of their difficulties was money. Money, in the form of coin or paper notes, paid bounties and wages to the soldiers, supplied them, and transported the armies to Saratoga and Yorktown. During the first three years the legislatures issued the usual tax anticipation notes, accompanied these with tax bills, and borrowed whatever they could. All of the New England states performed very well, as did South Carolina, but for various reasons people elsewhere did not loan as much or pay as high taxes. During this period the paper emissions depreciated only gradually, and the economy rested on a specie basis. The states tried by price restrictions, embargoes, and taxes to contain inflation. Historians have argued that they should have balanced budgets, but a balanced budget would not wage war. The people, especially in the South, lacked hard money; moreover, to have levied heavy taxes would have been suicidal in view of the loyalist and neutralist opposition. We must remember, too, that no one anticipated a long war, and every year the people supposed the next campaign to be the last. It seemed both necessary and reasonable to contract a debt, which a free, rich country could easily pay.

The villain, then, must be sought not in the people or

their representatives or in Congress but in the fortunes of war, which did not end in 1778 or 1779 or 1780, or even in 1781. By that time deficit financing had pulled the states through, though barely. During this period the states, which had collected about £4 million taxes previously, took in £120 million or so, inflation probably reducing the specie value to the earlier figure. By this time all of the states except Georgia were contributing, with Pennsylvania, Maryland, and the Carolinas now exceeding the New Englanders in their per capita burden. As inflation ate into the purchasing power of this money, the legislatures sought new sources. Almost all perceived in loyalist or British estates a perfect financial panacea: force one's enemies to pay for the war which they had begun. The need for money gradually overcame ethical scruples and sympathy, and almost every state now sold confiscated property to pay troops and other obligations or to serve as security for further currency emissions.

Confiscated property helped to supply a little cash, but the states needed millions. The use of quartermaster certificates and taxes payable in specific articles carried the armies through their final campaigns, as Georgia, the Carolinas, Virginia, Maryland, and New York in particular substituted forced sales to the army for purchases in a free market. These techniques financed ultimate victories without money. At the same time the governments reverted to a specie basis. This reform wiped out most of the currency held by the people generally, while leaving intact the loan-office certificates and other specie debts held by a small number of creditors. The widely held soldiers' depreciation notes, commissary certificates, and similar money substitutes were scaled down, and tax anticipation warrants virtually annihilated. The pressure for this change came from the mercantile centers, the creditor interest, and the areas where the favored notes were concentrated, such as coastal New Hampshire and Massachusetts, southeastern Pennsylvania, and southern Maryland. The states now levied further taxes amounting to £3 million specie, collecting just enough to bring their warships in to port.

By the end of the war the thirteen states had levied taxes of some £10 million currency, a respectable effort for a comparatively underdeveloped country, probably £3.3 per person. Blue ribbons go to South Carolina, Rhode Island, New Hampshire, and Connecticut, while New York, North Carolina, and Georgia must take the booby prize. In absolute sums, Pennsylvania led the way followed by Massachusetts, Virginia, and South Carolina. Of this total the states seem to have collected four-fifths. The combined debt also equalled about £10 million, distributed very unevenly. The four southernmost states owed half of it, resulting from their inability to finance the strenuous campaigns of 1780–1781 and (except for South Carolina) their lack of liquid capital. But these held such extensive lands that they need not worry. Of the Northern states only Massachusetts and Connecticut had contracted really heavy debts. Both had exerted themselves during the war and both, in 1781, treated the public creditors with unusual gratitude. The total value of the country's real and personal property exceeded the state debt by twenty-five times. Certain states, such as South Carolina and New York, had lost a significant portion of their property, but most ended fundamentally sound and with every hope of future growth. Even the enormous debt contracted by Congress seemed well within the people's capacity to pay.

Politically, too, the people in most of the states could look back with complacency and forward with anticipation. In the governors' chairs sat Jonathan Trumbull, Lyman Hall, William Paca, John Hancock, Mesech Weare, William Livingston, George Clinton, John Dickinson, William Greene, Benjamin Guerrard, Thomas Nelson, Alexander Martin, and Nicholas VanDyke, all well known at the time, some still familiar today, and as a group highly capable. They and their predecessors had presided over a badly divided people, yet defeated the greatest military power in the world. To most observers the thirteen states were progressing from a victorious past to a magnificent future.

# Chapter Twelve

# Retrospect and Prospect

THE ship bringing the news that the Treaty of Peace had been signed in Paris on January 21, 1783, sailed by way of Cádiz to halt the departure of the combined French and Spanish fleet. A thirty-two-day run then took her to Chester, just below Philadelphia, on Sunday, March 23. Philadelphians heard the good news the same day. Letters enclosing copies of a handbill then proceeded eastward quite slowly because the British still occupied New York City. One line of communication crossed New Jersey to the Atlantic and continued by sea around Long Island. The fastest route was up the Delaware to the New York line and then across to Fishkill on the Hudson, the communications center for the northern army, and thence safely north of the enemy lines into New England. Providence heard about it on the 27th, three days before the joyful tidings reached the town by the New Jersey route. A boat docked in Boston on the

30th with unofficial reports, and the next day James Bowdoin rode in from Philadelphia with confirmation. Not until
April 5 did the people of Portsmouth learn of the signing,
the day after Captain John Derby arrived in Salem direct
from France.

Celebrations seem to have been quite restrained or even
absent, perhaps because most people regarded the signing
as a foregone conclusion (military operations had virtually
ceased for a year), but more likely because in the past fes-
tivities had got out of hand and respectable folk preferred
restraint. The people of New London received the news on
a Sunday, so of course they waited until the next day, which
they spent "in Mirth and Jollity." At 11:00 the two forts
and several ships discharged their cannon, and the "principal
inhabitants" then met in a tavern and were "entertained in
a Manner suitable to the pleasing Occasion. The whole thing
being conducted with Propriety, and the Company dispersed
at 6 o'Clock." The day's delay doubtless gave the advocates
of Propriety a chance to enforce decorum. Most towns
waited even longer. Marblehead, Massachusetts, selected
April 20 (eight years almost to a day after Lexington).
After the usual firing of cannon and ringing of bells, all the
flags were displayed on the training field. The people then
divided. The "principal inhabitants," with out-of-town
guests, headed for the coffee house and a "genteel enter-
tainment," while the rest ate an ox and drank from a large
vessel kept filled with liquor. In the evening a number of
houses were "illuminated," and the townsmen lit a bonfire.
The people of New Jersey could choose between a celebra-
tion in Trenton on April 15, with the governor, public officials, and the trustees, director, and students of an acad-
emy, or another four days later in Princeton, this time with

the college crowd and the governor, like a good politician, again present.

The newspapers wasted little space on backward glances; Americans concerned themselves with the future, not the past. The treaty contained provisions protecting the rights of loyalists, and the prospect of former enemies regaining power and property alarmed many citizens. Emotional newspaper articles warned against readmitting the enemies. The *Boston Gazette* took the occasion to stress the danger of internal divisions and asserted that nothing was more destructive than "the raging of parties nearly balanced." An article in the same paper expressed some concern about the debt but concluded that trade, now relieved of British duties and restraints, would become much more profitable and that 36 million acres of unlocated land would pay the federal debt. The mood, on the whole, was optimistic: the people could point with pride and view with anticipation.

The war years had seen great economic and social dislocation. The country folk, who furnished most of the fighting men and provisions, ended poorer than they had begun. At first an abnormal demand for provisions enabled the commercial farmers to sell their surplus at high prices. Indeed, state and federal commissary officers had sometimes competed with local traders and speculators. The semi-subsistence farmers, who raised little beyond their own needs, could not take full advantage of this opportunity, but the increased supply of money enabled them to discharge their debts while taxes remained low. As the years passed, however, inflation began to injure even the commercial farmers. They were compelled to accept paper notes that declined very rapidly in purchasing power, sometimes to zero. The specie reforms of 1780 and 1781 came at the expense of agricultural profits. In their eagerness to buy the many imported articles that they had reluctantly forsworn in 1775, the farmers spent whatever money remained and incurred a new set of debts only to find, after 1783, that prices failed to meet their expectations. At the same time state governments were beginning to withdraw money from circulation through taxes in an effort to retire the debt and to balance expenditures with income. This policy almost always involved a net loss to the farmers because all paid taxes but few received interest on securities. To these difficulties we must add the destruction caused by the armies, locally quite serious as in the Southern loss of slaves, and probably a general decline in the number of livestock. In the end the poorer farmers and the Southern planters lost ground while the Northern commercial farmers, with exceptions, just held their own. To restore the nation's farms to full production took several years. Not until the 1790's would prosperity reward the country people for their sacrifices.

The artisans' experiences were quite similar. A shortage of British manufactured goods created by nonimportation agreements, combined with the high wartime demand for many products, brought them general prosperity. This happy state of affairs lasted until the general inflation began to eat into their earnings. The value of their certificates shrank, food prices shot up, and those who lived in port towns often faced damage if not bankruptcy when the British invaded, unless they accepted British protection and gold. By 1779 the artisans became disillusioned. In Philadelphia, and very likely elsewhere, they now joined the merchants in seeking fiscal reform, for they recognized their dependence upon commercial prosperity. As the war ended, the concentration of cash and certificates in the towns seemed to forecast a good local market. But these high hopes were dashed. British goods deluged the market, ruining some craftsmen, and those who did not face such competition found that their best customers had spent every shilling on imported luxuries. The merchant foresook his suit of home-spun for a suit in the latest London fashion, and then found that the commercial depression deprived him of the shillings for either. Within a year after the signing of the treaty, the skilled workers and their employers were back to their prewar situation; another year and their incomes declined still further. They would wait now (as so often before) for another war to stimulate an artificial prosperity. At least they no longer feared restrictive British laws and might hope that their government would some day pass laws to encourage domestic manufactures.

The fortunes of the traders varied greatly both over time and among individuals. The adoption of the Continental Association wiped out the profitable commerce with England and forced those who had specialized in it either to retire or to adjust to a totally new situation—unless they preferred to remain loyal and pursue their fortunes within the Empire. Those rebels who failed to explore new sources of profit never recovered financially. The other traders, including both established businessmen and newcomers, exploited very advantageously the many opportunities to combine their own profit with the national interest. Privateering, the export trade to Europe and the West Indies, and supplying the American and French armies both with imports and domestic goods all proved rewarding. Yet men lost as well as made fortunes. The British naval depredations wiped out the fishing and whaling industries, which would not recover for a decade. Men could lose as well as gain by army contracts, and inflation ate up paper fortunes. Those who suffered the most may well have been the most patriotic—the merchants who loaned money to the government and saw their paper certificates melt away, or who accepted treasurers' notes from customers and debtors. Indeed, the injury to businessmen by depreciation caused traders to take the initiative in pressing for financial reform.

The gloom that had settled on the mercantile community during the middle years of the war began to lift after 1780 with the new monetary policy, the accession to power of Morris in Philadelphia and others like him in the state government, and the growing prospect of peace. Some traders, at least, emerged with substantial specie reserves, others owned protected interest-bearing securities, while still others had bought, or given bond for, potentially valuable loyalist estates or other property. As soon as the war ended many merchants invested their cash and pledged their credit to import consumer goods, advancing these in turn on credit, as usual, to retailers and other purchasers. At this point most businessmen must have regarded the War for Independence, in its economic aspects, as highly successful.

They soon had reason to reconsider. As we know, the depression affected them perhaps more than any of their neighbors. Wartime profits vanished, debtors could not pay, states could not collect taxes sufficient to pay the promised interest on certificates, assets turned into liabilities, and all too often the traders saw even their political power evaporating. They too must wait for a return to prosperity in the 1790's, and by that time not the merchants of the Revolutionary generation but younger men would gather the new harvest.

In examining the economic consequences of the war, we must distinguish between the immediate and the long-range. The people entered the war with good prospects. British rule had constricted economic growth in some ways, and private debts had become burdensome, but the economy proved strong enough to carry the country through several years of conflict without serious strain. For awhile, wartime markets brought prosperity to most people. Thereafter, however, profits began to dissolve. The losses in slaves carried off, houses burned, crops impressed for depreciated paper, merchant vessels taken, and economic activities interrupted, counteracted occasional windfalls. The millions of dollars with which Congress and the states enriched the people vanished, while millions in certificates earned little interest and sold at a heavy loss. Debtors found themselves sued, and taxes burdened even the rich. The states owed nearly £9 million currency, and Congress owed three times as much. By 1784 most people were paying more taxes and more interest on private debts while receiving no more income than before the war. The depression hit everyone, even that segment of the people who had made money from the war.

Over the long haul, however, the Revolution freed Americans from the fiscal control of a self-interested empire and enabled them to determine their own economic policies. By the 1790's the rise in value of state and federal notes, an expanding foreign commerce, a booming economy, the development of banking, and the restoration of credit in Europe enabled the states to recoup their losses and attain new levels of wealth. The removal of most restrictions on trade permitted the merchants to seek out markets freely and temporarily to exploit the demand for American products stimulated by the European wars. The years of the Revolution saw the first steps toward a national economy. Business enterprises had united the various regions in a common effort to defeat the enemy. Interstate trade had expanded rapidly, and people everywhere had contributed money and goods to their Congress and their army. Americans would never again relapse totally into their former parochialism. Finally, the opening of the West released and rewarded the creative energies of the nation's young people. Within a few years the hardships of the war faded into the vision of unlimited prosperity.

Social changes are always difficult to document unless we take a very long view. Individuals died, were ruined, suffered exile, won fame and fortune, without affecting society as a whole. Clearly the war was not catastrophic. It neither destroyed an old order nor created a new one, but accelerated or modified certain trends already well in process.

The emancipation of Northern slaves and the decline of indentured servitude had begun before 1776 and perhaps might have been completed under British rule. Neither seriously affected the social order. In the North slavery had never been important, and the work force always consisted primarily of free laborers. Southern society remained untouched and indeed, as we know, slavery actually increased its hold as cotton culture expanded. It is even conceivable that slavery flourished more under an independent United States than if the colonists had remained part of the Empire.

The departure of the loyalists involved the exile of a disproportionate number of well-to-do, educated men. Some historians have lamented that the country thereby lost a conservative influence and a valuable political as well as a cultural leadership. Whether one deplores or applauds a lack of conservatism is a matter of opinion, but the history of the South, from whence few Tories fled, suggests that their emigration made little difference. Qualities of leadership are never confined to a social elite, so the country would suffer a deprivation only if the social order were so rigid as to prevent the replacement of the cultural loss from below. Actually society became, if anything, a little more open after the loyalists departed than it had been before, making it easier to replace the loss, if such it was. The same migration affected the exiles themselves, but it left society intact. So also the transfer of their property did not fundamentally alter the distribution of wealth. The dispossession of the proprietors and the transfer of the Crown land, however, did substantially help would-be farmers and elevated some renters to the status of freeholders.

Most historians think that the American social structure was becoming less equal during the late Colonial period. The Revolution did not touch some of the reasons for this trend, such as the growth of slavery in the South, increasing commercialization, and the persistent shortage of money relative to the needs of a growing population. It did, however, eliminate the danger of British restrictions on trade and halted the grant of huge landed estates to English noblemen. Perhaps most important, the removal of restrictions on the westward movement now relieved rising pressure on the available land. British policy, while not inflexible, had tended to discourage western expansion, whereas the new governments actively abetted it. Thousands of men who might have remained poor and obscure at home, became the founding fathers of flourishing new colonies. Geographical and vertical mobility went hand in hand with the advancing frontier.

The new opportunities offered to the average American strengthened those factors already breaking down the old deferential attitudes. The farmers and artisans who challenged the royal officials and (as they thought) defeated the British regulars, regarded themselves as equal to anyone. Victory confirmed the equalitarian spirit. The Whig elite, of course, did not lose their prestige, nor did the traditional status order vanish instantly, but the people increasingly challenged any pretensions to social superiority. Even though the actual distribution of wealth had not changed (and indeed, it would become more concentrated), and even though the country would soon contain richer people and poorer people than the colonists had known, "privilege" would not soon recover from its Revolutionary beating.

Social democracy inevitably encouraged political democracy. The citizen who celebrated the treaty in 1783 lived in a different political world than he who trembled at the news of Lexington and Concord. In the years since 1775 he had driven out governors, councilors, rich merchants, great landowners. He had joined local committees of observation, attended provincial congresses or conventions, helped to create governments responsible to the people, and served in a victorious army. As his role widened, he gained familiarity with the state's problems and confidence in his ability to resolve them. Experience ceased to be the monopoly of a local elite; the people need not invariably depend upon the great men. Occasions even arose when most of the leaders advocated measures opposed by the people. The result was a subtle psychological change. "How strangely things alter in a popular government!" wrote a bemused Massachusetts lawyer. "There was once a time when the arrival of Theodore Sedgewick in the Town of Richmont was in every bodies mouth—The children along the Street announced it as people passed by. But alas it is not so now." In Pennsylvania the lawyers thought to bring down the state's new constitution by refusing to accept appointments under it and by boycotting the courts, but they misread the times.

The gradual evolution toward popular government was accompanied by a growing democratic ideology. Independence removed some of the forces inhibiting those ideas, which now found expression in the new constitutions and their practical implications. Every aspect of government testified in some degree to the revolutionary changes. The freeman in each state now voted for a representative annually. He did not limit his choice exclusively to the community's great men, but might select someone of ordinary background and modest property. For example, in 1769 the victorious candidates in Westchester County, New York, had been the wealthy merchant and great landowner John DeLancey, the well-to-do judge and large landowner John Thomas, and Frederick Phillipse, owner of a huge manor, while Pierre Van Cortlandt represented his own manor. Only a specialist in local history would recognize the six delegates who held office as the war closed, except perhaps for Thomas Thomas, son of the above John, and John Lawrence, a prosperous merchant who had fled the city. The other four were just farmers.

During the same election, though perhaps not annually, the voter selected a senator. His choice narrowed somewhat, for as a rule only a prominent man sought or was persuaded to become available for this higher office, which indeed might require large property. Still, before 1776 the people seldom could even suggest a suitable person, for Crown officials made the decision. In the case of Westchester County they had not troubled to find anyone at all, the entire Council living in New York City, whereas our voter of 1783 would choose (along with candidates from other southern counties) the Eastchester farmer Stephen Ward. More often than before the war, the citizens would also elect local officials, who certainly would not owe their posts to the Crown.

In 1783 New Yorkers as usual re-elected General Clinton. In colonial days, of course, the executive bore no responsibility to local opinion but stood independent of it and all too often hostile to it. Nowadays it mattered less what the governor thought or did, since he lacked power to do harm (and, too frequently, to do good either). Moreover, the people need not wait upon royal action to rid themselves of an unpopular or unsuccessful governor, as some chief executives had already discovered.

At every level the governments became more responsible to public opinion than before 1776. We can perceive this process of democratization in several symbolic developments. One was the westward movement of the state capitols, following the geographical shift of power. During or shortly after the war, the legislatures ceased to meet at Savannah, Charleston, New Bern, Williamsburg, Philadelphia, New York, and Portsmouth. An effort to leave Boston, as we noticed, failed. These removals responded not only to western pressures for a more accessible location but to a conviction of the farmers that city folk exercised undue influence on policies. This feeling increased because of two other developments: the practice of opening legislative sessions to the public (guaranteed in several constitutions) and newspaper reports of legislative proceedings. Both enabled people to learn what the representatives proposed and to apply pressure if they lived close by. The principle of legislative responsibility also found expression in constitutional clauses requiring the publication of important bills for popular consideration and the prompt printing of the acts and proceedings of both houses.

Even more important in revealing to the voters the decisions of their delegates, and therefore restricting the independence of the legislators, was the practice of requiring roll-call votes on significant issues. During the Colonial period only the assemblies of Maryland and New Jersey had developed the habit with any regularity. Seven never did so, and the other four recorded votes only now and then, reaching crucial decisions without any publicity to indicate who favored and who opposed the measures. By the end of the war the Senates alone in New York, New Jersey, Delaware, and North Carolina were requiring and then printing more such votes than all the colonial legislatures combined, and the lower houses of these states and of Pennsylvania and Maryland were recording two dozen or more per session. By the end of the decade this practice became universal. Newspapers reported some of the most interesting, and unquestionably some delegates lost their seats as a result. Their anxiety is suggested by the incident following the printing of one Massachusetts vote, when members of the house absent on that occasion divulged through the newspapers the position they would have adopted.

These votes enable us to follow the legislatures as they fought the enemy and quarreled among themselves, settling the two great issues of home rule and who should rule at home. The prosecution of the war divided the delegates only rarely because most of them heartily approved of independence. Differences developed over the severity of anti-loyalist legislation, the strictness of militia laws, penalties for trading with the enemy, impressments of supplies, and similar questions, but no set alignments emerged except for certain persistent sectional divisions such as those in New Jersey and Delaware. As the war progressed, however, a much more significant and consistent alignment took shape, especially on economic issues. It would become increasingly apparent after the war. This division involved a struggle for power and led to the formation of persistent legislative blocs, or "parties."

Essentially this development signalized the accession to

political power of the farmers and in less degree of the artisans—of the small property holders generally. The core of this bloc, which furnished most of its votes, dictated its basic attitude, and supplied its rationale, was the least commercial component of the nation's economy and society—small property holders who farmed for a living. As we have seen, their limited experience and environment made them localists rather than cosmopolitans. Forming a majority of the people at that time, they adhered to democratic ideas which rationalized their desire for power. Weak before 1776 except in New England, they emerged either as the majority party or as an influential minority in every state.

Conflicts over the state constitutions first revealed the schism, which then quickly reappeared on a variety of issues. In Massachusetts, for example, the agrarian-localists wanted local courts to try most actions, opposed permanent salaries, tried to lower fees to public officials and lawyers, sought to aid debtors by evaluation laws and legal-tender clauses, favored the payment of taxes in farm produce, tried to lighten their own tax loan, supported the use of treasurers' notes, urged investigations to uncover fraud in army contracts, backed regulatory acts, and approved the confiscation and sale of loyalist estates. Allowing for local variations, similar groups of people advocated these policies in the other states. Thus the Pennsylvania Constitutionalists, though they originated as defenders of their democratic form of government, became associated with the same economic policies and, in addition, opposed the Bank of North America, the incumbent trustees of the College of Philadelphia, and the Quaker pacifists.

During the first few years of the war the agrarian-localist party derived considerable support from other segments of the voting public. The artisans, lesser shopkeepers, and small commercial farmers shared to some extent their political ideology, anti-Toryism, and preference for paper money instead of taxes. Even some traders, professionals, and large landowners joined with them out of mutual patriotism, especially if all had united behind "radical" policies with respect to England. But beginning about 1780 these last groups took the initiative in thoroughgoing financial reform and presently won over the other urban commercial and manufacturing interests. This opposing "party" derived its primary strength from the most commercial segment of the society—larger property holders and cosmopolitan men. Its leaders, who included practically all of the well-known men of the time, espoused Whig political theories which located power in their own hands, relatively independent of the people. During the later years of the war they advocated the monetary policies already described. They began to back political and economic nationalism, measures favorable to public and private creditors, energetic collection of taxes in specie, a centralized court system, independent and well-paid officials, protection of property rights including loyalist estates, and legislation to aid businesses such as the Bank of North America. Their success in regaining political power in several states where they had lost it reflected to some extent the failure of their opponents' fiscal policies and the appeal of their own program, but also their very great prestige, deriving not simply from old deferential attitudes but from superior education, experience, ability, and success.

The postwar years saw the further development of opposition between these two nascent parties—the commercial-cosmopolitan and the agrarian-localist. The latter drew strength from the economic and social discontent of the mid-1780's. In Pennsylvania, for example, the Constitutionalists briefly returned to power. The farmers of Rhode

Island reorganized about the same time, recaptured control of the legislature, and pushed through measures to increase the money supply and relieve debtors. The pro-Clinton bloc in New York, retaining the support of most farmers north of the city, adopted similar policies, as did the delegates from back-country North Carolina and Georgia, who indeed had never lost power. East Jersey representatives pushed through a paper-money bill despite their traditional opponents from the western counties. Simmering hostility in Massachusetts exploded in Shays' Rebellion, paralleling a comparable though more limited movement in central New Hampshire. Sectional divisions in Delaware, Maryland, Virginia, and South Carolina, already described, took much the same form and involved much the same issues.

These party controversies, which now became a permanent part of American life, were a major legacy of the American Revolution. Similar disputes had existed before 1776, but government under British rule prevented the agrarian-localists from exerting the weight appropriate to their numbers. The constititional reforms of 1776 democratized the distribution of power. Politics ceased to be the exclusive prerogative of the Whig leaders, of the commercial-cosmopolitans, and gradually became the instrument of a popular majority. Most of the men who began the movement for independence did not expect this revolution, did not want it, and tried to reverse it; but 1776 marked the end of an era.

# A Note on Sources

Most surveys of the period 1776–1783 concentrate on the national scene with only passing attention to the states. The only and therefore "standard" exception is Allan Nevins' *The American States During and After the American Revolution, 1775–1789* (New York, 1924). Nevins' work suffers from serious defects. Of the fourteen chapters, nine deal almost entirely with events after 1783, and his coverage is primarily political. The book is now badly out of date, recent research having rendered obsolete much of Nevins' material, and Nevins himself suffered from so strong a gold-standard, elitist bias that his interpretations lacked credence even when they had not become outmoded. We must now depend instead, for detail, upon the monographs noted hereafter. For interpretation we are on our own.

The special studies still leave many gaps, the worst of which I have tried to plug with temporary fillings, and anyone trying to develop a general understanding of the period must read the original sources. These are voluminous enough to occupy teams of scholars, and I have only riffled their pages. The laws and proceedings of the legislatures are all available on microfilm, depriving any writer of an excuse to skip them. Almost all the newspapers have been reproduced on microcard or microfilm. I have used these as well as issues still in the original. All the contemporary publications are also available on microforms. Major libraries either own these sources or can obtain them. I have also consulted a small part of the extensive manuscript collections held by the principal research libraries and archives. These include letters, petitions, journals, tax lists, and court records.

## CHAPTER I: AMERICAN SOCIETY IN 1776

The only recent general account of society during the War for Independence is my own *Social Structure of Revolutionary America* (Princeton, 1965). The book lacks the methodological rigor that historians are just beginning to require, but reflects extensive research. Critics have denied the existence of a "subsistence farm" society, arguing that all farmers produced whatever they could for sale, and that differences in degree do not justify drawing sharp contrasts in kind. Undoubtedly we must translate "subsistence" into "semi-subsistence," but pending further research I continue to postulate a distinction between two types of rural societies. Arthur M. Schlesinger's posthumously published *The Birth of the Nation: A Portrait of the American People on the Eve of Independence* (New York, 1968) draws indiscriminately from the entire late Colonial period. It subordinates fact to style, which makes for excellent reading but does not advance knowledge. Basic data concerning the distribution of population during the Revolution are contained in Evarts B. Greene and Virginia Harrington, *American Population Before the Federal Census of 1790* (New York, 1932), and Stella Sutherland, *Population Distribution in Colonial America* (New York, 1936).

Jack Sosin, *The Revolutionary Frontier, 1763–1783* (New York, 1967) has a chapter on frontier society and an up-to-date bibliography. Charles E. Clark, *The Eastern Frontier* (New York, 1970) covers northern New England and furnishes an interesting, readable background even though it stops in 1763. The Middle states still lack any such general treatment. One of the best state studies is Solon J. and Elizabeth H. Buck, *The Planting of Civilization in Western Pennsylvania* (Pittsburgh, 1939). For the Southern frontier see John R. Alden, *The South in the Revolution, 1763–1789* (Baton Rouge, 1957), and the

A Note on Sources

interpretive account of Thomas P. Abernethy, *Three Virginia Frontiers* (University City, La., 1940).

During the last few years historians have begun to study the society of New England systematically. So far they have published fragmentary essays, most of which have concentrated on the Colonial rather than the Revolutionary period. Representative are Richard L. Bushman, *From Puritan to Yankee* (Cambridge, Mass., 1967), an exceptionally able discussion of social change; Michael Zuckerman, *Peaceable Kingdoms* (New York, 1970), arguing for stability; and Philip J. Greven, Jr., *Four Generations* (Ithaca, 1970). I have benefited from the unpublished writings of Edward Cook and from Van Beck Hall's *Politics Without Parties: Massachusetts, 1780-1791* (Pittsburgh, 1972). Historians of the Middle colonies and states have not yet attempted this kind of social history, and one must draw from scattered sources. The quotation concerning New Jersey's society is from Hunter Dickinson Farish, ed., *Journal and Letters of Philip Vickers Fithian, 1773-1774* (Williamsburg, 1943), pp. 210-211.

Southern historians have also concentrated on studies of local areas rather than regions. A major exception is Carl Bridenbaugh's *Myths and Realities: Societies of the Colonial South* (Baton Rouge, 1952). A more specialized study with broad implications is Aubrey C. Land, "Economic Base and Social Structure: The Northern Chesapeake in the Eighteenth Century," *Journal of Economic History*, xxv (1965), 639-654. The material for descriptions of rural society in the South, as elsewhere, is abundant, but requires from the historian extensive travel, long days of reading, and careful quantitative analysis. I have relied upon but only scratched the surface of probate records and tax lists. The former include inventories of estates which enable one to discover what people owned and much about how they lived, while the latter reveal in more detail the social structures of various communities. County courthouses and the offices of town clerks contain the original documents, which increasingly are available on microfilm. Diaries and travel accounts also help one to re-create the life of the country people. Larger libraries usually have, on microfilm, all of the travel accounts described in Thomas D. Clark, ed., *Travels in the Old South: A Bibliography*, Vol. 1 (Norman, Okla., 1956).

The same sources exist for the towns, but for our discussion of urban society we can draw on more secondary sources. The basic general survey is Carl Bridenbaugh's *Cities in Revolt* (New York, 1955), now rather old-fashioned in its lack of precision and of statistical analysis. He covers only the five largest cities, and indeed we know much more about them than about the smaller but still important secondary towns. For Boston's society during the war, see Allan Kulikoff, "The Progress of Inequality in Revolutionary Boston," *William and Mary Quarterly*, 3rd series, xxviii (1971), 375–412. Thomas Jefferson Wertenbaker, *Father Knickerbocker Rebels* (New York, 1948), and Carl Bridenbaugh, *Rebels and Gentlemen* (New York, 1942) discuss New York and Philadelphia respectively, and Frederick P. Bowers surveys the principal Southern city in *The Culture of Early Charleston* (Chapel Hill, 1942). Esther Singleton, *Social New York Under the Georges* (New York, 1902) effectively uses estate inventories. These books tend to concentrate on the upper class, and, indeed, we lack any good book on urban laborers.

## CHAPTER 2: MAKING A LIVING IN THE COUNTRY

Curtis Nettels supplies us with a brief summary of economic developments and a useful bibliography in *The Emergence of a National Economy, 1775–1815* (New York, 1962). Research concerning agriculture has been limited recently to a few books on the Colonial period and some specialized publications. Anyone looking for facts about the farm economy may consult the old standbys, Percy Wells Bidwell and John I. Falconer, *History of Agriculture in the Northern United States* (Washington, D.C., 1925), and Lewis Cecil Gray, *History of Agriculture in the Southern United States to 1860*, 2 Vols. (Washington, D.C., 1933), but he will derive more pleasure from reading the contemporary treatise *American Husbandry*, edited by Harry J. Carman (New York, 1939). Historical geographers have contributed some interesting interpretations, such as Harry Roy Merrens' *Colonial North Carolina in the Eighteenth Century* (Chapel Hill, 1964). Tax lists and inventories of estates contain basic information about the people's economic activities. The Massachusetts assessment lists for 1771 are especially valuable. For the property of Joshua Hubbart, see Suffolk County Probate Records, Vol. 82, pp. 193–140; for Samuel Carne, South Carolina Inventory Book X, pp. 256–257, South Carolina Archives; for Theophilus Faver, Essex County Will Book 13, pp. 443–444, Virginia State Liberation. The inventories of James Gordon and James Caldwell are in the probate records of Suffolk County, Vol. 69 (1770) and Worcester County, Vol. 8 (1764). A description of great Southern planters which emphasizes their entrepreneurial activities is Aubrey C. Land's "Economic Behavior in a Planting Society: The Eighteenth-Century Chesapeake," *Journal of Southern History*, XXXIII (1967), 469–485.

We lack any study of free rural laborers during the Revolution. Abbot Smith's *Colonists in Bondage* (Chapel Hill, 1947) discusses indenture servitude during an earlier period, and I question whether his generalizations apply to the years after 1750. The recent development of black history has not yet produced a new book on the freedmen. Both Benjamin Quarles, *The Negro in the American Revolution* (Chapel Hill, 1961), and Arthur Zilversmit, *The First Emancipation: The Abolition of Slavery in the North* (Chicago, 1967) contain some information about slaves. Economic analyses of the slavery system apply to cotton culture of a later period. A brief, readable survey of artisans, both rural and urban, is Carl Bridenbaugh's *The*

*Colonial Craftsman* (New York, 1950). Joseph Cook's account book is in the Connecticut State Library.

Historians have not favored us with a study of professional men in the rural areas generally, though Alan M. Smith has written a dissertation on the Virginia group (Johns Hopkins University, 1967). The best source for these men and for ministers consists of the material in Clifford K. Shipton's *Biographical Sketches of Graduates of Harvard University* (Cambridge, Mass., in progress). The rural traders also await investigation. Local monographs include Margaret E. Martin, *Merchants and Trade of the Connecticut River Valley, 1750–1820* (Northampton, Mass., 1939), and Charles C. Crittenden, *The Commerce of North Carolina 1763–1789* (New Haven, 1936). See also Glenn Weaver, *Jonathan Trumbull: Connecticut's Merchant Magistrate, 1710–1785* (Hartford, 1956), and Albert E. Van Deusen, "The Trade of Revolutionary Connecticut," Ph.D. dissertation, University of Connecticut, 1948.

CHAPTER 3: MAKING A LIVING IN THE TOWNS

The historian must study economic developments in the towns piecemeal, relying upon specialized monographs. Bridenbaugh's *Cities in Revolt* is useful. No systematic study of urban laborers exists, but the books on various towns contain some information, especially Richard Walsh, *Charleston's Sons of Liberty* (Columbia, S.C., 1959). Bridenbaugh's *Colonial Craftsman* helps to understand the artisans. Charles S. Olton, "Mechanics and Sons of Liberty in Philadelphia, 1763–1789," Ph.D. dissertation, University of California, 1967, contains valuable information on political as well as economic history. For Benjamin Clark, see his account book, Joseph Downs Manuscript Library at Winterthur, Delaware. A sketch of the Sarazins appears in E. Milby Burton, *South Carolina Silversmiths* (Charleston, 1942), pp. 163–166.

The basic study of manufacturing is Victor S. Clark's *History* of *Manufactures in the United States, 1607–1860* (Washington, D.C., 1916). Nettels' *Emergence of a National Economy* contains many specific references. Isaac Roosevelt's career is unusual rather than typical, but then manufacturers did not usually serve in the legislatures. He became an exceptionally wealthy merchant and banker. The family is described in Charles Barney Whittelscy, *The Roosevelt Genealogy* (Hartford, 1902). For Ridgely, see *The Maryland Historical Magazine*, x (1915), 5–10, and LXII (1947), 96–101. The 1784 Baltimore and Anne Arundel County tax lists itemize his property.

Information on schoolteachers is scattered through primary materials such as newspaper advertisements. Those in Boston have attracted special attention but probably are not typical. See citations in Main, *Social Structure*, pp. 92–95. The same book indicates sources concerning other professional men. The quotation concerning popular suspicion comes from the *Pennsylvania Packet* (Philadelphia), February 21, 1787. Shipton's *Harvard Graduates* contains much information, as does Franklin P. Dexter, *Biographical Sketches of the Graduates of Yale University with Annals of the College History*, 3 Vols. (New York, 1885–1912).

We lack books on the town retailers and internal trade, but many historians have written about merchants and overseas commerce. Informative on late colonial trade are Virginia Harrington, *The New York Merchants on the Eve of the Revolution* (New York, 1935), Arthur L. Jensen, *The Maritime Commerce of Colonial Philadelphia* (Madison, 1963), and Leila Sellers, *Charleston Business on the Eve of the Revolution* (Chapel Hill, 1935). Studies of particular merchants include, notably, James B. Hedges, *The Browns of Providence Plantations, Colonial Years* (Cambridge, Mass., 1952), and Philip L. White, *The Beekmans of New York in Politics and Commerce*. See also Stuart Bruchey, ed., *The Colonial Merchant, Sources and Readings* (New York, 1966). Basic import and export figures are printed in U.S. Bureau of the Census, *Historical Statistics of the United States, Colonial Times to 1957* (Washington, D.C.,

1960), in Merrill Jensen, ed., *English Historical Documents: American Colonial Documents to 1776* (London, 1955), and in Sutherland, *Population Distribution*. George Boyd's phenomenal success is described in Charles Warren Brewster, *Rambles About Portsmouth*, 2 Vols. (Portsmouth, 1859, 1869), I, pp. 163–166. For William Elliott's estate, see Inventory Book X, pp. 305–313, South Carolina Archives.

There is no detailed study of the financial history of the late Colonial period, though several articles are useful. We especially need research into the question of private debts. Joseph A. Ernst, "Currency in the Era of the American Revolution," Ph.D. dissertation, University of Wisconsin, 1962, stops before the war. An excellent introduction to public monetary policy is furnished by E. James Ferguson's "Currency Finance: An Interpretation of Colonial Monetary Practices," *William and Mary Quarterly*, 3rd series, x (1953), 153–180. Lawrence H. Gipson correctly emphasizes the basic financial strength of the colonies in *The Triumphant Empire: Thunder-Clouds Gather in the West, 1763–1766* (New York, 1961), 53–110.

## CHAPTER 4: THE POLITICAL BACKGROUND

An article stressing the continued strength of the colonial governors is John M. Murrin, "The Myths of Colonial Democracy and Royal Decline in Eighteenth-Century America: A Review Essay," *Cithara*, v (1965), 53–69. For the councils on the eve of the Revolution, see Jackson Turner Main, *The Upper House in Revolutionary America* (Madison, 1965). Robert and Katherine Brown have led the way in arguing that a wide suffrage led to a democratic form of government. A considerable literature has developed which still continues, especially in the pages of the *William and Mary Quarterly*. The specialist will wish to consult J. R. Pole, *Political Representation in England and the Origins of the American Republic* (New York, 1966). My article "Government by the People: The American

Revolution and the Democratization of the Legislatures,"
*William and Mary Quarterly*, 3rd series, XXIII (1966), 391–407,
traces changes in the membership of the assemblies. Perhaps a
legislature controlled by the elite may respond as readily to
popular demands as one controlled by more ordinary folk, but
matters did not turn out that way during the Revolutionary
period. Jack P. Greene traces the increasing influence of the
lower houses during the prewar decades in *The Quest for
Power: The Lower Houses of Assembly in the Southern Royal
Colonies, 1689–1776* (Chapel Hill, 1963).

Tory ideas have attracted little attention because few colonials expounded them and because they perished in the successful War for Independence. Many historians have discussed
Whig ideology. Elisha Douglass draws a distinction between
Whig and democratic theories similar to mine in his *Rebels
and Democrats* (Chapel Hill, 1955), while Gordon Wood finds
a more unified body of thought in which the democratic elements became increasingly pronounced. His *The Creation of
an American Republic, 1776–1787* (Chapel Hill, 1969) deals
with the men and ideas that I call "Whig," and I am not so
much disagreeing as adding what seems to me a separate and in
some respects a conflicting strain—the "democratic." The able
article by Richard Buel, Jr., "Democracy and the American
Revolution: A Frame of Reference," *William and Mary
Quarterly*, 3rd series, XXI (1964), 165–190, in my opinion actually draws upon the writings of colonial leaders to describe
Whig, not democratic ideas, which circumstance explains the
many undemocratic features that Buel notes. Among the best
American expositions of Whig ideology are John Adams' influ-
ential *Thoughts on Government;* the articles by "Farmer,"
*Pennsylvania Packet*, November 5, 1776, and "A Republican,"
*New Hampshire Gazette*, February 8 to March 22, 1783; Carter
Braxton's *An Address to the Convention . . . of Virginia*
(Philadelphia, 1776); the anonymous *An Essay of a Frame of
Government for Pennsylvania* (Philadelphia, 1776); Jonathan
Jackson's *Thoughts on Government* (Worcester, Mass., 1788);

and, of course, the famous "Essex Result," printed in Theophilus Parsons, Jr., *Memoir of Theophilus Parsons* (Boston, 1859), pp. 359–402.

The best discussion of democratic ideas as they emerged at the end of the Colonial period is Merrill Jensen's "Democracy and the American Revolution," *Huntington Library Quarterly*, XX (1957), 321–341. The most informative statements include the anonymous pamphlet *The People the Best Governors*, republished in Frederick Chase, *The History of Dartmouth College and the Town of Hanover* (Cambridge, Mass., 1891), pp. 654–663; "Spartanus," in the *Freemans Journal or New Hampshire Gazette* (Portsmouth), June 15, 29, 1776; "Demophilus," *The Genuine Principles* . . . (Philadelphia, 1776); and "Philodemus" [Thomas Tudor Tucker], *Conciliatory Hints* . . . (Charleston, 1784).

Many accounts exist of late colonial politics. A general interpretation stressing ideological factors is Bernard Bailyn, *The Origins of American Politics* (New York, 1968). My forthcoming book, *Political Parties Before the Constitution* (Chapel Hill, 1972), elaborates material in the text and contains references.

The only history of the interim governments, Agnes Hunt's *Provincial Committees of Safety of the American Revolution* (Cleveland, 1904), does not discuss changes in the structure of power or the broader implications of the committees' work. The same fault characterizes the older books and forces the historian to rely on primary sources unless he can find recent research, usually doctoral dissertations. For New England see the following: "Records of the New Hampshire Committee of Safety," in *Collections of the New Hampshire Historical Society*, VII (Concord, 1863), 1–340; Nathanael Bouton, *et al.*, eds., *Documents and Records Relating to New Hampshire*, 40 Vols. (Concord and Manchester, 1867–1941), VII; Jere R. Daniell, *Experiment in Republicanism: New Hampshire Politics and the American Revolution, 1741–1794* (Cambridge, Mass., 1970), pp. 99–109; William Lincoln, ed., *The Journals* of each *Provincial Congress of Massachusetts in 1774 and 1775* (Boston, 1838); Stephen Everett Patterson, "A History of Political Parties in Revolutionary Massachusetts, 1770–1780," Ph.D. dissertation, University of Wisconsin, 1968; Harry Alonzo Cushing, *History of the Transition from Province to Commonwealth Government in Massachusetts* (New York, 1896). Connecticut and Rhode Island, of course, needed no special congresses.

For the Middle colonies, see J. Howard Hanson and Samuel Ludlow Frey, eds., *The Minute Book of the Committee of Safety of Tryon County* . . . (New York, 1905), which includes valuable biographical notes; *Journals of the Provincial Congress, Provincial Convention, Committee of Safety and Council of Safety of the State of New-York*, 2 Vols. in one (Albany, 1842); Bernard Mason, *The Road to Independence: The Revolutionary Movement in New York, 1773–1777* (Lexington, Ky., 1966), pp. 178–213; Roger Champagne, "New York Politics and Independence, 1776," *New-York Historical Society Quarterly*, XLVI (1962), 281–303; *Minutes of the Provincial Congress and the Council of Safety of the State of New Jersey* (Trenton, 1779), also containing the proceedings of various local groups; *Journal of the Votes and Proceedings of the Convention of New-Jersey* (Burlington, 1776); David Alan Bernstein, "New Jersey in the American Revolution," Ph.D. dissertation, Rutgers University, 1970; Charles H. Lincoln, *The Revolutionary Movement in Pennsylvania, 1760–1776* (Philadelphia, 1901); the proceedings of the 1775 convention, the 1776 conference, and the 1776 convention, all published contemporaneously in Philadelphia; and *Proceedings of the Convention of the Delaware State* (Wilmington, 1776).

Southern sources include *Proceedings of the Conventions of the Province of Maryland* . . . (Annapolis, 1775); John Archer Silver, *The Provincial Government of Maryland (1774–1777)* (Baltimore, 1895); Ronald Hoffman, "Economics, Politics and the Revolution in Maryland," Ph.D. dissertation, University of Wisconsin, 1969; the proceedings of the three Virginia conventions in 1775 and 1776, published contemporaneously in Williamsburg; Richard Barksdale Harwell, ed., *Proceedings of the County Committees, 1774–1776: The Committees of Safety of Westmoreland and Fincastle* (Richmond, 1956); Hamilton J. Eckenrode, *The Revolution in Virginia* (Boston and New York, 1916); *The Journal of the Proceedings of the Provincial Congress of North-Carolina* (Raleigh, 1831); Bessie Lewis Whitaker, *The Provincial Council and Committees of Safety in North Carolina* (Chapel Hill, 1908); Robert L. Ganyard, "North Carolina During the American Revolution," Ph.D. dissertation, Duke University, 1963; W. E. Hemphill and W. A. Waters, eds., *Extracts from the Journals of the Provincial Congress of South-Carolina* (Columbia, S.C., 1960); Allen D. Candler, comp., *The Colonial Records of the State of Georgia*, 26 Vols. (Atlanta, 1904–1916), XIV, and *The Revolutionary Records of the State of Georgia*, 3 Vols. (Atlanta, 1908), I, pp. 229–259; and Kenneth Coleman, *The American Revolution in Georgia, 1763–1789* (Athens, 1958), pp. 45–64.

## CHAPTER 5: CONFLICTS OVER THE CONSTITUTIONS

The constitutions adopted by the states during the Revolutionary era are printed in Francis N. Thorpe, ed., *Federal and State Constitutions, Colonial Charters, and Other Organic Laws*, 7 Vols. (Washington, D.C., 1909). Those which the states failed to adopt are noted below. Wood's *Creation of an American Republic* and Douglass's *Rebels and Democrats* are basic. Different aspects of the new governments are examined by Pole, Nevins, John Nees Shaeffer, "Constitutional Change in the Unicameral States, 1776–1793," Ph.D. dissertation, University of Wisconsin, 1968, and my own *Upper House*.

Daniell's *Experiment* discusses New Hampshire's constitutional history. The 1776 document is printed in *New Hampshire State Papers*, VIII, 2–4. "Spartanus" and the anonymous pamphlet are cited above. For the New Ipswich instructions of November 25, 1776, see Frederick Kidder and Augustus A. Gould, *The History of New Ipswich, from its first grant in MDCCXXXVI to the present time* (Boston, 1852), pp. 90–91. What little we know about the early constitutions of South Carolina is summarized in a revised, as yet unpublished version of Jerome Nadelhaft's Ph.D. dissertation, University of Wisconsin, 1965. See also a letter of J. L. Gervais, *South Carolina Historical Magazine*, LXVI (1965), 29.

Three books discuss Pennsylvania's constitution: J. Paul Selsam, *The Pennsylvania Constitution of 1776* (Philadelphia, 1936), David Hawke, *In the Midst of a Revolution* (Philadelphia, 1961), and Robert L. Brunhouse, *The Counter-Revolution in Pennsylvania, 1776–1790* (Harrisburg, 1942). Hawke's study, the latest and most detailed, presents the thesis that most Pennsylvanians opposed the radicals, but I find the votes of 1779 persuasive evidence to the contrary. "Demophilus" is cited above. The *Packet* contains the following articles on the same side: "The Considerate Freeman," November 12, 20, 26, 1776, and "A Watchman," June 17, 1776. On the other side, quoted in the text, are "K" and "Farmer," September 24, November 5, 1776. Philadelphia meetings are reported in *ibid.*, October 22, November 12, 1776. The petitions opposing a new convention are in the Assembly journals; for a sample remonstrance, see that of York County, Records of the General Assembly of Pennsylvania, Box 1, Archives of Pennsylvania.

Eckenrode's *Revolution* contains an account of the Virginia convention as does Irving Brant, *James Madison, Vol. I: The Virginia Revolutionist, 1751–1780* (Indianapolis, 1941). Eckenrode quotes Henry's opinion on p. 162. The ideas of Jefferson and Mason's plan are in Julian P. Boyd, ed., *The Papers of Thomas Jefferson* (Princeton, 1950), I, 329–386. Braxton's proposal appeared not only in pamphlet form as previously cited but in the *Virginia Gazette* (Dixon and Hunter), June 8, 15, 1776. "Democritus" offered some "loose thoughts" featuring an upper house chosen by county committees in the *Virginia*

*Gazette* (Purdie), June 7, 1776. Carter's letter is in Peter Force, ed., *American Archives*, 9 Vols. (Washington, D.C., 1837–1853), v, 390.

For New Jersey, the older work by Charles R. Erdman, Jr., *The New Jersey Constitution of 1776* (Princeton, 1929), is superseded by Bernstein's dissertation "New Jersey in the American Revolution." The petitions are in *Journal of the Votes and Proceedings of the Convention of New-Jersey* (Burlington, 1776). For Maryland, see Silver, *Provincial Government of Maryland*, and Hoffman, "Revolution in Maryland." The instructions and the "Watchman" article are in the *Maryland Gazette*, July 23, August 15, 27, 1776. Chase's account is in *ibid.*, Dec. 11, 1777. For Carroll's quotation, see Hoffman, "Revolution in Maryland," p. 286. See also the statement in the *Maryland Journal*, May 1, 1787. Beverly W. Bond, *State Government in Maryland, 1777–1781* (Baltimore, 1905), and Philip A. Crowl, *Maryland During and After the Revolution* (Baltimore, 1943) also contain some material.

Henry Clay Reed, *The Delaware Constitution of 1776* (Wilmington, 1930), and Harold Bell Hancock, *The Delaware Loyalists* (Wilmington, 1942) cover that state. Robert Ganyard argues in his dissertation, "North Carolina During the American Revolution," that North Carolina's constitution was more conservative than radical. The basic sources, including the Orange and Mecklenburg instructions, are in William L. Saunders, Walter Clark, and Stephen B. Weeks, eds., *Colonial and State Records of North Carolina*, 30 Vols. (Raleigh, Winston, Goldsboro, and Charlotte, 1886–1914), x, pp. 240, 870. For Hooper's ideas, see *ibid.*, pp. 867–868. Griffith J. McRee, *Life and Correspondence of James Iredell*, 2 Vols. (New York, 1857–1858), i, p. 276, contains Johnston's letter. For Georgia, see Coleman, *American Revolution in Georgia*, pp. 79–85.

My account of New York's convention follows that of Mason, *Road to Independence*, pp. 213–249. Jay's remark is quoted in Alfred F. Young, *The Democratic Republicans of*

*New York* (Chapel Hill, 1967), p. 21. For Vermont, see Chilton Williamson, *Vermont in Quandary* (Montpelier, 1949), and Nathaniel Hendricks, "A New Look at the Ratification of the Vermont Constitution of 1777," *Vermont History*, xxxiv (1966), 136–140. Robert J. Taylor has edited an excellent set of documents in *Massachusetts, Colony to Commonwealth* (Chapel Hill, 1961). It includes the return of Ashfield, Westminster, and Dorchester, the constitution of 1780, and selections from the *Essex Result*. Oscar and Mary Handlin include an even larger number of documents in their *Popular Sources of Political Authority: Documents on the Massachusetts Constitution of 1780* (Cambridge, Mass., 1966). Taylor's *Western Massachusetts in the Revolution* (Providence, 1954) describes events from one perspective while Patterson's dissertation, "Revolutionary Massachusetts," supplies a general study. For "A Faithful Friend" and "An Old Roman," see the *Independent Chronicle* (Boston), August 7, 1777, and the *Boston Gazette, and Country Journal*, April 15, 1778. A long defense of Rhode Island's government, attacking petitions from Scituate and Gloucester appeared, in the *Providence Gazette*, March 20, April 24, 1779. See also *ibid.*, September 7, 1776. For the abortive committee, Rhode Island Acts and Resolves, September 1777.

## CHAPTER 6: THE NEW GOVERNMENTS

Historians have devoted much time to examining the political theory behind the state constitutions and little to describing their practical consequences. In general, writers have advanced three theses concerning the effect of Revolutionary developments on the distribution of political power. One group maintains that democracy existed before 1776 and that subsequent events confirmed the people's control. A second agrees in a continuity but maintains that the upper class, or elite, controlled the governments during the entire period. My interpretation acknowledges the continuation of certain democratic elements, varying in strength, as well as of a strong upper-class tradition, but argues the greater significance of an increase in participatory democracy, or popular government. The advocates of the alternative hypotheses can cite supporting facts but in my opinion can only maintain their views by overlooking much evidence to the contrary. James Kirby Martin's Ph.D. dissertation, "Political Elites and the Outbreak of the American Revolution: A Quantitative Profile in Continuity, Turnover, and Change, 1774–1777," University of Wisconsin, 1969, supports my interpretation with respect to major offices, while Joel Alden Cohen finds that in Rhode Island the towns continued to elect representatives from the upper economic ranks ("Rhode Island and the American Revolution: A Selective Socio-Economic Analysis," Ph.D. dissertation, University of Connecticut, 1967).

The only book on the state executives, Margaret B. Macmillan's *War Governors in the American Revolution* (Columbia, S.C., 1943), is marred by three major defects. The author makes no effort to study the kind of people who held office, to trace changes from the Colonial period, or to assess the political significance of the new executives. She emphasizes the instability and brief tenure of the governors, taken collectively, without noting that her argument holds true for only two states, Georgia in particular contributing so many individuals that a general average becomes misleading. Finally, she itemizes every defect but does not grant due recognition for the many difficulties surmounted and victories gained. The book's usefulness therefore does not extend beyond its facts, and we need a fresh study. The biographies of these wartime leaders often make good reading, but individually they do not tell us much about the executive office because the authors lack any basis for broad comparisons. David Hawke furnishes a slightly longer list of governors in his *The Colonial Experience* (Indianapolis, 1966), pp. 686–698.

For the senates I have relied upon my research for *The Upper House*. Changes in the qualifications for voting are traced in Chilton Williamson, *American Suffrage from Prop-*

*erty to Democracy* (Princeton, 1960). More detail on the lower houses appears in my forthcoming *Political Parties*. We lack studies of the judges or of other officials. Wayne L. Bockerman finds only minor changes at the local level in "Continuity and Change in Revolutionary Pennsylvania: A Study of County Government and Officeholders," Ph.D. dissertation, Northwestern University, 1969. Jere Daniell discusses the revised New Hampshire constitution in his *Experiment in Republicanism*, pp. 164–179. The articles by "A Republican" appeared in the *New Hampshire Gazette*, February 8 to March 22, 1783. For Georgia, see Coleman, *American Revolution in Georgia*, pp. 271–275. The Savannah articles come from the *Gazette of the State of Georgia*, January 22, 29, February 5, 12, 19, 1784. The controversy in Pennsylvania, discussed in Brunhouse, *Counter-Revolution in Pennsylvania*, can best be followed in the newspapers. The *Packet* printed the "Principles and Articles of the Constitutional Society" on April 1, 1779, and the majority and minority reports of the Council of Censors on January 24, 1784; see also February 12, 1784. The most interesting account of the 1790 convention is in Alexander Graydon, *Memoirs of His Own Times* (Philadelphia, 1846), pp. 344–346.

Another volume in this Bicentennial History of the Revolution, by H. Trevor Colbourn, will discuss the significance of the constitutional changes for the history of religious liberty and will examine the declarations of rights. See in particular Leonard W. Levy, *Legacy of Suppression* (Cambridge, Mass., 1960), his *Origins of the Fifth Amendment* (New York, 1968), and Robert Rutland, *Birth of the Bill of Rights* (Chapel Hill, 1955).

## CHAPTER 7: ECONOMIC CHANGES DURING THE WAR

This chapter proved the most difficult to write and probably contains the most inaccuracies. Few reliable secondary works exist, and the primary sources are scanty and hard to interpret. Men at the time, even public officials, seldom kept precise track of their economic activities, nor did they systematically record incomes and expenditures. Fluctuating currencies create intolerable errors in our data. Crucial records have disappeared and in some cases never existed. Therefore, approximations replace accuracy. In addition, we must referee, remote from the arena, a major conflict over economic goals and means, some elements of which indeed remain just as controversial today.

Monetary policy, the key to the economic history of the period, receives such a distorted treatment from advocates of a specie standard that we can rely on none of the older works. The first accurate account is that of E. James Ferguson, *The Power of the Purse* (Chapel Hill, 1961), who concentrates almost entirely on congressional finance. The same is true of most other financial histories. We are forced to rely therefore on primary sources such as laws, legislative proceedings, the only-too-rare treasurers' reports, and newspapers.

The same difficulty impedes our discussion of other economic activities, including the support of the armies, handling of the debt, tax policy, the regulation of prices and wages, and state aid to business enterprises. We rarely find information about the actions of the state governments but only of congressional proceedings, usually in accounts highly critical of that body. Similarly, we know something about large-scale business enterprises but little about those within the states, important though these were. Most economic studies either concentrate on the Colonial period, halting about 1775, or begin with the Early National era, commencing after the war, so that during the years that interest us we encounter almost a vacuum.

Curtis Nettels' *Emergence of a National Economy* furnishes a general survey. Robert A. East's *Business Enterprise in the American Revolutionary Era* (New York, 1938) explains in detail the activities of leading merchants. Anne Bezanson, Robert D. Gray, and Miriam Hussy, *Prices and Inflation During the American Revolution: Pennsylvania, 1770–1790* (Philadelphia, 1951) provides a wealth of data concerning prices in

Philadelphia and a running account of factors affecting them. A few local studies contain useful information. Among them are Oscar and Mary F. Handlin, "Revolutionary Economic Policy in Massachusetts," *William and Mary Quarterly*, 3rd series, IV (1947), 3–26; W. Robert Higgins, "The South Carolina Revolutionary Debt and Its Holders, 1776–1780," *South Carolina Historical Magazine*, LXXII (1971), 15–29; Harold T. Pinkett, "Maryland as a Source of Food Supplies During the American Revolution," *Maryland Historical Magazine*, XLVI (1951), 157–172; James R. Morrill, *The Practice and Politics of Fiat Finance: North Carolina in the Confederation, 1783–1789* (Chapel Hill, 1969); and Thomas C. Cochran, *New York in the Confederation: An Economic Study* (Philadelphia, 1932), which concentrates on the state's relations with Congress. Helpful also are the dissertations by Ernst, "Currency in the Era of the American Revolution," and Van Deusen, "Trade of Revolutionary Connecticut." The latter traces the breakdown of regulatory acts in Connecticut, noting that price-fixing legislation remained in effect only from November 1776 to the following August, and again for three months during the spring of 1778.

My account differs from the standard interpretation by emphasizing the successes of the states rather than their failures, and by explaining the deficiencies as a result of circumstance rather than of ignorance or malice. On the basis of numerous newspaper articles, petitions, resolutions, and other expressions of opinion, I argue that the defenders of deficit financing presented as strong a case as their opponents, the preference depending upon one's economic convictions and (I think) social sympathies. The student might look through the *Pennsylvania Packet*, noting for example "Letters on Appreciation," January 18, 20, 1780 and "An American" (discussed in the text), February 17 to April 15, 1780. The Virginia State Library contains a revealing collection of petitions.

Developments in Rhode Island can be traced through the *Acts and Resolves* and the governor's summary in John Russell Bartlett, ed., *Records of the Colony of Rhode Island and*

*Providence Plantations in New England,* 10 Vols. (Providence, 1856–1865), IX, pp. 485–487. For the statements from Needham and Portsmouth, see the *Continental Journal, and Weekly Advertiser* (Boston), October 31, 1776, and *Freemans Journal,* January 14, 1777. Information concerning North Carolina's successful privateers comes from the *North Carolina State Records,* XV, pp. 68–69. The quotation from Walter Livingston is published in East, *Business Enterprise,* p. 104, that of Whipple is in Edmund Cody Burnett, ed., *Letters of Members of the Continental Congress,* 8 Vols. (Washington, D.C., 1921–1936), IV, pp. 222–223. Clarence Ver Steeg traces Morris's activities in *Robert Morris, Revolutionary Financier* (Philadelphia, 1954).

## CHAPTER 8: LOYALISM IN THE THIRTEEN STATES

Most books dealing with the loyalists concentrate on their experiences up to 1776, in exile, and in military service, omitting the subject of this chapter. The major exception is Claude H. Van Tyne's pathbreaking *The Loyalists in the American Revolution* (New York, 1902). Van Tyne concentrates on the laws, overlooking some executive decrees, legislative resolutions, and much other anti-loyalist activity. Wallace Brown's *The Good Americans: The Loyalists in the American Revolution* (New York, 1969) draws on his earlier study based upon loyalist claims, *The King's Friends* (Providence, 1965). Brown ignores the majority of loyalists, who never left the country, so his conclusions are misleading; but he publishes much useful data. The best study now available is William Nelson's *The American Tory* (Boston, 1961). Eugene Fingerhut emphasizes the unrepresentative character of the claimants in "Uses and Abuses of the American Loyalists' Claims: A Critique of Quantitative Analysis," *William and Mary Quarterly,* XXV (1968), 245–258. In the same issue, pp. 259–277, Paul H. Smith concludes that nearly one out of five white Americans actively supported the British.

The following special studies of loyalism in particular states proved useful for this chapter. Kenneth Scott, "Tory Associators of Portsmouth," *Wiliam and Mary Quarterly*, 3rd series, XVII (1960), 507–515; Alexander C. Flick, *Loyalism in New York During the American Revolution* (New York, 1901); Hancock, *Delaware Loyalists;* Richard Arthur Overfield, "The Loyalists of Maryland During the American Revolution," Ph.D. dissertation, University of Maryland, 1968; Isaac S. Harrell, *Loyalism in Virginia* (Durham, 1926); Peter Q. Mitchell, "Loyalist Property and the Revolution in Virginia," Ph.D. dissertation, University of Colorado, 1965 (which finds no redistribution of wealth); Robert O. DeMond, *The Loyalists in North Carolina During the Revolution* (Durham, 1940); Ralph Louis Andreano and Herbert D. Warner, "Charleston Loyalists, A Statistical Note," *South Carolina Historical Magazine*, LX (1959), 164–168; C. Ashley Ellefson, "Loyalists and Patriots in Georgia During the American Revolution," *Historian*, XXIV (1961–2), 347–356. See also references concerning loyalist property in Chapter 9 and the sources on state politics, Chapters 10 and 11. The article quoted from a New London paper may be found in the *Connecticut Gazette*, May 16, 1783. William Paterson's remarks are contained in his papers, Rutgers University Library, accession 888. For the address of Delaware's upper house, see *Minutes of the Council of the Delaware State from 1776 to 1792*, Papers of the Historical Society of Delaware, VI (Wilmington, 1887), p. 90 (February 22, 1777). The message from Maryland's Senate occurred on April 16, 1777, as reported in the *Journals*. These also contain the exchange between the two houses on December 19–23, 1779. Overfield summarizes the articles.

## CHAPTER 9: SOCIAL CHANGES IN THE REVOLUTIONARY ERA

The debate among historians over the questions in this chapter began with J. Franklin Jameson's *The American Revolution*

*Considered as a Social Movement* (Princeton, 1926). Research up to the early 1950's formed the basis for Frederick B. Tolles' article, "The American Revolution Considered as a Social Movement: A Reevaluation," *American Historical Review*, LX (1954), 1–12. Tolles left matters ambiguous and subsequent research has not resolved the issue, many aspects of which remain obscure.

Sources for the sale of loyalist property include those works cited in the last chapter and the following. Richard D. Brown, "The Confiscation and Disposition of Loyalists' Estates in Suffolk County, Massachusetts," *William and Mary Quarterly*, 3rd series, XXI (1964), 534–550; Harry B. Yoshpe, *Disposition of Loyalist Estates in the Southern District of the State of New York* (New York, 1939); Staughton Lynd, "Who Should Rule at Home? Dutchess County, New York in the American Revolution," *William and Mary Quarterly*, XVII (1961), 330–360; Beatrice G. Reubens, "Pre-Emptive Rights in the Disposition of a Confiscated Estate, Philipsburgh Manor, New York," *ibid.*, XXII (1965), 435–456; Catherine Snell Crary, "Forfeited Loyalist Lands in the Western District of New York: Albany and Tryon Counties," *New York History*, XXXV (1954), 239–258; Ruth M. Keesey, "Loyalism in Bergen County, New Jersey," *William and Mary Quarterly*, XVIII (1961), 558–571; Robert S. Lambert, "The Confiscation of Loyalist Property in Georgia, 1782–1786," *ibid.*, XX (1963), 80–94. Political histories mentioned in the next chapter also contain useful information.

The article estimating the wealth of the Middle colonies is Alice Hanson Jones, "Wealth Estimates for the American Middle Colonies, 1774," *Economic Development and Cultural Change*, XVIII (1970). Sosin's *Revolutionary Frontier* summarizes the migration into the frontier area.

The major authorities on Negroes during this period are Zilvermit's *First Emancipation* and Quarles's *Negro in the American Revolution*. The alternate account of emancipation in Connecticut is in Christopher Collier, *Roger Sherman's Connecticut* (Middleton, Conn., 1971), p. 194n. The key votes in the New York Assembly occurred on February 26, March 1–3, 9, 1785. For Pennsylvania's, February 16, March 1, 1780, September 22, 26, 1781, March 4, April 13, 1782. The roll call in Maryland's House of Delegates occurred on December 7, 1785. Virginia's petitions are in the state library. Examples on the pro-slavery side are Henrico, June 8, 1782, Halifax, November 10, 1785, and Lunenburg, November 20, 1785. An anti-slavery petition is that of Frederick, November 8, 1785, quoted in the text. The votes were recorded on December 14, 24, 1785, November 4, 1786, and January 1, 1788.

On primogeniture and entail see R. Ray Keim, "Primogeniture and Entail in Colonial Virginia," *William and Mary Quarterly*, 3rd series, xxv (1968), 545–586. I detected a break-up of estates in the older areas in research for my article "The Distribution of Property in Post-Revolutionary Virginia," *Mississippi Valley Historical Review*, xli (1954), 241–258. The remark concerning due subordination is Jonathan Trumbull's in a letter, June 7, 1783, Trumbull Papers, xx, Part 2, 354, Connecticut State Library. For John Langdon's complaint, see *Historical Magazine*, vi (1962), 240. Allan Kulikoff finds almost no social change in Boston resulting from the Revolution but only the continuation of long-term trends (cited above, Chapter 2).

## CHAPTER 10: NORTHERN POLITICS DURING THE WAR

I have drawn the material for this and the next chapter from monographs where these exist. All too often they do exist, and recourse to legislative records, session laws, and newspapers does not substitute for really thorough research. The generalizations in the text may seem more foolhardy than bold, but I preferred to risk error than to say nothing. The most serious gaps in the literature relate to state support of the war. Another major defect is the lack of books comparing the histories of the several states, for only such general comparisons enable us to understand what was taking place in particular instances.

Daniell's *Experiment in Republicanism* guides one carefully through New Hampshire's politics but supplies only a bare outline for economic developments. The quotations concerning monetary and tax policy come from the session laws, January 2, 1777, and July 2, 1776. For the vote on legal tender (September 1, 1781), see *New Hampshire State Papers*, VIII, 913.

The best guides to the political history of Massachusetts during this period are Patterson's dissertation "Revolutionary Massachusetts" and Van Beck Hall's *Politics Without Parties*, both referred to earlier. Taylor's *Western Massachusetts* and Lee N. Newcomer, *The Embattled Farmers: A Massachusetts Countryside in the American Revolution* (New York, 1953) trace western developments. For the Boston town meeting and the Plymouth County conventions, see *Boston Gazette*, June 2, 16, 1777. The legislature's statement on paper money can be found in the Journals of the House of Representatives, September 26, 1777. The votes on the legal-tender issue occurred on June 2, 6, 9, 10, 24, September 26-29, November 24, 1780, January 11, 16, 18, 24, June 13, 1781. See also *Boston Gazette*, February 5, 1781, for the position taken by some absent members. For economic policy, Andrew McFarland Davis, "The Limitation of Prices in Massachusetts, 1776-1779," Colonial Society of Massachusetts, *Transactions*, XI (1906-1907), 119-134, and the Handlins' "Economic Policy," cited above.

No adequate secondary work covers Rhode Island's internal history during the war years. David Lovejoy's *Rhode Island Politics and the American Revolution* (Providence, 1958) ends in 1776, while Polishook's account concentrates on the period after 1781. The present survey is based upon the published records, the *Acts and Resolves*, and newspapers. For Governor Greene's letter, see *Colonial Records of Rhode Island*, IX, pp. 485-487. The *Acts and Resolves* for July 1780 contain an informative financial summary. For the political controversy, see *Providence Gazette,* March 20, 1779, April 3, 24, 1780, February 24, 1781. The *Public Records of Connecticut* contain little information, and my observations draw on scattered sources. Van Deusen's dissertation, "Trade of Revolutionary Connecticut," is helpful. My book on the upper houses, pp. 180–182, briefly discusses the attack on the assistants. The quotation comes from the *Connecticut Courant,* September 12, 1783.

Both Cochran's *New York in the Confederation,* cited above, and E. Wilder Spaulding, *New York in the Critical Period* (New York, 1932) cast some light on our subject, but the former focuses on financial relations between the state and Congress while the latter concentrates on the postwar years. James Duane's observations come from a letter to R. R. Livingston in the latter's papers, New-York Historical Society. My discussion of wartime politics is based on an analysis of the legislative records, especially the roll-call votes, and biographical data on the delegates. The same sources for New Jersey supplement Bernstein's dissertation, "New Jersey in the American Revolution," and for the later years Richard P. McCormick, *Experiment in Independence: New Jersey in the Critical Period, 1781–1789* (New Brunswick, 1950). Leonard Lundin, *Cockpit of the Revolution: The War for Independence in New Jersey* (Princeton, 1940) covers the military aspects.

The basic study of Pennsylvania's political history is that of Brunhouse, *Counter-Revolution in Pennsylvania.* The legislature published many roll-call votes. Helpful petitions are preserved in the records both of the Assembly and the Supreme Executive Council, in the state archives, Harrisburg. Newspaper articles contain an exceptional amount of information. The quotation concerning the election of 1780 comes from a letter of Barnabus Bonney to Nicholas Brown, March 17, 1781, Brown Papers, Miscellaneous letters, John Carter Brown Library. The following quotation is taken from an article by "Reflector" in the *Freeman's Journal: Or, The North-American Intelligencer* (Philadelphia), September 25, 1782, and the next occurs in a circular letter sent by the Philadelphia Constitutionalists to their political supporters in other countries. August 1783, broadside, Historical Society of Pennsylvania.

## CHAPTER 11: SOUTHERN POLITICS
### DURING THE WAR

The only good history of Delaware during the war years is Hancock's *Loyalists*, which covers more than its title indicates but naturally not everything. I rely upon the laws and legislative records. Crowl, *Maryland During and After the Revolution*, furnishes a good guide. Hoffman's dissertation, cited above, supplements and in part replaces Crowl. See also Pinkett's article, *Maryland Historical Magazine*, XLVI (1951), 157–172. The legislative records and laws furnish basic information concerning economic developments and political divisions. The detailed financial summary of 1787 can be found in the journals of the House of Delegates for January 16. See also Jackson T. Main, "Political Parties in Revolutionary Maryland, 1780–1787," *Maryland Historical Magazine*, LXII (1967), 1–27.

For Virginia I have relied primarily upon the public records and the laws. The complaint about the draft came from Hanover County, May 24, 1782, Virginia State Library, which also contains the petition from Prince William County, December 10, 1781 (oversize).

The militia colonel's report is in William P. Palmer, ed., *Calendar of Virginia State Papers* (Richmond, 1875–1893), II, pp. 531–532. The first few volumes of the *Calendar* contain much essential material. I generalize about Virginia hesitantly; we need a monograph. The *State Records of North Carolina* furnish a great deal of information. The recent book by Morrill, *Practice and Politics of Fiat Finance*, deals with the postwar years but throws light upon the Revolutionary experience.

No recent book on South Carolina during the war years is available. Charles Gregg Singer, *South Carolina in the Confed-*

*eration* (Philadelphia, 1941) deals briefly with a later period. I have drawn on Jerome Nadelhaft's manuscript together with my own research. Richard Walsh's monograph on the Charleston artisans, *Charleston's Sons of Liberty*, is helpful. The only recent book on Revolutionary Georgia is that of Kenneth Coleman, *American Revolution in Georgia*.

CHAPTER 12: RETROSPECT AND PROSPECT

For sample accounts of the treaty's reception, see *Independent Gazetteer* (Philadelphia), March 29; *Boston Gazette*, April 7, May 5, July 7; *New London Gazette*, April 4; *Connecticut Courant* (Hartford), April 1; *Providence Gazette*, April 5; and the *New Jersey Gazette* (Trenton), April 16, 23. The hopeful article appeared in the June 30 and July 14 issues. The letter quoted from a lawyer is that of Henry Van Schaak to Theodore Sedgwick, January 2, 1784, Theodore Sedgwick papers, Vol. A, *Massachusetts Historical Society*. The Pennsylvania lawyers' position is outlined in Thomas R. Meehan, "Courts, Cases, and Counselors in Revolutionary and Post-Revolutionary Pennsylvania," *Pennsylvania Magazine of History and Biography*, xci (1967), 3–34. On the possible development of the South without slavery, see William N. Parker, "Slavery and Southern Economic Development: An Hypothesis and Some Evidence," in William N. Parker, ed., *The Structure of the Cotton Economy of the Antebellum South* (Washington, D.C., 1970), 115–126.

# *Index*

Adams, John, 140, 143, 180-82, 204; *Thoughts on Government* (pamphlet), 156
Adams, Samuel, 180-81, 182, 204
Allen, William and John, 292
Allen party (Vt.), 355
"American, An" (pen name), 255
Anglicans, 8, 59; and loyalism, 284, 285; in N.Y., 122; in Penn., 388; and slavery, 334; in South, 15, 121, 150
Arnold, Benedict, 412
Articles of Confederation, 377-78, 409
Artisans, 68-69, 452; economic effects on, 230-31, 245, 267, 442-43; in New England, 50-54; rural, 50-56; in South, 54-55; urban, 71-76
Ashe, John B., 275-76
Ashley, John, 57
Austin, Benjamin, 73

Baltimore (city; Md.), 10, 16; loyalism in, 325
Bank of North America (founded, 1781), 267, 391, 393-94, 408, 452, 453
Bankruptcy (of states), 243
Baptists, 8, 279; and slavery, 334, 344
Barnes, Richard, 402, 410
Bartlett, Josiah, 350
Bassett, Richard, 165
Benedict, Benjamin, 51
Bills of rights (state constitutions). *See* Declarations of rights
Bingham, William, 249
Blacks, free, 49-50

Blair, John, 156
Bland, Richard, 136
Blount, William, 306
Borland, John, 321
Boston (city; Mass.), 1, 67; British in, 223, 357; loyalism in, 270, 279, 281, 306, 320, 321; society in, 27-30; trade of, 4, 16-17
*Boston Gazette* (newspaper), 441
Boston Port Act, 124-25, 126. *See also individual states*—Revolutionary movement in
Bowdoin, James, 29, 180, 182, 190, 440
Boycotts. *See:* Continental Association; Nonimportation agreements
Boyd, George, 88
Braxton, Carter, 156
Brooks, John, 61
Broome, John, 173
Bryan, George, 84, 152, 390
Bull, Thomas, 386
Bull, William, 100, 272, 308
Bullett, Cuthbert, 416
Bulloch, Archibald, 429
Bunker Hill, Battle of, 223-24
Burgoyne, General John, 240, 242, 297, 351, 357, 372, 376, 382
Burke, Thomas, 57-58, 191, 421

Cabot family (Mass.), 247
Caldwell, James, 44, 198
Calvinists, 113, 122; and slavery, 334
Canada, expedition to, 224, 357
Cannon, Daniel, 73
Cannon, James, 151
Cape Cod (Mass.), loyalism on, 272
Carne, Samuel, 41
Carroll, Charles ("Barrister"), 161-62
Carroll, Charles (of Carrollton), 140, 161-63, 402
Carroll, Daniel, 325

Carter, Landon, 136, 157

Carter, Robert Wormeley, 419

Caswell, Richard, 191, 194

Charleston (city; S.C.), 10, 15, 67, 68; British in, 246, 306, 308, 420, 425-27; loyalism in, 272, 306, 308, 328-29; society of, 34-35, 424

Chase, Samuel, 161-63, 325, 410

Checks and balances, principle of, 142, 221

Chesapeake Bay area, geography of, 10-12, 16

Chesnut, John, 18, 425

Clark, Abraham, 84

Clarke, Benjamin, 75

Class conflicts, 122-23. *See also* Political parties

Clinton, George, 57, 189, 190, 191, 194, 212, 286, 287, 288, 315, 374, 377, 380, 438, 449, 454

Cluggage, Robert, 59

Clymer, George, 386

Coats, William, 73

Coleman, Robert, 386

Coles, Isaac, 63

Committees of Correspondence, 124-25, 129, 135, 141

Congregationalists, 6, 8, 27; and slavery, 334

Connecticut: British in, 370, 432; constitution of, 101, 184, 221; finances (war) of, 223, 370-71; loyalism in, 272, 282, 284-85, 321, 370; politics in, 121, 369-72; Revolutionary movement in, 126; slavery in, 336-37; wealth of, 330

Conscientious objectors, 295. *See also* Pacifist sects

Constitutionalists: Mass., 362-63; N.H., 274; Penn., 219, 220, 293, 339, 389-95 passim, 452, 453

Constitutions (state), 450; adoption of (conventions), 142, 187-88; Bills of rights in (*see* Declarations of rights); conflicts over, 452; Democratic ideology in (*see* Democratic ideology—in state constitutions); reform movements and, 183, 212-21; Whig ideology in (*see* Whig ideology—in state constitutions). *See also individual states*—constitution(s) of

Continental Army: creation of, 224-26; slaves in, 335-36; state contributions to, 351, 357, 364, 367, 370, 377, 383, 385, 392-93,

397, 402-403, 414, 420, 428, 429, 434; at Valley Forge, 382, 393, 405

Continental Association, 128, 129, 134, 135; adoption of, 137, 139, 443; enforcement of, 139, 275-76. *See also* Nonimportation agreements

Continental Congress (1st, 1774), 123, 125, 128

Continental Congress (2nd, 1775-1781), 129, 144; vs. loyalists, 276-77, 280, 283; and slavery, 336

Continental currency, collapse of, 250-51, 254

Cook, Joseph, 52

Cooke, Nicholas, 94

Cooper, John, 197

Copley, John Singleton, 29

Corbin, Thomas and Richard, Jr., 326

Corn production, 39

Cornwallis, General Charles, 259, 378, 412, 415, 421. *See also* Yorktown, Battle of

Cotton production, 446

Coxe, Daniel, 292, 323

Coxe, Tench, 292

Craftsmen. *See* Artisans

Creditors: and loyalists, 280, 283-84, 313; postwar, 261, 262-63; during war, 232, 245, 299, 356, 375

Cripps, Whitten, 198

Daivies, Thomas, 73

Dartmouth College (N.H.), 355, 362

Dawes, William, 29

Deane, Silas, 249

Debtors (postwar), political support for, 453-54

Debts (state), 260, 262-63, 264, 371, 439, 444. *See also* Creditors

Declarations of rights (state constitutions), 203, 209-11, 235; Del., 165; Ga., 172; Md., 164; Mass., 182; N.J., 161; N.C., 167, 170; Penn., 154; S.C., 150; Va., 159, 167, 170

Deflation. *See* Depression (postwar)

De Lancey, John, 449

De Lancey, Oliver, 322

De Lancey family (N.Y.), 131, 204, 271

Delany family (Md.), 402

Delaware: British in, 397, 432; constitution of, 165-66; depression (postwar) in, 262; finances (war) of, 224, 397-99; geography of, 8-10; loyalism in, 165, 234, 272, 273, 275, 294-95, 296, 312, 313, 324-25, 396-97, 433; politics in, 121, 396-99; Revolutionary movement in, 126, 134; slavery in, 210, 340-41, 342

"Delmarva" peninsula, loyalism on, 272-73

Democracy, social, 348, 448

Democratic ideology, 116-19, 146; growth of, 448-49, 221; in state constitutions, 151, 167-72, 176-77, 183, 185, 221, 449; in state legislatures, 198, 200-206

"Demophilus" (pen name), 151

Dennis, Henry, 410

"Depreciation notes," 245

Depression (postwar), 261-67, 441-46 passim

Derby, John, 440

De Witt, Charles, 173

Deye, Cockey, 161

Dickinson, John, 140, 190, 391-92, 438

Distilling industry, 77. See also Triangular trade

Doctors: rural, 60-61; urban, 83

Dougherty, Bernard, 59

Drayton, Charles, 60

Duane, James, 85, 140, 173, 197, 288, 374, 377-78

Dudley, John, 350

Duer, William, 172, 173

Dulany, Daniel, 325

Dunmore, John Murray, Governor (Va.), 123

Dutch minority (N.Y.), 8, 122; loyalism and, 273, 374-75, 380; and slavery, 334, 338, 339

Dutch Reformed church, 334

Dwight, Timothy and Josiah, 63


Edes, Benjamin, 29

Education, 42, 62, 82-83

Elliott, William, 89

Embargoes, 91, 124; effects of, 229, 231, 232, 238. *See also* Non-importation agreements

Entail, laws of, 345-46

"Essex Result" (pamphlet), 180, 215

Executive branch: in colonies, 99-102; in states, 188-95 (*see also individual states*—constitution(s) of). *See also* Governors

Executive councils: in colonies, 102-103; in states, 191-92

Eyre, Emanuel, 73


Factions (political). *See* Political parties

Fairfax, Denny Martin, 327

Fairfax, Thomas, Lord, 302, 327

Fairfax family (Va.), 327, 331

"Faithful Friend to his Country, A" (pen name), 178

"Farmer" (pen name), 154-55

Farming, 37, 40; in Chesapeake Bay area, 10-12; commercial, 24-26, 246, 441-42; in Delaware River area, 8-10; income from, 41-46; large landowners, 43-45 (*see also* Plantations); Long Island–N.Y. Sound area, 8; loyalism and, 271-74, 303; in New England, 4, 23-24, 38, 40-41, 66; and political parties, 452-54; in postwar period, 266, 441-42; small farms, 38-39; society of, 22-26

Faver, Theophilus, 43

Ferguson (loyalist leader, N.C.), 421

Fishing industry, 69, 247, 443

Fitch, Thomas, 111

Fitzhugh, William, 161, 419

Fleming, William, 50

Florida, raids into, 430

Folsom, Nathaniel, 350

Foster, Jedidiah, 63

France: aid from, 234, 242, 258, 365, 367, 381; exports to, 230, 249, 402

Franklin, Benjamin, 77, 79, 80, 191

Franklin, William, 100, 133

Frelinghuysen, Frederick, 324

French and Indian War, 8, 241

Frontier regions: expansion into, 318, 332-33, 446, 447, 450; geography of, 17-22; loyalism in, 272, 274; slavery in, 343; in state legislatures, 202, 204; war and, 410-11

Fruit production, 39-40


Gadsden, Christopher, 424

Gage, General Thomas, 223, 276, 279, 357

Galloway, Joseph, 292, 324

Gates, General Horatio, 247, 420-21

Geographic regions (in 1776), 2-4

Georgia: British in, 429-31, 432; constitution of, 170-72, 217-18; depression (postwar) in, 262, 263, 432; finances (war) of, 223, 429-32; geography of, 14-16; loyalism in, 272, 308-10, 314, 329-30, 429, 433; politics in, 190, 350, 429-32; Revolutionary movement in, 139; slavery in, 344-45. *See also* Savannah

German immigrants, 273, 308, 380, 386-87

Gerry, Elbridge, 131

Glorious Revolution, 107

Goldsborough, Robert, 161

Gordon, James, 44

Governors: colonial, 99-102; state, 188-95, 435, 438, 449 (*see also individual states*—constitution(s) of); royal vs. state, 191

Graham, John, 329

Grain production, 38-39, 45. *See also* Rice production

Granville, Earl of, 327, 328

Granville family (N.C.), 331

Great Awakening, 84

Great Britain: military control by, 432, 434 (*see also individual states and cities*—British in); trade with, 15-17, 89-90, 258 (*see also:* Embargoes; Nonimportation agreements)

Greene, Nathanaël, 329

Greene, William, 190, 194, 438

Grout, Jonathan, 58

Guerrard, Benjamin, 438

Gwinnett, Button, 94

Haig, Dr. George, 60
Hale, Ebenezer, 61
Hall, David, 80
Hall, Lyman, 438
Hamilton, Alexander, 85, 288
Hammond, Rezin, 161
Hancock, John, 29, 78, 94, 127, 190, 438
Hand, Jonathan, 198
Hard-money advocates, 97-98. *See also* Monetary policy, debate over
Harford, Henry, 325, 326
Harford family (Md.), 331
Harrison, Benjamin, 136
Hastings, John, 61
Henry, Patrick, 57, 120, 156, 191, 204, 419
Higginson, Stephen, 247
Hindman family (Md.), 410
Historians: and Revolution, 186-87, 446-47; and westward movement, 332-33
Hooper, William (N.C.), 168
Hooper, William Ennalls (Md.), 60
Hoops, Robert, 198
Hopkins family (R.I.), 364
Houses of Representatives (state), 200-206. *See also* Legislative branch
Howe, General William, 240, 242, 292, 382
Hubbard, William, 60
Hubbart, Joshua, 40-41
Hubly, Adam, 58
Hugg, Joseph, 197-98
Hurd, John, 29
Hurlburt, Samuel, 51
Hutchinson, Thomas, 29, 142, 320, 321

Immigrants, loyalism and, 273-74, 302-303, 308-309, 380, 386-87
Indentured servants, 48-49, 70
Indians, 322, 332, 432

Indigo production, 15, 266

Inflation (wartime), 233-35, 436; attempts to curb, 239-45; increase in, 243-45, 252-53. *See also individual states*—finances (war) of

Innkeepers: rural, 65; urban, 86, 87

Intolerable Acts, 276. *See also* Boston Port Act

Irish immigrants, 386

Iron manufacturing, 78

Iroquois Indians, 322, 332

Jay, Sir James, 197

Jay, John, 85, 140, 172, 173, 176, 288, 374

Jay's Treaty (1795), 302

Jefferson, Thomas, 57, 85, 143, 156, 157, 194, 412

Jernegan, William, 58

Johnson, Thomas, 58, 161, 191, 194, 402

Johnson, William, 73

Johnson family (N.Y.), 322, 331

Johnston, Samuel, 168, 190

Johnston, Sir William, 18

Jones, Joseph, 419

Jones, Robert, 18-19

Jones, Walter, 60

Jones, Willie, 306

Judicial branch: in colonies, 106; in states, 206-209

Justices of the peace, 58-59, 207

Kentucky, 332; constitution of, 156; expansion into, 411-12; slavery in, 343

Kershaw, Joseph, 18, 425

Kitchel, Abraham, 198

Knox, Henry, 86

Laborers (free), 46-48; skilled, 68-69 (*see also* Artisans)

Langdon, John, 191, 247, 348, 350, 351, 356

Laurens, Henry, 102, 147, 344

Laurens, John, 344, 345

Law, Richard, 337

Lawrence, John, 449

Lawyers: rural, 56-58, 62-63; urban, 84-86

Lee, Richard Henry, 419

Lee, Thomas Sim, 190, 194, 402

Legislative branch (colonies): lower houses, 103-106; upper houses, 102-103

Legislative branch (states): lower houses, 200-206; unicameral, 200, 218; upper houses, 195-200, 214. *See also individual states —constitution(s) of*

Leigh, Egerton, 102

Lexington and Concord, Battle of, 129, 131, 135, 227, 302, 448

L'Hommedieu, Ezra, 57, 374

Livermore, Samuel, 57

Livingston, Philip, 197

Livingston, Robert R., 172, 173, 286

Livingston, Walter, 249

Livingston, William, 190, 191, 194, 381, 385, 438

Livingston family (N.Y.), 288, 374

Livingston Manor (N.Y.), tenant revolt on, 19, 274

Loans (wartime), 240, 254, 255. *See also individual states— finances (war) of*

Local government (colonies), 106

Logan, George, 387

Long Island Sound area, 6-8, 16, 282. *See also:* Conn.; N.Y.; R.I.

Lowndes, Rawlins, 147

Loyalists, 28, 269-317, 433-35; death for, 312, 317; exile of, 272, 274, 277, 279, 283, 291, 296, 300, 307, 312-13, 317, 321, 346, 347, 378, 446-47; and finances (war), 239, 241-42; ideology of, 99, 106-109, 118-19; immigrants as (*see* Immigrants, loyalism of); laws against, 269, 271, 275-312; pacifists as (*see* Pacifist sects); postwar return of, 281, 285, 289, 291, 295, 300, 302, 308, 315-16; in Peace Treaty, 441; property confiscation, 264, 269, 270, 271, 275, 312-13, 317, 318-32, 346, 377, 379, 436; rural, 271-74; urban, 269-71. *See also individual states and cities—*loyalism in

Loyalty ("Test") oaths, 277, 282, 284, 286, 292-98 passim, 301, 307, 309, 310, 316, 390

McCulloch, Henry, 327-28

McKean, Thomas, 165, 397

McKinley, John, 397

McMechan, David, 84

Maccubin, Nicholas, 410

Mackall, John, 161

Madison, James, 57, 156, 157

Manufacturing, 76-77; in New England, 6; in Long Island Sound area, 8; postwar, 267; during war, 230-31

Marable, Matthew, 63

Martin, Alexander, 438

Martin, Ephraim, 198

Martin, James, 61

Martin, John, 190

Martin, Luther, 325

Maryland: British in, 432; constitution of, 161-65, 213; depression (postwar) in, 263; finances (war) of, 223, 298, 403-408; imports of, 12; loyalism in, 272, 273, 274, 295-300, 313, 314, 325-26, 399-401, 402, 408-409, 433; politics of, 120, 399-410; Revolutionary movement in, 124, 134-36; slavery in, 341-42, 403; Whig ideology in, 161, 164, 176, 184. *See also* Baltimore

Mason, George, 85, 140, 156-59, 162, 168, 184, 419

Massachusetts: constitutions of, 177-83, 214, 452; depression (postwar) in, 262, 361; finances (war) in, 223, 226, 256-57, 280-81, 357-61; geography of, 4-6; loyalism in, 272, 274, 276, 279-82, 320-21, 357; politics of, 357-64; Revolutionary movement in, 126-27, 130; separatist movement in, 362-63, 433; slavery in, 336; Whig ideology in, 178, 181, 185. *See also* Boston

Mathews, George, 191

Matlack, Timothy, 151-52, 387

Mennonites, 301

Merchants, 63-65, 68, 87-89, 94; in postwar period, 266, 443-44; during war, 231-32

Meredith, Samuel, 387

Methodists, 334

Mifflin, Thomas, 387

Ministers: rural, 59-60; urban, 83-84

Mitchel, Thomas, 44

Mobility (population), 203, 447

Mohawk Valley (N.Y.): loyalism in, 272; during war, 372

Monetary policy (debate over), 98, 123, 205, 213, 214; in post-war period, 453 (*see also* Shays' Rebellion); during war, 252-56, 260-61. *See also* Paper money

Money supply, 94-98, 222; during war, 229, 232, 241, 245, 435-36 (*see also individual states*—finances of)

Monmouth, Battle of, 382

Monopolics, 235-36, 237

Mooney, Hercules, 62

Moore's Creek Bridge (N.C.), 303

Morris, Gouverneur, 172

Morris, Richard, 286

Morris, Robert, 140, 249, 258, 263, 267, 367, 386, 391, 393-94, 444

Morris, Roger, 322, 323

Morris, Samuel, 387

Morris family (N.Y.), 197

Muhlenberg, F. A., 73

Mumford, Stephen, 248

Murray, John, 276

Mynderse, Jacobus, 63


Nantucket (island; Mass.), loyalism on, 272

Nash, Abner, 306

Nelson, Thomas, 190, 194, 415, 438

Nelson, Thomas, Jr., 419

New England: farming in, 4, 23-24, 38, 40-41, 66; loyalism in, 274; northern, 4-6, 16; slavery in, 336-37; southern, 6-8. *See also:* Conn.; Mass.; N.H.; R.I.; Vt.

New Hampshire: constitutions of, 144-47, 214-17; depression (postwar) in, 262, 356-57; finances (war) of, 223, 351-54; geography of, 4-6; loyalism in, 129, 274, 277-79, 319-20; politics in, 349-57; Revolutionary movement in, 125, 129; separatist movement in, 354-56, 433; slavery in, 336; Whig ideology in, 185, 216-17. *See also* Portsmouth

New Jersey: British in, 380, 382, 432; constitution of, 159-61; depression (postwar) in, 262; finances (war) of, 223, 381-83; geography of, 6-10; loyalism in, 273, 274, 289-91, 312, 314, 323-24, 383-84, 385, 433; politics in, 121, 381-85; Revolutionary movement in, 125, 133; slavery in, 339, 340; society of, 33

New London (city, Conn.), British in, 370

Newport (city, R.I.), British in, 227, 228, 282-83, 313, 365, 366; commerce in, 8; loyalism in, 270, 272, 283, 321

Newton, Willoughby, 50

New York: British in, 246, 372-73, 432; constitution of, 172-76; depression (postwar) in, 262; economic growth of, 8; finances (war) in, 224, 287, 375-76, 379; geography of, 6-8; loyalism in, 272-73, 285-89, 312, 321-23, 372, 377, 433; politics in, 120, 122, 204-205, 372-81; Revolutionary movement in, 131-32; slavery in, 338-39, 340; Whig ideology in, 172, 174, 175, 176, 185

New York City, 67; British in, 372-73, 378, 380; commerce in, 8; loyalism in, 270, 272, 289, 323; slavery in, 338; society in, 32-33

Nicholas, Robert Carter, 136

Nonconsumption agreements, 231

Nonimportation agreements, 91, 123, 124-25, 128, 139, 442. See also: Continental Association; Embargoes

Norfolk (city; Va.), 10; British in, 412; loyalism in, 272, 300, 326-27

North Carolina: British in, 420-21, 432; constitution of, 166-70, 346; depression (postwar) in, 262; finances (war) in, 223, 244, 421-24; geography of, 12-14, 433; loyalism in, 272, 273, 274, 276, 302-306, 312, 314, 316, 327-28, 419-21, 433; politics in, 419-24; Regulator movement in, 19, 122, 167; Revolutionary movement in, 126, 137-38; slavery in, 344; Whig ideology in, 168-69

Ogden, David, 323

Ohio region, 332

"Old Roman, An" (pen name), 178

Oliver, Andrew, 321
Ordinance of 1785, 21
Otis, James, 58


Paca, William, 161, 163, 325, 438
Pacifist sects, 274, 282, 289, 291, 295, 300, 305, 389. *See also* Quakers
Page, Mann, Jr., 419
Page, William Byrd, 326
Paine, Ephraim, 338
Paine, Thomas, 151, 386
Paine, Timothy, 276
Paper money: postwar advocates of, 453-54 (*see also* Shays' Rebellion); during war, 238-39, 252-54, 256, 259, 268. *See also:* Monetary policy; Money supply
Paterson, William, 198, 289, 324
Peabody, Nathaniel, 61
Peale, Charles Wilson, 390
Pendleton, Edmund, 85, 136, 137
Penn family (Penn.), 324, 331, 392
Pennsylvania: British in, 313, 390, 432; constitution of, 151-56, 165-66, 176-77, 218-20, 389; depression (postwar) in, 262, 263; finances (war) in, 224, 243, 390-93; geography of, 8-10; loyalism in, 272, 273, 291-94, 313, 316; politics in, 122, 385-95 (*see also:* Constitutionalists—Penn.; Republicans); population of, 387-88; religious groups in, 122, 386-87 (*see also* Quakers); Revolutionary movement in, 124-25, 133-34; slavery in, 339-40, 394; society in, 33; wealth of, 330. *See also* Philadelphia
"People the Best Governors, The" (pamphlet), 146
Person, Thomas, 18-19
Philadelphia (city; Penn.), 1, 10, 67, 388; British in, 240-41, 242, 291, 292, 380, 382, 390; College of, 394, 452; loyalism in, 270, 274
Phillipse, Frederick, 322, 323, 449
Pinckney, C. C., 147
Pinckney, Charles, 424

Pinckney, Thomas, 190

"Placemen," 102, 112

Plantations, 14, 25, 34, 40; income of, 44-45; slavery and, 68 (*see also* Slavery). *See also* Rice *and* Tobacco production

Plater, George, 161, 402

Plural officeholding, 207, 221

Point Judith farm (R.I.), 284, 321

Political parties (development of), 120-21, 123, 451-54

Popular sovereignty, doctrine of, 113, 221. *See also* Democratic ideology

Portsmouth (city; N.H.), loyalism in, 271, 277, 320, 353, 356

Potomac Valley, 16

Potts, John, 78

Presbyterians, 8, 122, 151, 386; and slavery, 334

Price regulation (wartime), 236-37, 238, 246, 358; opponents of, 254, 256

Primogeniture, laws of, 345-46

Principio Company (ironworks; Md.), 325

Privateering, 231, 240, 247, 249, 351, 443; losses from, 265

Professional men: rural, 56-63; urban, 68, 81-82

Property requirements: for officeholding, 200-201; for voting (*see* Voting requirements)

Proprietary party (Penn.), 122, 133-34, 271

Quakers, 8; Penn. party of, 122, 133-34, 161, 339, 387, 388; pacifism of, 282, 292-93, 301, 303, 309, 311, 385, 386-87, 389, 400-401, 452; and slavery, 334, 335, 338, 339, 342, 345

Quebec Act, 122

Race prejudice, 49-50, 333. *See also* Slavery

Ramsay, David, 344

Randolph, Edmund, 156, 190

Randolph, John, 326

Randolph, Peyton, 136

Read, George, 165, 397

Reed, Joseph, 194

Regulator movement, 19, 122, 167; loyalism and, 274, 306

Religion: in North, 6, 8; pacifism and (*see* Pacifist sects); and politics, 121-22; and slavery, 334, 344 (*see also* Quakers); in South, 150, 170, 210. *See also individual religions*

"Republican, A" (pen name), 216

Republicans (Penn.), 218-19, 220, 292-93, 386-95 passim

Revere, Paul, 29, 124

Revolution: economic effects of, 441-48 (*see also* Depression); financing of, 222-29 passim (*see also individual states- -finances* of); historians and, 186-87, 446-47; movement toward, 123-42; political effects of, 448-54; social effects of, 318-48 passim, 446-48; Whig concept of, 113, 139-140, 142. *See also individual states and cities*—British in

Rhode Island: British in, 282, 364, 365, 432; constitution of, 101, 183, 220-21, 364; depression (postwar) in, 369; finances (war) in, 223, 227-29, 243, 251-52, 365-68; loyalism in, 282-84, 312, 313, 321, 364; politics in, 120, 364-69, 453-54; Revolutionary movement in, 126; slavery in, 337, 340, 365. *See also* Newport

Rice production, 15, 39, 266, 424

Ridgely, Charles, 78, 134, 161

Rittenhouse, David, 152, 390

"River Gods" (western Mass.), 276

Robinson, Beverly, 322, 323, 413

Rodney, Caesar, 126, 134, 194, 397

Rodney, Thomas, 134

Roll-call votes (in state legislatures), 450-51

Roosevelt, Isaac, 77

Rotation in office, principle of, 194, 219

Rum. *See:* Distilling industry; Triangular trade

Rush, Dr. Benjamin, 386

*Rutgers vs. Waddington* (1784), 288

Rutherford, Robert, 63

Rutledge, Edward, 147, 307, 426, 427

Rutledge, John, 190, 191, 194


Sailors, 69-70

St. Thomas Jenifer, Daniel of, 61, 402

Sarazin, Moreau and Jonathan, 75

Savannah (city; Ga.): British in, 309, 425, 430, 431; loyalism in, 329, 372

Schoolteachers: rural, 62; urban, 82-83

Schuyler, Philip, 18, 204, 231, 249, 288, 374

Schuyler family (N.Y.), 197

Scott, John Morin, 173

Scott, John Morris, 374

Scottish immigrants, 273, 302-303, 386

Sectionalism (in politics), 121, 433. *See also individual states—politics in*

Sedgwick, Theodore, 281, 448

Senates (state), 195-200, 214. *See also* Legislative branch

Shays' Rebellion (Mass.; 1786-1787), 19, 214, 257, 454

Sherman, Roger, 337

Shipbuilding industry, 76-77, 232, 267

Shoemaker, Samuel, 292, 324

Shopkeepers: rural, 63, 64-65; urban, 86-87

Slavery, 34, 36; economics of, 25, 37, 45, 48, 50, 55; emancipation movement and, 210, 318, 333-40, 446; and politics, 122; religious groups and, 334, 344 (*see also* Quakers); in South, 12, 14, 15, 21, 446, 447 (*see also* Plantations); urban, 30, 68-69; in West Indian trade, 90 (*see also* Triangular trade). *See also individual states and cities—slavery in*

Smith, John, 402, 410

Smith, William (N.Y.), 173

Smith, William (N.C.), 386, 394

South Carolina: British in, 425-28 passim; constitution of, 147-51, 212-13; depression (postwar) in, 262; finances (war) of, 224, 244, 426-28; geography of, 14-16; loyalism in, 272, 273, 306-308, 313, 316, 328-29, 426, 428; politics in, 424-29; Regulator movement in, 19, 274, 306; Revolutionary movement in, 126, 138-39; slavery in, 428, 429, 433; trade of, 265; Whig ideology in, 149, 176, 184. *See also* Charleston

"Spartanus" (pen name), 146

Speculators (wartime), 233, 290, 299, 314, 324, 348, 411

Stagg, John, 73

Stamp Act crisis, 111, 275
Stark, General John, 420
Starkweather, William, 58
State militias, 225-26. *See also* Continental Army
Stephen, Adam, 61
Stevenson, John, 161
Stone, Thomas, 402
Stoutenburgh, Isaac, 73
Stuart, David, 60
Sullivan, John, 58, 191

Taxes: postwar, 261; wartime, 240-42, 251, 254-55, 436-37. *See also individual states*—finances (war) of
Tea Act, 235
Ten Broeck, Abraham, 286
Ten Broeck family (N.Y.), 197
Tennessee, 332
"Test laws." *See* Loyalty oaths
Thomas, John, 449
Thomas, Thomas, 449
Thompson, Ebenezer, 350
Thompson, Mark, 198
Thornton, Matthew, 350
*Thoughts on Government* (pamphlet; John Adams), 156
Tierce, Peter B., 58
Tilghman, Matthew, 161
Tilton, James, 134
Timothy, Peter, 424
Tobacco production, 45; in Delaware Bay area, 10-12, 401; in export trade, 91, 92, 230, 249, 265; New England importation of, 17; in N.C., 14, 420; in postwar period, 266; slavery and, 341-43; in Va., 411, 413; westward movement of, 21-22
Tomer, Anthony, 73
Tories. *See* Loyalists
Town meetings, 106
Townsend, Charles, 77

Trade, 8, 10; export, 91-94, 230, 249; import, 89-91; losses in, 264-65; postwar, 261-62, 264-65; triangular, 6, 77, 90-91; wartime, 229-30, 231-32, 249, 264-65, 443-44

Traders. *See* Merchants

Transportation facilities, 2, 233

Treaty of Paris (1783), 288, 315, 439-41, 448

Trenton, Battle of, 234, 242, 380

Triangular trade, 6, 77, 90-91. *See also* West Indies (trade with)

Trumbull, Jonathan, 65, 88, 90, 94, 111-12, 190, 194, 438

Tryon, William, 100

Tucker, Dr. Thomas Tudor, 60

Tyler, John, 419

Unicameral legislatures, 200, 218. *See also* Legislative branch

Urban society, 26-27; economic classes in, 67-98; loyalism in, 269-71

Valley Forge (Penn.), Continental Army at, 382, 393, 405

Van Cortlandt, Pierre, 449

Van Cortlandt family (N.Y.), 197

Van Dyke, Nicholas, 165, 190, 438

Van Schaak, Henry, 281

Vermont: constitution of, 156, 176-77, 220-21; and N.H. (separatist movement), 354-56; loyalism in, 274; slavery in, 336, 337

Virginia: British in, 412, 421, 432; constitution of, 156-59; depression (postwar) in, 262; exports of, 12; finances (war) of, 223, 224, 244, 415-19; frontier of, 18-19; geography of, 12-14, 16, 433; loyalism in, 272, 273, 300-302, 312, 314, 326-27, 411, 433; politics in, 120, 410-19; Regulator movement in, 19; Revolutionary movement in, 123-24, 136-37; slavery in, 342-44. *See also* Norfolk

Voting requirements: expansion of, 141; property qualifications, 38, 103-104, 195-96; in state constitutions, 200 (*see also individual states*—constitution(s) of)

Wadsworth, Jeremiah, 248-49, 371
Walton, George, 191
Ward, Stephen, 449
Ward family (R.I.), 364
Washington, George, 46, 60, 413; and war, 226, 228, 234, 242, 380, 415, 421
"Watchman" (pen name), 162
Watts, John, 322
Wayne, Anthony, 329
Weare, Mesech, 94, 144, 190, 191, 194, 350, 438
Wedgery, William, 58
Wentworth, John, 100, 144, 277, 278, 320
Wentworth family (N.H.), 197, 204, 271, 277, 350
West Indies (trade with), 6, 8, 15, 17, 88, 90-93, 229, 402 (*see also* Triangular trade); exports to, 39, 443; imports from, 77; St. Eustatius island, 265
Westward movement. *See* Frontier regions
Whaling industry, 443
Wharton, Thomas, 94
Wheat production, 38-39, 45
Whig ideology, 109-16, 143-44, 221; compared to Tory and Democratic, 118-19; loyalists and, 270-71; criticisms of (*see* Constitutions—reform movements and); and Revolution, 113, 139-40, 142; and monetary policy, 453; and slavery, 334-35; in state constitutions, 149, 161, 164, 168-69, 174, 176, 178-81, 184-85, 188, 199, 216-17
Whig leadership, 447; in Del., 294-95, 397; and loyalists, 277, 281; in N.Y., 172, 274; postwar, 454
Whipple, William, 249-50, 350
Willard, Abijah, 276
Williams, Israel, 276
Wilmington (city; Del.), British in, 397
Wilson, James, 85, 386
Wisner, Henry, 173
Wistar, Caspar, 80
Workmen, Benjamin, 390

Worthington, John, 276
Wright, James, 100, 139, 429
Wynkoop, Dirck, 58

Yates, Abraham, 84, 173
Yates, Robert, 173
Yorktown, Battle of, 194, 259, 293, 354, 405, 414, 417. *See also* Cornwallis, General
Young, Dr. Thomas, 152

Zane, Isaac, 78

## About the Author

Jackson Turner Main was born in Chicago
and received his B.A., M.A., and Ph.D. at the
University of Wisconsin, where a famous
ancestor of his, Frederick Jackson Turner, the
historian of the frontier, once taught. His own
teaching career has taken him to Stanford and
the University of Maryland.

He is now Professor of History and Director
of the Institute for Colonial Studies at the
State University of New York, Stony Brook.

His books include *The Anti-federalists*, *The
Social Structure of Revolutionary America*,
and *The Upper House in Revolutionary
America*. He is a leading authority on the
period of the American Revolution.